Salvaging Wesley's Agenda

Princeton Theological Monograph Series

K. C. Hanson, Charles M. Collier, and
D. Christopher Spinks, Series Editors

Recent volumes in the series

Matthew J. Marohl
Faithfulness and the Purpose of Hebrews: A Social Identity Approach

D. Seiple and Frederick W. Weidmann, editors
*Enigmas and Powers: Engaging the Work of Walter Wink
for Classroom, Church, and World*

Stanley D. Walters
Go Figure!: Figuration in Biblical Interpretation

Paul S. Chung
Martin Luther and Buddhism: Aesthetics of Suffering, Second Edition

Ralph M. Wiltgen
*The Founding of the Roman Catholic Church in Melanesia
and Micronesia, 1850–1875*

Steven B. Sherman
*Revitalizing Theological Epistemology: Holistic Evangelical
Approaches to the Knowledge of God*

David Hein
Geoffrey Fisher: Archbishop of Canterbury, 1945–1961

Mary Clark Moschella
*Living Devotions: Reflections on Immigration, Identity,
and Religious Imagination*

Abraham Kunnuthara
Schleiermacher on Christian Consciousness of God's Work in History

Salvaging Wesley's Agenda
A New Paradigm for Wesleyan Virtue Ethics

KEVIN TWAIN LOWERY

☙PICKWICK *Publications* • Eugene, Oregon

SALVAGING WESLEY'S AGENDA
A New Paradigm for Wesleyan Virtue Ethics

Princeton Theological Monograph Series 86

Copyright © 2008 Kevin Twain Lowery. All rights reserved. Except for brief quotations in critical articles or reviews, no part of this book may be reproduced in any manner without prior written permission from the publisher. Write: Permissions, Wipf and Stock Publishers, 199 W. 8th Ave., Suite 3, Eugene, OR 97401.

www.wipfandstock.com

ISBN 13: 978-1-55635-377-2

Cataloging-in-Publication data:

Lowery, Kevin Twain

Salvaging Wesley's agenda : a new paradigm for Wesleyan virtue ethics / Kevin Twain Lowery.

    Eugene, Ore.: Pickwick Publications, 2008
    Princeton Theological Monograph Series 86

    xx + 328 p.; 23 cm.

    Includes bibliographical references.

    ISBN 13: 978-1-55635-377-2

    1. Wesley, John, 1703–1791—Ethics. 2. Christian ethics. I. Title. II. Series.

BX8495.W5 L69 2008

Manufactured in the U.S.A.

To Jean

Contents

Acknowledgments ix

Abbreviations for Citations x

Introduction xiii

PART ONE: The Need to Develop Wesleyan Virtue Ethics

1. The Loss of Wesley's Agenda 3
2. The Call for a New Paradigm 41

PART TWO: The Intellectual Roots of Wesley's Thought

3. Wesley and Lockean Empiricism 65
4. Wesley and Lockean Ethics 95
5. The Rejection of Mystical Spirituality 122
6. The Cognitive Content of Emotions 152

PART THREE: Constructing a New Paradigm

7. The Basic Conceptual Elements 201
8. Incorporating Kantian Concepts 236
9. Reformulating Wesley's Two Distinctive Doctrines 270

Bibliography 315

Acknowledgments

I WOULD LIKE TO THANK JEAN PORTER FOR HER INPUT IN THE WRITING of this project. She has patiently and persistently helped me to nuance and clarify my thoughts, and I have greatly benefited from her experience and expertise as a scholar and writer. Also, Jennifer Herdt, Randy Maddox, Maura Ryan, and Gerald McKenny all provided comments on earlier revisions of this manuscript which have likewise been invaluable.

Abbreviations for Citations

Edwards

CF   *Charity and Its Fruits*. Edited by Tyron Edwards. Reprint, Carlisle, PA: Banner of Truth Trust, 1969.

DM   *The Distinguishing Marks of a Work of the Spirit of God*. 1741. Reprint, in *Jonathan Edwards on Revival*. Edinburgh: Banner of Truth, 1999.

FW   *Freedom of the Will*. Edited by Paul Ramsey. Vol. 1 of *The Works of Jonathan Edwards*. New Haven, CT: Yale University Press, 1957.

Im   *Images or Shadows of Divine Things*. Edited by Perry Miller. Westport, CT: Greenwood, 1977.

Misc1   *The "Miscellanies" (Entry Nos. a–z, aa–zz, 1–500)*. Edited by Thomas A. Schafer. Vol. 13 of *The Works of Jonathan Edwards*. New Haven, CT: Yale University Press, 1994.

Misc2   *The "Miscellanies" (Entry Nos. 501–832)*. Edited by Ava Chamberlain. Vol. 18 of *The Works of Jonathan Edwards*. New Haven, CT: Yale University Press, 2000.

NSC   *A Narrative of Surprising Conversions*. 1736. Reprint, in *Jonathan Edwards on Revival*. Edinburgh: Banner of Truth, 1999. (Referenced above in *The Distinguishing Marks of a Work of the Spirit of God*)

OS   *Original Sin*. Edited by Clyde A. Holbrook. Vol. 3 of *The Works of Jonathan Edwards*. New Haven, CT: Yale University Press, 1970.

RA   *Religious Affections*. Edited by John E. Smith. Vol. 2 of *The Works of Jonathan Edwards*. New Haven, CT: Yale University Press, 1959.

Ser1   *Sermons and Discourses, 1720–1723*. Edited by Wilson H. Kimnach. Vol. 10 of *The Works of Jonathan Edwards*. New Haven, CT: Yale University Press, 1992.

Ser2   *Sermons and Discourses, 1723–1729*. Edited by Kenneth P. Minkema. Vol. 14 of *The Works of Jonathan Edwards*. New Haven, CT: Yale University Press, 1997.

Ser4   *Sermons and Discourses, 1734–1738*. Edited by M. X. Lesser. Vol. 19 of *The Works of Jonathan Edwards*. New Haven, CT: Yale University Press, 2001.

ThR   *Thoughts on the Revival of Religion in New England*. 1740. Reprint, New York: American Tract Society, [18—].

TV   *The Nature of True Virtue*. Ann Arbor: University of Michigan, 1960.

Kant

CJ	*Critique of Judgment.* Translated by J. H. Bernard. Amherst, NY: Prometheus, 2000.
CPr	*Critique of Practical Reason.* Translated by Lewis White Beck. New York: Macmillan, 1993.
GMM	*Grounding for the Metaphysics of Morals.* Translated by James W. Ellington. Indianapolis: Hackett, 1981.
LE	*Lectures on Ethics.* Translated by Louis Infield. Indianapolis: Hackett, 1963.
LPT	*Lectures on Philosophical Theology.* Translated by Allen W. Wood and Gertrude M. Clark. Ithica, NY: Cornell University Press, 1978.
MM	*The Metaphysics of Morals.* Translated and edited by Mary Gregor. Cambridge: Cambridge University, 1996.
PP	*Perpetual Peace and Other Essays.* Translated by Ted Humphrey. Indianapolis: Hackett, 1983.
Rel	*Religion within the Boundaries of Mere Reason.* Translated and edited by Allen Wood and George di Giovanni. Cambridge: Cambridge University Press, 1998.

Locke

Disc	"A Discourse of Miracles." Included in *The Reasonableness of Christianity.* Edited by Ian T. Ramsey. Stanford: Stanford University Press, 1991.
Essay	*Essay Concerning Human Understanding.* Collated and annotated by Alexander Campbell Fraser. 2 vols.. New York: Dover, 1959.
Let	*A Letter Concerning Toleration.* New York: MacMillan, 1988.
RC	*The Reasonableness of Christianity.* Edited by Ian T. Ramsey. Stanford: Stanford University Press, 1991.

Wesley

CP	*The Christian's Pattern, or An Extract of "The Imitation of Christ" by Thomas à Kempis.* Reprint, Salem, OH: Schmul, n.d.
NNT	*Explanatory Notes upon the New Testament.* London: Epworth, 1976.
WHS	*The Work of the Holy Spirit in the Human Heart.* Abridgement of *The Distinguishing Marks of a Work of the Spirit of God* and *A Treatise on the Religious Affections.* Abridged by John Wesley. Reprint, Salem, OH: Schmul, 1998.
WW	*The Works of John Wesley.* Begun as "The Oxford Edition of the Works of John Wesley." Oxford: Clarendon, 1975–1983. Continued as "The Bicentennial Edition of the Works of John Wesley." Nashville: Abingdon, 1984–. 35 total vols. to be eventually printed.

WWJ *The Works of John Wesley*. 14 vols. Edited by Thomas Jackson. London: Wesleyan Methodist Book Room, 1872. Reprinted often. (For the sake of reference, all citations from the Bicentennial edition will also include the volume and page number from the Jackson edition in brackets, e.g. [J x:xxx].)

Introduction

My Interest in This Subject

As a descendent of a long line of Methodists, I was raised in that tradition for the first ten years of my life. My parents subsequently joined a Holiness church, and I was steeped in traditional Holiness teaching in the years that followed. However, I knew very little about John Wesley himself until I discovered him during my days as a seminary student. As I delved into his writings, I became convinced of several things. First, Wesley's thought is more nuanced than has been commonly assumed. Although he is certainly not the most profound thinker of his time, there are few figures in Christian history who are more eclectic than he is. Indeed, if anyone practiced "folk theology," it was Wesley's followers, not Wesley himself.

I also came to agree with the Holiness tradition that the doctrine of perfection is at the core of Wesley's theological agenda. However, it became apparent to me that, contrary to what I had been taught, Wesley's view of perfection is significantly different from that of the Holiness tradition. I found Wesley's view to be intellectually more sophisticated and appealing than the Holiness view, but this was not surprising to me, because the Holiness people have been shying away from their own teaching for the past few decades. Ironically, one would be hard pressed to hear Wesley's view articulated today, even in the local church. The vast majority of Methodists gave up on the doctrine of perfection over a century ago, and very few Holiness people know what Wesley actually taught. To their credit, the Holiness people did their best to carry the banner for Wesley, so to speak. Nevertheless, the traditional Holiness teachings on sanctification are based on an overly simplistic, mystical model of moral transformation that cannot be salvaged, but should be abandoned altogether.

Although Wesley's view is also insufficient by contemporary standards, it does show some promise as a basis for development, because it is founded upon an empirical account of the moral agent. It became my conviction that Wesley's view of perfection could be developed in a way that would make the doctrine more intellectually viable and more appealing to other Christian traditions. For instance, Catholic spirituality is replete with references to the pursuit of perfection. In contrast, a Protestant emphasis on perfection has been relatively absent outside the Wesleyan traditions. However, this lack can largely be attributed to the Reformation account of sin and depravity. When this difference is taken into consideration, one will find that the vast majority of Protestant traditions are not antinomian, but stress the importance of personal growth and piety. I cannot help but think that a nuanced account of the doctrine of perfection would be a useful resource for a number of Christian traditions.

Formulating a Particular Approach

When I began my doctoral studies at the University of Notre Dame, I intended to explore the compatibility of Wesley's view of perfection with that of Thomas Aquinas.[1] After all, Aquinas offers an account of perfection that is fairly nuanced, for he outlines the degrees of perfection that one can reasonably expect to attain, depending upon one's set of circumstances. Moreover, since his virtue theory is a fairly sophisticated development of Aristotelian ethics, Aquinas seemed to be a good resource for Wesleyan thought. This conclusion was grounded in my belief that that Wesley is, in many key respects, an Aristotelian at heart. I believe that it can reasonably be argued that Wesley never veered from his Aristotelian framework. The influence of Cambridge Platonism on Wesley seems to be superficial at best, and Wesley's attraction to the mystics was short-lived. Of course, Lockean empiricism was a formative influence on Wesley, but this is not incredible, since empiricism itself can be traced back to Aristotle.

---

1. My idea of bringing Wesleyan perfectionism into tension with Thomism is by no means novel. A year earlier, Ray Dunning had suggested that the thought of Aquinas would provide fertile ground for constructing a new paradigm for the Wesleyan doctrine of perfection. See Dunning, "Christian Perfection." More recently, Stephen Long has undertaken a similar project, arguing that Wesley's moral theology is akin to that of Aquinas. See Long, *John Wesley's Moral Theology*, 171–207.

It was my desire to develop Wesley's thought, not merely restate or recover it. As such, I began to research Wesley's immediate intellectual context, especially his dependence on Locke, the influence that Edwards had on him, and some of the more notable figures in British empiricism. Several things became apparent to me. First, Albert Outler is correct in characterizing Wesley as an eclectic thinker, and this is evidenced in his writings. However, since Wesley did not annotate his writings, his use of other sources will only be recognizable to those who have familiarity with them. Consequently, I came to believe that Wesley is best understood by those who have a certain mastery over the sources that were at his disposal.

Second, Wesley's thought, in particular ways, is much closer to the Enlightenment than has generally been recognized. George Cell Croft suggested this in the early twentieth century, but it seems that since he overstated his case somewhat, the thesis was too quickly dismissed out of hand. Wesley's relation to the Enlightenment is more comprehensible when the foundations and limits of his epistemology are more clearly defined. Third, Wesley developed his own thought over time and was thus opposed to dogmatism. Therefore, suggesting that his thought be developed further is actually in accord with his own concerns.

All of this led me to conclude that the best way to develop Wesley's thought is to follow the trajectory of his thought. From this perspective, the path to Wesleyan intellectual development does not primarily lead to Aquinas, the mystics, the Reformers, or to the Eastern church. Rather, since Wesley's thought reflects significant interaction with the Enlightenment thought of his day, his thought must now be brought into tension with subsequent elements of the Enlightenment. Wesley is a part of British empiricism, so it stands to reason that the place to start is with Kant, whose thought serves as a corrective to that tradition. My first exposure to Kant's writings was not very memorable, to say the least. However, I returned to his works several years later, and as I probed them more deeply, I began to have a growing fascination with Kant and his thought. The zenith of this attraction occurred with my first reading of *Religion within the Boundaries of Mere Reason*, which "awakened me from my dogmatic slumber."[2] Since that time, I have come full circle in my respect for Kant, and I now consider myself

---

2. In his *Prolegomena to Any Future Metaphysics*, Kant states that this is the effect that Hume's writings had on him.

better able to assess the strengths and weaknesses of his thought. I do not consider myself to be a Kantian per se, but I do admire the way that Kant addresses a number of key issues. Besides, he is one of the most pivotal figures in intellectual history.

It is obvious that Wesley's approach to ethics is vastly different from that of Kant in particular ways. For example, Wesley's empiricism and stress on the affections do not have Kantian counterparts, yet they cannot be compromised. Nevertheless, Wesley and Kant share some of the same concerns, and Kant's way of addressing them can inform the way that these concerns are addressed in Wesleyan ethics. My particular reading of Kant may be objectionable to some, but it is one that is defended by Kantian scholars like Barbara Herman and Christine Korsgaard, to name a few. As such, even if my interpretation of Kant is questioned, I do not feel that this prevents my appropriation of Kantian concepts in a Wesleyan schema.

The Significance of This Book for Wesleyanism

For about a century now, Wesleyans have been debating the nature of perfection, whether it should be regarded primarily as a process or as an event. This debate has become rather heated since Mildred Bangs Wynkoop's book, *A Theology of Love*, was published in 1972, and although she is now posthumously regarded as a bold voice for change in the Holiness traditions, there is still a strong element of resistance to some of her claims. Most recently, the issue itself has given rise to several polarized groups. Randy Maddox and John Cobb offer a more gradualist reading of Wesley, insisting that a Wesleyan understanding of grace emphasizes human responsibility. Kenneth Collins believes that this reading of Wesley ignores his stress on the instantaneous and unfairly stereotypes the nineteenth-century Holiness Movement.

Along those same lines, Laurence Wood argues that Wesley should be interpreted through the lens of John Fletcher, his intended successor. Fletcher teaches that entire sanctification is essentially a personal, instantaneous experience of the baptism of the Holy Spirit. Meanwhile, Thomas Oord leads a movement to integrate Wesleyan theology with the process thought of Whitehead and Hartshorne. This not only reinforces the more gradualist reading of Wesley (and Cobb is himself a process theologian), Oord believes that such process thought can be used to formulate a Wesleyan response to postmodernism.

What I want to do is offer a realistic account of perfection that sees it as a complex process in which particular processes may culminate in due course. I decided to include the doctrine of assurance in this project not only because it is Wesley's other distinctive doctrine, but also due to the fact that the quest for perfection and the quest for assurance seem to be at odds with one another. On one hand, when people feel secure about their salvation, they will be tempted to become complacent and not pursue perfection. On the other hand, when they feel the constant compulsion and need to progress morally, they might find it difficult to feel satisfied with their present state. I believe that this tension exists in Wesley's thought, and, as I will try to show, is one that must be upheld.

I am not offering a proposal that will fully address, let alone resolve, the epistemological debates that exist in Wesleyan circles. However, the very nature of this project requires an analysis of Wesley's epistemology, and this will be the focus of the third chapter. As my thesis unfolds, it will become apparent that I favor a more gradualist reading of Wesley. To be sure, the instantaneous is stressed in Wesley's writings, but I believe that the innermost workings of his thought suggest a view of grace like that championed by Wynkoop, Cobb, and Maddox. Wesley often held contrasting views in tension. I will suggest that some of these points of tension should be retained, but I will also propose that others be resolved in a particular direction.

The Broader Usefulness of This Project

This project was designed to function as a solid intellectual study on several counts. Of course, it is a constructive work in the theory of virtue ethics, and it is hoped that Wesley can be introduced as an interlocutor in future discussions on the subject. To date, Wesley's own views and agenda have not been given due consideration in this dialog. In a broader sense, this project is also a study in Enlightenment thought, focusing on Wesley, Kant, Locke, and Edwards. Perhaps this project can serve as a resource for other studies of these and other Enlightenment figures. Moreover, it is my desire to locate Wesley in the intellectual history of the Enlightenment and introduce him in such discussions.

Nevertheless, the major focus of this project is the development of Wesley's thought, and it is my belief that if this is carried out sufficiently, his thought can be a helpful resource for a number of Christian traditions. This would seemingly be the case judged by his eclecticism alone. The relevance of Wesley's doctrines of assurance and perfection may not be quite so apparent. Since these doctrines represent his distinctive contributions to Christian thought, it might be assumed that they would not be useful to other traditions. However, I reject this assumption on two counts. First, assurance and perfection are central to Christianity in general, so they are the proper concerns of every Christian. In virtually every Christian tradition, believers desire to have some measure of assurance regarding their salvation. Granted, every tradition does not embrace perfection as a goal. Nevertheless, the pursuit of perfection is essentially the pursuit of holiness, and this is certainly a vital part of Christianity and relevant to all Christian traditions.

Second, I am offering a development of Wesley that is more fully engaged with the empirical sciences, especially an empirical knowledge of the self. To the extent that other Christian traditions share this objective, this project will be relevant to them. Science is increasingly providing us with a greater empirical account of the human psyche, and I believe that theology is better served when it utilizes science as a resource. Although this project is not interdisciplinary in the fullest sense of the word, it represents an attempt to develop a particular Christian tradition in that direction. As such, it can be a useful resource for moving other traditions in that same direction.

Key Terms in the Book

There are several terms that are used repeatedly throughout the book, each of which may require some explanation as to my precise usage of them. First of all, when I refer to "Wesleyan ethics," I have in mind the broad, underlying principles of Wesley's virtue ethics, not his "special ethics" which addresses specific issues. In effect, the book is concerned with the formation of Wesleyan moral theory.

The main objective of the book is to construct a paradigm for Wesleyan virtue ethics that is based on a more cognitivist approach to epistemology. I am aware that the term "cognitivist" has some technical connotations. For example, as Noah Lemos points out,

> Critical cognitivism . . . [recognizes] . . . just four sources of our knowledge: external perception, memory, self-awareness or inner consciousness, and reason. It asserts (1) that we do know facts about the external world, other minds, and the past, (2) that we have no other sources of knowledge, and, therefore, (3) our knowledge of the external world, other minds, and the past is yielded by these four sources.³

The position I am advocating for Wesleyanism, and the one that I believe best represents Wesley's view, is a modified form of this type of cognitivism, distinguished by two qualifications. First, this view would allow belief that God subtly speaks to us through natural means, i.e., the four sources of knowledge. This suggests that God generally communicates to us in ways that do not unduly coerce us or abrogate our responsibility to actively seek truth. In this way, even the truth given in special revelation (i.e., Scripture) is ascertained through our natural cognitive processes. Second, a Wesleyan perspective would certainly hold that since God is not limited, God's self-disclosure and communication with us are not limited to natural means or to the normal course of events. God certainly has the ability to speak to us directly, and God can likewise choose to act in supernatural ways (i.e., ways that are out of the ordinary). Nevertheless, since there is integrity in divine truth, any knowledge that would presumably be received directly or supernaturally from God will nonetheless coincide with knowledge acquired through natural means. Consequently, even if knowledge were received directly and supernaturally, it would still be empirically or logically verifiable. The important thing is that knowledge is generally attained the natural way, so it is irresponsible to neglect this pursuit in hopes of receiving a direct or supernatural revelation.

This speaks to the type of *mysticism* that Wesley rejects. He certainly believes that God speaks to us, but he vehemently opposes the notion that natural means can be regarded as secondary or neglected altogether. On the other hand, Wesley also rejects *naturalism* that does not acknowledge God's activity or communication with us. Therefore, when I argue that Wesleyan ethics needs to be distanced from mysticism and become more naturalized, I am suggesting that: (1) knowledge is usually mediated through natural means, (2) exceptions to this rule

---

3. Lemos, 73.

are verifiable through natural means, and (3) we have a duty to pursue knowledge through whatever natural means are at our disposal.

In a cognitivist schema, our knowledge is foundational to our beliefs, feelings, and dispositions. This implies that moral transformation itself is cognitive in nature. Once again, since this occurs through our natural cognitive processes, we are morally derelict if we seek it apart from natural means. This does not mean that one cannot hope for supernatural transformation, but it does mean that one cannot hope for such to the neglect of natural means.

PART ONE

The Need *to* Develop Wesleyan Virtue Ethics

1

The Loss of Wesley's Agenda

JOHN WESLEY HAS BEEN CALLED "THE SINGLE MOST INFLUENTIAL Protestant leader of the English-speaking world since the Reformation."[1] That Wesley should be regarded so highly should be of little wonder, for he is a central religious figure in several respects. He is most readily recognized as the founder of Methodism, which not only has been a major influence in British and American religious history over the past two centuries, but continues to be a prominent Christian tradition in the world today. Moreover, Wesley is essentially the progenitor of the subsequent Holiness, Keswick, Pentecostal, and Charismatic Movements, all of which have their roots in the Methodist tradition.

However, Wesley's importance goes beyond his impact on Christian history, for his eclecticism makes him a key figure for understanding the diverse strands of philosophy and theology that developed in the eighteenth century. According to Albert Outler, the intricacies of Wesley's thought have often been overlooked, and Wesley is often not fully appreciated.

> Obviously, Wesley can be read, and usually has been read, without the broad and intricate tapestry of his sources unfolded as a background for interpretation. This was part of the price he paid for self-divestiture of his theological apparatus. Even so, it is just as this background is recovered and reevaluated that Wesley emerges as a more interesting and impressive theologian than his stereotypes have presented—precisely because he was a folk theologian.[2]

---

1. Ayling, *John Wesley*, 318; quoted by Matthews, "Religion and Reason Joined," 21.
2. Outler, "John Wesley: Folk Theologian," in *Wesleyan Theological Heritage*, 123.

There has been a renewed interest in Wesley scholarship in the past few decades thanks to the efforts of scholars like Outler and Frank Baker.[3] However, too little attention has been devoted to the intellectual development of Wesley's ethical thought. Historically, there has been an apparent lack of interest in Wesley beyond Wesleyan circles, and those who have examined Wesley's ethics have either limited their investigations to his casuistry (i.e., his "special ethics") or they have predominantly focused on theological themes to the neglect of their philosophical underpinnings.

Wesley's Two Distinctive Doctrines

Wesley did not formulate his own systematic theology, much less a comprehensive moral theory. However, he had two ubiquitous concerns that arguably represent his most distinctive contributions to Christian thought: assurance and Christian perfection. I believe that the basic elements of a Wesleyan moral theory are best reflected in these two doctrines. However, I will suggest that these doctrines have not been substantially developed since Wesley formulated them himself. It is my theory that developing these doctrines will require the concepts that support them to be developed as well. I will propose the type of development that I believe will prove the most fruitful yet remain faithful to Wesley's own concerns. Creating a new paradigm for Wesleyan ethics will be the first step toward the construction of a more comprehensive Wesleyan moral theory.

The doctrines of assurance and perfection are actually held in tension for Wesley. On the one hand, he wants to be certain of his standing with God. He wants to know not only that his sins are forgiven, but also that God is pleased with his life. On the other hand, Wesley contends that Christians must strive to be perfect as God is perfect, at least in a moral sense. There must be both progress and attainment in the Christian life. As such, the quest for perfection requires that there be some dissatisfaction with one's present state.

Wesley's understanding of these two doctrines matured throughout the course of his life, and this maturation of thought was not merely theoretical in nature, because Wesley allowed his views to be shaped by the experiences that he and others encountered. Regarding

---

3. Maddox, *Responsible Grace*, 24.

his understanding of assurance, the defining moment for Wesley was his well-known experience at Aldersgate.

> In the evening I went very unwillingly to a society in Aldersgate-Street, where one was reading Luther's preface to the Epistle to the Romans. About a quarter before nine, while he was describing the change which God works in the heart through faith in Christ, I felt my heart strangely warmed. I felt I did trust in Christ, Christ alone for salvation: And an assurance was given me, that he had taken away *my* sins, even *mine*, and saved *me* from the law of sin and death.[4]

This event would later become the cornerstone of Wesley's doctrine of assurance. At first, he did not interpret this experience as the witness of the Spirit, but as his true conversion. Five days later, he related this experience to a group of people gathered at the Hutton home, alleging that he had not been a Christian prior to that event. This led to an exchange of words between Wesley and Mr. Hutton. Wesley defended himself by arguing that we are saved through faith alone, and he now believed that he had lacked real faith before that time.[5] It is not surprising that Wesley should take this stance, considering: 1) his Aldersgate experience occurred while someone was reading Luther's preface to Romans, and 2) he was being heavily influenced at the time by the Moravians, a Lutheran pietist group.

Five more months passed, and Wesley felt that he had not yet received the "witness of the Spirit" that his sins were forgiven and that he was a child of God, yet he continued to wait patiently. Doing so was difficult, since he had observed others receiving this "witness" in less than an hour.[6] Within a year of his Aldersgate experience, Wesley was already expressing serious doubts concerning his status as a child of God. It is important to note here the source of these doubts. For that reason, it is imperative to examine the passage in its entirety.

> My friends affirm I am mad, because I said I was not a Christian a year ago. I affirm, I am not a Christian now. Indeed, what I might have been I know not, had I been faithful to the grace then given, when, expecting nothing less, I received such a sense of the forgiveness of my sins, as till then I never knew. But

---

4. Wesley journal, 24 May 1738, §14, *WW*, 18:249–50 [J 1:103].
5. Mrs. E. Hutton to Samuel Wesley, 5 June 1738, *WW*, 18:252 n. 90.
6. Wesley to his brother, Samuel Wesley, 30 October 1738, *WW*, 25:576–77 [J 12:34].

that I am not a Christian at this day, I as assuredly know, as that Jesus is the Christ.

For a Christian is one who has the fruits of the Spirit of Christ, which (to mention no more) are love, peace, joy. But these I have not. I have not any love of God. I do not love either the Father or the Son. Do you ask, how do I know whether I love God, I answer by another question, "How do you know whether you love me?" Why, as you know whether you are hot or cold. You *feel* this moment, that you do or do not love me. And I *feel* this moment, I do not love God, which therefore I *know*, because I *feel* it. There is no word more proper, more clear, or more strong.

And I know it also by St. John's plain rule, "If any man love the world, the love of the Father is not in him." For I love the world. I desire the things of the world, some or other of them, and have done all my life. I have always placed some part of my happiness in some or other of the things that are seen. Particularly in meat and drink, and in the company of those I loved. My desire, if not in a gross and lustful, yet in a more subtle and refined manner, has been almost continually running out towards this or that person. For many years I have been, yea, and still am, hankering after a happiness, in loving, and being loved by one or another. And in these I have from time to time taken more pleasure than in God. Nay, I do so at this day. I often ask my heart, when I am in company with one that I love, "Do I take more delight in you or in God?" And cannot but answer, *In you*. For in truth I do not delight in God at all. Therefore I am so far from loving God with all my heart that whatever I love at all, I love more than God. So that all the love I have is flat idolatry.

Again, joy in the Holy Ghost I have not. I have now and then some starts of joy in God: But it is not that joy. For it is not abiding. Neither is it greater than I have had on some worldly occasions. So that I can in no wise be said to "rejoice evermore," much less to "rejoice with joy unspeakable and full of glory."

Yet again: I have not "the peace of God," *that* peace, peculiarly so called. The peace I have may be accounted for on natural principles. I have health, strength, friends, a competent fortune, and a composed, cheerful temper. Who would not have a sort of peace in such circumstances? But I have none which can with any propriety be called, a "peace which passeth all understanding."

From hence I conclude (and let all the *saints of the world* hear, that whereinsoever they boast, they may be found even as I), though I have given, and do give, all my goods to feed the poor, I am not a Christian. Though I have endured hardship, though I have in all things denied myself and taken up my cross, I am not a Christian. My works are nothing, my sufferings are nothing; I have not the fruits of the Spirit of Christ. Though I have constantly used all the means of grace for twenty years, I am not a Christian.[7]

It is my contention that Wesley was driven by an ascetic moral rigorism, especially in his earlier years. He seemed to believe that all of our thoughts should be continually centered on God. One wonders whether the attainment of such an ideal is even psychologically possible. Likewise, the slightest offense or omission caused him great anguish. For instance, it is a well-known fact that throughout the course of his life Wesley lived as frugally as possible and gave the bulk of his income away to the poor. Moreover, he believed that each of us has a moral obligation to live the same way.

> Perhaps you have not seen it in this light before. When you are laying out that money in costly apparel which you could have otherwise spared for the poor, you thereby deprive them of what God, the proprietor of all, had lodged in your hands for their use. If so, what you put upon yourself, you are, in effect tearing from the back of the naked, as the costly and delicate food which you eat, you are snatching from the mouth of the hungry. For mercy, for pity, for Christ's sake, for the honor of his gospel, stay your hand! Do not throw this money away! Do not lay out on nothing, yea, worse than nothing, what may clothe your poor, naked, shivering fellow-creature![8]

When Wesley is judged in light of these moral preconceptions, he can hardly be faulted for desiring to be assured that his life is pleasing to God. Nevertheless, this does not obviate the need to scrutinize these preconceptions so that a more acceptable doctrine of assurance may be formulated. I believe that Wesley's ascetic moral rigorism is countered by the positive place that he gives to self-love and by the duties we have to ourselves. This will also be addressed in subsequent chapters.

---

7. Wesley journal, 4 January 1739, WW, 19:29–31 [J 1:170–72].
8. Wesley, Sermon 88, "On Dress," §15, WW, 3:254 [J 7:20–21].

After Wesley felt that he better understood the witness of the Spirit, he defined it as follows:

> The testimony of the Spirit is an inward impression on the soul, whereby the Spirit of God directly witnesses to my spirit, that I am a child of God, that Jesus Christ hath loved me, and given himself for me, and that all my sins are blotted out, and I, even I, am reconciled to God.[9]

The connection between this statement and Wesley's account of Aldersgate is patent. Not only are the same themes expressed, there is great similarity in the language as well. Apparently, this account is Wesley's way of overcoming his own self-doubt and fear, and he practically admits as much, since he claims that the direct witness of the Spirit brings peace to those who are otherwise plagued with doubts.[10] The direct witness also gives assurance to those who strive to be pleasing to God, but have "no consciousness that they are forgiven."[11] Once again, it seems that Wesley has himself in mind.

Wesley also acknowledges the necessity of the "indirect witness," which is essentially the witness of conscience.[12] The content of this judgment is primarily the observance of the fruit of the Spirit in one's own life. Nevertheless, Wesley asserts that there is a direct witness of the Spirit beyond one's self-evaluation, and he believes that this assertion is validated both by the "plain natural meaning" of Scripture and by the experience of many.[13] Even if Wesley does not assume that other people share in his doubts and fears, he certainly supposes that all Christians experience trials and temptations, at least from time to time. When faith is tested in this way, only the direct witness can grant assurance.[14]

One might think that Wesley would eventually back away from these claims, especially after he had been repeatedly criticized for making them, but such was not the case. Instead, he continued to defend his basic definition twenty years later. In fact, he added to it. Whereas

---

9. Wesley, Sermon 10, "The Witness of the Spirit, Discourse I," §1.7, WW, 1:274 [J 5:115].

10. Wesley, Sermon 11, "The Witness of the Spirit, Discourse II," §3.7, WW, 1:291 [J 5:128].

11. Ibid., §3.9, WW, 1:292 [J 5:129].

12. Ibid., §2.6, WW, 1:287–88 [J 5:125].

13. Ibid., §5.1, WW, 1:296–97 [J 5:132].

14. Ibid., §5.2, WW, 1:297 [J 5:133].

he had earlier claimed that the Spirit witnesses to us "directly," he later asserts that this takes place "immediately and directly."[15] The emphasis on feeling is increased as well, for his later discourse describes the "immediate influence" of the Spirit as bringing a "sweet calm."[16]

Wesley is indeed aware of the possibility (perhaps probability) that his insistence on the direct witness of the Spirit might lead to exaggerations and aberrations. "If we deny it, there is a danger lest our religion degenerate into mere formality.... If we allow it, but do not understand what we allow, we are liable to run into all the wildness of enthusiasm."[17] However, he is willing to run this risk, because he regards this as preferable to the omission of the doctrine altogether.

> It more nearly concerns the Methodists, so called, clearly to understand, explain, and defend this doctrine, because it is one grand part of the testimony which God has given to them to bear to all mankind. It is by his peculiar blessing upon them in searching the Scriptures, confirmed by the experience of his children, that this great evangelical truth has been recovered, which had been for many years well nigh lost and forgotten.[18]

According to Randy Maddox, many aspects of Wesley's thought weave around his doctrine of assurance.[19] Likewise, John Cobb indicates that Wesley's doctrine of assurance is closely linked to his pneumatology, for it is in this doctrine that Wesley's belief in the immediate working of the Holy Spirit is most clear. In this way, the doctrine of assurance is closely tied to the Wesleyan understanding of grace.[20]

The other major focus of Wesley's ethics is his doctrine of Christian perfection, which he regards as "the grand depositum which God had lodged with the people called Methodists, and for the sake of propagating this chiefly he appeared to have raised us up."[21] Basically, Wesley defines Christian perfection as deliverance from all sin.

---

15. Ibid., §2.3, *WW*, 1:287 [J 5:125].
16. Ibid., §2.4, *WW*, 1:287 [J 5:125].
17. Ibid., §1.2, *WW*, 1:285 [J 5:123].
18. Ibid., §1.4, *WW*, 1:285–86 [J 5:124].
19. Maddox, *Responsible Grace*, 124.
20. Cobb, *Grace and Responsibility*, 46.
21. Wesley to Robert Carr Brackenbury, 15 September 1790, *WWJ*, 13:9.

> In conformity, therefore, both to the doctrine of St. John, and the whole tenor of the New Testament, we fix this conclusion: a Christian is so far perfect, as not to commit sin. This is the glorious privilege of every Christian, yea, though he be but a babe in Christ. But it is only of grown Christians it can be affirmed, they are in such a sense perfect, as, Secondly, to be free from evil or sinful thoughts.[22]

In effect, at conversion believers experience (1) justification, i.e., they are pardoned of their sins and declared righteous on the merits of Christ's atonement; (2) regeneration, i.e., they are "born again" and made alive unto God; (3) adoption, i.e., they become God's sons and daughters and joint heirs with Christ. At this point, sanctification (i.e., the process of perfection) is begun. All Christians, even "newborn babes in Christ," are expected not to commit sin, for such is a part of repentance. This is essentially the most basic degree of perfection, and one must attain it in order to be genuinely a Christian. However, Christian perfection involves the process of cleansing one's thoughts, dispositions, and attitudes. Consequently, Wesley is only willing to affirm the attainment of this higher level of perfection in mature believers, since he evidently does not believe that God typically makes this transformation in us in a short period of time, let alone in an instant.

Wesley is not speaking of flawless perfection, but of a relative state of moral perfection. Nevertheless, this type of perfection exceeds mere sincerity, since those who would be perfect must be "cleansed from pride, anger, lust, and self-will."[23] In order for this to take place, the Holy Spirit must reveal to believers the depths of their own depravity. "And now first they do see the ground of their heart, which God before would not disclose unto them, lest the soul should fail before him, and the spirit which he had made." Once believers are cognizant of their own carnality, they begin to experience "the inexpressible hunger [for] a full renewal in [God's] image."[24] One by one, carnal dispositions are renounced and essentially reversed, and this frees the soul to love God and others unconditionally and unreservedly. "Yea, we do believe that [God] will in this world so 'cleanse the thoughts of our hearts, by the

---

22. Wesley, "A Plain Account of Christian Perfection," §12, *WWJ*, 11:376–77.
23. Ibid., §25.Q12, *WWJ*, 11:418.
24. Ibid., §13, *WWJ*, 11:381.

inspiration of his Holy Spirit, that we shall perfectly love him, and worthily magnify his holy name.'"[25]

Wesley contends that the moment in which perfection is attained "is constantly both preceded and followed by a gradual work."[26] Inward sanctification thus begins within the believer at the moment of justification, and "yet sin remains in him, yea, the seed of all sin, till he is sanctified throughout. From that time a believer gradually dies to sin, and grows in grace."[27] Death to sin is typically a gradual process. Nevertheless, there must still be a terminus, a point at which the process is culminated.[28] For Wesley, the process of crucifying sinful desires is rarely, if ever, accomplished in a short amount of time. In fact, he clearly maintains that in referring to those who have attained perfection, "we are not now speaking of babes in Christ, but adult Christians."[29] The entirely sanctified[30] can likewise be regarded as those who are "grown up into perfect men."[31] In other words, "perfect" Christians are neither those who indefinitely progress but never attain, nor are they immature believers.

Wesley's desire for assurance is not nearly as strong in Christian perfection as it is in justification. He acknowledges that a certain degree of uncertainty is inherent in perfection, most likely since it is more a process (which culminates at a particular point in time) than it is an event. Even the precise moment when the process is complete can be

---

25. Ibid., §28, *WWJ*, 11:445–46.
26. Ibid., §26, *WWJ*, 11:442.
27. Ibid., §17, *WWJ*, 11:387.
28. Ibid., §19, *WWJ*, 11:402.
29. Ibid., §12, *WWJ*, 11:374.
30. For those unfamiliar with Wesleyan jargon, it should be noted that Wesley sometimes used the term "entire sanctification" to denote the attainment of Christian perfection. In their efforts to promote perfection as a definite experience, the Holiness people preferred this term over that of "Christian perfection." Thus, Holiness people have historically spoken of being "sanctified" to indicate that they have been "entirely sanctified" or "sanctified holy." Also, Holiness people have consistently used the term "holiness" both in its traditional, broader sense and in a more narrow sense to refer to the doctrine and experience of Christian perfection (i.e., entire sanctification).
31. Wesley, "A Plain Account of Christian Perfection," §15.(2), *WWJ*, 11:383.

difficult to perceive.³² This is much different from the witness of the Spirit (at justification), which is an instantaneous event.³³

Similar to his views on the assurance of justification, Wesley suggests an account of assurance for Christian perfection that includes both empirical self-knowledge and direct impressions made by the Holy Spirit. This assurance comes as believers participate in the various facets of perfection. First, seekers gain a "deeper and clearer conviction" of their own carnality. A further exploration of this knowledge (as well as conscience itself) will appear in chapters 3 and 4, which will focus on Wesley's epistemology. Second, there must be a gradual yet complete mortification of sin. Here, Wesley understands consecration to be an evidence of perfection, namely, "total resignation to the will of God, without any mixture of self-will."³⁴ Again, the fact that Wesley's standards are so high explains why he sees consecration as the culmination of a long, difficult, and gradual process of crucifying sinful, selfish desires and thoughts. "I believe [Christian perfection] is usually [achieved] many years after justification, but that it may be within five years or five months after it, I know no conclusive argument to the contrary."³⁵ Third, the subject is filled with the love of God and is thus renewed in God's image. Wesley firmly believes that our awareness of our own desires, motives, and intentions allows us to evaluate whether this is a reality in our own lives. Fourth, the entirely sanctified person also receives a direct witness from the Holy Spirit.

---

32. Ibid., §26, *WWJ*, 11:442.

33. Wesley did believe that assurance could also be granted, through a witness of the Holy Spirit, to those who attain Christian perfection. As such, the terms "assurance" and "witness of the Spirit" do not refer exclusively to justification. In general, they reflect the belief that the Holy Spirit communicates to individuals (whether through conscience or otherwise) their current standing with God. Therefore, the terms can refer to either justification or sanctification, depending upon which is being held in question. However, Wesley believed that the event of justification is not only always possible in this life, it is required for salvation. In contrast, Christian perfection is a process that cannot always be completed in this life, so its attainment before death is not necessary to salvation, although the pursuit of perfection essentially is necessary. Consequently, when salvation is being discussed in general, the terms "assurance" and "witness of the Spirit" typically refer to justification. I will try to be judicious in my use of these terms, so as to avoid confusing the reader.

34. Wesley, "A Plain Account of Christian Perfection," §25.Q23, *WWJ*, 11:422.

35. Wesley, "Brief Thoughts on Christian Perfection," §3, *WWJ*, 11: 446.

Subjects can only be certain of avoiding delusional experiences when all four of these facets are realized. For those who do experience all four of them, Wesley considers it impossible that they should be deceived regarding their own perfection.[36] Nevertheless, in contrast with the direct witness of the Spirit at justification, the direct witness of sanctification "is not always clear at first.... Yea, and sometimes it is withdrawn." However, Wesley concludes that as long as the believer has no doubt, the Spirit's direct witness regarding perfection is unnecessary.[37]

Wesley's doctrines of assurance and Christian perfection are related in that they are both driven by Wesley's perfectionistic tendencies, i.e., his ascetic moral rigorism. Nevertheless, the two doctrines are formed in different ways. On the one hand, Wesley's doctrine of assurance was essentially an interpretation of his Aldersgate experience. In other words, Wesley theorized about what he had definitely experienced. On the other hand, Wesley never clearly testified to having attained Christian perfection, so this doctrine remained more theoretical and less focused on experience. It is true that Wesley was willing to allow the experiences and claims of others to influence his views on perfection, but this can largely be attributed to Scripture's silence concerning whether sanctification should be regarded as a process or as an event.[38]

Another similarity between the two doctrines involves their significance in salvation. Although Wesley truly believes that "without holiness no one shall see the Lord," he does not believe that attaining it in this life is ultimately necessary for salvation. Rather, he avers that many Christians will not attain Christian perfection until death or a little before.[39] This fact will not alter their eternal destiny, because not all of those who are sealed by the Spirit for the day of redemption attain perfection in this life.[40] In the final analysis, Wesley does exhort others to pursue Christian perfection, but he does not claim that salvation is contingent on attaining it. In the same way, the witness of the

---

36. Wesley, "A Plain Account of Christian Perfection," §19, *WWJ*, 11:401–2.
37. Ibid., §25.QQ16–18, *WWJ*, 11:420.
38. Maddox, *Responsible Grace*, 46.
39. Wesley, "A Plain Account of Christian Perfection," §25.Q25, *WWJ*, 11:423. Charles Wesley held an even stronger position. He objected to John's insistence that Christian perfection can be attained in this life, and he became increasingly convinced that it is not attainable until death. See Maddox, *Responsible Grace*, 186.
40. Wesley, "A Plain Account of Christian Perfection," §13, *WWJ*, 11:380 n. 2.

Spirit is not necessary for salvation, yet it does testify to the reality of justification, which is what ultimately determines one's eternal destiny. However, the key difference between the two doctrines is that striving for perfection is portrayed as a duty while the witness of the Spirit is seen as a privilege.

Ironically, Wesley's doctrines of assurance and Christian perfection would later prove to be problematic to the Methodist tradition that he started. According to Rex Matthews, these two doctrines created the greatest difficulty for Wesley, since they exposed him to repeated charges of "enthusiasm."[41] This particular term occurs most prominently in the seventeenth and eighteenth centuries and can be understood to denote "religious fanaticism" within this context. Robert Crocker describes it as a conflict between the "magical" perspectives of the Renaissance and the secular rationalism that emerged after the Reformation.[42]

Ronald Knox notes that although many of the behaviors and practices associated with enthusiasm have a long history, there are two particular strands of enthusiasm that flourished during this period of history. First, *mystical enthusiasm* uses the Incarnation as its model, exhorting human beings to experience "union with God" or "oneness with Christ." Thus, Christ dwells within the individual, in the person of the Holy Spirit, to the extent that self-will is lost and the subject becomes a conduit for divine, ecstatic activity. Second, *evangelical enthusiasm* seeks affirmation for redemptive works of grace, i.e., to know whether one has been born again, sanctified, etc. This type of enthusiasm centers on the atonement.[43] In general, Knox prefers using the term "ultra-supernaturalism" to summarize the trend as a whole.[44]

Whether or not one accepts Knox's analysis of enthusiasm, when Wesley's doctrines of assurance and Christian perfection are examined, it is easy to see why Wesley was continually defending himself against these kinds of charges. He tried to distinguish himself from other so-called enthusiasts, but this distinction is a rather fine one to make for two reasons. First, since Wesley was generally willing to validate religious experience, the distinction he tried to make is not one of *kind*, but

---

41. Matthews, "Religion and Reason Joined," 331.

42. Crocker, "Mysticism and Enthusiasm," 137.

43. Knox, *Enthusiasm*, 581. Overall, Knox gives a rather inimical interpretation of Wesley. See chapters XVIII through XXI.

44. Ibid., 2.

one of *degree*. He was thus willing to embrace subjective experiences within certain limitations. Had he simply rejected them outright, the charges of enthusiasm would have much less force. Second, Wesley was unwilling to decry many of the experiences that others claimed to have, even when these exceeded the limits of what he was willing to claim for himself. For instance, Wesley was constantly exhorting others to expect that they should attain perfection, even though he never clearly testified to this himself.

The question of whether Wesley should be regarded as an enthusiast will be discussed further in a later chapter. The point that is being made here is that Wesley's doctrines of assurance and perfection are susceptible to distortion and exaggeration, and this is what makes him vulnerable to such criticisms. Consequently, it should not be surprising that the tradition that followed him splintered in different directions, most often in controversy over these two issues. As Donald Dayton points out, the concern for assurance came to the forefront at the time of Puritanism and classical Methodism, but it was intensified by the Holiness and Pentecostal Movements.[45] Perfectionism was emphasized even more.

Related Aspects of Wesley's Thought

The vulnerabilities of Wesley's doctrines of assurance and perfection were only intensified by several other facets of his thought. For instance, Wesley's doctrine of sin, even in its more mature, nuanced form, has contributed to some of the distortions that followed Wesley in the nineteenth century. Wesley defines sin as follows:

> Nothing is sin, strictly speaking, but a voluntary transgression of a known law of God. Therefore, every voluntary breach of the law of love is sin, and nothing else, if we speak properly. To strain the matter farther is only to make way for Calvinism. There may be ten thousand wandering thoughts and forgetful intervals without any breach of love, though not without transgressing the Adamic law, but Calvinists would fain confound these together. Let love fill your heart, and it is enough![46]

---

45. Dayton, *Theological Roots*, 176–77.
46. Wesley to Elizabeth Bennis, 16 June 1772, *WWJ*, 12:394.

Wesley's firm commitment to Scripture as the authoritative rule of life and conduct often allows his ethics to be construed as a type of divine command ethics, and it seems that this type of an emphasis is incompatible with his stress on Christian perfection. Outler argues that Christian history has repeatedly shown that deontological ethics in general and the goal of Christian perfection do not readily mix.[47] Harald Lindström states, "If the Christian life is regarded as a process towards the goal of perfection, the idea of perfection will be seen as a typical expression of the teleological alignment of [Wesley's] view of salvation."[48] Likewise, it would seem that his ethics should also be construed teleologically. Ironically, this has not been the practice of many Wesleyans, especially those who stressed Christian perfection most stridently, i.e., the Holiness Movement.

Ray Dunning believes that the nineteenth-century emphasis on experiencing entire sanctification is to a great extent what caused Wesleyan ethics to be emphasized deontologically. Rather than seeing entire sanctification as a "perfectible perfection," the Holiness people too often viewed it as a "perfected perfection."[49] In short, perfection ceased to be seen as a means to a greater end (e.g., kingdom of God, union with God, etc.). Instead, the experience of perfection became an end in itself. More and more people wanted to claim that they had attained the experience, and this was facilitated by a distinct shift in emphasis. By not insisting that perfection requires a certain level of maturity, the Holiness people essentially lowered the bar with respect to inner dispositions and attitudes. At the same time, they raised the bar with respect to outward conduct.[50]

This seems to run counter to Wesley's emphasis. As I indicated earlier, although Wesley clearly testified to receiving the witness of the Spirit, he never made any such claims regarding perfection. I believe that this is due in large part to his ascetic moral rigorism, which would

---

47. Outler, *Wesleyan Spirit*, 81.
48. Lindström, *Wesley and Sanctification*, 126–27.
49. Dunning, *Reflecting the Divine Image*, 35–36.
50. Of course, the Holiness people did not see themselves as lowering the bar, so to speak, because they believed that God would supernaturally produce in an instant the same results that Wesley felt must be obtained over a long period of time. Not only was this type of mysticism rejected by Wesley himself, I believe that it is untenable for a number of reasons, and this is what I will endeavor to show.

never allow him to confidently speak of having attained Christian perfection. In fact, Maddox indicates that around 1760 Wesley seemed to have concluded that his portrayal of Christian perfection was too demanding and thus hindered people from seeking and claiming the experience. After the 1759 Methodist conference, Wesley qualified his doctrine of Christian perfection by more clearly defining the concept of sin. As a result, Christian perfection was not only limited to the *known* laws of God, it was also limited specifically to *voluntary* transgressions of those laws. This shift did result in more people claiming entire sanctification, but it also increased the risk of "enthusiasm."[51]

Clarence Bence is essentially correct in pointing out that Wesley's "focus on intentionality keeps his perfectionism from becoming a harsh legalism of external religion."[52] However, this assertion must be qualified in two ways. First, although Wesley's doctrine of perfection cannot be equated with an external legalism of action, it is still based upon an ascetic moral rigorism with regard to motive and intention, and this can become a type of internal legalism. Of course, we have just noted that Wesley softened these demands over time. Second, while Christian perfection does not necessarily entail legalism, it is still interconnected with one's conduct. After all, Wesley saw Christian perfection as the means to fulfilling the moral demands of the gospel. Love for God and for others not only qualifies our actions by making them truly moral, it also provides the motivation that is necessary for keeping the moral law. Hence, Wesley clearly attempts to define morality in a way that maintains a tension between purity of intention and obedience to the law of God, not only in inner disposition, but in outward conduct as well.

However, it is a strange coincidence that the nineteenth-century and early twentieth-century Wesleyan traditions that have placed the greatest emphasis on perfection (i.e., sanctification, baptism of the Holy Spirit) have also tended to be the most legalistic. Granted, many American evangelicals during this time period were rather austere in opposing "worldliness," and there were various factors that contributed to this mindset.[53] Nevertheless, Wesley's focus on intention did little to

---

51. Maddox, *Responsible Grace*, 183.

52. Bence, "John Wesley's Teleological Hermeneutic," 65.

53. There are many helpful works on this subject, such as Marsden, *Fundamentalism and American Culture.*

detract from the attention given to external standards of conduct. In fact, it was sometimes used to reinforce them.

Charles Edwin Jones believes that the Holiness Movement's rigorous standards and personal disciplines stemmed from its belief that the carnal nature must be identified so that the crisis event of entire sanctification can remove it.[54] It was thus believed that carnality could be evidenced in a person's unwillingness to live a "godly life." Two corollaries of this proposition were also held as true. First, many people assumed that outward conformity to standards of conduct demonstrates purity of heart. This claim is fallacious, because an action may be performed from a variety of motives, both pure and impure. Second, pure motives were equated with a willingness to conform. In other words, these standards were revered as the most accurate expression of Biblical principles. There was no room for disagreement. "If people really love Christ," it was believed, "then they will keep *these* commandments," so to speak.

In the last half of the twentieth century, most evangelicals, including the Holiness and Pentecostal groups, began to distance themselves from their legalistic past, and it seems that some contemporary evangelical groups are intentionally attempting to avoid the pitfalls of legalism. The problem of legalism is not caused by holding moral standards per se, for the gospel itself makes many demands on the Christian. The problem arises whenever ethics is narrowly defined as a set of specific rules. Dunning agrees, for he states that understanding ethics as rules can lead to either legalism or permissiveness, depending upon the way the rules are defined.[55]

In this way, Wesley's ethics has at times been unfairly reduced to *sola scriptura*, even though his epistemology is commonly understood to be much broader. Additionally, the legalistic focus on rules does not do justice to Scripture itself, for the rules can often go well beyond the principles of Scripture and essentially obviate them. Dunning feels that Wesley's understanding of ethics is more consistent with Scripture than much of what the legalistic factions of Wesleyanism have taught.[56] Wesley was more attuned to the development of character and virtue.

---

54. C. Jones, *Perfectionist Persuasion*, 83–88.
55. Dunning, *Reflecting the Divine Image*, 27.
56. Ibid., 7.

And yet, the Wesleyan traditions at large have not attempted to develop Wesley's focus on intentions.

This is not to say that Wesley was always clear about his conception of pure intentions. For one thing, his position on self-love is somewhat ambiguous. In one respect, he does appear to be a eudemonist, since he asserts that happiness and virtue are in harmony when love is present.[57] Outler eventually came to view Wesley's ethics as eudemonistic, believing that Wesley's "emphases on duty and discipline are auxiliary to his main concern for human happiness."[58] Wesley unmistakably understands human happiness to ultimately be grounded in love for God, but at times he does not leave much room for self-interest. For example, he asserts,

> Purity of intention is equally destroyed by a view to any temporal reward whatever. . . . Any temporal view, any motive whatever on this side eternity, any design but that of promoting the glory of God and the happiness of men for God's sake, makes every action, however fair it may appear to men, an abomination unto the Lord.[59]

It thus seems that Wesley is reluctant to affirm the goodness of natural human abilities, and this is most evident in his doctrine of prevenient grace. He attempts to reconcile an orthodox view of original sin with a robust conception of human freedom. Of course, he is ever careful to avoid falling into Pelagianism. The result is that he affirms human abilities without recognizing them as natural. Cobb notes that for Wesley, prevenient grace is not the restoration of natural free-will. Rather, it ensures that "a measure of free-will is restored to the person, not to human nature."[60] The same can be said of conscience, which is also only "natural" in the sense that it is restored through prevenient grace.

Judged within its context, Wesley's doctrine of prevenient grace was a rather clever way for him to balance orthodoxy and Enlightenment thought. It also helped Wesley to maintain a certain distance from

57. Wesley, "An Earnest Appeal to Men of Reason and Religion," §3, *WW*, 11:45 [J 8:3].
58. Outler, *Wesleyan Spirit*, 81.
59. Wesley, Sermon 26, "Upon Our Lord's Sermon on the Mount, Discourse VI," §2.2, *WW*, 1:576 [J 5:331].
60. Cobb, *Grace and Responsibility*, 38–39.

Roman Catholic theology, and the motivation for this was essentially fostered by the religious climate of his time. However, in denying that human abilities are natural, claiming instead that they are the result of the direct influence and activity of the Holy Spirit, Wesley helped to set the stage for accounts of assurance and perfection that understand change and transformation to be largely supernatural in nature. Later I will argue that when Wesley's cognitivist tendencies are taken into consideration, a more naturalized account of grace (particularly prevenient grace) will be more suitable for Wesleyan ethics.

Distortions in Subsequent Wesleyan Movements

Although Wesley fought to prevent any excesses that might be engendered by his emphasis on experience, the various Wesleyan groups that sprang from Methodism were not always as cautious, and distortions to Wesley's doctrine ensued. Jones says that these groups (especially the Holiness Movement) considered themselves to be true followers of Wesley, and they likened the changes they made in Methodism to the changes Wesley made in Anglicanism a century earlier.[61] However, it would be unfair to put the entire onus on the Holiness Movement, for the controversy over Christian perfection in nineteenth-century Methodism arose over the fact that the doctrine was never included in the articles of religion. Wesley had adapted the thirty-nine Anglican articles of faith for the Methodist statement of faith, and he never added an article for the doctrine of Christian perfection. Therefore, it should not be surprising that Wesley's followers were divided over the doctrine's importance.

The seeds of dissent grew from within Methodism itself, for the early catalysts of the Holiness Movement were predominantly Methodists. Even though most of the dissenters broke away from the Methodist Episcopal Church, a significant number of Methodists have historically been a part of the Holiness Movement. It is therefore more proper to refer to these historic developments as movements, since they had adherents in various ecclesial bodies and since the influence of these groups was more widespread than is reflected in the formal organization of these bodies. After the Civil War, a plethora of splinter groups left Methodism, but the vast majority of these eventually either united

---

61. C. Jones, *Perfectionist Persuasion*, 83.

to form larger groups (like the Church of the Nazarene) or returned to the Methodist Church by the time of World War I.

It should also be pointed out that a few groups, like the Wesleyan Methodist Church (now the Wesleyan Church) and the Free Methodist Church, were started on abolitionist grounds before the Civil War. After the issue of slavery had been decided by the Civil War, a number of these people returned to the Methodist Episcopal Church. However, those who remained separate soon became involved in the Holiness Movement, and these denominations consequently redefined their purpose for existing as separate bodies.[62]

A Greater Emphasis on Experience

The Holiness people were not satisfied to merely emphasize the doctrine of entire sanctification, as they preferred to refer to it. Rather, they chose to be innovative. However, as I have already indicated, the desire to develop Wesley's doctrine is indeed legitimate, but developments need to be consistent with Wesley's own commitments and concerns, especially at a deeper theological and philosophical level. Such was not the case with the innovations made to Wesley's doctrine of perfection in the nineteenth century.

According to Stephen Gunter, a methodology for pursuing Christian perfection was never discussed until the nineteenth century.[63] Developing such a methodology naturally entailed granting a greater epistemic role to experience, and this had other ramifications. Outler claims that American Wesleyanism's concept of fourfold authority—Scripture as the base, tradition and reason as the hermeneutical pillars, and experience as confirmation—was drastically altered. Scripture was retained as the base, but tradition was ignored altogether, reason degenerated into polemical justification, and experience was enlarged beyond the realm of assurance and given an authority of its own.[64]

---

62. Even though all of the constituent groups within the Holiness Movement shared similar views regarding Christian perfection (i.e., "entire sanctification"), they did not all make the propagation of this doctrine their primary focus. In fact, the movement itself gave rise to foreign missions organizations (e.g., World Gospel Mission) and organizations dedicated to social outreach (e.g., Salvation Army). These organizations have their parallels in other branches of Evangelicalism.

63. Gunter, "Aldersgate," 131.

64. Outler, "'Biblical Primitivism' in Early American Methodism," in *Wesleyan Theological Heritage*, 151.

Holiness proponents thus began to rely increasingly on personal experience. For instance, the Methodist Daniel Steele, first president of Syracuse University and later professor at Boston University, claimed that while all salvific truth is revealed in the Bible, "facts of a personal nature" are revealed directly by the Holy Spirit.[65] However, the Holy Spirit grants us much more than self-knowledge.

> The same large view of the possibilities of grace is seen in these words: "Eye hath not seen, nor ear heard, neither have entered into the heart of man, the things which God hath prepared for them that love him, but God hath revealed them unto us by his Spirit," in the glories of a present experience, as a foretaste of the glories of heaven.[66]

Another striking example of this mode of thought is that of S. A. Keen, Methodist Bishop of the Ohio Conference. He proposed that beyond the witness of the Holy Spirit, one could also receive what he referred to as "the witness of faith." As he describes it,

> The witness of faith is just as conscious an experience as is the witness of the Holy Spirit. It comprises emotions of joy, peace, and gladness peculiar to itself. There is a faith-feeling just as there is a fear-feeling or a love-feeling. There is no true faith without feeling.[67]

Perhaps the most notable shift occurred with Phoebe Palmer, one of the founders of the Holiness Movement. Building on the ideas of early Wesley protégés John Fletcher and Adam Clarke, she developed a pentecostal model of Christian perfection.[68] Whereas Wesley viewed perfection as a process that can reach a point of culmination, she equated it with an event, i.e., the instantaneous baptism of the Holy Spirit. As a result, she placed a greater stress on experience. According to Dayton, this alteration paved the way for the Pentecostal view of spirituality.[69]

65. D. Steele, *Defense of Christian Perfection*, 65–66.
66. Ibid., 57.
67. Keen, "Faith Papers," 55.
68. Here, the term "pentecostal" indicates that the model is based on the event of Pentecost in the book of Acts. The groups that originated in the Pentecostal Movement adopted this term for that very reason. Others, like the Holiness denomination the Church of the Nazarene, initially had the word "Pentecostal" in their names, but they later dropped it to avoid being identified with the tongues-speaking Pentecostals.
69. Dayton, *Theological Roots*, 76.

In fact, Palmer is often regarded as the forerunner of Aimée Semple McPherson and the Pentecostal Movement, which elevated the role of experience to an even higher level.[70]

Paul Bassett contends that the difference between Wesley and Palmer is that for Palmer Scripture must be experienced, whereas Wesley believed that experience must be assessed by Scripture.[71] However, the difference between Wesley and his followers like Palmer is greater than this. Wesley was only willing to give credence to experience that has specific warrant in Scripture, e.g., the witness of the Holy Spirit. As Maddox indicates, Wesley was willing to permit experiences and expressions, even those of which he himself remained skeptical. This is why he insisted that everything must be tested by Scripture.[72] Moreover, Wesley did not go to Aldersgate Street seeking an experience, rather, the experience came to him. In contrast, Wesleyans like Palmer specifically sought for experiences that would bring them assurance, even when there was no basis for them in Scripture, which is considerably more than Wesley would affirm.

The problem with granting religious experience so much epistemic status is that theology is altered in the process. Palmer's use of the pentecostal model reflects such a change.

> [Palmer's] pentecostal model not only redefines perfection as a singular event (as opposed to the culmination of a process), it also moves away from theology toward experience. The significance here is the fact that one is usually used to define the other. While Wesley wants experience to confirm and nuance his theology, Palmer uses experience to derive hers. As such, the pentecostal model changes the theological content of perfection, adding some concepts and overlooking others.[73]

Novel religious experiences need to be validated theologically, and this almost always requires theology to be adjusted accordingly.[74] In this particular case, theology is not the only part of Wesley that has been reinterpreted. In an effort to promote entire sanctification as a

70. See Lowery, "Wesleyan Road," 218–21.
71. Bassett, "Theological Identity," 86.
72. Maddox, *Responsible Grace*, 136.
73. Ibid., 192.
74. For a more detailed account of how Palmer altered Wesley's theology, see Lowery, "Wesleyan Road," 189–208.

distinct experience, some within the Holiness Movement have even attempted to reinterpret Wesley's Aldersgate experience as his attainment of Christian perfection.[75] Efforts such as these actually represent attempts to force Wesley to conform to Palmer, since their teachings do not coincide at key points. Consequently, Wesley's name has been invoked even in instances when his thought has not been followed as closely as Palmer's.

The Appeal to Supernaturalism

The heightened focus on instantaneous experience within the Wesleyan traditions naturally led to a greater stress on supernatural change and transformation. What Wesley believed could be accomplished over time, his followers claimed could be realized in an instant. However, Wesley did indeed believe in the supernatural transforming power of the Holy Spirit, especially in regeneration. As Matthews puts it, "By the 'new birth,' then, Wesley means a real transformation, almost an ontological change, in human nature."[76] Nonetheless, Wesley does not oversimplify the process, for he clearly acknowledges its more gradual, cognitive elements.

Once again, the Wesleyan traditions took this aspect of Wesley's thought and exaggerated it. For example, consider Nazarene theologian Richard S. Taylor's comments regarding regeneration.

> Psychologists of religion are at a loss to try to describe and explain on naturalistic or purely psychological grounds the change that occurs in the new birth. The biblical explanation is that the change is an immediate action of the Holy Spirit upon the human spirit. It involves a change in us and a presence in us.[77]

In another place, Taylor makes even stronger claims.

> All true experiences of regeneration require the direct action of the Spirit upon the self in creating a real change, by which the self is made spiritually alive and dispositionally turned toward heaven. This is the divine culmination of the previous

---

75. Gunter, "Aldersgate," 121–31.
76. Matthews, "Religion and Reason Joined," 315.
77. R. Taylor, *Theological Formulation*, 143.

preparatory influences which we call Gospel, Providence, and Prevenient Grace.[78]

The real difficulty with this position is that it downplays the causal role that knowledge has in change. For instance, Clarke proposes that the change of regeneration effected by the Holy Spirit cannot be produced through natural causes or human efforts.[79] If he is simply suggesting that the change cannot be effected *solely* through human efforts but requires some level of divine activity, then the statement is not problematic. This seems to be what Clarke intends, for in other places he indicates that knowledge, most specifically self-knowledge, increases one's capacity for perfection.[80]

Nevertheless, others like Steele take matters further. He claims that Christian perfection can be obtained by someone "having very little knowledge."[81] Then he adds,

> Moreover, we do not find in the Bible any such limitation of the work of the sanctifying Spirit to the narrow range of human knowledge. We read that it is possible for the believer "to know the love of Christ, which passeth knowledge" (Eph 3:19), surpassing not only our ability to comprehend, but also overleaping the boundaries of self-knowledge, and going down into the unexplored depths of our nature with its cleansing power. For love is the element in which holiness dwells.[82]

Leon Hynson notes that the Holiness Movement at large thus tended "to treat reason as of lesser significance" than the other facets of Wesley's epistemology.[83] However, this phenomenon was not limited to Wesleyans. Mark Noll details how anti-intellectualism has historically been characteristic of many evangelicals, but he does believe that a greater stress on supernaturalism, like that found in the Holiness, Keswick, and Pentecostal Movements, magnified this tendency. He

78. R. Taylor, "Relation of the Holy Spirit," 87–88.
79. Clarke, *Christian Theology*, 146.
80. Ibid., 387.
81. D. Steele, *Christian Perfection*, 53.
82. Ibid., 56.
83. Hynson, "Wesleyan Quadrilateral," 30. Outler was the first to suggest that Wesley's epistemology has four foundations: Scripture, reason, tradition, and experience. This has become popularly known as the "Wesleyan Quadrilateral." More will be said about this in a later chapter.

quotes Martyn Lloyd-Jones, who was asked in 1941 to speak on the anti-intellectualistic drift that had occurred among British evangelicals, as saying:

> The Keswick, "higher-life" movement . . . also contributed to a reduction of interest in biblical theology and deeper scholarship. No Christian in his right mind will desire anything other than true holiness and righteousness in the church of God. But Keswick had isolated one doctrine, holiness, and altered it by the false simplicity contained in the slogan, "Give up, let go and let God." If you want to be holy and righteous, we are told, the intellect is dangerous and it is thought generally unlikely that a good theologian is likely to be a holy person. . . . You asked me to diagnose the reasons for the present weakness and I am doing it. . . . If you teach that sanctification consists of "letting go" and letting the Holy Spirit do all the work, then don't blame me if you have no scholars![84]

There are some Holiness people who do allow a limited role for knowledge in Christian experience. For example, John Barker says that "Entire Sanctification is a fullness of love and grace up to the capacity of the moment."[85] For Taylor, the limitation is that we can purge ourselves "as far as we know and are able, but beyond that [we] must be perfected by the sanctifying work of the Holy Spirit."[86] According to Thomas Oden, this still falls short of a balanced view of grace, for the "zap theory" of conversion and sanctification ignores the transformation of the will.[87]

And yet, these distortions of Wesley's doctrine are not driven by the thirst for experience alone. A strong account of original sin leads many Wesleyans to discount natural human abilities. Clarke not only asserts that human beings have a natural propensity to do evil, he maintains that we have no propensity toward the good. Even "the great principles of self-love and self-interest weigh nothing against the sinful propensities of [the] mind."[88] In other words, even when human beings realize that the good is in their best interest, they will still not be inclined to

---

84. Noll, *Scandal*, 124.
85. Barker, *Will of God*, 88.
86. R. Taylor, *Theological Formulation*, 165.
87. Oden, *Transforming Power*, 95.
88. Clarke, *Christian Theology*, 95.

pursue it. This leads Clarke to conclude that divine intervention is necessary. "So strong is the propensity to do what is evil that nothing less than the power by which the soul was created can conquer these habits, eradicate these vices, and cause such a leper to change his spots."[89]

Barker holds similar sentiments, for he believes that holiness is not in human nature at all, including all aspects of our personalities. All righteousness was lost in the fall.[90] Thomas Cook elaborates on this position:

> Before the fall Adam was complete in his mental structure, in the enthronement of his moral sense, and in the harmony and balance of all his faculties. He could reason rightly and always judge correctly, and therefore was adapted to the law of perfect obedience. . . . But through lack of knowledge, defective memory, a fallible judgment, slowness of understanding, and numerous other infirmities, we are as liable to err as it is natural for us to breathe, and every error is a breach of the perfect law which allows no deviation from perfect rectitude.[91]

According to Methodist thinker William Burt Pope, this is why human beings are in need of prevenient grace. Without it the unregenerate "can do nothing good."[92] In contrast, contemporary, progressive Holiness thinkers more readily recognize the role of natural factors in their account of grace. For instance, regarding the faculty of conscience Dunning states, "We may say that formally conscience is the work of the Spirit (prevenient grace), but that materially it is the result of background, experience, and education."[93]

These accounts of grace often include supernatural empowerment. Cook asserts that when someone is "born of God," the love of God strengthens the will so that sin will be resisted.[94] Keen claims that entire sanctification empowers people to the extent that "finite capabilities are raised to superhuman power."[95] Taylor adds that the crisis of entire sanctification effects a second change within the individual that results

89. Ibid., 146.
90. Barker, *Will of God*, 19–20, 93–94.
91. Cook, *New Testament Holiness*, 9.
92. Pope, *Higher Catechism of Theology*, §6.3.6, 216.
93. Dunning, *Grace, Faith, and Holiness*, 433.
94. Cook, *New Testament Holiness*, 18.
95. Keen, "Faith Papers," 83.

is "released power and freedom, more rapid progress, new learning and advanced discoveries, increased strength, knowledge, and usefulness."[96] Even many contemporary Wesleyans are reluctant to espouse a more naturalized account of grace. For instance, Oden asserts that without grace, the fallen will "cannot long persevere in good works."[97]

Frequently overlooking the merits of natural human knowledge, these highly supernatural accounts of grace stress mystically imparted knowledge. In the words of H. Orton Wiley,

> The first effect of the Spirit's work is contrition, or godly sorrow for sin. . . . In its truest and deepest sense, however, contrition is a new moral consciousness of sin, in which the sinner identifies himself with God's attitude toward sin, and thinks God's thoughts about it.[98]

He says that conscience is subjectively moral self-consciousness, but it is ultimately "the utterance of God's voice in the soul, and is thus beyond the power of education or development."[99]

Steele was one of the first Wesleyans to promote a dualistic view of conscience. He distinguishes the more rational *discriminating power* from the more emotional *impulsive power* of the conscience. The latter is lacking in sinful human beings and must be imparted through the operations of divine grace. "In the entire cleansing from inward sin, and the impulsive power imparted to the conscience, [entire sanctification] is instantaneous; in the discriminating power of the moral sense, through exercise, it is gradual."[100] Consequently, "In all holy beings, this impulse toward the right is round, full, and complete, a movement of the soul along the line of perceived rectitude, with no drawbacks, antagonisms, nor counter-currents within itself."[101] In this regard, conscience infallibly judges our own motives.[102]

However, the divinely imparted mystical knowledge extends beyond morality to the apprehension of spiritual realities. Cobb suggests

---

96. R. Taylor, *Theological Formulation*, 146.
97. Oden, *Transforming Power*, 206.
98. Wiley, *Christian Theology*, 2:361.
99. Ibid., 3:33.
100. D. Steele, *Milestone Papers*, 109.
101. Ibid., 104.
102. Ibid., 106.

that the twentieth-century Pentecostal Movement "has reintroduced 'enthusiasm' in the sense of understanding the Holy Spirit as working immediately and speaking directly."[103] Although this practice has been particularly characteristic of the Pentecostals and Charismatics, it has traditionally occurred in varying degrees among Wesleyans in general. In early Methodism, Clarke taught that the Holy Spirit "brings a light, a power, and conviction, more full, more clear, and more convincing to the understanding and judgment, than they ever had, or ever can give, of any circumstance or fact brought before the intellect."[104] Today, Wesleyans like Oden are still making similar, albeit weaker claims. "Grace works through all the faculties of human consciousness: illumining the intellect, strengthening the will, and guiding the senses."[105] Whereas Steele, over a century ago, spoke of the witness of the Spirit as "direct spiritual perception,"[106] the modern-day Taylor still refers to it as "a divinely imparted sense of peace and assurance."[107]

In making these criticisms, I am not suggesting that a Wesleyan view of grace should exclude the possibility of supernatural change and transformation. Rather, I believe that a Wesleyan account of grace will recognize that (1) God generally works through natural means; (2) God's influence over us is usually subtle so as to not override free will; (3) God is not limited, but can still work in ways that are out of the ordinary; (4) when God does work supernaturally, this can by and large be confirmed in other ways. I will explain this in greater detail in a later chapter. For now, it will be sufficient to state that my primary objection with these accounts of grace is that natural means are either neglected or relegated to a place of insignificance, and I believe that this is inconsistent with Wesley's view of grace.

Oversimplifying Virtue

These innovations to Wesley's thought naturally led to an oversimplified account of virtue. To begin with, carnality is regarded as a precognitive

---

103. Cobb, *Grace and Responsibility*, 45.
104. Clarke, *Christian Theology*, 151.
105. Oden, *Transforming Power*, 206.
106. D. Steele, *Milestone Papers*, 157.
107. Taylor, *Theological Formulation*, 139.

state that opposes both the intellect and the will.[108] It is not the result of faulty reasoning or disordered values; rather, it is the foreign entity that causes them. As such, it must be "removed" and replaced by the virtue of Christ, which is supernaturally conveyed into the soul through faith.[109] However, this is not a cognitive process, because the love of God is transmitted to the human spirit, and this is sufficient to produce the other virtues. Nineteenth-century Methodist and Holiness advocate J. A. Wood states it as such:

> A "pure heart" is one that is cleansed from all indwelling sin, and is morally clean and right before God . . . and it cannot be clean until all inbred sin is removed by the cleansing blood of Christ. In the pure heart all the Christian virtues exist to the exclusion of their opposite vices, as love without hatred, submission without rebellion, faith without unbelief, humility without pride, meekness without anger, patience without impatience, and peace with no strife.[110]

Moreover, Wesley's ambiguity on the moral status of self-love was translated into the tradition as well. On one hand, some Wesleyans have followed the path of the Quietists in identifying self-love as the core of carnality, and they have maintained that it must be eliminated if one wishes to be truly holy. Pope is one who apparently favors this line of interpretation, since he believes that the love of God "must needs extinguish the very principle of self which is the true defilement of original sin."[111] On the other hand, there are other Wesleyans who have not viewed self-love so suspiciously. Although he was a staunch Holiness polemicist, A. M. Hills still believed that it is a mistake to equate sinfulness with self-love. He preferred to view sin as willfully choosing the desires and passions over the dictates of reason and intelligence that,

---

108. R. Taylor, *Right Conception*, 102.

109. Clarke, *Christian Theology*, 133.

110. J. A. Wood, *Purity and Maturity*, 49, quoted in Quanstrom, "Doctrine of Entire Sanctification," 31.

111. Pope, *Higher Catechism of Theology*, §6.4.3.4, 261.

consequently, lead to virtue.¹¹² If self-interest is guided by right reason, a desire for holiness will ensue.¹¹³

The Propagation of Questionable Claims

In the end, the ongoing distortion of Wesley's views led to claims that are highly implausible. The Holiness Movement's stress on entire sanctification led to some of these exaggerations. Although Wesley viewed perfection as a process that is brought to completion in this life, the Holiness people generally understood it to be an event that is realized instantaneously. Clarke asserts that in a moment the sanctified heart is "emptied of sin, filled with holiness, and becomes truly happy."¹¹⁴ Steele's words are even stronger and certainly unequivocal. "The evil in man . . . such as pride, malice, envy, etc. . . . It is the Wesleyan theory that these may all be destroyed at once in the removal of this indwelling evil without presenting each form of depravity separately to be burned up by the purifying Spirit."¹¹⁵ However, this assertion is antithetical to the approach that Wesley took, for he believed that unholy passions, dispositions, and tempers must be identified and crucified individually. Mark Quanstrom is absolutely correct when he indicates that Wesley's emphasis on gradual change was novel to Holiness people two centuries later.¹¹⁶

To the Holiness preachers and teachers, the experience of entire sanctification was sufficient to remove "the last trace of the indwelling or pollution of sin."¹¹⁷ Indeed, it was even claimed that one would thus be given deliverance over dispositions like impatience and anger.¹¹⁸ As

---

112. Hills is appropriating the thought of James Harris Fairchild, who taught moral philosophy and theology at Oberlin College, where Hills was a student. Fairchild went on to succeed Charles Finney as the third president of the institution.

113. Hills, *Scriptural Holiness*, 148–59.

114. Clarke, *Christian Theology*, 208–9.

115. D. Steele, *Christian Perfection*, 54.

116. Quanstrom, "Doctrine of Entire Sanctification," 188–89. Quanstrom also indicates that while the Church of the Nazarene has been committed to propagating the Holiness message since its inception, Wesley's "A Plain Account of Christian Perfection" was not a part of the denomination's ministerial training until 1952 (185). A general neglect of Wesley can be observed in other Wesleyan denominations as well.

117. Pope, *Higher Catechism of Theology*, §6.4.3.3, 256. Also, see Hills, *Scriptural Holiness*, 63–82.

118. Brengle, *Helps to Holiness*, 17–18.

such, entire sanctification is believed to be more than the mere repression of sinful proclivities, because the very "roots" of sin are removed and destroyed.[119] According to Taylor, this is what happened to the apostles on the day of Pentecost. When these believers were baptized with the Holy Spirit,

> ... [their] motives were purified of self-seeking, dispositions were cleansed of malice, and devotion became an undivided and unquenchable flame.... Their carnal nature was not merely overcome by the effulgent glory of the pentecostal power, but was cleansed out. The very impulses of their natures were deeply altered.[120]

He believes that the same experience is to be expected today. Whenever someone is baptized with the Holy Spirit, "the predispositional bent toward self-sovereignty and self-willfulness ... can be radically displaced with a bent toward pliancy, submissiveness, and humility before God."[121] All of this is understood to take place in an instant.

Holiness proponents felt this change to be so radical that some were willing to assert that the "sanctified" believer cannot sin.[122] For instance, Samuel Brengle claimed that since the "very roots of sin" are destroyed in entire sanctification, an alcoholic would "no longer be tempted in the least to get drunk."[123] However, many Holiness people were skeptical of such optimism, and yet they still recognized the need to maintain the highest standards of "holiness of heart and life," to coin a phrase from Wesley himself. Methodist bishop R. S. Foster issued a stern warning in that regard. "Would you maintain a sanctified state? Then must there be on your part an absolute refusal to comply with temptation under any circumstance, to *any degree*. The slightest compliance is death."[124] Indeed, a number of Holiness people felt a strong

---

119. Cook, *New Testament Holiness*, 30.

120. R. Taylor, *Right Conception*, 33.

121. R. Taylor, "Relation of the Holy Spirit," 89–90.

122. Quanstrom, "Doctrine of Entire Sanctification," 60.

123. Brengle, *Helps to Holiness*, 27–28. At the turn of the twentieth century Brengle was commissioner of the Salvation Army, which has been a part of the Holiness traditions since its origin. He wrote a number of books that are representative of Holiness teaching at that time.

124. Foster, "How to Retain the Blessing," 37.

sense of urgency, for they truly believed that one would ultimately be damned if entire sanctification were not achieved and retained.[125]

This teaching does not accurately represent the substance of Wesley's thought. He does not insist that unless one attain Christian perfection before death, one will be damned for hell. Furthermore, he does not embrace the notion of supernatural, instantaneous change as some of his followers do. Although he was told by the Moravians that conversion is an instantaneous and complete deliverance from all sin, he concludes that full spiritual transformation is not realized in an instant.[126] Maddox contends that Wesley's conception of "responsible grace" suggests variability in personal experience. Since we are expected to respond to God's grace without coercion, it is only logical to expect responsiveness to vary from person to person.[127]

Methodism's Neglect of Wesley's Distinctive Doctrines

It can be said that the Methodist neglect of Christian perfection is what sparked the Holiness Movement, but it can also be argued that the excesses of the Holiness Movement fueled the Methodist aversion to the doctrine. John Leland Peters concludes that the nineteenth-century emphasis on Christian perfection essentially created a division in Wesleyanism. "Thus two groups with antithetical points of view were mutually repelled by the extremes each saw in the other. . . . Reaction provoked reaction, and extreme begot extreme."[128] Outler provides a similar account of events.

> The nineteenth-century conflicts that swirled around Wesley's emphasis upon "holiness of heart and life" [led to] its alterations and distortions at the hands of men and women who were seeking to be faithful Wesleyans (on both sides!) without having experienced anything close to the theological and spiritual struggles out of which his own original synthesis had emerged. The ironic outcome of this process (especially in America) was that the keystone in the arch of Wesley's own theological "system" came to be a pebble in the shoes of standard-brand Methodists,

---

125. Quanstrom, "Doctrine of Entire Sanctification," 52. In fact, W. B. Godbey authored a short book in the twentieth century entitled *Holiness or Hell*.

126. Maddox, *Responsible Grace*, 153.

127. Ibid., 156.

128. Peters, *Christian Perfection*, 192.

even as a distorted version of Wesley's doctrine of sanctification (as "a second and separate work of grace *subsequent to* regeneration") was becoming a shibboleth of self-righteousness amongst a pious minority of Methodists who professed themselves holier than the rest. That conflict and its abrasions had the effect of leaving the average Methodist (and many much above average) alienated even by the bare terms—"holiness," "Christian perfection," "sanctification"—not to speak of an aversion toward those persons who actually profess such spiritual attainments.[129]

As a result of the controversy over Christian perfection, Methodists shied away from the doctrine altogether. Peters believes that this antipathy continues to be felt among twentieth-century Methodists, for whom the doctrine does not hold "anything like the significant place given it by Wesley."[130] Cobb concurs that it was the insistence on an instantaneous experience of entire sanctification that "had so many negative consequences that much of the Wesleyan movement abandoned, to its loss, the entire doctrine of perfection."[131]

Methodists have thus distanced themselves from the other Wesleyan traditions. Oden points out that although United Methodists have initiated dialog with many other traditions (e.g., Reformed, Lutheran, Eastern Orthodox, Catholic), they have not yet reached out to other Wesleyan groups, especially the conservative Wesleyan traditions (e.g., Wesleyan Church and Free Methodist Church) and the Holiness and Pentecostal traditions that sprang from "nineteenth-century Methodist, holiness, and sanctificationist revivalism."[132] Moreover, Methodists have sought to distance themselves from the rest of Wesleyanism not only in relationship, but sometimes theologically, too. For example, Quanstrom believes that John Miley's writings on sanctification were largely a polemic against the Holiness Movement.[133]

Robert Chiles outlines a gradual theological shift in American Methodism from 1790 to 1935, evidenced most clearly in the thought of Richard Watson, John Miley, and Albert Knudson. This shift occurred mainly in three areas. First, Methodists came to rely less upon

129. Outler, *Wesleyan Spirit*, 66–67.
130. Peters, *Christian Perfection*, 195–96.
131. Cobb, *Grace and Responsibility*, 110.
132. Oden, *Doctrinal Standards*, 127.
133. Quanstrom, "Doctrine of Entire Sanctification," 77.

revelation and more upon human reason. Second, human nature was seen less as sinful and corrupt and more as inherently good and moral. Third, there was a change in emphasis from free grace to free will.[134] In and of themselves, these developments are not bad. In fact, they can be embraced to a significant extent. However, it appears that these shifts were not intended to be developments of Wesley's thought, but departures from it.

Outler adds that Methodism was altered in the twentieth century by three other transmutations: (1) embracing liberal Protestantism; (2) adopting the Social Gospel; (3) "the tragic immoderations of the late nineteenth-century controversies between the 'liberals' and partisans of 'holiness.'"[135] Whereas the changes noted by Chiles could perhaps be reconciled with Wesley's thought, these latter alterations do not seem to be as compatible with Wesley, with the exception that the Social Gospel has some key similarities with Wesley's views on social action and ministering to the poor. In any event, with all of these modifications to Methodist thought, it is not surprising that twentieth-century Methodists have tended to neglect Wesley himself. As Maddox notes, even most Methodist academic theologians did not show an interest in Wesley's thought until the last half of the century.[136]

Outler says that Methodists' unfamiliarity with Wesley can even be evidenced in the ordination ritual. Ordinands are asked the following questions: (1) "Have you faith in Christ?" (2) "Are you going on to perfection?" (3) "Do you expect to be made perfect in this life?" and (4) "Are you earnestly striving after it?" Outler believes that too often these questions are affirmed without any deep understanding of the issues involved.[137] This seems like a rather harsh indictment until one realizes just how few Methodists actually grapple with the issues of perfection and assurance.

Too often, Wesley's teachings on these subjects are either flatly denied or treated in a superficial way. For instance, Philip Wogaman explains, "Thus, when Wesley speaks of Christian perfection . . . he means

---

134. Chiles, *Theological Transition*, 198.
135. Outler, "Biblical Primitivism," 156.
136. Maddox, "Reclaiming an Inheritance," 220.
137. Outler, *Wesleyan Spirit*, 66.

growth in love. To be perfect is to be loving as God is loving."[138] I am sure that Wogaman's understanding of Wesley's views on perfection are more nuanced than is suggested by such vague generalities. However, one would be hard pressed to find a significant number of Methodists who address these issues in a theologically informed and philosophically sophisticated way.

This can perhaps be illustrated by a pair of essays presented at the consultation, "Wesleyan Theology in the Next Century: United Methodism Reviews Its Theological Task," which was held in commemoration of the bicentennial of Methodism. In one of the essays, Robin Lovin offers a solid exposition of Wesley's understanding of virtue, then he assesses its relevance in several respects.[139] In the other, Stanley Hauerwas gives several reasons why he feels that Wesley's view of perfection is too vague and unfashionable today. He then proceeds to defend the account of perfection promoted by William Law, a man whose views Wesley ultimately rejected.[140] Although Wesley considered this doctrine the "grand depositum" of Methodism, Hauerwas brushes Wesley's account of perfection aside because it does not fit neatly into his agenda. He defends Law's account of perfection because it is based on concrete examples, rather than characterizations, and this more easily reinforces his claim that virtue is learned through example.[141] Granted, Hauerwas does not claim to be a devoted and loyal Wesleyan, but this raises the question as to why someone who has very little commitment to Wesley would be chosen to represent Methodism at its bicentennial.

Cobb ponders the effect of this general neglect (at times, disdain) of Wesley. "After the decline of Boston Personalism, we United Methodists have lost our way theologically. We are fragmented in the extreme, although a certain ethos, derived from our Wesleyan heritage, enables the denomination as an institution to hold us together."[142] The Wesleyan tradition is essentially fragmented because the inner workings of Wesley's thought have not been developed intellectually. Instead, some particular aspect of Wesley is cited apart from the broader and

---

138. Wogaman, *Christian Moral Judgment*, 36.
139. Lovin, "Physics of True Virtue," 264–72.
140. Hauerwas, "Characterizing Perfection," 252.
141. Ibid., 260.
142. Cobb, *Grace and Responsibility*, 8.

deeper context of his thought and life. If one were to lend equal credence to all of the ways that Wesley has been appropriated, he would seem to be a rare figure indeed, for he would appear to be on both sides of virtually every issue that has historically confronted humanity.

Toning Down the Message

Within the last century, Holiness people have begun to temper many of the more radical assertions that had been characteristic of the earlier tradition. According to Jones, the emergence of Pentecostalism was the turning point. Early Holiness people sought assurance of entire sanctification, and this led to an external legalism and to an emphasis on testimony and emotional demonstration, especially the practice of shouting in worship services. However, when the Pentecostal Movement began to insist on tongues as the evidence of the baptism of the Holy Spirit, the Holiness people began to decrease their emphasis on personal experience.[143]

Just as Wesley felt the need to modify his doctrine of sin (in order to make it more compatible with his doctrine of Christian perfection), the Wesleyans made similar alterations to their teaching. The Keswick Movement taught that believers must be filled (i.e., baptized) by the Spirit, but they never insisted that this implies a deliverance from sinful inclinations. Although the Pentecostals did initially have the stronger emphasis, it was soon abandoned and began to resemble Keswick teaching in that respect.

In contrast, the Holiness movement insisted on full deliverance from sin, but in order to defend this, they had to make a distinction between purity and maturity. Purity is achieved instantaneously, but maturity is a perpetual process.[144] Cook explains that the heart is supernaturally purified in entire sanctification so as to be free of hatred, unbelief, and anger. Nevertheless, this purity is distinct from "the ripeness and fullness of Christian virtues."[145] According to Kenneth Grider, unintentional breaches in God's will do not require God's forgiveness.

---

143. C. Jones, "Tongues-Speaking," 117–24.

144. Many Holiness authors have made this distinction. See J. A. Wood, *Purity and Maturity*.

145. Cook, *New Testament Holiness*, 33–34.

They only require cleansing, and this is an ongoing effect of walking in the light.[146]

At first glance, this seems like a logical way to rescue the holiness message, because it retains Wesley's distinction between action and motive, but this attempt is ultimately found wanting. The more simplistic approach to this issue is to create a false dichotomy between "carnal nature" and "human nature." Grider is a representative of this line of thought, and he claims that motives can arise from either of the two natures. In the entirely sanctified, carnality is "cleansed away," but motives arising from human nature are not necessarily pure in the "wider sense" of being acceptable to God.[147]

In 1972, the appearance of Mildred Bangs Wynkoop's book *A Theology of Love*, sparked a controversy within Holiness circles, because Wynkoop challenged many of the conventions that had dominated Holiness thought and practice for over a century. This debate helped to foster a growing interest in deeper scholarship, particularly in theological matters, and most especially in the study of Wesley himself. Wynkoop found herself dissatisfied with the status quo, and she not only called many assumptions into question, she suggested that the movement had indeed misinterpreted Wesley.

Wynkoop argues against what she refers to as a "magical" interpretation of salvation. Instead, salvation should be given a "moral" interpretation. Wynkoop feels that although the intellectual roots of this misconception can be traced back to early Christianity, Wesleyanism has historically embraced it par excellence. She sees the "magical" view as resting on two longstanding but faulty notions: ontological dualism and salvation as a reality of substance.[148] First, a dualistic conception of human nature (as pure spirit and corrupt body) is favored over a more holistic view of the human being, which regards the person as an integrated unity. Wynkoop believes that human personality is not dualistic in any sense, but always "acts as a single unity."[149]

Second, salvation is described in substantial, rather than relational, terms. When salvation is depicted this way, concepts like sin, holiness,

---

146. Grider, *Wesleyan-Holiness Theology*, 293.
147. Ibid., 458.
148. Wynkoop, *Theology of Love*, 48–49.
149. Ibid., 339.

and love are regarded as entities, not as properties. Wynkoop explains that a notion like holiness cannot be regarded as an entity, because holiness is not something that is imparted from without, like superadded grace, nor is it simply the presence of the Holy Spirit. Also, it is not a substantial change within the soul, but it is certainly more than mere judicial standing. Rather, holiness can be likened to spiritual health, in which the individual is in proper relationship with God, with others, and with herself.[150]

She proceeds to explain why she considers these two assumptions to be problematic.

> The inadequacy—even danger—of the above positions lies exposed in the next logical step. It is the contrast between the magical versus moral interpretation of salvation. This means that a sub-rational, psychological mutation defines cleansing from sin. The problem here is that men come to expect a substance alteration of the soul in salvation which occurs below the level of rational life and which, apart from personal involvement, changes the impulsive reactions of the self. Anger and pride and all other normal human emotional equipment is said to be removed, so that responsibility for discipline and proper channeling of the emotions is considered a suppression which denies what God ought to do.
>
> The moral interpretation stresses the full participation of the self in every step in grace, strengthening rather than weakening moral integrity and taking responsibility for the ordering of all human impulse and powers around a central and controlling love. Nothing human is despised or rejected but made to serve a new master.
>
> These three assumptions—(1) the Greek versus Hebrew concept of man, (2) the substantial versus relational concept of sin, and (3) the magical versus moral concept of salvation—create a vastly different "Wesleyanism" (if that term could any longer be used) than Wesley himself taught.[151]

Wynkoop avers that Wesley was not as concerned with ontological questions as he was with moral motivation.[152] The latter is a more appropriate place for Wesleyans to focus.

---

150. Ibid., 359–60.
151. Ibid., 49–50.
152. Ibid., 166.

Nevertheless, it should not be assumed that Wynkoop is discounting supernaturalism altogether, for she distinguishes magic from what she regards as legitimate faith in the supernatural.

> Magic is always amoral and a-causal, whether it is religious or otherwise. Some critics of evangelicalism have called supernaturalism belief in magic. This charge cannot stand up under scholarly investigation, but a supernaturalism that supposes it can bypass the moral dimension of human experience *is* belief in magic. The Bible stands squarely opposed to just such perversions of truth. Its supernaturalism is preserved from the amorality of speculation precisely by the incarnation of Christ and the involvement of human experience in truth. Faith as taught in the Scripture is not credulity but is intellectually and morally relevant. Supernaturalism is not super-history but God's grace met by human faith.[153]

I fully concur with Wynkoop's analysis, especially her belief that it is possible to construe Wesleyan ethics in a way that underscores the need for moral development and progress. This will entail a more naturalized account of grace, but this does not necessarily dismiss supernaturalism out of hand, as I shall endeavor to show.

---

153. Ibid., 243.

2

The Call for a New Paradigm

Justifying the New Approach

AS WE HAVE SEEN, THE DOCTRINES OF ASSURANCE AND PERFECTION were central to Wesley's theological concerns. Indeed, they are the cornerstone of Wesleyan virtue ethics. However, these two doctrines, along with other doctrines that support them, have some glaring weaknesses and vulnerabilities. As such, they are in need of development. Although the subsequent Wesleyan traditions attempted to develop Wesley's doctrine of perfection in particular ways, they essentially distorted Wesley's views and produced accounts that cannot be rationally defended. Moreover, many Methodists have abandoned Wesley's project altogether and moved on to other issues.

If Wesley's agenda is to be salvaged, it will require the construction of a new paradigm, one that retains Wesley's core concerns and commitments in a way that is intellectually defensible. It is my contention that a more cognitivist version of Wesleyan ethics will not only avoid the pitfalls of the past, it will capture the more intellectual side of Wesley that has so often been ignored. Wesley was not as mystical as he has sometimes been portrayed. Rather, he had a high regard for the use of reason, and this suggests the possibility of the type of development I am proposing.

Wesley's Rejection of Mysticism

Early in his life, Wesley was attracted to mysticism, especially the writings of William Law, with whom he carried on correspondence for quite some time. Wallace Gray speculates, "Probably the emphasis upon heart holiness attracted him more than any other aspect of mysticism."[1] John Cobb outlines two areas of agreement between Wesley and the mystics: (1) they both saw perfection as the all-encompassing goal of the Christian life; (2) they believed that those who would be perfect must focus more on internal motivation than on external action. However, Wesley felt that while some of the mystics underemphasized human responsibility, others failed to stress sinfulness and the need for divine grace. The latter claimed that human beings should enlarge the divine presence within them.[2] To be sure, Wesley is not objecting to human effort itself. What he opposes is stressing human effort without recognizing the operation of divine grace that makes it possible.

Wesley's attraction to mysticism was always qualified, and he eventually came to reject the mystical approach to religion. One of his most basic complaints against the mystics is that they spoil "plain Christianity" by continually refining it beyond the tenets of Scripture.[3] He claims that they "find hidden meanings in everything" and "seek mysteries in the plainest truths."[4] This is not to say that the role of reason should be diminished. On the contrary, Wesley asserts, "There are many, it is confessed, 'particularly those who are styled mystic divines,' that utterly decry the use of reason, thus understood, in religion—nay, that condemn all reasoning concerning the things of God, as utterly destructive of true religion."[5] According to Gray, "Wesley seems also to have objected to that extreme emphasis in mysticism upon mystery which occasionally borders on a-rationalism or even anti-rationalism."[6] In fact, Wesley also accuses Luther of disdaining reason.[7]

As Wesley told Law, the danger is that "they who stop the workings of their reason lie the more open to the workings of their imagination."[8] In the case of Madame Guyon, she "imagined herself to be infallible"

---

1. Gray, "Place of Reason," 144.

2. Cobb, *Grace and Responsibility*, 49–50.

3. Wesley, letter DCCCXVIII to Miss Newman, Cheltenham, 23 Oct 1772, *WWJ*, 13:165–66.

4. Wesley, preface to "A Christian Library," *WWJ*, 14:221–22.

5. Wesley, "An Ernest Appeal to Men of Reason and Religion," §30, *WW*, 11:55–56 [J 8:12].

6. Gray, "Place of Reason," 22.

7. Wesley, journal entry, 15 June 1741, *WW*, 10:200–201 [J 1:15].

8. Wesley to William Law, 6 January 1756, *WWJ*, 9:503.

because she believed that the strong impressions she felt were all placed on her by God.⁹ Wesley asserts that all spiritual knowledge must meet the test of "the law and the testimony," i.e., Scripture and the tradition of Christian orthodoxy.¹⁰ In Wesley's mind, the mystics ultimately failed this test, because they exceeded the boundaries of both reason and Scripture.¹¹ In so doing, they made personal experience the standard of religion and consequently created a plethora of religions.¹² This same mistake has been made in Wesleyanism.

Wesley's High Regard for Reason

Wesley most likely depicted the mystics this way since he possessed a strong inclination toward reason throughout his life. Even as a child, he was noted for having a "sober and serious disposition," which was guided compellingly by his reason and conscience.¹³ Gray surmises that Wesley was predisposed to theoretical and speculative matters more than he could either recognize or justify.¹⁴ He states,

> Those who misunderstood Wesley as an anti-intellectual, because of his work with the unlettered, were overlooking his quite rationalistic method of controversy, his many intellectual interests, and the rather definite, though non-creative, place he assigned to reason in theology.¹⁵

Wesley was also well-read, for his own recorded bibliography includes over 1,400 different authors with nearly 3,000 separate items ranging from pamphlets to twelve-volume sets. Moreover, he frequently quoted the classics from memory with a high degree of accuracy.¹⁶ According to Albert Outler, "Wesley had a vast repertoire of obscure lore on which he drew almost casually."¹⁷ He also was interested in

---

9. Wesley, preface to "An Extract of the Life of Madame Guion," *WWJ*, 14:276.
10. Wesley to Law, 6 January 1756, §2.6, *WWJ*, 9:466, 503.
11. Wesley, Sermon 123, "On Knowing Christ after the Flesh," §15, *WW*, 4:105 [J 7:296].
12. Wesley to Miss Bishop, 19 September 1773, *WWJ*, 13:25.
13. Matthews, "Religion and Reason Joined," 3–4.
14. Gray, "Place of Reason," 64.
15. Ibid., 50.
16. Outler, "John Wesley: Folk Theologian," in *Theological Heritage*, 114.
17. Ibid., 116.

scientific experiments and even dabbled in medicine and electrical shock therapy.[18]

Donald Thorsen claims that Wesley was "predisposed by the Anglican tradition toward reason, the Aristotelian tradition of logic, and the validity of reason as a source of religious authority."[19] He adds that Wesley had "great confidence in the power of people to think logically, especially in spiritual matters."[20] Rex Matthews concurs, affirming the notion that Wesley's understanding of reason "is derived directly from the Oxford Aristotelian logical tradition."[21]

Wesley extensively used logical argumentation. One of his contemporaries during his college days described him as "a very sensible and acute collegian, baffling every man by his subtleties of logic, and laughing at them for being so easily routed."[22] In fact, Wesley was worried that he might get carried away with his penchant for logic and the sciences.

> So I am convinced, from many experiments, I could not study, to any degree of perfection, either mathematics, arithmetic, or algebra, without being a Deist, if not an Atheist. . . . Every man must judge for himself and abstain from whatever he in particular finds to be hurtful to his soul.[23]

Outler believes that this apprehension over mathematics is one of the places where Wesley agrees with the Cambridge Platonists, who "broke with the strongest and most fruitful scientific force of the seventeenth century, exact mathematics." Wesley thus appears to embrace their notion that nature has a certain mystery that cannot be quantified or reduced by mathematics and science.[24] A comment made by Wesley in a letter to John Robertson seems to confirm Outler's conclusion. After reading Andrew Michael Ramsey's *Principles of Religion*, Wesley told Robertson, "The treatise itself gave me a stronger conviction than I

---

18. Ibid., 117.
19. Thorsen, *Wesleyan Quadrilateral*, 174.
20. Ibid., 170.
21. Matthews, "Religion and Reason Joined," 157.
22. See Telford's note, *Letters of the Rev. John Wesley*, 1:7n, quoted by Matthews, "Religion and Reason Joined," 145.
23. Wesley, Sermon 50, "The Use of Money," §1.2, WW, 2:270 [J 6:128].
24. Outler, WW, 2:270 n. 17.

ever had before both of the fallaciousness and unsatisfactoriness of the mathematical method of reasoning on religious subjects."[25]

One of the reasons that Wesley has been mischaracterized is the fact that he often seems vague. In part this can be attributed to the fact that, once he gave up his academic life at Oxford, he turned his attention to evangelism and to the more pressing matter of organizing the Methodist movement that he started. Moreover, Wesley was a highly eclectic thinker. As Outler puts it, "He was, of course, trying to hold too many disparate concerns together, and this helps explain why he left so few successors who were interested in, or capable of, repeating his special accomplishments."[26] In the early 1960's, Outler argued that Wesley's value as a major theologian was to be found in his "folk theology," i.e., his ability to synthesize and simplify theology for the laity. By the mid-1980's, after two decades of critically studying Wesley's writings, Outler was claiming that Wesley's methodology was "an authentic and creative form in its own right" and was not inferior to "academic theology."[27]

Outler thus believes that Wesley's desire to simplify complicated matters for his audience often camouflages the depth of his thought. "Most of the quotations in Wesley's writings are uncited (and rarely verbatim). Most of his allusions are unidentified. It is as if he never expected to have a critical edition of his works."[28] As a result,

> [Wesley's] deliberate oversimplifications have helped many of his readers to miss the range and richness of his theological learning. In this way, though, they also miss . . . his grasp of the tangled web of controversies which he was inclined to resolve without exposing his readers to their complexities. A consequence of this has been an obscuration of his theological sophistication and originality, which remain largely unacknowledged.[29]

However, Wesley's depth is much greater than is often recognized.

> As the offspring of an Oxford-educated father and an extraordinarily intelligent and theologically acute mother, the product

25. Wesley to John Robertson, 24 September 1753, *WW*, 26:515 [J 12:211].
26. Outler, "Pietism and Enlightenment," 254.
27. Maddox, "Reclaiming an Inheritance," 225.
28. Outler, "John Wesley: Folk Theologian," 113.
29. Outler et al. "Wesley Studies," 54.

of Christ Church and Lincoln Colleges, Fellow of Lincoln and Lecturer there in Greek and Logic, voracious reader and, when necessary, tenacious controversialist, John Wesley was very much more a child of the "Age of Reason" and a citizen of the Eighteenth Century Commonwealth of Ideas than many students of his thought, or the period, seem to have realized.[30]

It has been said that the pietism of Wesley's mother Susanna made her value reason less than her husband Samuel, and this created a tension within John's thought and life.[31] Whether or not this tension can be ascribed to Wesley's parents, it is obvious that his loyalties were divided between orthodox Christianity, pietism, and the intellectual currents of the Enlightenment.[32] Outler believes that Wesley's doctrine of grace is a good example of this tension, for his stress on free grace can be regarded as a more orthodox prototype of the Enlightenment notion of liberty.[33] What Wesley actually did was propose an account of grace that could better reconcile the Enlightenment notion of liberty with the Arminian notion of free will.

In any event, Wesley was conscious of both the value and the ambiguities of reason, and he thus tried to avoid the extremes of valuing reason too much or too little. On one hand, "Among them that despise and vilify reason, you may always expect to find those enthusiasts who suppose the dreams of their own imagination to be revelations from God."[34] On the other hand, those who regard reason as virtually infallible are almost always the same people who reject divine revelation.[35] Wesley thus sought a "happy medium" between these two extremes.[36] Rebekah Miles points out that in distancing himself from the Deists, Wesley rejected the notion that reason is an independent source of knowledge of God.[37] He believed that with the exception of divine revelation, our knowledge of God does not come from inward impressions,

---

30. Matthews, "Religion and Reason Joined," 5.
31. Gray, "Place of Reason," 241.
32. Outler, "Pietism and Enlightenment," 252–55.
33. Ibid., 253.
34. Wesley, Sermon 70, "The Case of Reason Impartially Considered," §2, *WW*, 2:587 [J 6:351].
35. Ibid., §§3–4, *WW*, 2:588 [J 6:351].
36. Miles, "Instrumental Role of Reason," 83.
37. Ibid., 85.

but is limited to the empirical.[38] We acquire knowledge of God from the Scriptures, and the Holy Spirit assists us in this endeavor.[39] Although Wesley gradually tempered his confidence in reason by asserting more strongly the need for grace, he continued to maintain that religious belief can be rationally assessed and justified.[40]

For Wesley, reason is also limited in that it is incapable of producing the theological virtues (faith, hope, and love). It cannot produce faith, because faith ultimately lies beyond the reach of the natural senses. Rather, faith involves the perception of spiritual realities. As such, reason must work with perceptions that are supplied by "spiritual senses."[41] Since Wesley believes that faith produces hope—after which love, virtue, and happiness are produced in succession—reason is likewise unable to produce these properties on its own.[42] What is vitally important, according to Wesley, is that we be aware of our own ignorance, and this awareness should stir within us humility, faith in God, and resignation to obey God's will.[43]

There is no conflict between religion and reason, in Wesley's mind. It is the human thirst for knowledge that elevates our thoughts above the mundane and turns our attention ultimately toward God.[44] Indeed, religion and reason complement each other. "It is a fundamental principle with us, that to renounce reason is to renounce religion, that religion and reason go hand in hand, and that all irrational religion is false religion."[45] To the extent that we depart from "true, genuine reason,"

---

38. Wesley, Sermon 69, "The Imperfection of Human Knowledge," §1.4, WW, 2:571 [J 6:339].

39. Wesley, Sermon 70, "The Case of Reason Impartially Considered," §1.6, WW, 2:592 [J 6:354].

40. Thorsen, Wesleyan Quadrilateral, 197.

41. Wesley claimed that believers receive "spiritual senses" at conversion, enabling them to perceive spiritual realities. He borrows this analogy from sources like the Macarian homilies, Malebranche, and John Norris, among others. This will be explained in greater detail in a subsequent chapter.

42. Wesley, Sermon 70, "The Case of Reason Impartially Considered," §§2.1–10, WW, 2:593–600 [J 6:355–60].

43. Wesley, Sermon 69, "The Imperfection of Human Knowledge," §§4.1–3, WW, 2:584-6 [J 6:349–50].

44. Ibid., §1, WW, 2:568 [J 6:337].

45. Wesley to Thomas Rutherford, 28 March 1768, §3.4, WW, 9:382 [J 14:354].

we depart from Christianity itself.⁴⁶ "Passion and prejudice govern the world, only under the name of reason. It is our part, by religion and reason joined, to counteract them all we can."⁴⁷

Hence, maintaining harmony between religion and reason was of the utmost importance to Wesley. "Now I believe and reason too: For I find no inconsistency between them. And I would just as soon put out my eyes to secure my faith, as lay aside my reason."⁴⁸ He firmly declares, "I wish to be, in every point, great and small, a scriptural, rational Christian."⁴⁹

The Type of Change That Is Being Proposed

A New Context for Wesleyan Ethics

Before any type of change or development can be suggested, Wesley must be seen in his historical and intellectual context so that Wesleyan moral theory can be developed without disconnecting itself from the inner workings of Wesley's thought. In this way, the ethic can still be truly labeled as Wesleyan. Care must be taken to avoid the narrow stereotypes that Outler believes have been attached to Wesley. "In America, especially, Wesley has been invoked oftener than he has been read and usually has been read with a low-church anti-intellectualist bias that celebrates his warm heart and worn saddlebags, unconcerned with his theology."⁵⁰ Rather, what is needed is a resurgence of Wesleyan intellectualism.

> We have, by now, a nearly irreversible tradition of "anti-intellectualism" in Methodism which neither nourishes nor cherishes theology as top priority. . . . Most of our Methodist theological professors have been trained in ecumenical centers (which is altogether right and proper) but with often little or no

---

46. Wesley, "An Earnest Appeal to Men of Religion and Reason," §27, *WW*, 11:54-55 [J 8:11].

47. Wesley to Joseph Benson, 5 October 1770, *WWJ*, 12:412-13.

48. Wesley, "A Dialogue Between and Antinomian and His Friend," *WWJ*, 10:267. Obviously, Wesley assumes the position of the friend in debating with the "antinomian."

49. Wesley to Freeborn Garrettson, 24 January 1789, *WWJ*, 13:73; cf. Wesley to Miss Bishop, 1767, *WWJ*, 13:17.

50. Outler, "Towards a Re-Appraisal of John Wesley," in *Theological Heritage*, 53.

acquaintance with Wesley himself as a resource for ecumenical theologizing. The result is, that Wesleyan theologians are rare enough to be listed as an "endangered species."[51]

Matthews points out that even some of the intellectual studies of Wesley have been short-sighted. In discussing the role of reason in Wesley's thought, he notes that all of the earlier works on the subject fail "to consider carefully enough the implications of the intellectual environment within which Wesley lived for his understanding of the nature and function of reason or for the role of faith in his epistemology."[52] Therefore, the first task at hand is to place Wesley within his historical and intellectual context. This includes recognizing the trajectories of his thought as he developed his views over time, a detail that is sometimes overlooked.[53]

This is merely the starting point, because Wesleyan ethics does indeed need to progress beyond Wesley himself. Cobb is of the opinion that Wesley's thought cannot be simply repeated today. Rather, it needs to be reappraised as to its relevance for our time.[54] Randy Maddox adds that "authentic Wesleyan theological activity today" is not simply restating Wesley's views and emphases, for it entails relating "responsible grace" to "situation-related theological activity." It may even mean disagreeing with Wesley at times and perhaps suggest "that there is an even more adequate orienting concern that should guide our practical-theological activity than 'responsible grace.' But if that day should come, it will be itself a contribution from taking Wesley as a theological mentor."[55]

Nevertheless, if an ethic is to be called a genuinely Wesleyan ethic, then it must remain consistent with the primary theological concerns

---

51. Outler, "John Wesley as Theologian—Then and Now," in *Theological Heritage*, 73.

52. Matthews, "Religion and Reason Joined," 10–11.

53. To cite a recent example, Stephen Long attempts to distance Wesley in particular ways from the intellectual currents of the Enlightenment. However, it is my opinion that Long does not give enough attention to the progression of Wesley's own thought, and this allows the analysis to be skewed to some extent. In several places Long correctly notes the ambiguity of Wesley's views, and this is indicative of Wesley's attempt to hold contrasting strands of thought in tension with one another. However, as Wesley nuanced his views over time, these points of tension often shifted. See Long, *John Wesley's Moral Theology*.

54. Cobb, *Grace and Responsibility*, 9.

55. Maddox, *Responsible Grace*, 256.

and goals that Wesley held. It is my conjecture that Wesley's thought, in spite of the fact that it is couched in theological and mystical terminology and imagery, has a cognitivist foundation that can be built upon. This would imply that Wesley's ethics can be developed philosophically without abandoning the inner workings of his thought. I am also suggesting that the future development of Wesleyan ethics is better served through a broader intellectual context and not merely through a broader experiential context.

It should be noted, however, that a comprehensive historical interpretation of Wesley's ethical thought is not being attempted. Rather, I will outline a fresh context for the intellectual development of Wesleyan ethics, one that will avoid the distortions and narrow interpretations that typically have been attached to Wesley. Locating Wesley within his wider intellectual context will allow him to be related to his contemporaries, and this should provide some needed options for addressing Wesley's concerns in a more comprehensive manner. The goal is to recast Wesleyan ethics in a paradigm that more adequately emphasizes the cognitive aspects of religious knowledge and moral development.

In order to accomplish this, a new paradigm for Wesleyan ethics will be constructed in two basic stages. In the first stage, I will explore the cognitivist roots of Wesley's thought. This will begin with an analysis of his reliance upon Lockean empiricism. Even though Wesley's dependence on Locke is limited in specific ways, Wesley is still an empiricist at heart, and his thought should be understood from that perspective. I contend that Wesleyan epistemology should remain more closely tied to empirical knowledge and distance itself from mystical and intuitionist models like Wesley's own "spiritual sense" analogy. Not only would a more empirically grounded version of Wesleyan ethics be more compatible with Wesley's general theory of knowledge, it would also be more consistent with the types of authors that appealed most to him.

Wesley's cognitivist tendencies are apparent not only in his empiricism, but also in his view of emotions. I will attempt to show that Wesleyan ethics should not regard emotions as something to be passively experienced. Rather, emotions have cognitive content that allows them to be shaped and scrutinized. Viewing the emotions this way implies that inner change and transformation begin in the mind. This perspective is reflected in Wesley's rejection of mysticism, especially that which disdains or otherwise neglects the means of grace. For Wesley, the means of grace are not magical rituals that are disconnected from natural processes. On the contrary, they are practices that shape the individual at the cognitive level. The cognitivist understanding of emotion is even more evident in the way that Wesley appropriates Edwards' *Treatise Concerning Religious Affections*. In that regard, a chapter will be devoted to an exposition of Wesley's abridgement of this work.

In the second stage of my constructive effort, the new paradigm will be completed by suggesting ways that Wesley's own concepts should be revised and expanded. This will allow more of Wesley's concerns to be incorporated into the paradigm without sacrificing his core commitments. Oddly enough, I will suggest that some of Wesley's categories can be informed by Kant's concepts. In relating Wesley to Kant, it is not my intention to build a strong link between the two of them. Indeed, I am not even suggesting that Wesley and Kant had any familiarity with one another, only that Wesleyan concepts can in certain respects be informed by Kant's ethical thought. Wesley and Kant share some key similarities in their ethics, and this should not be surprising, considering the fact that they are both responding to the developments in moral thought that followed Locke throughout the eighteenth century. Of course, it cannot be assumed that Wesley and Kant mean the same thing even when using the same terminology. As such, particular terms will be carefully nuanced so that Kant's concepts can appropriately inform a Wesleyan intellectual framework.

In the final chapter I will provide a sketch of what the doctrines of assurance and perfection will look like in the new paradigm. Essentially, assurance will be based on religious faith and on self-knowledge, both empirical and psychological, and perfection will be understood in a more teleological context. Hopefully, the end-result will be a version of Wesleyan ethics that is a more faithful development of Wesley's own thought and can withstand the scrutiny of higher intellectual standards.

Developing Wesley's Two Distinctive Doctrines

Up to this point, I have contended that Wesley's doctrines of assurance and perfection were regarded by him as central to his theology and are perhaps his most distinctive contributions to Christian thought. I also suggested that these doctrines have not been developed intellectually, and this lack of development is what permitted the two doctrines to be distorted in ways that are both inconsistent with particular aspects of Wesley's thought and unacceptable by higher intellectual standards. It is my belief that since these doctrines more generally represent concerns that have been held throughout the history of Christianity, they should not be abandoned. For instance, Cobb affirms that, "Although [Wesley's] doctrine of assurance never attained full clarity and certainly cannot be adopted by us in any of his specific formulations, the concern for knowing God's forgiving work in our lives is important for us as well."[56] I propose that these doctrines can be developed along more cognitivist lines and that this development will remain consistent with Wesley's primary concerns and motivations.

Within the type of development I am suggesting, assurance will still begin with an immediate sense of pardon, but it will be solidified through the assessment of one's own psychological state and moral progress. Experience will still have a more limited epistemic function. If Wesleyan ethics is to avoid the distortions that have historically been produced by an overemphasis on experience, then religious experience such as Wesley wishes to recognize will have more of an affirming role in assurance.

In addition, Wesleyan ethics must move away from Wesley's "spiritual sense" analogy, since it lends itself to validating subjective experiences that can be neither supported nor falsified. Furthermore, this approach to assurance does not regard divinely imparted, mystical knowledge to be the norm of human experience. This does not deny the possibility of God communicating directly with individuals. Nevertheless, it suggests that this communication seldom, if ever, supplies superadded knowledge to the individual. In this way, it would generally be the case that conscience only functions within the limits of the knowledge it has been supplied.

Kant's position on the issue of assurance is helpful in this regard, but I believe that he eliminates too much. He asserts that one's religious state is assessed by one's faith in satisfaction and by one's moral progress. As useful as this framework may be in judging one's long-term standing with God, it does not provide a basis for assurance at the time of conversion, which is Wesley's primary concern. A mediating position

---

56. Cobb, *Grace and Responsibility*, 10.

must be found between objective criteria and subjective experience, and I believe that such a position is what Jonathan Edwards is seeking in his evaluation of the Northampton revival and of religious affections in general.

Edwards is concerned with distinguishing what he regards as true and false conversion experiences. He proposes that the affections are perhaps the best way to gauge one's own spiritual status. He also suggests that subjective experiences should be evaluated in light of the attitudes and behaviors they produce. However, Edwards is a predestinationist, so his underlying motive for evaluating conversion experiences is to identify the elect. He believes that the non-elect (i.e., reprobates) can have false conversion experiences that resemble true conversions, yet these people will finally be unable to persevere in the Christian life. In his effort to make a clear distinction between true and false conversions, Edwards finally appeals to the same "spiritual sense" analogy that Wesley invokes.

In a Wesleyan paradigm (which is consequently Arminian), this would be regarded as a false dichotomy. According to Wesleyan soteriology, salvation can be forfeited, so it is believed possible that people can be genuinely converted and then fall away later. As such, conversion experiences are not neatly sorted into two categories. Rather, these experiences are judged across a spectrum according to their effectiveness in producing changed lives. Obviously, either Kant's criteria for assurance or Edwards' depiction of the religious affections could be used to make this assessment over time, but a Wesleyan doctrine of assurance needs to assess the conversion itself. Since I do not find the "spiritual sense" analogy (used by both Wesley and Edwards) to be compelling, I am suggesting that the best that can be hoped for is an accurate self-assessment by converts themselves. One must ultimately be able to evaluate one's own psychological state.

In the end, I believe that Wesley's two-fold model of the witness of the Spirit is the most satisfactory way to address these concerns. Before a new convert can attain a clear conscience, there must be faith in satisfaction and pardon, i.e., that one's sins have been forgiven. Whenever this faith is present, it is logical to conclude that a sense of immediate assurance would be granted by God. This seems to hold true even in a purely natural sense, since the exercise of faith would already include the seeds of assurance. However, the immediate sense of assurance would still need to be validated and solidified over time, and this corresponds with what Wesley refers to as the indirect witness of conscience (or reason). Consequently, religious experience does indeed play an important role in Wesleyan epistemology, but it must be confirmed by other sources, especially the subject's long-term moral progress.

This development of Wesleyan ethics also agrees with Mildred Bangs Wynkoop, Ray Dunning, and Clarence Bence in suggesting that perfection should be construed teleologically, not deontologically. In other words, the change that occurs in the process of perfection is not one of substance (e.g., eradication of a "carnal nature"). Instead, the change is one in which one's motives are purified and one's actions are improved, not by supernatural intervention that overrides human responsibility, but through a divine-human synergism. As Wynkoop states it, Wesleyan ethics must become less magical and more focused on moral progress.

If perfection is understood as being rooted in perfect love, as it is in Wesley's doctrine of Christian perfection, then there must be a concomitant commitment to being utterly moral if love is to have any content beyond the mere experience of affection or emotion. In other words, loving God and others must mean more than simply being enraptured by them. Even if perfection itself is depicted as perfect love, there must still be more to perfection than the mere experience of love. Instead, perfect love should provide the motivation to strive for moral perfection, and this includes the perfection of the intentions as well as the improvement of actions.

Kant's analysis of perfection speaks directly to this issue. Kant asserts that we have a duty to increase our natural perfection, i.e., we must develop our "natural powers as means to all sorts of ends."[57] Additionally, he believes that we have a duty to increase our moral perfection through (1) the purity of our dispositions and incentives, and (2) completely attaining our moral end by fulfilling all of our duties.[58] Too often, Wesleyan ethics has limited its definition of perfection to the purity of motives, ignoring the other obligations Kant mentions. Kant's

---

57. Kant, *MM*, 194 [6:445]. Henceforth, references to Kant will include, whenever available, the volume and page number of the standard German (originally the Royal Prussian) Academy of Sciences *Kants gesammelte Schriften*. These references will be placed in square brackets [ ].

58. Ibid., 196 [6:446].

approach to perfection is broader, because it understands moral perfection to include action as well as intention and it extends beyond moral perfection to the perfecting of all human faculties and abilities.

I agree with the assessments given earlier that perfection is most compatible with a teleological view of ethics. Understanding ethics primarily as rules often leads to legalism, and it has been historically demonstrated in the Wesleyan traditions that this tendency is magnified by an emphasis on perfection. If perfectionism is to avoid legalism, then ethics should be goal-oriented. My use of Kant at this point will be objectionable to those who view his ethics deontologically, since he stresses the inherent duty to uphold certain principles. To be sure, Kant determines the morality of actions deontologically. The same can be said of the maxims that produce action. In other words, he believes that actions and maxims are moral insofar as they conform to specific principles (e.g., they are universalizable, they are motivated by a respect for duty, etc.).

Nevertheless, when Kant speaks of the moral progress of agents, he construes the matter teleologically. Everything must tend toward a kingdom of ends.

> Teleology considers nature as a kingdom of ends; morals regards a possible kingdom of ends as a kingdom of nature. In the former the kingdom of ends is a theoretical idea for explaining what exists. In the latter it is a practical idea for bringing about what does not exist but can be made actual by our conduct, i.e. what can be actualized in accordance with the very idea.[59]

Christine Korsgaard interprets this as follows:

> Speculative and practical reason are linked in that their ultimate ideal, their conception of a rationally intelligible world, is of a system of purposes organized around free rational beings taken as the final purpose of the system, a Kingdom of Ends. But while speculative reason is already realized in the world, practical reason—or morality—is the attempt to impose this ideal on action and on the world insofar as action shapes the world.[60]

This construal can be a helpful construct for Wesleyan ethics with regard to the way it generally relates the perfection of agents to the moral

---

59. Kant, *GMM*, 42 [4:437, n. 28].
60. Korsgaard, *Creating the Kingdom of Ends*, 243.

perfection of all creation. Of course, the ends themselves will be significantly different in a Wesleyan paradigm than they are in Kant's ethics. Even the Wesleyan concept of perfection is different, as we shall see.

Laying a Foundation for the Development

Developing Wesley's doctrines of assurance and perfection along more cognitivist lines will require several other concepts to be nuanced. First, a more naturalized view of grace will be part of this new paradigm. The Holy Spirit cannot be viewed as the imparter of mystical knowledge (according to the definition I gave earlier), as has sometimes been advanced in Wesleyan teachings. Likewise, the Holy Spirit does not necessarily need to be portrayed as the bestower of natural virtue and conscience, which is what Wesley's doctrine of prevenient grace suggests. Rather, the role of the Holy Spirit is to assist natural human faculties, which are not utterly depraved. In short, the Holy Spirit does not do for us what we otherwise can do for ourselves. Therefore, a more naturalized view of grace does not deny divine activity. It merely advances the notion that divine activity does not supersede human responsibility. Essentially, grace is viewed less as the altering of human faculties and more as God's willingness to forgive, accept, and assist us, even though we cannot typically assess the extent of this assistance.[61]

---

61. There are two key presuppositions that underlie the view of grace that I am proposing for Wesleyan ethics. First, it suggests that human beings are not utterly depraved, but have inclinations toward both good and evil. The goodness of God can thus be seen in both redemption and creation, since creation has not been completely corrupted. As such, there is no need to assert prevenient grace as the restoration of natural faculties (e.g., conscience), because these faculties were never lost. Rather, prevenient grace can denote the communication of the Holy Spirit with the unregenerate, the offer of salvation to all, etc. Second, this view of grace proposes that God intervenes for people at the boundaries of their limitations. However, as humanity continues to progress, these boundaries are constantly being pushed back. Therefore, although God is still active in the world and in the personal lives of people, God's intervention in human affairs has changed over time. For example, we can now routinely cure illnesses that would have required miraculous healing a century or two ago. This does not preclude belief in divine healing, for the more we learn about restoring health, the more we also learn about the body's defects and maladies. Along those same lines, the more we understand the human psyche, the more responsibility we must assume in promoting its health and development. In the final analysis, God is understood to be helping humanity to evolve, gently guiding it, so that it becomes neither too dependent on God nor too independent from God.

A more naturalized understanding of grace will partially redefine the Wesleyan view of conscience, and this will have implications regarding the way Wesleyans should regard intuition in general. Rather than view conscience as the mystical receptacle of divine knowledge, conscience can be regarded as a type of reasoning. This proposed change will highlight a facet of Wesley's thought that is often overlooked, namely, his strong belief in the value of education, both morally and otherwise. Again, this does not imply that the Holy Spirit does not interact with human conscience. What it denies is the claim that the Holy Spirit provides superadded knowledge to conscience. Instead, the Holy Spirit simply helps the mind to reason and remember.

Leonard Hulley notes that although Wesley attributes natural conscience to prevenient grace (through the operation of the Holy Spirit), his views on natural conscience are still conditioned by other presuppositions, for he admits that sophisticated cultures tend to produce people who are "well-bred" and "well-natured." Wesley also believes that the Golden Rule is so consonant with human nature that people will generally accept it. Hulley thus concludes that Wesley's doctrine of prevenient grace does not really resolve the dilemma he sees in the fact that many unregenerate people live what would generally be considered to be moral lives.[62] The more naturalized account of grace (and conscience) I am recommending will resolve this dilemma. Furthermore, it will underscore Wesley's emphasis on education.

Second, this new paradigm includes a focus on the cognitive content of emotions. This is imperative if a more cognitivist account of perfection is to be developed. As Cobb states,

> Whether Wesley had a consistent position on perfection is hard to say, and even if he did, it is doubtful that it could be transposed unchanged into our own time. But we can say that in the United Methodist churches today it would be very valuable to renew the goal of perfect love, recognizing with Wesley that it is the work of grace in those who believe. The meaning of love would need to be carefully formulated to avoid the exaggerations to which Wesley was rhetorically prone. We would have to pay much more careful attention to unconscious motivations and causes than did he.[63]

---

62. Hulley, *To Be and To Do*, 13–16.
63. Cobb, *Grace and Responsibility*, 112.

More attention will need to be given to the cognitive element of affections, and this will shape the Wesleyan understanding of religious and moral affections. Religious experiences such as conversion must be seen as being informed by reasoned reflection. Christian perfection must be understood to be more than feelings and emotions. It will also involve moral progress, and this will include, among other things, the purity of one's intentions and the maturity of one's beliefs. Evaluating affections can be helpful in assessing moral character, yet they must in turn be judged by other criteria.

Contrary to what one might suppose, Wesley's emphasis on the role of affections in the religious life does not ignore their cognitive element. Kenneth Collins points out that Wesley understands our tempers (i.e., affective dispositions) to be shaped by our beliefs.[64] When viewed in this way, the Wesleyan emphasis on love can be construed in a cognitivist fashion, noting how the affections are largely dependent upon beliefs. Ted Runyon has expressed similar sentiments regarding the place of reason in Wesley's understanding of the affections. He suggests that even though Wesley's theology is best characterized as "orthopathy" (i.e., right affections), reason still plays an important function in the formation and governance of the affections.[65]

Third, the new cognitivist context will have a more expansive definition of sin. It will move beyond understanding sin merely as disobeying law and see sin more generally as the neglect of duty. Thus, Wesleyan ethics does not need to be construed as a type of divine command theory. Rather than be limited by Locke's emphasis on law, it can utilize Kant's category of duty. This will be especially helpful for the Holiness and Pentecostal traditions, which have historically been legalistic in their moral codes. The stress on duty will also underscore the need for proper attitudes and dispositions, a theme that is central to the Wesleyan understanding of virtue and character. Moreover, it will allow room for the inclusion of what Wesley calls "sins of omission."

However, if this intellectual development is to remain consistent with Wesley's primary concerns, then Scripture must be upheld as

---

64. Collins, "Topography," 166.
65. Runyon, *The New Creation*, 164–65.

the authoritative guide to Christian living.⁶⁶ This emphasis is not supported by either Locke or Kant, so it must be reinforced elsewhere. It seems that Wesley looked to the writings of Peter Browne in that regard. Browne appropriates Locke's empiricism such that he claims that we cannot have any knowledge of God or of spiritual things without special revelation.

In maintaining the authority of Scripture, Wesley sees himself as remaining faithful to the true spirit of Protestantism.

> The faith of the Protestants, in general, embraces only those truths as necessary to salvation which are clearly revealed in the oracles of God. Whatever is plainly declared in the Old and New Testaments is the object of their faith. They believe neither more nor less than what is manifestly contained in, and provable by, the Holy Scriptures. The word of God is "a lantern to their feet, and a light in all their paths." They dare not on any pretense go from it to the right hand or to the left. The written Word is the whole and sole rule of their faith, as well as practice. They believe whatsoever God has declared and profess to do whatsoever he hath commanded. This is the proper faith of the Protestants; by this they will abide, and no other.⁶⁷

Wesley thus aspired to be *homo unius libri* (i.e., "a man of one book").⁶⁸ Nevertheless, Wesley never insisted on *sola scriptura*, for he declares that limiting oneself to reading only Scripture is "rank enthusiasm." Even St. Paul read other books.⁶⁹ What is most important is that theology (and ethics) must remain consistent with Scripture. For Wesley, personal claims of revelatory experiences are to be rejected, because the Holy Spirit always guides us in accordance with Scripture.⁷⁰

---

66. Scripture can be regarded as an authoritative source without resorting to an uncritical foundationalism. Rather, the biblical texts are considered trustworthy to the extent that they withstand the scrutiny of canonization, scholarship, etc. When expressed within the framework of a Wesleyan schema, this asserts that the authority of Scripture has been historically established through the sources of reason, tradition, and experience. This process of authorization permits Scripture to then scrutinize the other three sources.

67. Wesley, Sermon 106, "On Faith," §1.8, *WW*, 3:496 [J 7:198].

68. Wesley, preface to the 1746 edition of *Sermons on Several Occasions*, §5, *WW*, 1:105 [J 5:3].

69. Wesley, "Minutes of Several Conversations Between the Rev. Mr. Wesley and Others, 1744–1789," Q. 32, *WWJ*, 8:315.

70. Maddox, *Responsible Grace*, 133.

This was one of Wesley's frustrations with mysticism. Gray states that Wesley "felt that because mysticism lacks a steadying scriptural foundation, it is the easy prey to all sorts of ridiculous extremes."[71]

Wesleyan ethics cannot be truly Wesleyan if Scripture is not regarded as an authoritative source of moral knowledge. Nevertheless, it should not be assumed that Wesley had a simplistic understanding of Scripture. Quite the opposite is true. For Wesley, the authority of Scripture is not undermined by a historical-critical approach. In fact, the better we understand both the text and the context of Scripture, the better we can perceive the inspired truth.

Benefits of a More Cognitivist Approach

I believe that a more cognitivist approach to Wesleyan ethics will have several basic advantages over other approaches. First, this project will give a fresh and distinct interpretation of Wesley that can prove useful as an intellectual resource for future appropriations of Wesley. It will indeed follow a recent trend to place Wesley in his intellectual context more clearly than conventional treatments of his thought have done in the past. More importantly, this is a unique attempt to situate Wesleyan ethics within a particular, more cognitivist context.

Cobb apparently holds the position that a fresh understanding of Wesley might bring some intellectual unity to Methodism.[72] I believe the same holds true for Wesleyanism at large. A new paradigm will allow Wesleyan doctrines to be developed and nuanced in a way that better reflects the culture and the intellectual environment of the twenty-first century, and this may help to unite a splintered tradition that can once again become a powerful voice in Christianity.

Next, this will be a more attractive development of Wesleyan ethics, one that (1) avoids some of the drawbacks of other versions, (2) is more intellectually suitable for our time, and (3) addresses some of Wesley's neglected concerns. As Maddox reminds us, Wesley "rejected both antirational Christian enthusiasm and antisupernatural Enlightenment rationalism; though, on balance, he appears to have been more worried about the rejection of reason than its exaltation."[73] Although some

---

71. Gray, "Place of Reason," 144.
72. Cobb, *Grace and Responsibility*, 177.
73. Maddox, *Responsible Grace*, 40.

may fear that the type of development I am suggesting could eventually erode other Wesleyan commitments, I am confident that the Wesleyan tradition will continue to preserve its rich heritage as it continues to progress intellectually.

Finally, providing a more cognitivist context for Wesleyan ethics should give it a broader basis for relating to other ethical systems and theological traditions. For one thing, it appears that there has been little effort (if any) to relate Kantian and Wesleyan ethics to one another. This research project could provide a basis for future interactions between the two traditions. Additionally, given the significance that Kantian ethics continues to have in contemporary ethical discussions, a bridge between Wesleyan and Kantian ethics may help relate the Wesleyan tradition to a broader base of religious and intellectual traditions.

I also believe that other religious and ethical traditions, especially those that have historically included pietistic and mystical elements, can truly benefit from Wesleyan ethics if it is developed philosophically. Since 1960, there have been over one hundred book-length studies on Wesley's theology, but many are unpublished dissertations.[74] It is unfortunate that other traditions have not benefited from Wesley's insights. However, I am in agreement with Outler when he suggests that if Wesley is studied more carefully within his own intellectual context, he can become accessible to the Christian community at large as a "fruitful resource for Christian self-understanding and hope."[75]

---

74. Ibid., 24.

75. Outler, "A New Future for Wesley Studies: An Agenda for 'Phase III,'" in *Theological Heritage*, 142.

PART TWO

The Intellectual Roots of Wesley's Thought

3

Wesley and Lockean Empiricism

IN ORDER TO JUSTIFY A MORE COGNITIVIST APPROACH TO WESLEYAN ethics, it will be necessary to show that such a development is consistent with the inner workings of Wesley's thought. This does not mean that the development will be a recovery or a restatement of Wesley himself, otherwise it would not be a development of his thought. Rather, I will attempt to demonstrate that the new paradigm can be truly regarded as Wesleyan in three respects. First, I believe that the intellectual roots that underlie Wesley's primary concerns are broad enough to allow these concerns to be developed along more cognitivist lines. In other words, Wesley's eclecticism presents a number of options for developing his thought. In the first chapter I identified some developments that I believe both distorted Wesley's views and led to exaggerations that are intellectually indefensible. However, I contend that Wesley's intellectual roots also permit a more cognitivist development of his thought. An examination of these roots will expose the other possibilities.

Second, when we look more closely at the way Wesley appropriated the various sources he used, we will see that he was more often attracted to cognitivist, rather than mystical, strands of thought. This does not deny the fascination that Wesley had for particular mystical writers. However, this fascination was by no means categorical, but was focused on particular themes, and in each case Wesley's adherence to mystical themes was both qualified and limited. In fact, as Wesley's thought matured, he tended to drift away from the mystical authors that he had held in such high esteem earlier in life.

Third, the paradigm will be Wesleyan to the extent that it remains consonant with Wesley's basic theological framework and religious commitments. I believe that Wesley's thought is sufficiently deep for this goal to be realized. Also, Wesley's basic theological commitments will define the limits for the cognitivist development of his thought. Wesley himself recognized the danger of valuing reason either too little or too much, and he tried to maintain a point of tension between what he regarded as the extremes. Other aspects of his thought also display a certain tension between conflicting views. I would suggest that as long as Wesleyan ethics remains faithful to Wesley's primary commitments, these points of tension will define boundaries for the development of his thought. My criticism of historic Wesleyan developments is precisely that they did not retain these points of tension and thus exceeded the boundaries of the true spirit of Wesleyanism.

I will not attempt to provide a comprehensive analysis of Wesley's intellectual roots. This would be an immense project in and of itself. Instead, this project is centered on Wesley's doctrines of assurance and perfection, so the goal will be to investigate the ways in which Wesley developed these two doctrines as well as the intellectual backdrop that is behind them. Even though the investigation is being limited to these particular doctrines, a fair amount of research is required.

This chapter will focus on Wesley's dependence on Lockean empiricism. I do not argue that Wesley was unqualifiedly a Lockean. There are particular places where Wesley clearly diverges from Locke. However, I do believe that Wesley follows Lockean empiricism to a significant degree. Some of the points of divergence can be attributed to Wesley's loyalty to an Aristotelian understanding of reason. At other points of divergence, Wesley follows some conventional innovations of his time. This is especially evident in his use of the "spiritual sense" analogy, which he and Jonathan Edwards both employ. Ultimately, I will argue that these innovations are unsatisfactory by higher intellectual standards. As such, Wesleyan ethics (and Wesleyan thought in general) would be better served if it abandoned them in favor of a more cognitivist approach. This is facilitated if Wesleyan epistemology remains more closely tied to its Lockean roots.

Wesley's General Regard for Locke

John Locke was one of the most influential thinkers of his day. He was not only a formative influence in the thought of Wesley; his psychological account of reason underlay much of the philosophy of the

Enlightenment.¹ The imprint of Locke can be seen not only in empiricists like Jonathan Edwards and David Hume, but also in other intellectual circles like Scottish Commonsense Philosophy.² John English suggests that about the time Wesley was finishing his undergraduate studies, Oxford was moving away from Aristotle and Descartes and starting to embrace Locke, (Samuel) Clarke, and Newton.³

Although Wesley did not make many direct references to Locke, he certainly was familiar with Locke's writings. His mother Susanna was even acquainted with Locke's epistemology and saw its benefit for understanding the Christian life.⁴ On more than one occasion, Wesley himself recommended Locke's *Essay Concerning Human Understanding* as foundational reading.⁵ He also noted the inclusion of the *Essay* in the curriculum at the Kingswood School, one of the institutions he oversaw.⁶ However, Wesley did not consider Locke to be everyday reading, for he admitted that the *Essay* may not be understood by the average person. He thus affirmed his commitment to provide reading material "for the sake of the learned as well as the unlearned readers."⁷

This may partially explain why Wesley never included an abridgment of Locke's *Essay* in the multi-volume *Christian Library* he edited and published, a collection "consisting in extracts from, and abridgments of, the choicest pieces of practical Divinity which have been published in the English Tongue."⁸ Of course, the immense length of Locke's *Essay* may have also been a factor in that decision. However, in the spring of 1781, he did compose "Remarks upon Mr. Locke's *Essay on Human Understanding*," and this provides some insight regarding Wesley's opinion of Locke.⁹

---

1. Andrews, "John Wesley and the Age of Reason," 31.
2. Brantley, "Common Ground," 272.
3. English, "Undergraduate," 37.
4. Wallace, "Susannah Wesley's Spirituality," 166–67.
5. Wesley to Miss L—, §14, *WWJ*, 12:262; also Wesley to Miss Bishop, 18 August 1784, *WWJ*, 13:39.
6. Wesley, "A Short Account of the Kingswood School, in Bristol," *WWJ*, 13:288.
7. Wesley, preface to vol. 7 of *The Arminian Magazine: Consisting of Extracts and Original Treatises on Universal Redemption*, §8, *WWJ*, 14:293.
8. Wesley, preface to *A Christian Library*, *WWJ*, 14:220.
9. Wesley, *WWJ*, 13:455–64.

In general, his assessment of Locke was favorable. He likens the difference between Locke and Montesquieu to that between an adult and a child, placing Locke on the same par with Pascal and Malebranche, both of whom he respected.[10] Wesley approves of the *Essay* with a few reservations. He says that the work's popularity is well deserved, and then he commends Locke for his display of "a deep fear of God, and reverence for his word." He qualifies this through the observation, "And though there are some mistakes, yet these are abundantly compensated by many curious and useful reflections."[11]

Wesley remains in basic agreement with Locke throughout the first two parts of the *Essay*, since they focus more on epistemology, especially the process of cognition. His major objections to the work lie in the third and fourth parts, where Locke begins his discussion of "nominalism."[12] Wesley applauds Locke for coming close to the "middle way" of esteeming reason. In other words, he properly estimates its importance as well as its limitations, and this is the type of approach Wesley ultimately wishes to embrace.[13] In the end, Wesley concludes,

> From a careful consideration of this whole work, I conclude that, together with several mistakes, (but none of them of any great importance,) it contains many excellent truths, proposed in a clear and strong manner, by a great master both of reasoning and language. It might, therefore, be of admirable use to young students, if read with a judicious Tutor, who could confirm and enlarge upon what is right, and guard them against what is wrong in it. They might then make their full use of all the just remarks made by this excellent writer, and yet without that immoderate attachment to him which is so common among his readers.[14]

Wesley's attraction to Lockean epistemology was not limited to the writings of Locke himself. According to Richard Brantley, many of the

---

10. Wesley, "Thoughts upon Baron Montesquieu's 'Spirit of Laws,'" §10, *WWJ*, 13:416.

11. Wesley, "Remarks upon Mr. Locke's *Essay*," *WWJ*, 13:455.

12. Although the term "nominalism" has other connotations, especially in Medieval philosophy, this discussion is restricted to Locke's and Wesley's own use of the word "nominal."

13. Wesley, Sermon 70, "The Case of Reason Impartially Considered," §5, *WW*, 2:589 [J 6:352].

14. Wesley, "Remarks upon Mr. Locke's *Essay*," *WWJ*, 13:464.

theologians Wesley studied "were philosophical, and even sometimes Lockean." These included the likes of Benjamin Hoadly, Isaac Barrow, John Tillotson, Nicolas Malebranche, John Norris, George Berkeley, William Wollaston, William Derham, Samuel Clarke, Richard Fiddes, and Isaac Watts.[15] More importantly, Wesley was influenced by Peter Browne's *The Procedure, Extent, and Limits of Human Understanding*, and he felt that Browne properly corrected Locke at particular points.[16]

There can be no doubt that Wesley was shaped by Lockean thought. As Frederick Dreyer puts it, Wesley's thought can only be understood in the context of Lockean empiricism.[17] However, Dreyer seems to overstate the case by asserting, "In explaining how the mind acquired the knowledge it possessed, Wesley's agreement with Locke was complete."[18] This is a claim that I would like to challenge, for I believe that Wesley's alliance with Locke is limited in some specific ways.

General Epistemology

It is my contention that Wesleyan ethics should remain more closely tied to Lockean empiricism. For one thing, Wesley founded a significant portion of his epistemology on Locke's thought, and even his use of the "spiritual sense" analogy can to a certain extent be regarded as an adaptation of this method. However, I feel that this analogy, as well as similar aspects of Wesley's thought, places too much emphasis on intuition, not only because it leads to a much higher degree of subjectivity, but also because it veers away from Wesley's general synthesis of Aristotle and Locke and his heavy emphasis on logic.

A foundation for this line of argumentation will be established here as Wesley's appropriation of Locke's empirical method is explored. It will also be beneficial to note the agreement that Wesley has with Thomas Reid. In particular, Wesley and Reid both feel that ideas are conceptual in their content and should not be viewed simply as mental pictures or images. Wesley also echoes some of Reid's sentiments regarding epistemic certainty. Since it is generally accepted that Reid's empiricism is indebted to Locke, the purposes of this chapter do not

15. Brantley, *English Romanticism*, 27.
16. Wesley, "Remarks upon Mr. Locke's *Essay*," *WWJ*, 13:463.
17. Dreyer, "Edmund Burke," 115.
18. Ibid., 114.

require giving a fuller explanation of Locke's influence on Reid or Reid's influence on Wesley. In the end, the exposition of Wesley's epistemology given here will provide a baseline for proposing new boundaries for Wesleyan epistemology.

Basic Epistemic Principles

The fundamental principle in Lockean empiricism is the notion of *tabula rasa*—i.e., the denial of all innate ideas.[19] Locke asserts, "God having endued man with those faculties of knowledge which he hath, was no more obliged by his goodness to plant those innate notions in his mind, than that, having given him reason, hands, and materials, he should build him bridges or houses."[20] Wesley agrees with the principle of *tabula rasa*, and he believes that Locke has proven the point beyond all noteworthy objection.[21]

Brantley insists that Wesley and Locke hold equivalent, if not identical, conceptions of the human cognitive process.[22] However, this does not appear to be the case, at least in Wesley's mind. He adheres to the Aristotelian cognitive schema, and he accuses Locke of complicating it. According to this representation, reason has three basic functions: (1) simple apprehension, (2) judgment, and (3) discourse.[23] In simple apprehension, ideas are formed from sensations, whereupon judgment takes the ideas and compares them to determine their agreement or disagreement with one another. Finally, the mind "reasons" the judgments, inferring one from another—i.e., connecting them syllogistically. This is the process of discourse.[24] As such, the role of the senses is crucial to a proper understanding of the world. "True judgments" must be founded upon "clear apprehensions," which, in turn, are formed from sensory data.[25]

---

19. Locke, *Essay*, §1.2, 1:13–32.
20. Locke, *Essay*, §1.3.12, 1:102.
21. Wesley, "Remarks upon Mr. Locke's *Essay*," *WWJ*, 13:455.
22. Brantley, *English Romanticism*, 67.
23. Wesley, "Remarks upon Mr. Locke's *Essay*," *WWJ*, 13:456; also Sermon 70, "The Case of Reason Impartially Considered," §1.2, *WW*, 2:590 [J 6:353].
24. Wesley, Sermon 116, "What Is Man?" §5, *WW*, 4:21 [J 7:226].
25. Wesley, "An Earnest Appeal to Men of Reason and Religion," §§32–34, *WW*, 11:56–57 [J 8:13–14].

When we examine Wesley's conception of ideas more closely, we find that it also has some intriguing similarities with the epistemology of Reid.[26] Like Reid, Wesley understands cognition to be impossible without the existence of ideas, yet he does not agree with theories that portray ideas as mental images. Rather, Wesley seems to visualize ideas as being more conceptual in their content.[27] As such, ideas are the building blocks of truth claims about realities that are empirically perceived. On the whole, Wesley expressed mixed emotions regarding Reid. He was "greatly delighted" by the first part of Reid's *Essay on the Intellectual Powers of Man*. He claimed that the latter part was too obscure and disappointing, though he admitted that his negative sentiments were probably tainted by his detestation of Reid's admiration for Rousseau, whom he considered to be exceeded in arrogance only by Voltaire.[28]

It is interesting to note that Wesley shares Locke's belief in the association of ideas. Locke suggests that ideas often become inseparably connected, and when this takes place the two ideas will occur together. The occurrence of one generates the occurrence of the other. This connection can be established in one of two basic ways. First, ideas can be associated through habit, whether or not the habit is voluntary. For example, if I get in the habit of drinking a cup of coffee every morning, then I will begin to think of coffee automatically when I awaken, even when I am away from home and do not have access to coffee. The second way that ideas become connected is through some physiological change or condition. Perhaps I eat so much chocolate that I get nauseous. If the impression is strong enough, any future thoughts of chocolate may also make me nauseous.[29]

Wesley sees the validity in both types of connection. He acknowledges that ideas can become associated through mental and physical habits.[30] Moreover, he devotes a significant portion of his sermon "Wandering Thoughts" to the notion that physical ailments and conditions can wreak havoc on the mind, introducing thoughts over which the subject has no control. He does not believe that such thoughts are

26. Thomas Reid's epistemology is represented primarily in *Essays on the Intellectual Powers of Man* and secondarily in *Essays on the Active Powers of the Human Mind*.
27. Wesley to Miss Ritchie, 12 August 1776, *WWJ*, 13:57.
28. Wesley journal, 30 June 1774, *WWJ*, 4:16.
29. Locke, *Essay*, §2.33, 1:419–27.
30. Wesley journal, 29 May 1745, *WW*, 20:66–67 [J 1:496].

blameworthy, because they are not voluntary.[31] As such, Wesley seeks an approach to salvation that is holistic, addressing the person in both body and spirit. He believes that the various facets of our humanity are interrelated. Consequently, religious experience cannot be compartmentalized, since it affects every aspect of life to some degree. Every part of a Christian's life must be disciplined, because this is how dispositions and habits are shaped.

Epistemic Certainty

According to Locke, belief cannot be compelled externally, especially in the case of religious faith. "True and saving religion consists in the inward persuasion of the mind, without which nothing can be acceptable to God. And such is the nature of the understanding that it cannot be compelled to the belief of anything by outward force."[32] Even penalties cannot compel belief, in spite of the fact that they are necessary in the enforcement of laws.[33] Rather, it is evidence that produces belief. The strength of the evidence supporting a proposition determines the probability that the proposition is true. Therefore, belief occurs in degrees of certainty.[34] This "probabilistic" view of knowledge, espoused by both Locke and Newton, brought Scripture under unprecedented scrutiny.[35] In addition, this led Locke to ultimately regard faith as opinion, because it lacks the degree of certitude requisite for knowledge.[36]

Locke essentially classifies himself as a nominalist, for he maintains that we only perceive particulars, not universals. He believes that complete accuracy could be achieved were we able to name every particular that we encounter. However, doing this would be highly impractical, not to mention impossible.[37] With the exception of proper names, which we assign to particulars, we give general names to things. Even so, Locke claims that these general names are nothing more than

---

31. Wesley, Sermon 41, "Wandering Thoughts," *WW*, 2:126–37 [J 6:23–32].
32. Locke, *Letter*, 18.
33. Ibid., 19.
34. Wolterstorff, *John Locke*, 73.
35. S. J. Jones, *John Wesley's Conception*, 26–27.
36. Wolterstorff, *John Locke*, 122.
37. Locke, *Essay*, §§3.3.2–4, 2:14–16.

abstract ideas.³⁸ They denote similarities that we observe in the objects, yet we cannot speak of the objects themselves, only our ideas of them. Hence, the general names that we assign to things say nothing essential about them. They only describe our ideas of them.³⁹

Wesley finds this portrayal to be appalling. He distinguishes the nominal from the real, referring to the "nominal definition" as the "derivation of the word" and to the "real definition" as the "nature of the thing."⁴⁰ He assumes that objects have real essences that determine their properties.⁴¹ In contrast, Locke denies the validity of classifying objects by genus and species, attacking the medieval scholastics for their propagation of the method.⁴² Wesley comes to their defense, decrying Locke's understanding of them. Thereupon, he defends the use of genus and species, citing the Biblical doctrine of creation.⁴³

Locke's nominalism also leads him to denigrate the role of testimony. His premise is that we can only trust our senses, not the descriptions we give of our experiences. For this reason, every time a personal testimony is passed to an additional party, the account becomes less credible.⁴⁴ According to Nicholas Wolterstorff, "Whereas tradition had once been regarded and treated as a repository of wisdom, Locke unwaveringly saw it as a source of error and vice."⁴⁵

Wesley has four concerns in this regard. First, he wants Christian tradition to be regarded as an authoritative source of knowledge, especially in the interpretation of Scripture. He feels that certainty can be based on testimony, as it is in history.⁴⁶ Second, Wesley perceives that Locke's nominalism also brings Scripture itself under fire, for it is a testimony of God's revelation to humanity. This is especially crucial with respect to the apostolic witness of the death and resurrection of Christ, which Wesley claims is as credible today as it was when it happened.⁴⁷

38. Locke, *Essay*, §§3.3.5–9, 2:16–19.
39. Locke, *Essay*, §§3.3.13–17, 2:23–28.
40. Wesley, "A Compendium of Logic, Book I," §1.7, *WWJ*, 14:164.
41. Wesley, "Remarks upon Mr. Locke's *Essay*," *WWJ*, 13:462.
42. Locke, *Essay*, §§3.3.15–17, 2:25–28.
43. Wesley, "Remarks upon Mr. Locke's *Essay*," *WWJ*, 13:461.
44. Locke, *Essay*, §4.16.10, 2:377.
45. Wolterstorff, *John Locke*, 151.
46. Wesley to the Rev. Dr. Conyers Middleton, 4 January 1749, §5.11, *WWJ*, 10:65.
47. Wesley, "Remarks upon Mr. Locke's *Essay*," *WWJ*, 13:463.

He realizes that the authority of Scripture can only be defended if communication itself is regarded as reliable. Third, Wesley seeks not only to protect the authority of Scripture, he wants to preserve the integrity of preaching and teaching, two activities central to his ministry. Fourth, Wesley repeatedly asserts the "Law and the Testimony" as the only "certain test" of subjective experience.[48]

The reference to Scripture is obvious, coinciding with his assertion that spiritual matters are "conjectural" and "uncertain" without special revelation.[49] Nevertheless, since he does not refer to Scripture directly, I surmise that he indicates "testimony" in a broader sense, incorporating traditional Christian orthodoxy. The term "Law and the Testimony" seems to broadly denote divine revelation and the human witness that attests to it. At the end of the day, if Locke's nominalism goes unchecked, it can lead to subjectivism. Since Wesley already endorses certain kinds of subjective experience, he needs to retain the "Law and the Testimony" as an objective safeguard. Without it, the result could be utter subjectivism.

The nominalism of Locke also causes him to disdain the use of logic in discourse, because he believes that the art of rhetorical debate leads to the obscuring of language. Words are twisted and nuanced in such a way as to render their meanings unintelligible.[50] Syllogistic logic, of which Wesley is a staunch advocate, is also deemed as problematic in certain ways. For instance, Locke claims that since knowledge progresses from the particular to the general, very little can be asserted in relating the general categories to one another.[51] Wesley finds these conclusions unsettling. He admits that many abuses of logic have brought about confusion. However, he contends that the antidote lies in clarifying the misconceptions through pure logic, not in discarding logic altogether. Wesley accuses Locke himself of confusing his audience through his

---

48. Wesley journal, 22 June 1739, *WW*, 19:72 [J 1:206]; cf. Wesley to Bishop Lavington, 1 February 1750, *WWJ*, 9:12; Wesley to Bishop Lavington, 8 May 1752, *WWJ*, 9:33; Wesley to the Bishop of Gloucester, 26 November 1762, *WWJ*, 9:143.

49. Wesley, Sermon 132, "On Faith," §§15–7, *WW*, 4:198–99 [J 7:334–35]; cf. Sermon 128, "On the Deceitfulness of the Human Heart," §2.8, *WW*, 5:158–59 [J 7:342]; "An Earnest Appeal to Men of Reason and Religion," §65, *WW*, 11:72–73 [J 8:27]; Wesley to the Rev. Mr. Law, 6 January 1756, *WWJ*, 9:491.

50. Locke, *Essay*, §§3.10.6–7, 2:126–27.

51. Ibid., §4.7.11, 2:277–78.

neglect of logic.[52] According to Wesley, logic has a way of focusing discourse on the point at hand, eliminating not only much confusion, but a significant amount of verbiage as well.[53]

Locke wishes to argue for the co-existence of simple ideas in substances, which renders them only partially intelligible. In other words, we only have fragmentary knowledge of objects. Once complex ideas are formed about a particular object, the variations from person to person in these ideas will be so great as to render terminology useless.[54] Wesley is not so skeptical concerning complex ideas, for he notes that they are commonly used without any difficulty. His confidence in everyday language is strong enough to boast, "Yes, we know what [words] stand for perfectly well, and no sophister can persuade us to the contrary."[55] In Wesley's opinion, partial knowledge of an object is not an inherent flaw in the cognitive process. It is usually attributed to the lack of a clear apprehension.

At one point, Wesley appears to contradict his otherwise "realist" stance. In the introduction to *A Survey of the Wisdom of God in the Creation: Or, A Compendium of Natural Philosophy* he states,

> I endeavor throughout not to account for things, but only to describe them. I undertake barely to set down what appears in nature, not the cause of those appearances. The facts lie within the reach of our senses and understanding, the causes are more remote. That things are so, we know with certainty, but why they are so, we know not. In many cases we cannot know, and the more we inquire, the more we are perplexed and entangled. God hath so done his works, that we may admire and adore, but we cannot search them out to perfection.[56]

Dreyer interprets this passage as indicating that Wesley "disclaimed all knowledge of things in their real natures." In regards to Wesley's empiricism he thus concludes, "In the visible world, the best that human reason could do was to describe and classify the information that

---

52. Wesley, "Remarks upon Mr. Locke's *Essay*," *WWJ*, 13:462.
53. Wesley, "Address to the Clergy," §2.1.(5), *WWJ*, 10:492.
54. Locke, *Essay*, §§3.9.12–14, 2:111–14.
55. Wesley, "Remarks upon Mr. Locke's *Essay*," *WWJ*, 13:462.
56. Wesley, preface to *A Survey in the Wisdom of God in Creation*, §5, *WWJ*, 14:301.

the senses provided. The metaphysical nature of things lay beyond the reach of human understanding."[57]

I believe that this overstates Wesley's position. In the first place, Wesley seems to be referring to the "why" of creation, not the "how." In other words, the thrust of the passage is theological, alleging that we can never fully understand or be overly certain of the creative purposes of God. Wesley is thus asserting that we cannot claim to know the Divine reason, except where it has been revealed to us (in Scripture). Nevertheless, even if Wesley *is* saying that we cannot know the *effective* cause of being, this does not imply that he is denying all knowledge of being itself. In other words, there is a vast difference between saying (1) we can only have perceptions that are partially valid, and (2) we can have valid perceptions, but only a partial knowledge of an object. The former is the more skeptical position and appears to be Dreyer's interpretation of Wesley. However, it seems that Wesley would be more likely to assert the latter. Regardless of how the passage is interpreted, Wesley is most certainly *not* saying that we can have *no* knowledge of things in themselves. If he is making any kind of ontological claim at all, it is that such knowledge, while perfectly valid, is limited both in scope and in extent. In the final analysis, the passage in question gives us no reason to seriously doubt Wesley's identity as a "realist."

Locke describes judgment as the mind's ability to compare its ideas to one another, but he asserts that this function occurs in the absence of "clear and certain knowledge," proposing that judgment compensates for the lack of "demonstrative evidence."[58] Wesley does not accept this definition, for it limits the function of judgment to matters that are only probable and not certain.[59] Wesley desires an epistemology that allows a high degree of certainty.

Oddly enough, Wesley still comes rather close to Locke's probabilistic approach to certainty. In general, Wesley asserts that certainty cannot be based on hearsay or "subtle and uncertain reasonings," but must be founded upon empirical observation.[60] More specifically, a "certain" proposition is one against which "nothing of weight" occurs.

---

57. Dreyer, "Faith and Experience," 24.
58. Locke, *Essay*, §4.14.3, 2:361.
59. Wesley, "Remarks upon Mr. Locke's *Essay*," *WWJ*, 13:463.
60. Wesley, "The Doctrine of Original Sin, Part I," §2.11, *WWJ*, 9:224.

Certainty can occur in degrees, depending upon the amount of opposition that can be mounted against the proposition.[61] Wesley assesses the spectrum of certainty as follows:

> If, therefore, we were to make a sort of scale of assent, it might consist of the following steps:
> 1. Human faith, an assent to a doubtful proposition,
> 2. Opinion, to a probable,
> 3. What we may term sentiment, an assent to a certain proposition,
> 4. Science, to a certain and evident conclusion,
> 5. Intelligence, to a self-evident axiom,
> 6. Divine faith, to a Divine revelation.[62]

Within this scale of assent, we once again find some strong agreement between Wesley and Reid. For example, Wesley does believe that we see "self-evident axioms" with "certainty and clearness."[63] He defines a self-evident proposition as one that "extorts the assent as soon as it is understood." Additionally, Wesley places all propositions in one of two categories: self-evident axioms and propositions that are deduced from them.[64] This part of Wesley's construal parallels Reid's account rather closely.[65]

Spiritual Empiricism

As an empiricist, Wesley believed that all knowledge is founded upon some type of sense perception. Unlike Locke, he saw himself as a realist, not a nominalist, and he was especially interested in assuming a realist stance with regard to spiritual matters. This is why he appealed to a "spiritual sense." Through his doctrine of prevenient grace, he was able to explain the existence of natural conscience without appealing to a "moral sense" like many of his contemporaries. However, the perception of spiritual realities is a different matter, for it is limited to regenerate believers. Hence, the "spiritual sense" must be divinely bestowed at regeneration, allowing believers to perceive realities that previously had

---

61. Wesley, "Compendium of Logic, Book II," §1.2, *WWJ*, 14:177.
62. Ibid., §3, *WWJ*, 14:178.
63. Wesley, Sermon 71, "Of Good Angels," §1.2, *WW*, 3:7 [J 6:363].
64. Wesley, "Compendium of Logic, Book II," §1.2, *WWJ*, 14:177–78.
65. For example, see Reid, *Intellectual Powers*, §6.6, 358, and §7.2, 429.

been hidden to them. Wesley came to equate the "spiritual sense" with the gift of faith that is received at regeneration.

It is interesting to note that Edwards' appeal to the "sense of the heart" has striking similarities to Wesley's "spiritual sense," and yet it does not appear that Edwards can be credited with Wesley's use of the general model. In fact, the "spiritual sense" analogy was used rather broadly during that time period. Nevertheless, it is highly possible that Wesley's use of the term was shaped more by the homilies of Macarius than by any other single source. Wesley indeed was criticized for making appeals such as the "spiritual sense," and I shall suggest that this analogy should be abandoned in favor of a more cognitivist model that allows subjective experiences to be scrutinized without destroying epistemic certainty.

The "Spiritual Sense"

Wesley's scale of assent is not very controversial until the final point. Wesley wishes divine revelation to be the most certain, since it is immediately perceived. Even though divine faith occurs on the scale of certainty with other types of belief, he is careful to preserve divine faith as a separate entity from the others. "It is where sense can be of no further use, that faith comes in to help."[66] Basically, empirical knowledge can only produce certainty about the physical world, since that is its domain. In contrast, the spiritual (i.e., invisible) world must ultimately be ascertained by a "spiritual sense," since God's presence is generally not manifested in the physical realm. For Wesley, the natural senses cannot "reach beyond the bounds of this visible world. . . . They furnish us with no information at all concerning the invisible world." However, God grants faith "to supply the defect of sense . . . and help us over the great gulf."[67] Once faith is attained, the change is most notable. "How different is the case, how vast the pre-eminence, of them that 'walk by faith!' God, having 'opened the eyes of their understanding,' pours divine light into their soul, whereby they are enabled to 'see Him that is invisible,' to see God and the things of God."[68]

66. Wesley, Sermon 119, "The Difference Between Walking by Sight, and Walking by Faith," §12, WW, 4:53-54 [J 7:259].

67. Wesley, Sermon 117, "On the Discoveries of Faith," §§3-4, WW, 4:30 [J 7:232].

68. Wesley, Sermon 119, "The Difference Between Walking by Sight, and Walking by Faith," §13, WW, 4:54 [J 7:260].

Wesley thus bases spiritual epistemic certainty on an analogy between the natural senses and the "spiritual senses." He feels that the natural senses must be trusted for the material world to be intelligible.[69] In the same way, the spiritual senses (e.g., faith) give certainty to spiritual matters.[70] Wesley's overall rejection of innate ideas parallels his contention that the natural self has no perception of God. It is only through prevenient grace that God can be perceived before conversion. However, this perception is partial and unclear at best. At regeneration the new Christian receives new senses, ideas, passions, and tempers, and this new "spiritual sense" is what enables the believer to perceive God.[71] This new sense functions in a manner similar to the natural senses, for it must likewise have "clear apprehensions" before "true judgments" can be formed regarding spiritual matters. In contrast, those who would deny God's existence cannot perceive God, similar to the way that natural sensations will not lead to perception if the senses are not trusted.[72]

For Wesley, this analogy is a logical extension of empiricism.

> You know, likewise, that before it is possible for you to form a true judgment of them, it is absolutely necessary that you have a clear apprehension of the things of God, and that your ideas thereof be all fixed, distinct, and determinate. And seeing our ideas are not innate, but must all originally come from our senses, it is certainly necessary that you have senses capable of discerning objects of this kind, not those only which are called natural senses, which in this respect profit nothing, as being altogether incapable of discerning objects of a spiritual kind, but spiritual senses, exercised to discern spiritual good and evil....
>
> And till you have these internal senses, till the eyes of your understanding are opened, you can have no apprehension of divine things, no idea of them at all, nor, consequently, till then, can you either judge truly or reason justly concerning them, seeing your reason has no ground whereon to stand, no materials to work upon.[73]

---

69. Wesley, "Thoughts Upon Necessity," §4.3, *WWJ*, 10:470–72.

70. Wesley to Middleton, §6.2.9, *WWJ*, 10:74.

71. Wesley, Sermon 130, "On Living Without God," §14, *WW*, 4:175 [J 7:353].

72. Ibid., §§3–11, *WW*, 4:170–73 [J 7:349–52].

73. Wesley, "An Earnest Appeal to Men of Reason and Religion," §§32–33, *WW*, 11:56–57 [J 8:13].

Wesley equates this "spiritual sense" with faith itself. He generally regards faith as "a power wrought by the Almighty" that enables the perception of spiritual realities. "In its more particular notion, it is a divine evidence or conviction wrought in the heart that God is reconciled to me through his Son."[74] Faith is (1) the soul's eye, whereby it "seeth the light of the glory of God in the face of Jesus Christ;" (2) the soul's ear, whereby it hears the voice of God; (3) the soul's palate, whereby it "tastes the good word and the powers of the world to come . . . and sees that God is gracious;" and (4) the soul's feeling, whereby it senses the presence of God.[75] For the child of God, Christ is revealed in the heart.[76]

The Source of the Analogy

This teaching was also Wesley's attempt to reconcile the notion of *tabula rasa* with the doctrine of original sin. On one hand, the denial of innate ideas was the starting point of an eighteenth-century movement to eliminate the Christian notion of depravity, according to W. M. Spellman.[77] Many thinkers of this time period rejected the premise that human nature is utterly depraved, and began to view it more favorably. Denying innate ideas was another way of saying that human nature begins in a morally neutral state. However, in another sense, "the denial of innate ideas was a corollary to the doctrine of Original Sin" for Wesley.[78] He believed that human beings have neither any innate ideas of God nor any natural ability to perceive spiritual realities. The "spiritual sense" analogy allowed Wesley to deny the existence of innate ideas and still explain how believers can somehow overcome the limitations of original sin.

It has often been proposed that this spiritual empiricism is an adaptation of Lockean epistemology. For example, Brantley suggests that it is a "theologizing of Locke's empiricism."[79] He sees it as an attempt to

---

74. Wesley to Middleton, §§6.2.6–7, *WWJ*, 10:73.

75. Wesley, "An Earnest Appeal to Men of Reason and Religion," §7, WW, 11:46–47 [J 8:4].

76. Wesley, Sermon 117, "On the Discoveries of Faith," §§13–14, WW, 4:35–36 [J 7:236].

77. Spellman, *John Locke and the Problem of Depravity*, 106.

78. Runyon, "Role of Experience," 188.

79. Brantley, "Common Ground," 281.

link sense to reason, matter to mind, and nature to grace.[80] However, Wesley draws this analogy from a variety of sources, not merely from Locke. Rex Matthews points out that Wesley's understanding of sensation in general was also shaped by the writings of Malebranche, Norris, and Browne.[81] Nevertheless, it is not likely that Wesley relied on Browne in deriving this analogy, because Browne only makes isolated references to the spiritual senses, and they do not play a significant role in his system.[82]

In contrast, Malebranche spoke of knowing God through "perception" and through union with God, even in our minds.[83] English indicates that Wesley frequently cited Malebranche, who was a devotee of Descartes.[84] Malebranche believed that an immediate knowledge of God is possible. Wesley esteemed him, along with Pascal and Fénelon, for holding this view.[85] Even Wesley's parents admired Pascal and Henry Scougal, both of whom asserted the possibility of direct and immediate knowledge of God.[86] Pascal specifically emphasized the need for special revelation, and this goes beyond the revelation provided through Scripture and Christ, for it includes "inspiration," which is effected through "participation in divinity itself."[87]

Norris, the foremost English proponent of Malebranche's philosophy, also proposed the notion of "spiritual senses."[88] According to English,

> Norris himself referred to the spiritual senses with some frequency. He called for "the conversion of the Mind to the Ideal World," that is to say, fixing "the Eye of the Mind upon the *Intellectual Sun*, upon him who is Substantial Truth, and the Light of the World," namely, "the Eternal Word of God."

---

80. Ibid., 271.
81. Matthews, "Religion and Reason Joined," 235.
82. English, "John Norris," 60.
83. English, "French Catholic Tradition," 442.
84. English, "Undergraduate," 37.
85. English, "French Catholic Tradition," 442.
86. English, "John Norris," 62.
87. English, "French Catholic Tradition," 443.
88. English, "English Enlightenment," 401.

Elsewhere he mentioned the "intellectual eye," the "spiritual eye," and the "eye of the heart." He also spoke of the "taste of the soul" and the "spiritual" as contrasted with the "outward senses."[89]

Whereas Locke and Browne both believed that knowledge of God is indirect and mediated, Norris claimed that this knowledge can be direct and immediate.[90] English estimates that between 1725 and 1735 Wesley read at least fifteen of Norris's published works, including the *Essay towards the Theory of the Ideal or Intelligible World*. Furthermore, Wesley produced extracts of Norris's *Treatise upon Christian Prudence* and *Reflections upon the Conduct of Human Life*.[91]

Notwithstanding these examples, the use of this analogy was more widespread than one might suppose. Randy Maddox indicates that references to a "spiritual sense" can also be found in the Macarian Homilies and in the works of Western Spiritualist, Pietist, and Puritan writers.[92] To be specific, the Puritan authors Richard Baxter, William Perkins, Richard Sibbes, John Owen, William Ames, and John Smith all used this analogy.[93] Similar analogies can even be traced back to the writings of Origen, William of St. Theiry, William of Auxierre, Alexander of Hales, Bonaventure, and Ignatius of Loyola.[94] Dreyer argues that Hutcheson's "moral sense" is similar to Wesley's "spiritual sense," because they are both derived from Lockean empiricism.[95] Although the Lockean nexus between the two analogies is certainly identifiable, Hutcheson's "moral sense" is somewhat different from Wesley's "spiritual sense," because it is a natural account, based on human affections. In fact, Wesley repeatedly condemns Hutcheson for offering an account of morality that is completely independent of God and special revelation.[96]

---

89. English, "John Norris," 59–60.
90. Ibid., 60.
91. Ibid., 56–57.
92. Maddox, *Responsible Grace*, 28.
93. Matthews, "Religion and Reason Joined," 236.
94. Ibid., 234–35.
95. Dreyer, "Edmund Burke," 116–17.
96. See Wesley, Sermon 105, "On Conscience," §§1.8–10, WW, 3:483–84 [J 7:188–89]; Sermon 106, "On Faith," §2.2, WW, 3:499 [J 7:201]; Sermon 120, "The Unity of the Divine Being," §18, WW, 4:68 [J 7:270]; and Sermon 128, "On the Deceitfulness of the Human Heart," §§1.2, 2.8, WW, 4:153, 158–59 [J 7:238, 242].

A notable contemporary of Wesley who also adheres to this analogy is Jonathan Edwards. He asserts that at the moment of regeneration, believers are given supernatural faculties that enable them to perceive spiritual realities.[97] Richard Steele says that it is faulty to classify Edwards solely as a "rationalist" and Wesley only as an "empiricist," because such characterizations overlook Edwards' advocacy of the "spiritual sense" and Wesley's high regard for reason.[98] He also points out, "Edwards' complaint against Wesley was not that he verged on philosophical skepticism, but that he espoused moral perfectionism. Similarly, Wesley objected not to Edwards' rationalism but to his predestinarianism."[99]

In this regard, Matthews outlines three ways in which Edwards' thought parallels that of Wesley: (1) Wesley's "spiritual sense" is like Edwards' "sense of the heart," (2) Wesley's "witness of the Spirit" is comparable to Edwards' "divine and supernatural light," and (3) Wesley's "inward fruits of faith" are similar to Edwards' "religious affections."[100] It is unclear whether Edwards was much of a factor in Wesley's development of the "spiritual sense" analogy. However, there is good reason to believe that Wesley was influenced by Edwards' account of the religious affections, and this theme will be developed later in the book.

Another likely source for Wesley's understanding of this analogy is the Homilies of Macarius the Egyptian. Wesley names Macarius among the ancient Christian writers who "describe true, genuine Christianity and direct us to the strongest evidence of the Christian doctrine."[101] Macarius asserts that there are five "rational senses of the soul."[102] These "senses of the soul" must be exercised through "much labor and patience and affection toward [God]."[103] These senses are essentially activated through union with God. Specifically, the soul that is in communion with the Holy Spirit "becomes all light, all face, all eye, and there is no part of her that is not full of the spiritual eyes of

---

97. Edwards, *RA*, §3.1, 107.
98. R. B. Steele, *"Gracious Affection,"* 88.
99. Ibid., 89.
100. Matthews, "Religion and Reason Joined," 368–69.
101. Wesley to Middleton, §§6.2.11–12, *WWJ*, 10:79.
102. Macarius, §4.7, 24.
103. Ibid., §50.4, 310.

light."[104] The "whole soul" becomes both a "spiritual eye" and "light."[105] Consequently, those who are spiritual can perceive the spiritual realms of good and evil with the "heart's eye."[106] However, the most important function of the "inward, spiritual eyes" is to sense God's beauty and love.[107] This description is very close to Wesley's claim that the joy of the Christian only arises after "the eyes of the understanding" are opened, in which "spiritual senses, fitted to discern spiritual good and evil" are received.[108]

According to English, the concept of "spiritual senses" can be traced all the way back to Plato.[109] This fact is what leads John Cobb to conclude that Wesley combined Lockean-Aristotelian empiricism with the Cambridge Platonist belief that there is immediate knowledge of the spiritual world.[110] Matthews argues at length that, although Wesley was influenced by the Cambridge Platonists, his epistemology remained true to the Aristotelian tradition.[111] He believes that the reason that Albert Outler attributes Wesley's epistemology to Cambridge Platonist intuitionism is that he overemphasizes the innateness of the spiritual senses, which Wesley clearly understood to be supernaturally activated at regeneration.[112] Rebekah Miles summarizes the matter by stating that "Wesley developed an empiricist model with a Platonic twist."[113]

The Inadequacy of the Analogy

Although the "spiritual sense" analogy was widely used, it was not universally accepted, and Wesley received some criticism for his use of it. For instance, Richard Thompson balked at Wesley characterizing faith as a "spiritual sense," since he believed that the term contradicts

---

104. Ibid., §1.2, 2.

105. Ibid., §1.12, 10–11.

106. Ibid., §14.4, 103.

107. Lee, "Experiencing the Spirit in Wesley and Macarius," 208.

108. Wesley, Sermon 12, "The Witness of Our Own Spirit," §18, *WW*, 1:311 [J 5:142–43].

109. English, "John Norris," 58–59.

110. Cobb, *Grace and Responsibility*, 72.

111. Matthews, "Religion and Reason Joined," 255–80.

112. Ibid., 296–97, 302–5.

113. Miles, "Instrumental Role of Reason," 86.

defining faith as trust, something that Wesley certainly wanted to do.[114] Nevertheless, this analogy represents the sort of simple solution that Wesley sought in his efforts to resolve the deep struggle he felt within.

> By this faith we are saved from all uneasiness of mind, from the anguish of a wounded spirit, from discontent, from fear and sorrow of heart, and from that inexpressible listlessness and weariness, both of the world and of ourselves, which we had so helplessly labored under for many years, especially when we were out of the hurry of the world, and sunk into calm reflection. In this we find that love of God, and of all mankind, which we had elsewhere sought in vain.[115]

Maddox points out that at the same time Wesley was being exhorted by the Moravians to seek the witness of the Spirit, he was also reading the writings of Macarius.[116] It is easy to see how these separate influences intersected at this early stage in his life. While his doctrine of prevenient grace allowed him to recognize natural morality without compromising his doctrine of original sin, the "spiritual sense" analogy helped him to incorporate religious experience within his empiricist framework. Specifically, the analogy gave some validity to the experience of assurance he sought and eventually found. Wesley was ultimately driven by his quest for epistemic certainty, i.e., his need to buttress his doctrine of the witness of the Holy Spirit. In a letter to his mother, he expressed his sentiment that if people cannot be certain of their salvation, they will be most fearful and miserable.[117] He contended that these uncertainties are dispelled by knowledge of God, especially that which is apprehended directly.[118]

However, Wesley was well aware that the real difficulty he faced was that of subjectivity. Although he believed that reason and life experience help to counterbalance the subjectivity of intuition, they do so insufficiently.[119] He thus felt that individuals must be scrutinized by

---

114. Matthews, "Religion and Reason Joined," 365.

115. Wesley, "An Earnest Appeal to Men of Reason and Religion," §8, WW, 11:47 [J 8:5].

116. Maddox, *Responsible Grace*, 125.

117. Wesley to Susannah Wesley, 18 June 1725, WW, 25:170 [J 12:9].

118. Wesley, "A Farther Appeal to Men of Reason and Religion, Part II," §3.19, WW, 11:267 [J 8:196].

119. Wesley, Sermon 37, "The Nature of Enthusiasm," §§24–26, WW, 2:55–56 [J 5:474–75].

some external source if they are to avoid self-presumption about their spiritual state. He naturally appealed to Scripture for some sort of objective criteria, and he concluded that the fruit of the Spirit must be evidenced in the life that claims to be Christian. The outward effects of these virtues can be judged by others, but the inward motives must be judged by personal conscience.[120] This is about all that can be reasonably expected.

> Q. What is reasonable proof? How may we certainly know one that is saved from all sin?
>
> A. We cannot infallibly know one that is thus saved, (no, nor even one that is justified,) unless it should please God to endow us with the miraculous discernment of spirits. But we apprehend those would be sufficient proofs to any reasonable man, and such as would leave little room to doubt either the truth or depth of the work:
>
> 1. If we had clear evidence of his exemplary behavior for some time before this supposed change. This would give us reason to believe, he would not "lie for God," but speak neither more nor less than he felt,
> 2. If he gave a distinct account of the time and manner wherein the change was wrought with sound speech which could not be reproved, and,
> 3. If it appeared that all his subsequent words and actions were holy and unblamable.
>
> The short of the matter is this:
>
> 1. I have abundant reason to believe, this person will not lie,
> 2. He testifies before God, "I feel no sin, but all love; I pray, rejoice, and give thanks without ceasing, and I have as clear an inward witness, that I am fully renewed, as that I am justified." Now, if I have nothing to oppose to this plain testimony, I ought in reason to believe it.[121]

In summary, Wesley wishes to allow a subjective experience of assurance, but the door is left open for many illegitimate claims, even on his own terms. The best that can be done is to judge the lifestyle and the character of the person making the claim. Inconsistencies will thus

---

120. Wesley, Sermon 10, "The Witness of the Spirit, Discourse I," §§2.1–14, *WW*, 1:277–84 [J 5:117–23].

121. Wesley, "A Plain Account of Christian Perfection," §19, *WWJ*, 11:398–99.

invalidate the profession of assurance. The claim itself must be accepted on the testimony of the subject, judged according to the person's apparent truthfulness and ability to evaluate her own psychological state. The bottom line is that the experience can only be judged externally. Its internal dynamics cannot be scrutinized by others.

It appears that there is no way to prevent illegitimate professions. On one occasion, Wesley noted that after he left a revival, "enthusiasm" set in. People were imagining false revelations from God and the like. Should this type of abuse be prevented altogether? Wesley says not, for he concludes that Satan always "sows tares among the wheat." Trying to eliminate the false experiences would result in the elimination of the valid ones as well.[122] Therefore, the unfortunate result must be tolerated.

Obviously, there is no way to eliminate delusion and hypocrisy from religion altogether. However, claims of personal experience must be scrutinized in some way. The history of the Wesleyan tradition (and other traditions as well) has shown that legalistic standards are ineffective in this regard, for they only exacerbate the problem. Rather than scrutinize personal experience, external standards are often used to validate it. Outward conformity endorses whatever inward experience is being claimed. Wesley was right to search for an internal standard in gauging personal experience, but a simple analogy like a "spiritual sense" is inadequate. Instead, a more sophisticated intellectual paradigm will provide some criteria for evaluating and limiting the claims of personal experience.

Furthermore, Wesley's use of this analogy and his conception of faith both point to the need for a more cognitive approach. For example, Steven O'Malley explains that Wesley does not so much describe faith as a movement from the passive trust in pardon to the active expression of love. Rather, he emphasizes faith as a "holy discernment" at each point in the Christian life.[123] Although Wesley believes in spiritual perception, he recognizes the role of cognition in the process, for he admits that "there may be infinite degrees of seeing God."[124] Even Macarius asserts

---

122. Ibid., §20, *WWJ*, 11:406–7.

123. O'Malley, "Recovering the Vision of Holiness," 10.

124. Wesley, "Minutes of Some Late Conversations between the Rev. Mr. Wesleys and Others," Conversation II, 2 August 1745, *WWJ*, 8:282.

that the mind and conscience govern the "natural faculties that spring from the heart."[125]

Wesley indeed believes that the fruit of the Spirit will be produced when the "spiritual senses" are rightly disposed.[126] O'Malley says that for Wesley, spiritual discernment is not possible for those who are not also "manifesting the fruit of Christian holiness." There is thus a "close correlation between a 'reasonable Christianity,' grounded in the spiritual senses, and the truly moral life."[127] Wesley believes that "rational assent to the truth of the Bible is one ingredient of Christian faith." Nevertheless, because faith is given through grace, it is "properly supernatural." It is given "in an instant," but only with respect to the "fitness" of the recipient.[128] This "fitness" is a state of repentance. Elsewhere, Wesley asserts that repentance is what leads to faith, and then this produces good works.[129] Moreover, repentance itself is cognitive, since it requires the self-knowledge attained in conviction.[130]

Wesley appreciates the role that cognition plays in conversion and throughout the Christian life. Additionally, he sees the need for the individual to be scrutinized before and after the event of conversion. To state it more generally, inasmuch as Wesley gives credence to personal experience, he realizes that it must be judged according to objective criteria. In the end, personal experience is of little epistemic value, because delusion is always possible. Even though Wesley apparently intends the "spiritual sense" analogy to provide believers with some degree of inner certainty, in reality it only aggrandizes the degree of subjectivity that is already inherent in religious experience, and this multiplies the problems associated with subjectivity. I would suggest that this analogy should be abandoned in favor of a more cognitivist construal of religious and moral transformation, one that will allow subjective experience to

---

125. Macarius, *Fifty Spiritual Homilies*, §15.34, 123.

126. Wesley, Sermon 10, "The Witness of the Spirit, Discourse I," §2.12, *WW*, 1:283 [J 5:122].

127. O'Malley, "Recovering the Vision of Holiness," 7.

128. Wesley to John Smith, 28 September 1745, §11, *WW*, 26:156–57 [J 12:60]. It has been long believed that the letters written to Wesley under this pseudonym were actually written by Dr. Thomas Secker, then Bishop of Oxford and later Archbishop of Canterbury. See *WWJ*, 12:56 n.

129. Wesley, "A Farther Appeal to Men of Reason and Religion, Part I," §1.2, *WW*, 11:106 [J 8:47].

130. Cannon, *Theology of John Wesley*, 139, 216.

be scrutinized without destroying epistemic certainty. This task will be undertaken later in the book.

Some Thoughts on the Quadrilateral

Wesley's doctrine of assurance, especially its emphasis on the direct witness of the Holy Spirit, is based on the premise that personal religious experience should have epistemic value. In Wesley's own thought, the role of experience is limited, and experience must come under the scrutiny of the other facets of his epistemology. However, Wesley's followers did not always retain these limits, nor did they require personal experience to be scrutinized to the extent that Wesley did. As a result, Wesleyan epistemology became rather subjective at times, and this helped to validate the distortions made to Wesley's doctrines. I suggest that Wesleyan ethics will be better served if it once again places limits on the epistemic value of experience and subjects it to the scrutiny of empirical method. Moreover, it would be helpful to construct a general hierarchy of the elements of Wesleyan epistemology.

Several decades ago, Outler suggested that Wesley's epistemology can be represented by a quadrilateral of Scripture, tradition, reason, and experience. According to Outler, Anglicanism was equally loyal to reason, Scripture, and tradition. In adding experience to the triad, Wesley was "trying to incorporate the notion of conversion into the Anglican tradition." Outler did say that the term "Wesleyan quadrilateral" should not be taken literally. He only intended it to be used as a metaphor.[131] He later regretted coining the phrase, because "it has been so widely misconstrued."[132]

Scott Jones asserts that Scripture, for Wesley, clearly holds preeminence over the other facets of the quadrilateral.[133] However, a Wesleyan view of Scripture should not be simplistic. Jones adds, "We can safely assume that [Wesley] would oppose the biblicism of later Protestants who pitted the Bible against all secular knowledge." Moreover, the heart of Wesley's approach to Scripture is not "fundamentally altered"

---

131. Outler, "The Wesleyan Quadrilateral—in John Wesley," in *Theological Heritage*, 26–28.

132. Ibid., 35–36.

133. S. J. Jones, "The Rule of Scripture," 42–43.

by modern scholarship.[134] These claims all seem to be widely accepted among Wesleyans, and I also find myself in full agreement with them. Wesleyans should be able to have a sophisticated view of Scripture and still be able to regard it as an authoritative source of moral and religious knowledge.

The source of controversy in Wesleyan circles has been in determining other sources of epistemic authority and their relative importance in the overall schema. I have tried to support the claim that many of Wesley's followers have not appreciated the great epistemic role that reason played for him, neither has their own esteem of reason been as high as that of Wesley. Nevertheless, Wesley was careful not to elevate reason above Scripture, as he perceived the Deists and Latitudinarians to have done. As such, he recognized the limits of reason and he affirmed the relevance of special revelation, particularly Scripture.

It has long been assumed that Wesley held tradition (if not experience also) in equal regard with reason. However, Wesley not only valued reason more highly than many have recognized, it seems that Wesley relied upon reason as an arbitrator for determining which parts of the Christian tradition to give the most weight. Clearly, Wesley was an eclectic thinker who had a broad appreciation of both Christian thought and Western philosophy in general. Nevertheless, he favored particular streams of thought over others. It cannot be said that he blindly followed the Church of England in making these distinctions. Although he remained committed to its tenets, he introduced many reforms and challenged the conventional Anglican thinking of his day.

Wesley's epistemology is clearly more complex than can be represented by a simple model like a quadrilateral. As we have seen, Wesley advocates an empiricism that is a synthesis of Aristotle and Locke. As such, all knowledge is rooted in experience, but experience itself does not constitute knowledge. Rather, knowledge is produced through rational discourse. Essentially, experience supplies the raw data, and reason organizes it into knowledge.

The main problem is that of subjectivity, and Wesley grappled with this in several respects. First of all, he rejected Locke's nominalism, which asserts that we cannot speak of things in general categories, but only refer to particulars. Wesley was not only a realist in this regard,

---

134. Ibid., 58–59.

he believed that reason is able to construct generalizations from particulars and then apply these generalizations to new particulars. When Stanley Hauerwas claims that perfection cannot be learned from laws and principles, but only from concrete examples, he is taking a position that is completely at odds with genuine Wesleyan epistemology.[135] Although abstract principles may be of lesser use in a Wesleyan paradigm, principles that are generalizations of concrete experiences are not only a useful source of knowledge, they help to safeguard against the distortions engendered by subjectivism.

Notwithstanding this emphasis, Wesley was very reluctant to make generalizations. He was willing to affirm the validity of personal experiences, but he only allowed generalizations to become normative to the extent that the experiences they represented were widely shared. Even though his Aldersgate experience was perhaps the most definitive moment in his life, Wesley consistently interpreted it within the context of Scripture, reason, and tradition. In contrast, many of his followers did not exercise such restraint.

In Wesleyan epistemology it would be best to understand tradition as a collective body of thought, not as the arbiter of knowledge. I believe that Wesley ultimately regards reason itself as the arbiter of knowledge, and this locates him much closer to the Enlightenment than has commonly been assumed. In fact, when Wesley's intellectual commitments are carefully scrutinized, it will be discovered that his intellectual outlook was shaped more by the Enlightenment than it was by the Reformation.[136] What separates Wesley from other Enlightenment thinkers, including the British Empiricists, is his epistemic optimism. It is not the case that Wesley valued reason less than his contemporaries. Instead, he refused to adopt their level of skepticism with regard to Scripture, tradition, and experience. Also, the fact that he placed little trust in philosophical speculation is not a denigration of reason itself, but an insistence that reason is more reliable when it is (1) consistent with Scripture, (2) rooted in experience, not imagination, and (3) kept in check by the collective reasoning of others.

Since Wesleyan epistemology is rooted in empiricism, it regards experience as the foundation of knowledge. However, we have already

135. Hauerwas, "Characterizing Perfection," 260.
136. Dreyer, "Faith and Experience," 29.

noted that experience alone does not constitute knowledge. There must be reasoned reflection about experience in order to form ideas and concepts. As such, knowledge is acquired through the exercise of reason, which uses experience as its raw material. Of course, once ideas and concepts are formed, they can be related to one another, allowing new concepts to be formed. After people reason collectively about their individual and shared experiences, tradition comes into being. As such, tradition itself represents a body of collective thought, one that sanctions Scripture through the process of canonization. The four elements of Wesleyan epistemology are consequently all held in tension with one another. The canon of Scripture is still ultimately accountable to the authority of Christian tradition, and its text is subject to the scrutiny of higher criticism. Reason must adhere to the tenets of Scripture, be accountable to the collective thought of tradition, and be ultimately rooted in experience. Tradition is scrutinized by Scripture and reason, and it is shaped by the ongoing saga of human experience. Finally, experience is judged and interpreted by the other three.

A general hierarchy between the four elements can be established. Scripture clearly takes precedence over the other three for Wesley, and I believe that he would consider experience to be the least important of the four. Donald Thorsen says, "Although experience adds little to the substance of biblical truth, it confirms, illumines and vitalizes such truths in the believer."[137] Outler offers a similar assessment. He suggests that for Wesley, "Christian experience adds nothing to the substance of Christian truth; its distinctive role is to energize the heart so as to enable the believer to speak and do the truth in love."[138] In short, experience has a limited epistemic role. It can confirm, clarify, and motivate. However, unique personal experiences are only of worth to the individual. Groups can only benefit from shared experience. The subjective nature of experience both limits its scope and makes it more dependent on external validation.

The relationship between reason and tradition is a bit more complicated. Whenever the issue at hand is one that has been addressed in the past, it seems that individual reason must be accountable to the collective reason of tradition. However, this does not mean that there can-

---

137. Thorsen, "Experimental Method," 129.
138. Outler, "The Wesleyan Quadrilateral—in John Wesley," 25.

not be and should not be fresh ways of addressing issues. Moreover, as circumstances change, the relevance of tradition may be lessened from time to time. Human reason must continually process information that was unavailable in the past, so the collective reason of the past may have limited relevance in some present circumstances. Although reason does not always have the upper hand over tradition, it always has a degree of relevance that tradition sometimes cannot have.

Conclusion

In broader terms, I am making two suggestions. First, Wesleyan epistemology should remain rooted in empiricism, specifically in the thought of Locke. I have attempted to outline the ways in which Wesley was indebted to Locke, and this is more than a cursory relationship. Many have tried to downplay this connection, because they are uncomfortable with Locke's approach to Christianity and morality. I most certainly will not portray Locke as a grand defender of Christian orthodoxy, but I believe that he has too often been needlessly disparaged. As Matthews puts it, Locke was not only a philosopher, he was a "theological philosopher."[139] Indeed, Locke even concedes the possibility of direct supernatural activity in our lives.

> In what I have said I am far from denying that God can or doth sometimes enlighten men's minds in the apprehending of certain truths, or excite them to good actions by the immediate influence and assistance of the Holy Spirit, *without any extraordinary signs accompanying it*. But in such cases too we have reason and Scripture, unerring rules to know whether it be from God or no.[140]

Second, the "spiritual sense" analogy needs to be abandoned. Matthews characterizes Wesley's epistemology as "thoroughly empiricistic, not intuitionist," yet it allows spiritual experience.[141] He believes that Wesley's "transcendental empiricism" has its practical application in his doctrine of assurance.[142] In reality, it is Wesley's attempt to justify his experience at Aldersgate in empiricist terms. I agree with Cobb

---

139. Matthews, "Religion and Reason Joined," 37.
140. Locke, *Essay*, §4.19.16, 2:440.
141. Matthews, "Religion and Reason Joined," 307.
142. Ibid., 312.

when he asserts that few people today will find this account convincing. In fact, Wesley himself expressed doubts about his faith several times.[143] Wesley knew that conversion and transformation are not simple events, yet he was correct in declaring that certain changes (e.g., repentance) are necessary.[144] In fact, at one point, he notes that there may be more than two degrees of conversion.[145] Cobb maintains that regardless what intellectual framework might be used, the important thing is that we understand how becoming a Christian changes our perception of reality.[146] According to Dreyer, "In the end all knowledge for Wesley can be reduced to a kind of self-knowledge."[147] I believe that a more cognitivist account of assurance can be constructed, and this will not only prove to be more adequate than the "spiritual sense" analogy, it will eliminate the need for it altogether.

---

143. Cobb, *Grace and Responsibility*, 72.
144. Ibid., 127–28.
145. Maddox, *Responsible Grace*, 331–32, n. 17.
146. Cobb, *Grace and Responsibility*, 75.
147. Dreyer, "Evangelical Thought," 180.

4

Wesley and Lockean Ethics

Morality

IT SEEMS THAT WESLEY'S APPROPRIATION OF LOCKE EXTENDS BEYOND epistemology, for Wesley uses many of Locke's moral constructs. At times, Locke has been classified as a hedonist, and although he generally defines good and evil in terms of pleasure and pain, he believes that moral rectitude can only be determined in reference to law. Wesley's understanding of morality is very similar, for he defines sin as willful disobedience to God's law. Obviously, Wesley stresses the importance of Scripture much more than Locke, and although he does not necessarily associate good and evil with pleasure and pain per se, he believes that moral goodness is conducive to happiness. Also, both Locke and Wesley make a distinction between moral action and moral intention, placing the greatest emphasis on the latter.

I believe that Wesleyan ethics can benefit from a somewhat broader definition of sin, for in limiting sin to willful action itself, Wesley is restricted in his ability to address sins of omission, i.e., positive duties. However, Wesley does express concerns that extend beyond his own definition of sin. Not only does he specifically speak of sins of omission and of positive duties, he also asserts that both intentions and actions must be moral. Since Locke is already a major resource for Wesley, it would be appropriate to (1) examine the extent of agreement between Locke and Wesley regarding their understanding of morality, and (2) explore the possibilities of using Locke as a resource for expanding the Wesleyan definition of sin.

Good and Evil

Locke defines good as that which increases pleasure or decreases pain. Inversely, evil is that which increases pain or decreases pleasure.[1] This is not quite as hedonistic as it may seem, for Locke believes that pleasure and pain are part of the grand Divine plan. He asserts that God has joined virtue and happiness together for the preservation of society.[2] The desire for pleasure and the aversion to misery are indeed innate, "but these are inclinations of the appetite to good, not impressions of truth on the understanding."[3] Locke recognizes the fact that inclinations may vary from person to person. This implies that although these inclinations generally lead to the good, people may not always be inclined to the greatest good. On one hand, they may not understand what the greatest good is in a given situation. On the other hand, even when they do recognize the greatest good, they still may not be inclined to pursue it, because what may be good for the individual might not be good for society.

For Wesley, virtue and happiness are united through love.[4] In effect, when we seek the well-being of others, we will bring them happiness and discover happiness for ourselves in the process. Randy Maddox surmises that this premise explains why Wesley did not regard his strict spiritual disciplines as legalism.

> He understood the General Rules [of the Methodist Societies] to be character-forming disciplines that nurture Christian holiness. Since he also believed that holiness was integrally related to happiness, he could insist that only a Christian could be truly happy in this life.[5]

Moral Rectitude

Given the fact that inclinations cannot always be trusted, Locke concludes that *moral* good and evil concern the conformity of our voluntary

---

1. Locke, *Essay*, §2.20.2, 1:303.
2. Ibid., §1.2.6, 1:70.
3. Ibid., §1.2.3, 1:67.
4. Wesley, "An Earnest Appeal to Men of Reason and Religion," §3, *WW*, 11:45 [J 8:3].
5. Maddox, *Responsible Grace*, 243.

actions with some law.[6] Consequently, moral rectitude entails goodness but does not necessarily coincide with it.[7] Locke contends that duty cannot be known without law, and law cannot be made without a lawgiver.[8] "Without a notion of a lawmaker, it is impossible to have a notion of a law, and an obligation to observe it."[9] Nevertheless, moral obligation itself is derived from the worthiness of the lawgiver, i.e., the lawgiver must be a rightful superior with the right and power to govern.[10] The lawmaker must have the right to command obedience, otherwise the command is a mere exercise of power.[11] Obviously, God is the Supreme Lawgiver, qualified to be such by his wisdom and power.[12] Locke claims that this wisdom and power are apparent in creation.[13] If God is the Supreme Lawgiver, then it necessarily follows that the true foundation for morality is the law of God.[14] The law of God thus proceeds from the divine wisdom, and this provides moral law with a rational basis. Hence, rules are only moral and binding insofar as they are rational.[15]

Locke does not limit law to the law of God. Rather, there are three levels of law: (1) divine law, (2) civil law, and (3) opinion or reputation.[16] All three types of law are used to judge moral rectitude.[17] Nevertheless, Locke does assert that divine law "is the only true touchstone of moral rectitude."[18] The "true ground of morality . . . can only be the will and law of a God."[19] Locke believes that the moral law originates in the nature of God. Consequently, it is "of eternal obligation" and cannot be

---

6. Locke, *Essay*, §2.28.5, 1:474.
7. Chappell, "Locke on the Intellectual Basis of Sin," 200, n. 4.
8. Locke, *Essay*, §1.2.12, 1:76.
9. Ibid., §1.3.8, 1:96.
10. Drury, "John Locke," 534.
11. Wolterstorff, *Ethics of Belief*, 137.
12. Drury, "John Locke," 535.
13. Locke, *Essay*, §1.3.9, 1:99.
14. Drury, "John Locke," 533.
15. Snook, "Moral Education," 367.
16. Locke, *Essay*, §2.28.7, 1:475.
17. Ibid., §2.28.13, 1:480.
18. Ibid., §2.28.8, 1:475.
19. Ibid., §1.2.6, 1:70.

changed, else the world would be full of "irregularity, confusion, and disorder."[20]

According to Locke,

> [Civil law] is the force of the Commonwealth, engaged to protect the lives, liberties, and possessions of those who live according to its laws, and it has power to take away life, liberty, or goods from him who disobeys, which is the punishment of offences committed against his law.[21]

Indeed, Locke believes that life, liberty, and ownership of property are the basic necessities of a happy life.

The law of reputation, although the lowest level of law, is heeded most often. People often ignore God's law in hopes of future reconciliation, and they sometimes ignore civil law in hopes of impunity. In contrast, reputation is followed most often because its consequences are more immediate.[22] As a result, social mores often provide the clearest notions of obligation, since they are founded on human inclinations and carry immediate reward and punishment.[23] In fact, the law of reputation is so effective that it often governs what people generally regard as virtue and vice. Locke does acknowledge that virtue and vice are ultimately determined by divine law, yet he believes that these two terms commonly refer to nothing more than reputation or discredit, shaped according to each particular culture.[24]

Wesley is in basic agreement with Locke's definition of the good. "By good I mean conducive to the good of mankind, tending to advance peace and goodwill among men, promotive of the happiness of our fellow-creatures."[25] Along with Locke, he believes that the law of God is the only legitimate basis of morality. He contends that the will of God is the "sole law of every intelligent creature."[26] Even though Wesley acknowledges Locke's other two levels of law (i.e., civil law and reputation),

---

20. Locke, *RC*, §180, p. 46.
21. Locke, *Essay*, §2.28.9, 1:476.
22. Ibid., §2.28.12, 1:479.
23. Flage, "Locke and Natural Law," 451.
24. Locke, *Essay*, §2.28.10, 1:476–47.
25. Wesley, "An Earnest Appeal to Men of Reason and Religion," §16, *WW*, 11:50 [J 8:7].
26. Wesley, Sermon 96, "On Obedience to Parents," §2.1, *WW*, 3:369 [J 7:105].

he is skeptical regarding their ability to produce virtue. For one thing, Wesley restricts "genuine virtue" to the love of God and others that produces "every divine and amiable temper."[27] He is reticent about defining virtue and vice, in a secondary sense, as public opinion.

Wesley recognizes the power of interpersonal influence, but he does not believe that this necessarily leads toward the good. Rather, our natural tendency is to try to make others like ourselves. Good people tend to make others better, but bad people make others worse.[28] For Wesley, what the world calls a "sense of honor," i.e., a desire for approbation and a fear of disapprobation or shame, is what St. John refers to as the "pride of life."[29] It does not foster a love for God, neither does it necessarily lead to the good. Furthermore, Wesley contends that private interest tends to oppose justice.

> Everyone is likewise prone, by nature, to speak or act *contrary to justice*. This is another of the diseases which we bring with us into the world. All human creatures are naturally partial to themselves, and when opportunity offers, have more regard to their own interest or pleasure as strict justice allows.[30]

For this reason, private interest usually has to be hidden. In contrast, public interest is most beneficial when it is known by the public.[31] Essentially, Wesley seems to believe that although public interest can unite people, private interest eventually divides them.

Locke underscores the need for law, because he feels that law establishes morality. Without it, there would be no such thing as sin and everyone would be equally righteous.[32] He also asserts that law is crucial to maintaining morality in society. Locke claims that moral principles curb our appetites that would otherwise lead to our self-destruction, and yet law itself is insufficient for producing moral behavior. People tend to overlook long-term consequences and base their judgment primarily on more immediate factors. This shortsightedness must be

27. Wesley to the author of "The Craftsman," 1745, *WW*, 26:149 [J 8:513].
28. Wesley, Sermon 81, "In What Sense We Are to Leave the World," §14, *WW*, 3:148–49 [J 6:470].
29. Wesley, Sermon 14, "The Repentance of Believers," §1.7, *WW*, 1:339 [J 5:159].
30. Wesley, Sermon 95, "On the Education of Children," §11, *WW*, 3:352 [J 7:90].
31. Wesley, Sermon 137, "On Corrupting the Word of God," §5, *WW*, 4246 [J 7:470].
32. Locke, *RC*, §21, 30.

altered if religion and virtue are to be esteemed.[33] Our faulty judgment in comparing the present with the future comes from our general inability to enjoy pleasure in the presence of either pain or another pleasure.[34] Moreover, an absent good usually loses to present considerations.[35] As a result, "certain and unavoidable punishment" must accompany a law if it is to be inculcated and obeyed.[36] Rewards also provide a needed incentive for obeying law. Locke believes that the promise of heaven and the threat of hell carry enough weight to counterbalance any temporal considerations that might be made.[37]

Wesley also views law as a necessary instrument in maintaining a certain level of morality in society. He surmises that the interests of society would conform to virtue more closely if people had a deeper sense of the impending judgment of God.[38] Of course, since the law of God is the only legitimate source of morality, civil law will only preserve societal virtues inasmuch as it parallels divine law. Nevertheless, this does not abrogate the Christian's obligation to obey civil law. Following the scriptural injunction of 1 Pet 3:13–17, Wesley asserts that the Christian has a clear duty to obey the civil law as unto Christ. However, this obedience is not blind and cannot lead to disobeying Scripture.[39] For Wesley, law additionally has a salvific role that is fulfilled in three functions: (1) law convicts us of sin, (2) it drives us to Christ for pardon, and (3) it keeps Christians growing in the renewal of their nature.[40] In agreement with Locke, Wesley also claims that law must be reinforced by reward and punishment if it is to fulfill its societal and salvific roles. Although Wesley's virtue ethic teaches that Christians must be motivated by love that is free of "self-will," he still acknowledges reward and punishment as the initial motives to holiness.[41]

---

33. Locke, *Essay*, §2.21.62, 1:355–56.
34. Ibid., §2.21.66, 1:358.
35. Ibid., §2.21.67, 1:359.
36. Ibid., §1.2.13, 1:77.
37. Ibid., §2.21.72, 1:364.
38. Wesley, Sermon 15, "The Great Assize," §3, *WW*, 1:356 [J 5:172].
39. Hulley, *To Be and To Do*, 71.
40. Maddox, *Responsible Grace*, 101.
41. Reist, "John Wesley and George Whitefield," 35.

Intention

Locke does make a distinction between actions and intentions. He admits that outward conformity to rules cannot be the sole measure of morality, because intentions may not be proper. Moreover, people can assent to moral rules, be convinced of their obligation to obey them, and approve of them out of self-interest without the least consideration of God, the lawgiver.[42] For example, even outlaws can honor contracts and commitments without embracing justice.[43] Nevertheless, Locke does not feel that intentions should be the primary gauge of morality in matters of justice. Although actions may originate from sincere intentions, if these intentions are misguided and the actions do not comply with "the eternal law and nature of things," then the actions are still punishable.[44]

However, Locke's moral interpretation of Christianity still stresses the centrality of the intentions. He does not believe that faith alone is sufficient for justification. It must be accompanied by "the works of sincere obedience to the law and will of Christ."[45] Faith and sincere obedience are the conditions of the new covenant.[46] Indeed, God judges us according to these two criteria. Nevertheless, Christ does not expect "perfect obedience, void of slips or falls." He knows our weakness, but he still expects "sincere obedience," which is reflected in the laws he gave us.[47]

Intentions are significant for Wesley as well. He asserts that God cares more about our attitudes and affections than the correctness of our ideas.[48] Hence, we must be cautious in judging others because we cannot know their thoughts or their intentions.[49] He proceeds to claim that outward works are only acceptable to God if they "spring from

---

42. Locke, *Essay*, §§1.2.6–8, 1:70–71.
43. Ibid., §1.2.2, 1:66.
44. Ibid., §2.21.57, 1:353.
45. Locke, *RC*, §179, 46.
46. Ibid., §213, 49.
47. Ibid., §182, 47.
48. Wesley, Sermon 130, "On Living without God," §15, *WW*, 4:175 [J 7:354].
49. Wesley, Sermon 69, "The Imperfection of Human Knowledge," §4, *WW*, 2:570–71 [J 6:350].

holy tempers."⁵⁰ As Leonard Hulley notes, Wesley believes that the good works of the unregenerate are not truly good, in the Christian sense, because they are not rooted in faith in Christ.[51] Of course, Wesley relates this emphasis to his spiritual empiricism. Just as the eye can only focus effectively on one object at a time, so must the intention be focused on pleasing God, since the intention itself is the eye of the soul. This focus is necessary for accurate spiritual perception.[52]

Nevertheless, Wesley knows that our actions cannot be evaluated solely on the basis of intention. Not only are we to have pure intentions (i.e., "simplicity"), all we think, say, and do must be "actually conducive" to the glory of God. In effect, we must have "godly sincerity" so that "in our whole lives, we are moving straight toward God and that continually, walking steadily on the highway of holiness, in the paths of justice, mercy, and truth." Simplicity indicates that the intentions are free of ulterior motives. Godly sincerity indicates that they are guided by the standard of God's will. This is what distinguishes godly sincerity from the sincerity of the heathen.[53] Wesley's standards of simplicity and godly sincerity underscore his understanding of morality as justice, mercy, and truth.

Conclusion

Wesley does agree with Locke that moral rectitude should be measured according to the degree of one's conformity with the moral law. He also resonates with Locke's claim that morality goes much deeper, because it starts with intention. To this extent, it would seem that Locke might be helpful in expanding Wesley's definition of sin. However, Locke's willingness to more generally equate good and evil with pleasure and pain greatly limits his usefulness in this regard. Consequently, Locke will not be the most appropriate source for this development, for making Wesleyan ethics more eudemonistic would not only subject it to charges of hedonism, like those that were leveled at Locke, it would also fail to correct the subjectivism that has often been characteristic of Wesleyan

---

50. Wesley, Sermon 92, "On Zeal," §3.10, *WW*, 3:320 [J 7:66].
51. Hulley, *To Be and To Do*, 18.
52. Wesley, Sermon 148, "A Single Intention," §1.4, *WW*, 4:374.
53. Wesley, Sermon 12, "The Witness of Our Own Spirit," §§11–13, *WW*, 1:306–8 [J 5:138–39].

perfection. Later I will recommend that sin be defined more broadly as the neglect of duty. This development will largely be shaped by Wesley's own concerns, but it will also draw from Kant at certain points.

Moral Epistemology

This next section investigates Wesley's understanding of moral knowledge. Like Locke, Wesley denies the existence of innate moral ideas, and although he does not affirm Locke's assertion that morality can be logically demonstrated like mathematics, he agrees with Locke that morality is rooted in natural law, i.e., the "fitness of things." However, intuitive moral knowledge of this sort is insufficient for Wesley. Whereas Locke displays a certain respect for Scripture, Wesley believes that it is the essential foundation of true moral knowledge. On this point he departs from Locke and echoes the sentiments of Peter Browne.

Overall, Wesley sees moral knowledge as more cognitive than intuitive, and this is evidenced in his view of conscience, which contains both natural and supernatural elements. His theological commitments lead him to define conscience in terms of divine grace, yet the inner workings of conscience can be explained in natural terms. This is why he agrees with Locke that conscience can only function properly if it is adequately educated, developed, and followed. This introduces a theme that will be developed throughout the remainder of the book, namely, that divine grace for Wesley generally operates through natural means.

General Principles

Locke's denial of innate ideas excludes the possibility of innate moral principles as well. Indeed, he claims that moral principles are not even self-evident.[54] As S. B. Drury indicates, Locke denies that moral laws are innate in three ways: (1) they are not self-evident or known by intuition, (2) they do not receive universal consent, and (3) they are not continually operative in human inclinations.[55] According to Locke, things learned by intuition alone carry their own evidence. We thus understand the laws of nature through reason and intuition. However, such is not the case for moral principles. Since they are complex ideas

---

54. Locke, *Essay*, §1.2.1, 1:64.
55. Drury, "John Locke," 538.

that require "intermediate ideas," they are not understood through mere intuition.[56] Locke says that moral principles only seem self-evident because they are taught to us at an early age.[57] Virtually all of Locke's contemporaries believed in innate moral ideas. They felt that self-evident truths are necessary for the stability of morality and religion, else one would be left with a Hobbesian relativism.[58] In contrast, Locke believed that "it is impossible that [any] practical principle should be innate, i.e., imprinted on the mind as a duty, without supposing the ideas of God, of law, of obligation, of punishment, of a life after this [to be] innate."[59]

Locke makes the bold claim that "morality is capable of demonstration as well as mathematics."[60] He regards certainty as "the perception of the agreement or disagreement of our ideas," where ideas are our abstract notions about our perceptions. In other words, we perceive concrete realities, then we form ideas about these perceptions. Although all of our ideas ultimately have their origin in sense perceptions, the ideas themselves are abstract, and they can be used to form other abstract ideas. So when Locke asserts that "moral knowledge is as capable of real certainty as mathematics," he is speaking of abstract morality.[61] Hence, moral truth is "speaking of things according to the persuasion of our own minds, though the proposition we speak agree not to the reality of things."[62]

According to Locke, demonstrating morality fully like mathematics requires us to presuppose that God exists and that human beings are "understanding, rational creatures." These two assumptions make morality almost seem self-evident.[63] Moral demonstration involves breaking down moral ideas from complex ideas into simple ideas, after which the simple ideas can be analyzed as to their "congruity and incongruity." This analysis is what supplies moral rules with certainty.[64] Indeed, "it is our own fault if we come not to a certain knowledge of

56. Ibid., 532.
57. Locke, *Essay*, §1.2.22, 1:87.
58. Spellman, *Problem of Depravity*, 111–12.
59. Locke, *Essay*, §1.2.12, 1:76.
60. Ibid., §4.12.8, 2:347.
61. Ibid., §4.4.7, 2:232. See footnote 57.
62. Ibid., §4.5.11, 2:249.
63. Ibid., §4.3.18, 2:208.
64. Ibid., 3.11.15–16, 2:156.

them."[65] When Locke speaks of demonstrating morality like mathematics, he is obviously referring to the derivation of moral rules and laws. Assessing the morality of individuals simply entails judging their conformity to the moral rules themselves. Moral rectitude is measured by one's conformity to law. As such, even if a rule is erroneous, the individual's conformity to the rule can still be assessed. Evaluating the rule itself is a different matter.[66]

However, this is the precise point on which Locke remains vague. Molyneux once asked Locke to compose a treatise on morals, because he was intrigued by the "hints" Locke frequently gives about his view that morals can be demonstrated according to mathematical method.[67] The most that Locke says is that moral ideas can be evaluated as to their "agreement or disagreement," yet this statement itself is unclear. On one hand, Locke could be asserting that morality must simply be coherent, i.e., moral ideas must agree with one another. He comes quite close to saying this when he claims that moral ideas do not necessarily need to agree with reality. On the other hand, he could be saying that moral ideas must coincide with human inclinations in general, even when our personal inclinations may differ, and in spite of the fact that our conception of human inclinations may sometimes be mistaken.

Natural Law

Francis Oakley indicates that Locke occasionally speculates that God can only choose the good, and this is a necessary consequence of God's wisdom and goodness.[68] Locke thus concludes that divine omnipotence operates within the confines of the natural order that was ultimately chosen by the divine will because of its goodness.[69] Regardless of whether Locke should or should not be labeled as a voluntarist, he does see a natural order that he feels we must follow, even with respect to human inclinations. Although he declares that there are no innate principles, the fact that all humans seek pleasure and avoid pain gives us the same basic disposition with respect to our behavior, and this leads us

---

65. Ibid., §1.2.1, 1:65.
66. Ibid., §2.28.20, 1:485.
67. Locke, 1:65, n. 2.
68. Oakley, "Locke, Natural Law, and God," 650.
69. Ibid., 649.

to form similar ideas of goodness.[70] This distinction supports Nicholas Wolterstorff's claim that Locke's moral system is more eudemonistic than hedonistic.[71]

Wesley views morality as rooted in the "fitness of things," but he ultimately sees it as a copy of God's goodness. Kenneth Collins interprets this as representing a Platonic view of the moral law.[72] According to Wesley, God has designed the moral law such that our obedience to it leads to the continual increase of our happiness, since it adds to the perfection of our nature and entitles us to higher rewards.[73] Obedience to law is what leads to true freedom and happiness. "This is perfect freedom: thus to keep [God's] law and to walk in all his commandments blameless."[74] Wesley thus recognizes a certain order, balance, and harmony in the world, which was imprinted upon it at creation.

> In like manner, when God, in his appointed time, had created a new order of intelligent beings, when he had raised man from the dust of the earth, breathed into him the breath of life, and caused him to become a living soul, endued with power to choose good and evil, he gave to this free, intelligent creature, the same law as to his first-born children [i.e., angels], not written, indeed upon tables of stone, or any corruptible substance, but engraved on his heart by the finger of God, written in the inmost spirit both of men and of angels, to the intent it might never be far off, never hard to be understood, but always at hand, and always shining with clear light, even as the sun in the midst of heaven.[75]

Scott Jones points out that Wesley does accept some of the tenets of natural religion as proposed by the Deists, e.g., unassisted reason teaches the existence of God and it teaches that God rewards people for their lives on earth.[76] Wesley even suggests that the heathen have

---

70. Flage, "Locke and Natural Law," 444–45.
71. Wolterstorff, *Locke and the Ethics of Belief*, 135.
72. Collins, "Platonic Conception," 118–21.
73. Wesley, Sermon 34, "The Origin, Nature, Property, and Use of the Law," §1.2, *WW*, 2:6 [J 5:436].
74. Ibid., §4.9, *WW*, 2:18–19 [J 5:446].
75. Ibid., §1.3, *WW*, 2:7 [J 5:436].
76. Jones, *John Wesley's Conception*, 70.

"the law written in their hearts."[77] Nevertheless, the unregenerate (heathen or otherwise) are incapable of perceiving the moral law apart from the operations of prevenient grace and the provision of special revelation. This is what distinguishes Wesley's version of moral law from other accounts of "natural law."[78]

Special Revelation

Locke feels that genuine revelation must be accepted as true. However, reason must determine what is to be regarded as genuine revelation, and this cannot be done definitively. On the other hand, the places where Scripture coincides with the maximization of pleasure are most likely divine laws. Once again, this points to Locke's assumption that human dispositions are generally consistent with the goodness of God.[79] In short, Locke maintains that the purpose of Scripture is to assist reason in the areas where it falls short.[80]

For instance, Locke claims that "the coming of Jesus the Messiah" brings us many advantages. First, the incarnation helps us to see God, since God cannot be seen adequately in nature, and especially since most people make little use of their reason. Second, Christ as king and lawmaker reveals to us our duty. This is a "surer and shorter way" than philosophical speculation, because such speculation requires "long and sometimes intricate deductions of reason," which "the greatest part of mankind have neither leisure to weigh, nor, for want of education and use, skill to judge of." Locke thus claims that "all the moral rules of the philosophers" fall short of the morality taught by Christ and his disciples. The moral teachings of Christ are "a full and sufficient rule for our direction and conformable to that of reason." The truth and moral obligation of Christ's teachings are confirmed by his mission.[81]

Locke argues that some aspects of truth are too deep to be ascertained easily and thus require "light from above." Many things, once they are learned, seem obvious. This causes us to underestimate the

---

77. Wesley, Sermon 12, "The Witness of Our Own Spirit," §6, *WW*, 1:302 [J 5:136]; cf. Sermon 96, "On Obedience to Parents," §1, *WW*, 3:361–62 [J 7:99].

78. Collins, "Platonic Conception," 118.

79. Flage, "Locke and Natural Law," 448–50.

80. J. T. Moore, "Need for Christianity," 65.

81. Locke, *RC*, §§236–42, 56–63.

importance of special revelation. However, the gospel is still the most effective means of teaching morals to the common people.[82] In fact, when Molyneux asked Locke to derive a system of morality, Locke ultimately replied,

> The Gospel contains so perfect a body of ethics that reason may be excused from that inquiry, since she may find man's duty clearer and easier in revelation than in herself. This is the excuse of a man who, having a sufficient rule of his actions, is content therewith, and thinks he may employ the little time and strength he has in other researches wherein he is more in the dark.[83]

The third advantage that the Incarnation brings is that Christ reformed our worship of God. Fourth, Christ gives us encouragement in living a "virtuous and pious life." Fifth, Christ promises to assist us in living this life. "If we do what we can, he will give us his Spirit to help us" fulfill our moral obligations.[84] Note how this emphasis describes a synergism of human responsibility and divine assistance.

Locke believes that the truth of Christ's moral teaching and the obligation it imposes on us is validated by his Messianic mission.[85] In turn, the miracles of Christ authenticate his mission, since these miracles can be regarded as divine signs.[86] This validation is necessary, because it gives us evidence whereby we may believe that Jesus is the Messiah. The condition for receiving God's forgiveness is that we possess this faith and receive Christ as our "King and Ruler."[87] If we do not accept Jesus as the Messiah, then we are left with a legalistic "law of works."[88] However, Locke's religion is ultimately a moral one that avoids the pitfalls of "antinomianism." He asserts, "These two, faith and repentance, i.e., believing Jesus to be the Messiah, and a good life, are the indispensable conditions of the new covenant, to be performed by all those who

---

82. Ibid., §243, 65–67.
83. Locke, *Essay*, 1:65, n. 2.
84. Locke, *RC*, §§244–46, 67–70.
85. Ibid., §242, 63.
86. Locke, *Disc*, §3, 84–85.
87. Locke, *RC*, §178, 45.
88. J. T. Moore, "Need for Christianity," 66.

would obtain eternal life."[89] Nevertheless, Locke believes that we must be careful to not add to the basic requirements of salvation that God has ordained.[90] For this reason, he concludes that only certain tenets of Scripture must be believed for salvation.[91]

A key book in understanding Wesley's view of Scripture is Peter Browne's *The Procedure, Extent, and Limits of Human Understanding*. Brantley says that Locke's *Essay*, as interpreted by Browne's *Procedure*, "not only informed young Wesley's understanding, but also settled into Wesley's philosophical theology."[92] Wesley even abridged the *Procedure* and included it in the *Christian Library*. It is a work that develops Locke's empiricism while granting a higher status to Scripture. Browne's underlying premise is: "We have no other faculties of perceiving or knowing anything divine or human but our five senses and our reason."[93] He adheres to this empiricism, for he makes no substantial appeal to the "spiritual sense" analogy that Wesley, Edwards, and others employed.[94] "Divine information gives us no new faculties of perception, but is adapted to those we already have." Moreover, it does not give us direct spiritual impressions, but works through our natural senses and the "ideas which are already in the mind."[95] In essence, Browne built upon Locke by proposing a higher view of Scripture, then Wesley built upon Browne by insisting that we need "spiritual senses."

Browne asserts that "evangelical faith" requires us to know before we can believe. Before this faith can be attained, we must assent to certain truths of Christianity.[96] However, since we cannot form any "simple or direct idea" of God, we must understand God analogously.[97] At best, we have mediate and indirect notions about God.[98] Although the existence and attributes of God cannot be logically demonstrated, they must be accepted for "evangelical faith" to be possible. Scripture

89. Locke, *RC*, §172, 44–45.
90. Ibid., §248, 71.
91. Ibid., §§250–52, 74–75.
92. Brantley, *English Romanticism*, 96.
93. Browne, *Limits of Human Understanding*, 53.
94. Maddox, *Responsible Grace*, 31.
95. Browne, *Limits of Human Understanding*, 473.
96. Ibid., 250.
97. Ibid., 82.
98. Ibid., 453.

is necessary because it provides sufficient evidence to give these notions moral certainty. Also, Scripture provides us with analogies of God as well as all of the "mysteries of Christianity."[99] It not only gives us a deeper understanding of the truths of natural religion, it explains concepts that are inaccessible to natural religion, e.g., the doctrine of the Trinity.[100]

In light of the fact that our natural "faculties and powers" have been corrupted by sin, God has given us special revelation so that our minds may be enlightened without violating our free will.[101] Scripture thus elevates morality above the limits of natural morality. It exalts "moral virtues" into "evangelical graces" by shifting the focus from outward conduct to "the inward disposition of the mind and conscience."[102] It also reinforces morality by promising rewards and punishments in the afterlife.[103]

Overall, Browne's trust in Scripture is greater than Locke's, because Browne is more optimistic about the reliability of testimony itself. Nevertheless, he outlines four criteria for evaluating testimony: (1) the content must be intelligible; (2) the content must be possible, if not probable; (3) the person providing the testimony must be reliable (i.e., competent and sincere); and (4) although revelation from God comes through human beings (i.e., personalities, language, etc.), it is still confirmed by external sources (e.g., miracles, fulfillment of prophecies, moral superiority of the message, etc.).[104]

For Wesley, the sole measure of morality is Scripture. Indeed, "the law of man binds only so far as it is consistent with the word of God." He offsets this remark by affirming his allegiance to civil and ecclesiastical authority. "I obey [church authorities] in all things where I do not apprehend there is some particular law of God to the contrary."[105] However, Wesley believes that Scripture provides us with moral truth

99. Ibid., 246–47.
100. Winnett, *Peter Browne*, 119.
101. Browne, *Limits of Human Understanding*, 469–72.
102. Ibid., 336.
103. Ibid., 345.
104. Ibid., 276–84.
105. Wesley, "A Farther Appeal to Men of Reason and Religion, Part I," §6.11, *WW*, 11:185 [J 8:120]; cf. "The Principles of a Methodist Farther Explained," §3.4, *WW*, 9:188 [J 8:438].

that cannot be obtained elsewhere. He thinks that the knowledge of God that can be acquired through natural theology is insufficient for salvation.[106] For the Christian, Scripture is the whole and sole outward rule whereby conscience is to be directed in all things.[107]

In giving Scripture such a central place in his moral and religious epistemology, Wesley is fully aware of the need for proper scriptural interpretation. One cannot substitute "precarious inward motion in the place of the written word."[108] For Wesley, scriptural interpretation must be publicly defensible.[109] On one hand, Wesley stood with the Protestant Reformers in stressing the need for the Holy Spirit to illumine the reader when interpreting Scripture.[110] According to Rob Staples, Wesley's belief that the Holy Spirit assists us in understanding and interpreting Scripture is reminiscent of Luther's and Calvin's teaching on the "inner witness."[111] On the other hand, Wesley (and the Reformers) knew that Scripture cannot be understood properly without the use of critical thinking.[112]

Wesley's view of the scriptural text was by no means unsophisticated. He relied on the scholarship of his day in interpreting Scripture. Harold Kingdon asserts that this is reflected in Wesley's *Explanatory Notes* on the Old and New Testaments.[113] Wesley engaged with the biblical criticism (source and textual) of his time. He departed from the 1611 Authorized Version in over 12,000 instances, and about two-thirds of his textual emendations were incorporated into the English Revised Version of 1881.[114]

Furthermore, he insisted that any serious study of the Scriptures requires them to be read critically in their original languages.[115] When

---

106. Hulley, *To Be and To Do*, 18.
107. Ibid., 67.
108. Wesley to Count Zinzendorf, 8 August 1741, §14, *WWJ*, 1:330–31.
109. Maddox, *Responsible Grace*, 41.
110. Williams, *Wesley's Theology Today*, 26.
111. Staples, "Doctrine of the Holy Spirit," 98–99.
112. Thorsen, *Wesleyan Quadrilateral*, 118.
113. Kingdon, "Bible Scholar Extraordinaire," 43–45.
114. Ibid., 45; cf. Wesley journal, 13 September 1785, *WW*, 23:377 [J 4:320–21].
115. Wesley, "Address to the Clergy," §2.1.2, *WWJ*, 10:491.

using a translation, the most original text and the best translation available should be used.[116]

Outler indicates that although Wesley defended the Protestant doctrines of *sola fide* and *sola Scriptura*, he interpreted *solus* to mean "primarily" rather than "solely" or "exclusively."[117] First of all, Wesley looked to Christian tradition as a measuring stick of his own interpretations. Even in matters of spirituality, he considered the ancient church fathers to be a more reliable resource than the "modern Mystics" whom many of his contemporaries were following.[118] Wesley did not feel that any of the doctrines he taught were novel or new, for he found precedents for them in church history. Next, the faculty of reason is perhaps the most indispensable tool for interpreting Scripture. Donald Thorsen points out that the Anglican emphasis on reason allowed Christian belief to be confirmed and illuminated by knowledge from intellectual disciplines other than theology.[119] Moreover, evangelical Anglicans like Wesley did not regard the Bible as a textbook on all subjects. In contrast with the Dissenters, the Anglican evangelicals more often emphasized the authority of Scripture for issues related specifically to salvific knowledge.[120]

The use of logic is a particularly important part of Wesley's scriptural hermeneutic. In fact, on a scale of importance, he ranks the knowledge of logic just below the knowledge of Scripture.[121] Stressing the need for logic in understanding Scripture not only views humans as rational beings, it assumes Scripture itself to be logical and coherent. If Wesley's construal of the mind's operations is applied here, it can be inferred that logic assists in (1) gaining clear perceptions or apprehensions of scriptural truths, (2) determining the agreement between various scriptural tenets, and (3) inferring some scriptural teachings from others. Consequently, doctrine, Biblical theology, and systematic theology are all dependent upon logic, because they require these three functions in varying degrees.

---

116. S. J. Jones, *John Wesley's Conception*, 126.
117. Outler, *John Wesley*, 28.
118. Wesley to Count Zinzendorf, 8 August 1741, §12, *WWJ*, 1:330.
119. Thorsen, "Experimental Method," 119.
120. Gunter, "The Quadrilateral," 17.
121. Wesley, "Address to the Clergy," §1.2, *WWJ*, 10:483.

I suggest that several noteworthy implications arise from these premises. First, construing the hermeneutical process in a more logical way assumes the coherence of Scripture. Otherwise, there could be no agreement between its various teachings. This consequently implies a certain teleology in Scripture. The various teachings of Scripture are coherent because they have an overarching purpose—the redemption of the human race. To the readers of Scripture, Wesley recommends, "Have a constant eye to the analogy of faith, the connection and harmony there is between those grand, fundamental doctrines."[122]

Second, if scriptural principles can be inferred from one another, then each part of Scripture is best understood as a particular part of the whole. Not only is the immediate context important for interpreting Scripture, the broader context is as well. Wesley exhorts us:

> No less necessary is a knowledge of the Scriptures, which teach us how to teach others, yea, a knowledge of all the Scriptures, seeing Scripture interprets Scripture, one part fixing the sense of another . . .
> In order to do this accurately, ought he not to know the literal meaning of every word, verse, and chapter, without which there can be no firm foundation on which the spiritual meaning can be built? Should he not likewise be able to deduce the proper corollaries, speculative and practical, from each text . . . and to make a suitable application of all to the consciences of his hearers?[123]

Third, if we believe that the Holy Spirit supernaturally assists us in understanding Scripture, then the Spirit either bypasses our reason, giving us logical understanding through mystical means, or the Spirit heightens our powers of reason so that our minds might think more logically. In the first chapter, I made several allusions to ways in which the Wesleyan tradition has seemingly embraced the first of these two options. In my opinion, this was a mistake and has led to many difficulties. I believe that the second option is not only more intellectually defensible, it is actually closer to what Wesley himself believed.

> Is it not reason (assisted by the Holy Ghost) which enables us to understand what the Holy Scriptures declare concerning the

---

122. Wesley, preface to *Explanatory Notes upon the Old Testament*, §18, *WWJ*, 14:253.

123. Wesley, "An Address to the Clergy," §1.2, *WWJ*, 10:482–83.

being and attributes of God? Concerning his eternity and immensity, his power, wisdom, and holiness? It is by reason that God enables us in some measure to comprehend his method of dealing with the children of men. . . . It is by this that we understand (his Spirit opening and enlightening the eyes of our understanding) what repentance is, not to be repented of; what is that faith whereby we are saved. . . . By the due use of reason we come to know what are the tempers implied in inward holiness and what it is to be outwardly holy . . . in other words, what is the mind that was in Christ, and what it is to walk as Christ walked.[124]

Conscience

Wesley's definition of conscience is as follows: "Conscience, then, is that faculty whereby we are at once conscious of our own thoughts, words, and actions, and of their merit or demerit, of their being good or bad, and, consequently, deserving either praise or censure." Every person has conscience "as soon as the understanding opens, as soon as reason begins to dawn."[125] In fact, "Every person capable of reflection is conscious to himself when he looks back on anything he has done, whether it be good or evil."[126] Wesley knows that conscience is only as good as the education and training that shape it, yet there are certain moral principles that seem to be universally held. For example, he asks, "Do not all men, however uneducated or barbarous, allow it is right to do to others as we would have them do to us?"[127] Since God has joined happiness and holiness together, and since prevenient grace restores a modicum of human goodness, every person is inclined to acknowledge the validity of the most basic moral principles.

Wesley asserts that "conscience" implies more than the mere consciousness of what we feel or do.[128] Rather, it serves a threefold role. It is a *witness*, i.e., it testifies to what we have done in thought, word, and

---

124. Wesley, Sermon 70, "The Case of Reason Impartially Considered," §1.6, *WW*, 2:592 [J 6:354–55].

125. Wesley, Sermon 105, "On Conscience," §1.3, *WW*, 3:481–82 [J 7:187].

126. Wesley, "An Earnest Appeal to Men of Reason and Religion," §14, *WW*, 11:49 [J 8:7].

127. Wesley, Sermon 105, "On Conscience," §1.4, *WW*, 1:482 [J 7:187].

128. Wesley, Sermon 12, "The Witness of Our Own Spirit," §4, *WW*, 1:301–2 [J 5:135].

deed. Next, it is a *judge*, i.e., it passes sentence on our actions, whether they are good or bad. Then, it is an *executioner*, i.e., it gives us a feeling to accompany the judgment.[129] In order for conscience to serve this threefold role, it must have three kinds of knowledge. First, we must have self-knowledge. Second, we must have knowledge of the law to which we are accountable. As stated earlier, this is ultimately Scripture. Third, we must know whether or not our thoughts, words, and deeds conform to that law.[130] Hence, if we are to have a "good conscience," i.e., one that is "void of offense," we must have (1) a right understanding of Scripture; (2) true self-knowledge; (3) congruence between our thoughts, words, deeds, and Scripture; and (4) a perception of this agreement.[131]

Wesley's construal of conscience is a peculiar mixture of the natural with the supernatural. The term "natural conscience" is one that Wesley prefers not to use, because he argues that conscience is only "natural" in the sense that everyone has it. Properly speaking, it is a "supernatural gift of God above all natural endowments."[132] For Wesley, conscience is basically a function of reasoning, and yet several things are required if moral reasoning is to function properly. Besides reason, conscience also requires liberty, education, and a sense of pardon. Even though Wesley clearly asserts that natural conscience cannot exist without prevenient grace, I will attempt to show that this is merely a convenient theological construct to account for liberty and education in the conscience of the unregenerate.

Although Wesley first associated prevenient grace with infant baptism, he later related it to natural conscience.[133] He was concerned with preserving a doctrine of original sin that teaches that human beings are utterly depraved, unable to make moral judgments without divine aid. Nevertheless, he knew that all human beings possess conscience in some degree, so he concluded that prevenient grace is what supplies conscience to the unregenerate. As such, the doctrine of prevenient grace allowed him to account for natural abilities without compromising his

---

129. Wesley, Sermon 105, "On Conscience," §1.7, *WW*, 1:483 [J 7:188].

130. Ibid., §1.11, *WW*, 3:485 [J 7:189-90].

131. Wesley, Sermon 12, "The Witness of Our Own Spirit," §7, *WW*, 1:303-4 [J 5:136-37].

132. Wesley, Sermon 105, "On Conscience," §1.5, *WW*, 3:482 [J 7:187].

133. Maddox, *Responsible Grace*, 228.

doctrine of original sin. John Cho says that the doctrine is consequently a mediating position between Pelagianism and Augustinianism.[134]

This doctrine also represents his attempt to find a compromise between predestinarianism and works righteousness, i.e., it is a justification of Arminianism.[135] Nevertheless, prevenient grace is not a concept that Wesley pulled out of the air. In the Thirty-Nine Articles of the Anglican Church, there is reference to "preventing grace," and this seems to include both the grace needed for good works and the special grace that leads to conversion.[136] In fact, the Anglican thinker Thomas Hooker distinguished "precedent grace" from "subsequent grace." He even delineated "the grace whereby God doth incline towards man, the grace of outward instruction, and the grace of inward sanctification."[137]

According to Donald Dorr, Wesley understands prevenient grace to also provide natural conscience with a desire for God, over and above its normal functions.[138] Hulley speculates that Wesley relates the restoration of natural conscience through prevenient grace to the restoration of free will, which enables moral judgment.[139] Essentially, the function of conscience in all people (both Christian and unregenerate) is a reflection of divine activity, for it is the Holy Spirit who gives us an inner feeling of uneasiness when we transgress.[140] In formulating his view of conscience, Wesley draws significantly from the writings of his grandfather, Dr. Annesley. However, it is interesting to note that Dr. Annesley never asserts that the Holy Spirit activates human conscience.[141]

What Wesley really wants to assert is that conscience must have freedom if it is to function properly. Skevington Wood explains, "It has been claimed that Wesley's conception of grace is basic to his idea of free will. It might also be argued that his conception of free will underlies his idea of grace."[142] In fact, Wesley believes that freedom is a necessary concomitant to reason itself. "The right of private judgment . . . is

---

134. Cho, "Adam's Fall," 210.
135. Heitzenrater, "God with Us," 93.
136. Dorr, "Total Corruption," 308.
137. Heitzenrater, "God with Us," 89–90.
138. Dorr, "Total Corruption," 309.
139. Hulley, *To Be and To Do*, 12–13.
140. Wesley, Sermon 105, "On Conscience," §1.5, WW, 3:482 [J 7:188].
141. Monk, *John Wesley: His Puritan Heritage*, 134.
142. A. Skevington Wood, "Contribution of John Wesley," 214.

indeed unalienable from reasonable creatures." Moreover, a "conscience void of offense" can only be a reality if the right to private judgment is upheld.[143] Although Wesley distinguishes the natural, political, and moral aspects of the image of God, the capacity for reason is an important part of all three. This leads Wesley to conclude that, as humans, we have certain rights that entitle us to exercise reason in following our conscience.[144] Similar to Locke, Wesley feels that people must have the right to private judgment if they are to be held morally accountable.[145] However, this is not a rationale for moral relativism, because it is precisely accountability that limits the freedom of conscience.[146]

For both Wesley and Locke, the education of conscience is crucial, given the fact that they deny the existence of innate ideas.[147] This is why Wesley claims that the heathen are bound to continue in the same cycles with "no possibility of any better education" than their parents can offer. They are thus consigned to living lives of "ungodliness and unrighteousness."[148] Locke says that children must be taught to take pleasure in virtue, and he regards the judicious use of praise and blame as the most effective method of accomplishing this.[149] His reason for making this claim is his belief that we tend to reverence the things we are taught in early childhood.[150] Locke does not hold much confidence in corporal punishment, because he does not think that it is capable of producing moral motives within children. I. A. Snook indicates that for Locke, "the whole purpose of moral education is to secure respect for the will of the lawmaker."[151] Nevertheless, childhood education is also a struggle to teach the child "to get a mastery of her inclinations and submit her appetite to reason."[152] Locke thus believes that some people

---

143. Wesley, "An Earnest Appeal to Men of Reason and Religion," §17, *WW*, 11:50 [J 8:7].

144. English, "Rights of Conscience," 353.

145. Hynson, "Concept of Liberty," 41.

146. Ibid., 45.

147. Spellman, *Problem of Depravity*, 112–13.

148. Wesley, Sermon 69, "The Imperfection of Human Knowledge," §3.1, *WW*, 2:582–83 [J 6:347–48].

149. Snook, "Locke's Theory of Moral Education," 366.

150. Locke, *Essay*, §4.20.9, 2:449.

151. Snook, "Locke's Theory of Moral Education," 366.

152. Spellman, *Problem of Depravity*, 109.

can be educated to the point where education can effectively override their baser instincts.[153]

Locke and Wesley both hold the view that children are born with a bias in their nature that must be corrected through education.[154] Wesley emphatically states, "The bias of nature is set the wrong way. Education is designed to set it right."[155] Hence, children must be shaped in their dispositions and attitudes, for this is true religion, in Wesley's estimation. To impose merely external religion is worse, because it fosters pride.[156] Robert Monk feels that Wesley's Puritan heritage contributed to his understanding in this regard. Two of Wesley's great-grandfathers (Bartholomew Westley, grandfather of Samuel, and John White, grandfather of Susanna) were Puritans.[157] Puritanism often taught that the child's "self-will" must be broken, and Wesley clearly adopted this stance in his approach to child education.[158] Nevertheless, Locke and Wesley share the view that moral training includes instruction as well as control over the children.[159]

The underlying premise of Wesley's theory of education is that knowledge is necessary for virtue, and virtue is a prerequisite to piety.[160] Education thus helps children resist evil by their own strength when they come of age. However, this does not obviate the necessity of religious conversion.[161] The words of John Prince capture the final goal of education for Wesley: "The purpose of religious education is to instill in children true religion, holiness, and the love of God and mankind and to train them in the image of God."[162] Elmer Towns adds, "Wesley deeply believed that a genuine and deeply religious life is possible in childhood."[163]

---

153. Ibid., 125.

154. Tracy, "Christian Education," 43.

155. Wesley, "A Thought on the Manner of Educating Children," §7, *WWJ*, 13:476.

156. Ibid., 13:475–76.

157. Monk, *John Wesley: His Puritan Heritage*, 8.

158. Ibid., 161.

159. Towns, *Religious Education*, 320.

160. Tracy, "Christian Education in the Wesleyan Mold," 45.

161. Towns, *Religious Education*, 322.

162. John W. Prince, *Wesley on Religious Education*, 87–88, quoted by Towns in *Religious Education*, 323.

163. Towns, *Religious Education*, 323.

In Wesley's mind, moral education begins with Scripture. Essentially, conscience judges what is right or wrong in our "tempers, thoughts, words, and actions" by the standard of the word of God. Most particularly, we are to judge our lives in comparison to the perfect life of Christ. Wesley contends that whatever Scripture does not forbid or require is morally neutral and should not be a concern of conscience.[164] This is what leads him to define a "scrupulous" (i.e., overly sensitive) conscience as one that assumes duties that are not enjoined by Scripture. Inversely, a "hardened" conscience is much more dangerous, because it either ignores Scripture or violates it without any remorse.[165] This heavy emphasis on Scripture does not preclude private moral judgment, because Wesley believes that Scripture coincides with natural law. Thomas Oden asserts, "Scripture does not override the private sphere of conscience, but points to it. Conscience is the internal witness testifying to moral rightness present within every human being."[166]

Tradition is another of Wesley's resources in the quest for moral truth. Stephen Gunter surmises that this commitment is in large part attributable to Wesley's Anglican heritage, which tended to value tradition more than its Puritan counterpart.[167] Furthermore, Wesley most certainly valued tradition more than the Deists and the Latitudinarians of his day. Thorsen maintains that these two groups, although deeply indebted to Locke, were less committed to orthodoxy than Locke himself was.[168] However, Locke gave them an intellectual basis for elevating reason above Scripture and tradition.

Ted Campbell points out that Wesley's appeals to tradition were often "programmatic," i.e., he used tradition to justify the reforms he introduced through the Methodist revival.[169] For this reason, when Wesley refers to "tradition," he most often means Christian antiquity and the early Church of England.[170] Nevertheless, Wesley's eclecticism still comes through. Campbell states,

164. Wesley, Sermon 12, "The Witness of Our Own Spirit," §§5–8, *WW*, 1:302–4 [J 5:136–37].
165. Wesley, Sermon 105, "On Conscience," §§1.16–17, *WW*, 3:487 [J 7:191].
166. Oden, *Scriptural Christianity*, 59.
167. Gunter, "The Quadrilateral," 32–34.
168. Thorsen, *Wesleyan Quadrilateral*, 48.
169. Campbell, "Interpretive Role," 72–74.
170. Ibid., 65; cf. S. Jones, *John Wesley's Conception*, 64.

> Methodist people can take Wesley as one bridge to the whole Christian past, but we cannot find in Wesley a hidden path that leads to a secret garden of, say, Eastern Orthodoxy or Catholicism or even Anglo-Catholicism, for that matter. This would require an extensive denial of the complexity of Wesley's own roots, and an equally extensive fantasy about the relevance of Wesley's roots to us two hundred years later.[171]

The eclecticism of the Anglicans is a product of their attempt to derive a *via media* between Catholicism and Calvinism. Besides Wesley, Hooker is a good example of one who employed the Anglican theological method, which allowed theologians the ability and freedom to assimilate diverse sources of theology.[172] Basically, Anglicans considered reason the "synthesizing medium between Scripture and tradition, Continental Protestantism and Roman Catholicism, and so on." Wesley fits very well into this tradition.[173]

According to Wesley, a "good conscience" can only be attained if a sense of pardon has been obtained, i.e., we must have assurance that God has forgiven us of our sins. Simplicity and godly sincerity in conscience cannot be attained solely through human effort, even education. Rather, the direct witness of pardon enables the "testimony of conscience."[174] This "testimony" is essentially the objective aspect of the witness of the Spirit.[175]

This facet of Wesley's teaching reflects a particular tension created by two opposing streams of thought that were prevalent in his day. On the one hand were those to whom Wesley referred as "antinomians." They stressed the doctrine of justification by faith so strongly that it became difficult to portray Christians as being culpable for a failure to progress morally. On the other hand were those whom Wesley believed to advocate "works righteousness." Their heavy emphasis on moral progress left little room for the doctrine of justification by faith. These two points of tension are represented by Wesley's doctrines of

---

171. Ibid., 74.

172. Thorsen, *Wesleyan Quadrilateral*, 41.

173. Ibid., 117.

174. Wesley, Sermon 12, "The Witness of Our Own Spirit," §§14–15, *WW*, 1:308–9 [J 5:140–41].

175. Wesley, Sermon 10, "The Witness of the Spirit, Discourse I," §1.6, *WW*, 1:273–74 [J 5:115].

assurance and perfection, and Wesley struggled throughout his life to counterbalance these two concerns, because he saw the importance of both of them. Wesley knew that God expects us to pursue perfection, yet he felt that it is virtually impossible to achieve pure motives without a clear conscience. Otherwise, we would perpetually be attempting to merit God's favor, and this is a self-centered motive, not the ideal of perfection that serves God and others freely and unconditionally. All of this necessitates a sense of pardon.

While others have shrunk away from Wesley's doctrines of assurance and perfection, I believe that they must be developed if this tension is to be retained in Wesleyan ethics (and, more generally, in Christianity itself). Wesley did the best that he could with the intellectual tools that were at his disposal. The time has come for the Wesleyan tradition to use the intellectual tools that are now available and construct a more intellectually sophisticated account of these doctrines. This will require several of Wesley's conceptual categories to be expanded. Later on, I will suggest that some of this expansion can be gained from Kant, because several of his categories are broader than those used by Wesley and can be suitably adapted to fit within a Wesleyan paradigm. In the end, I believe that if Wesleyan ethics can be situated within a paradigm that will better promote its intellectual development, it can recapture its relevance in broader ethical debates.

5

The Rejection of Mystical Spirituality

UP TO THIS POINT I HAVE ARGUED THAT WESLEY'S DOCTRINES OF assurance and perfection need to be developed intellectually. To be specific, they need to be developed along more cognitivist lines, veering away from the mystical approaches that have already been tried. In the previous chapters, I discussed Wesley's epistemology and suggested some limitations for it. This will be most helpful with regard to the doctrine of assurance, although it will carry implications for the doctrine of perfection as well.

Wesley's doctrine of perfection focuses on the purity of the affections, intentions, etc.; the various Wesleyan traditions that have promoted the doctrine have often assumed that emotions are supernaturally transformed by the direct activity of the Holy Spirit (i.e., apart from natural means). As I stated earlier, I am not suggesting that Wesleyan ethics should be naturalized to the exclusion of divine influence and activity. Nevertheless, Wesleyan ethics is founded on the belief that salvation is a divine-human synergism, presupposing God's initiative of prevenient grace. As such, divine activity never supersedes human responsibility, and this implies that human beings must participate in their own transformation as much as they are able. Analyzing the means by which moral transformation takes place does not deny the role of divine influence, for Wesley himself believed that God often uses natural means to accomplish his purposes.

In the next two chapters, I will attempt to further corroborate my claim that the Wesleyan doctrine of perfection can be construed along more cognitivist lines. In this chapter, I will show that Wesley's interest in Christian perfection was not mystical, for it emphasized the role of cognition. Wesley drew from a number of sources in formulating his views on perfection, and when these sources are closely examined, a consistent pattern emerges. Wesley relied mostly on authors who tended to recognize the role of reason in the process of perfection, and he distanced himself from those who took a more mystical (especially quietistic) approach. In my opinion, this suggests that Wesley's goals of perfection can and should be pursued within a more cognitivist paradigm.

Wesley's Pietistic Spirituality

Early Affinities with Mysticism

With its mixture of Anglican and Puritan roots, the Wesley family was very pietistic. According to Ernest Stoeffler, both Samuel and Susanna Wesley were avid supporters of the society movement, which propagated a "mystical-pietistic spirituality." He adds that the early spirituality of John and Charles seems to be a blend of two pietistic strands. First, they had affinities with the spirituality of Jean de Labadie, which was "a mixture of early Reformed Pietism and Romanic spirituality." Second, they resonated with "the practical, outgoing, ethically sensitive, duty-oriented type of piety that had been the mark of the native Puritan tradition." These emphases are reflected in the structure of the Holy Club that John and Charles helped to form at Oxford, because this group had two main foci—"spiritual exercises and concern for the neighbor."[1]

Newton Flew says that "the essential mark of Pietism is its quest for individual holiness."[2] This was the type of pietism that John Wesley sought to propagate at Oxford. Indeed, when he was nominated as a fellow at Lincoln College, other candidates complained that his "excessive seriousness of conduct" would dampen the morale of his colleagues.[3] During his Holy Club days at Oxford, Wesley read Richard Lucas's *An Inquiry after Happiness*, and he later included it in his *Christian Library*. Wesley seems to mirror Lucas's view of perfection, especially later in life. In this regard, Lucas makes the following claims: (1) happiness and perfection are inseparably dependent on one another, (2) perfection is the maturity of virtue, (3) those in a perfect state are not free from

---

1. Stoeffler, "Pietism," 186–87.
2. Flew, *The Idea of Perfection*, 275.
3. Runyon, *The New Creation*, 94.

trials and temptations, (4) perfection is usually attained later in life, and (5) the perfect are still capable of improvement.[4] All of these tenets are present in the mature form of Wesley's doctrine of perfection.

Regarding the theology of holiness, Wesley read Thomas à Kempis, William Law, the French and Spanish mystics, Juan de Castanica (Lorenzo Scupoli), Macarius, and Ephraem Syrus. These people represent three distinct traditions of "holiness" that Wesley attempted to mediate. First, Kempis et al. aim at the total resignation of the will to God through self-denigration. Second, the Quietists (e.g., Molinos, Madame Guyon, and François de Sales) espouse an antinomian mysticism. Third, Eastern spirituality emphasizes active holiness in this life.[5] Wesley tried to incorporate the concerns of each group into his own thought, and this provides another example of the eclectic theology that is so characteristic of him. Maximin Piette states, "A great mistake has sometimes been made in attributing to Wesley's work a novelty it did not possess. Originality, besides, was at a low ebb in all religious movements, and especially in Protestant sects."[6] Essentially, Wesley did not view his doctrine of perfection as an innovation, but as the recovery of a neglected yet vital part of Christian spirituality.

In general, it was ancient ascetic Christianity that shaped Wesley's conception of the Christian life. He was aware of Anglican, Pietist, and Catholic devotional literature that relied on ancient Christian asceticism.[7] Moreover, he regarded the time of the early church as the pristine period of Christian history. Although he never made it explicit, Wesley seems to have understood true Christianity, after the age of Constantine, to lie principally in isolated pockets of Eastern Christendom, among the ascetics in particular.[8] He not only valued the theology of the ancient ascetics, he believed that they truly modeled the life of Christ-like holiness.[9] According to Ted Campbell, Wesley's respect for the ancient Christians was due more to their "spiritual and moral purity" than to

---

4. D. Moore, "Wesley's Thought," 30.
5. Outler, *John Wesley*, 251–52.
6. Piette, "Revolution of Protestantism," 474.
7. Campbell, "Church Fathers," 61–63.
8. Campbell, *Christian Antiquity*, 50.
9. Campbell, "Church Fathers," 63.

"their representation of a consensus of doctrine and practice."[10] He believed that the moral purity of ancient Christians qualifies them as an authoritative source for interpreting Scripture and for "suggesting and confirming Christian teachings and practices not specifically enjoined in Scripture."[11]

Wesley was particularly drawn to the Greek fathers who saw the goal of the Christian life as the restoration of the lost image of God.[12] He appropriated but modified the Patristic doctrine of Theosis. According to Michael Christensen, "By dismissing the Platonic notion of 'becoming gods according to grace' in favor of the less ambitious notion of becoming *like* God, by grace through faith, 'Christian perfection' suddenly emerged as an attainable goal."[13] The quest for perfection is what attracted Wesley to the mystics as well. Brazier Green points out that Wesley "had a deep appreciation of religion as an ultimate union of the soul with God, which is the essence of mysticism."[14] He agreed with the mystics that perfection is the true aim and essence of religion.[15]

Both Wesley and the mystics believe that a private devotional life is essential for Christians, especially in the matter of prayer. Wesley's emphasis on constant prayer as communion with God is reminiscent of the mystics' "ascending scale of prayer."[16] Robert Tuttle points out that the life of contemplation likewise had a certain appeal for Wesley. "Not only did the mystical pursuit of holiness appeal to his innate sense of morality, but the love of contemplation also appealed to his natural inclination for solitude."[17] However, he also believed that solitude should not be overemphasized since it hinders the Christian in living a life of good works, which is perfectly modeled in the life of Christ. Since he generally associated mysticism with solitude, the issue became a point

---

10. Campbell, "Interpretive Role," 70.
11. Campbell, *Christian Antiquity*, 110–11.
12. Runyon, "Role of Experience," 192.
13. Christensen, "Theosis and Sanctification," 88.
14. Green, *John Wesley and William Law*, 191.
15. Lindström, *Wesley and Sanctification*, 60.
16. Wilson, "Mystical Prayer," 64–67.
17. Tuttle, *Mysticism in the Wesleyan Tradition*, 59.

of separation between Wesley and the mystics.[18] It also explains why Wesley was most influenced by the more practical mystics.[19]

Mysticism Ultimately Rejected

Wesley's fascination with the mystics did not last. Later in life he reflected, "The Mystic Divines . . . we had once in great veneration as the best explainers of the gospel of Christ. But we are now convinced that we therein greatly erred, not knowing the Scriptures, neither the power of God."[20] John English states that the aspects of mysticism that Wesley found unsatisfactory were solitude, Pelagianism (i.e., works righteousness), sanctification before justification, and quietism that deprecates the means of grace, especially Scripture, prayer, and the sacraments.[21] This builds upon George Croft Cell's assessment, in which he claims that Wesley offers four general critiques of mysticism: (1) it de-emphasizes the role of Christian fellowship in spiritual formation, (2) its stress on solitude can degenerate into an attitude of retreat and withdrawal from the world, (3) some types of mysticism undervalue the role of the intellect in religion, and (4) it gravitates toward effusive sentimentality in which union with God is described in sensual (sometimes sexual) terms.[22] In a nutshell, Wesley believes that spirituality should not devalue the role of reason and the natural means of grace, and he feels that good works are a necessary part of the Christian life, not as an attempt to merit God's favor, but as a response to it.

According to Wesley, some mystics base justification on personal righteousness. He strongly disagrees with this, asserting, "Holiness of heart, as well as holiness of life, is not the cause of [justification], but the effect of it."[23] More generally, Wesley believes that the Reformers understand justification but misunderstand sanctification. Conversely, he feels that the Catholics understand sanctification but misunderstand

---

18. Ibid., 95.

19. C. Williams, *John Wesley's Theology Today*, 173.

20. Wesley, preface to *A Collection of Hymns and Sacred Poems* (1739), §1, *WWJ*, 14:319.

21. English, "Francis Rous," 33.

22. Cell, *The Rediscovery of John Wesley*, 125–29.

23. Wesley, preface to *A Collection of Hymns and Sacred Poems* (1739), §2, *WWJ*, 14:319–20.

justification.[24] He sees the Reformers as the champions of justification by faith in Christ alone, and he regards the Catholics as the proponents of Christian perfection. In his mind, only the Methodists properly understand the relationship between these two aspects of salvation.[25]

However, Wesley accuses other mystics of going to the opposite extreme of antinomianism. They believe that virtue and perfection can be attained apart from outward works. For instance, they do not stress the importance of doing good works for others. Wesley feels that this neglect is contrary to Scripture. "The gospel of Christ knows of no religion but social, no holiness but social holiness. 'Faith working by love' is the length and breadth and depth and height of Christian perfection."[26] Moreover, these mystics trivialize outward works to the point of asserting that reading Scripture is unnecessary, because they claim to communicate with God directly.[27] Wesley objects, for he feels that Christian perfection does not mitigate our need and duty to do good works and to attend to all of the means of grace.[28]

Wesley explains his use of this term. "By 'means of grace' I understand outward signs, words, or actions, ordained of God and appointed for this end, to be the ordinary channels whereby he might convey to men preventing, justifying, or sanctifying grace." He uses the term because of its use in Christian history, especially in the Anglican Church, and because he knows no better expression for describing it.[29] Wesley's insistence on the means of grace stems from his belief that God will not grant the end without the means.[30] However, these means are worthless in and of themselves. "If they do not actually conduce to the knowledge and love of God, they are not acceptable in his sight; yea, rather, they are an abomination before him, a stink in his nostrils; he is weary to bear them." They cannot achieve their end "separate from the Spirit of

---

24. Cannon, "Doctrine of Sanctification," 93.

25. Rivers, *Reason, Grace, and Sentiment*, 1:210.

26. Wesley, preface to *A Collection of Hymns and Sacred Poems* (1739), §§4–5, *WWJ*, 14:321.

27. Wesley to his brother Samuel, 23 November 1736, *WW*, 25:488 [J 12:28]

28. Wesley, preface to *A Collection of Hymns and Sacred Poems* (1745), §2, *WWJ*, 14:328.

29. Wesley, Sermon 16, "The Means of Grace," §2.1, *WW*, 1:381 [J 5:187].

30. Knight, *Presence of God*, 46.

God."[31] One of the key ends that these means produce is the habituation of our affections, and this will become more evident later in the chapter when the discussion shifts to the cognitive content of emotions.[32]

The means of grace can be divided into two categories, according to Wesley. First, the *instituted means* are those which are specifically ordained in Scripture, including prayer, Scripture, the Lord's supper, fasting, and "Christian conference" (i.e., accountability to others). These are means that every Christian is obliged to use, and they are effective to some degree in all persons. Second, Wesley identifies what he calls the *prudential means*, which are context-specific rules that help us grow in grace. These will vary from person to person and from situation to situation, because what is effective in one context may not be effective in another. However, all Christians should see some evidence of growth when they attend to the following prudential means: self-scrutiny, self-denial, "taking up our cross" (i.e., performing duties that are difficult and sacrificial), and "exercise of the presence of God" (i.e., staying focused on God and remembering that he is watching us).[33]

In formulating the rules for the prudential means of grace, reason plays a large role, since these usually extend beyond the specific guidance of Scripture. As Kenneth Collins indicates, they are "subject to change as common sense and circumstances dictate."[34] This is another reason why Wesley finds the mystical attitude toward reason to be destructive. He says that there are many people, especially the so-called "Mystic Divines" who "utterly decry the use of reason." They essentially "condemn all reason concerning the things of God as utterly destructive of true religion."[35] For Wesley, the opposite is true, for he sees the use of reason as crucial to true religion. In any event, he believes that in order for the means of grace to be effective, the following principles must be heeded: (1) remember that God is not limited to particular means; (2) be aware that the means have no intrinsic power in themselves; (3) seek

---

31. Wesley, Sermon 16, "The Means of Grace," §2.3, WW, 1:382 [J 5:188].

32. Maddox, "A Change of Affections," 20.

33. Wesley, "Minutes of Several Conversations between the Rev. Mr. Wesley and Others; From the Year 1744, to the Year 1789," Q. 48, WWJ, 8:322–24.

34. Collins, "Means of Grace," 26.

35. Wesley, "An Earnest Appeal to Men of Reason and Religion," §30, WW, 11:55–56 [J 8:12].

God alone and use the means only as a means, not as an end; and (4) do not allow the means of grace to cultivate pride in our attitude.[36]

Wesley also feels that the way of the mystics is frequently too austere. As stated earlier, he claims that the mystics advocate seclusion even though Christ commands us to build up one another.[37] They also stress self-denial almost to the point of self-loathing, and this is certainly more rigid than Wesley's conception of perfection. He clearly states that perfection is not freedom from "ignorance, or mistake, or infirmities, or temptations."[38] In its most basic sense, "true Christian perfection is no other than humble love."[39] The way of the perfect is not laborious, for Christian perfection leads to the "full enjoyment of God."[40]

Wesley acknowledges the fact that believers can experience periods of doubt and discouragement, like John of the Cross's "dark night of the soul," yet he believes that these are not caused by God, as the mystics claim. Rather, God delivers us from them through the witness of the Holy Spirit, which is often reaffirmed in the believer's heart.[41] Wesley does not see "darkness" as something that comes from God, for he associates the term with sin.[42] In his comments on John 16:22, Wesley asserts

> [There is] no manner of authority to assert that all believers must come into a state of darkness. They never need lose either their peace, or love, or the witness that they are the children of God. They never can lose these, but either through sin, or ignorance, or vehement temptation, or bodily disorder.[43]

In the end, Wesley's assessment of the mystics is rather unfavorable. "I think the rock on which I had the nearest made shipwreck of

---

36. Wesley, Sermon 16, "The Means of Grace," §5.4, *WW*, 1:395–97 [J 5:200–201].

37. Wesley, preface to *A Collection of Hymns and Sacred Poems* (1739), §3, *WWJ*, 14:320.

38. Wesley, "An Earnest Appeal to Men of Reason and Religion," §55, *WW*, 11:66 [J 8:22].

39. Wesley, "A Farther Appeal to Men of Reason and Religion, Part I," §3.5.Q2, *WW*, 11:126 [J 8:65].

40. Wesley, Sermon 48, "Self-Denial," §2.6, *WW*, 2:247 [J 6:111–12].

41. Wesley, preface to *A Collection of Hymns and Sacred Poems* (1740), §§9–10, *WWJ*, 14:326–27.

42. Tuttle, *Mysticism in the Wesleyan Tradition*, 96.

43. Wesley, *NNT*, John 16:22.

the faith was the writings of the mystics, under which term I comprehend all, and only those, who slight any of the means of grace."[44] In fact, Wesley refers to mysticism as the "mystery of Satan," the "mystery of iniquity," the "specious snare of the devil," and as the "fairest of Satan's devices."[45] G. E. Clarkson suggests that although Wesley's critiques of the mystics are valid, they are somewhat exaggerated, due in part to the fact that he (like many others of his day) had a simplistic understanding of mysticism and tended to think only of the ecstatic type.[46] Tuttle adds that we must be careful in assessing Wesley's opinions regarding mystical writers, for he frequently cited one source to refute the errors of another.[47] Obviously, Wesley's criticisms do not apply equally to all those who might be regarded as "mystics," for mystic writers vary in their particular emphases.[48] Nevertheless, it does not seem these criticisms are as misguided or as misleading as some might suppose. Wesley's objections are clear and apply to mystics to the extent that they neglect the natural means of grace.

The Quest for Perfection

Early Influences on Wesley

Onva Boshears suggests that besides the Bible and the *Book of Common Prayer*, the main influences on Wesley during his Oxford days were Kempis's *The Imitation of Christ*, Jeremy Taylor's *Holy Living*, Law's *A Serious Call to a Devout and Holy Life* and *A Practical Treatise upon Christian Perfection*, and Henry Scougal's *The Life of God in the Soul of Man*.[49] With respect to the formulation of his views on Christian perfection, Wesley himself distinctly acknowledges the first three.

> In the year 1725, being in the twenty-third year of my age, I met with Bishop Taylor's "Rule and Exercises of Holy Living and Dying." In reading several parts of this book, I was exceedingly affected, that part in particular which related to purity of

---

44. Wesley to his brother Samuel, 23 November 1736, *WW*, 25:487 [J 12:27].
45. Tuttle, *Mysticism in the Wesleyan Tradition*, 95.
46. Clarkson, "John Wesley and William Law's Mysticism," 541.
47. Tuttle, *Mysticism in the Wesleyan Tradition*, 53.
48. Wilson, "Mystical Prayer," 62.
49. Boshears, "The Books in John Wesley's Life," 51.

intention. Instantly I resolved to dedicate all my life to God, all my thoughts and words and actions, being thoroughly convinced there was no medium, but that every part of my life (not some only) must either be a sacrifice to God or myself, that is, in effect, to the devil.

Can any serious person doubt of this or find a medium between serving God and serving the devil?

In the year 1726, I met with Kempis's "Christian Pattern." The nature and extent of inward religion, the religion of the heart, now appeared to me in a stronger light than ever it had done before. I saw that giving even all my life to God (supposing it possible to do this and go no father) would profit me nothing unless I gave my heart, yea, all my heart to him.

I saw that "simplicity of intention and purity of affection," one design in all we speak or do, and one desire ruling all our tempers,[50] are indeed "the wings of the soul," without which she can never ascend to the mount of God.

A year or two after, Mr. Law's *Christian Perfection* and *Serious Call* were put into my hands. These convinced me, more than ever, of the absolute impossibility of being half a Christian, and I determined, through his grace (the absolute necessity of which I was deeply sensible), to be all-devoted to God, to give him all my soul, my body, and my substance.[51]

Wesley's thus relied on the writings of Taylor, Kempis, and Law to strengthen his own spiritual life.[52] Moreover, this body of literature reinforced the piety that he had been taught at home. From Taylor, Wesley learned that goodness comes from dedicating one's life to God. From Kempis, he learned that obedience begins in the heart with pure intentions. From Law, Wesley learned to associate self-denial with the absolute fulfillment of God's law.[53] In general, these men taught Wesley that Christian perfection involves purity of intention, the imitation of Christ, and the love of God and others.[54]

---

50. Wesley's use of the word "temper" seems to denote a disposition of the affections. This seems to be consistent with the common usage of the term at that time. See Collins, "Topography," 165.

51. Wesley, "A Plain Account of Christian Perfection," §§2–4, *WWJ*, 11:366–67.

52. Piette, *Evolution of Protestantism*, 259.

53. Cannon, *Theology of John Wesley*, 56–63; cf. Tuttle, *Mysticism in the Wesleyan Tradition*, 58.

54. Lindström, *Wesley and Sanctification*, 129.

Jeremy Taylor

According to John Tyson, it was the influence of Taylor's *Holy Living* that effected an intellectual conversion for Wesley, in which he "moved beyond the uncritical acceptance of an external authority that dictates morality to an internalized and critical appropriation of moral love."[55] Taylor emphasizes three ways in which vitality is to be retained in the Christian life: (1) the judicious use of our time, (2) purity of intention, and (3) the practice of God's presence.[56] This represents a pietistic approach to spirituality, for it stresses the need to cultivate the inner thought life as well as put religion into practice. Taylor says, "Let all your spare moments be employed in prayers, reading, meditation, the necessities of nature, recreation, charity, friendliness, neighborliness, and those things pertaining to spiritual and bodily health."[57] The concept of using time judiciously resonated with Wesley, who devoted an entire sermon to the subject.[58] Like Wesley, Taylor believes in the practice of constant prayer, for his exhortation is to "make frequent conversations between God and your own soul."[59] Additionally, the exercise of practicing God's presence "enkindles holy hunger for him because it produces joy when we do experience his presence."[60]

However, the key to holiness is purity of intention, according to Taylor. "Without a holy intention, our actions are sinful, unprofitable, and vain."[61] Even the spiritual disciplines are of no avail unless they are motivated by pure intentions. For example, those who pray merely out of habit are Pharisees and hypocrites in their devotion.[62] It is the intention that makes an action pure. Nevertheless, intentions neither purify unholy actions, nor do they justify them.[63] Some actions are unacceptable regardless of the intentions behind them, and yet the intentions are what make our actions pleasing to God. It therefore behooves us to

---

55. Tyson, "John Wesley's Conversion at Aldersgate," 30–31.
56. J. Taylor, *Holy Living*, 2–3.
57. Ibid., 5.
58. Wesley, Sermon 93, "On Redeeming the Time," *WW*, 3:323–32 [J 7:67–75].
59. J. Taylor, *Holy Living*, 25.
60. Ibid., 28.
61. Ibid., 13.
62. Ibid., 12.
63. Ibid., 19.

evaluate the purity of our intentions, and the best way that this can be accomplished is through despising the world.[64] In essence, the simpler our motives are, the easier it is to gauge their purity.

Thomas à Kempis

John Murray Todd states that Kempis "had much to do with stinging Wesley into a serious study of the demands of a life lived solely for God."[65] Indeed, Wesley abridged Kempis's *Imitation of Christ* and called it *The Christian's Pattern*. Wesley gives the book a hearty endorsement.

> The whole treatise is a complete and finished work, comprehending all that relates to Christian perfection, all the principles of that internal worship with which alone we worship God "in spirit and in truth." A serious mind will never be sated with it, though it were read a thousand times over, for those general principles are as fruitful seeds of meditation, and the stores they contain can never be exhausted. And herein it greatly resembles the holy Scriptures that, under the plainest words, there is a divine, hidden virtue, continually flowing into the soul of a pious and attentive reader, and by the blessing of God, transforming it into his image.[66]

What Wesley appreciated most about Kempis was his emphasis on purity of intention. Kempis says that intentions must be simple and affections pure.[67] Wesley would later take this concept and express it as "godly simplicity and godly sincerity," an expression that we have seen earlier. The first phrase, "godly simplicity," indicates that intentions must be free of ulterior motives. "Godly sincerity" implies that intentions must be focused on the proper end, i.e., the will and glory of God. Kempis declares that pure love is "unmixed with any gain or love of self." We are to "retain nothing of self-love."[68]

Kempis also asserts that we must be "free from all temporal care." Only God should be loved or regarded as pleasing, yet spiritually-

---

64. Ibid., 18.
65. Todd, *Wesley and the Catholic Church*, 36.
66. Wesley, preface to *The Christian's Pattern*, §2.2, *WWJ*, 14:202.
67. Kempis, §2.4.1; Wesley, *CP*, §2.4.1, 37.
68. Kempis, §§2.11.3–4; Wesley, *CP*, §§2.11.3–4, 45–46.

minded people still put the care of themselves above all other cares.[69] It would seem that Kempis is allowing a positive role for self-love here, but it will soon become evident that this is not the case. In this passage, self-love is needed simply to generate concern over one's own spiritual condition. Nevertheless, God cannot be loved out of self-love; rather, God must be loved for his own sake. In this respect, Kempis believes that we can be easily deceived by our motives, so it is necessary that our affections be tested by trouble and adversity.[70]

Wesley basically agrees with Kempis's concept of perfection, though he is not as mystical about the means through which it should be pursued. Note the following passage (the portions deleted by Wesley are italicized):

> Blessed are the eyes which are closed to things without, but are fixed upon [W: "open to"] things within. *Blessed are they who search inward things and study to prepare themselves more and more by daily exercises for the receiving of heavenly mysteries.* Blessed are they who long to have leisure for God, and free themselves from every hindrance of the world.[71]

Wesley is averse to implications that God supernaturally imparts knowledge to us apart from natural means. For example, Kempis prays, "Enlighten me, Blessed Jesus, with the brightness of Thy inner light, and cast forth all darkness from the habitation of my heart. Restrain my wandering thoughts and carry away the temptations which strive to do me hurt." Wesley replaces the term "inner light" with "shining light."[72] He is comfortable with praying for divine assistance, but knowledge is not received apart from natural means. Although he endorses the direct witness of the Spirit, this must be verified by other knowledge gained from natural means, i.e., the "witness of our own spirit."

Kempis displays a particular leaning toward quietism, though he does not go as far as his successors later would. He states, "In silence and quiet the devout soul goeth forward and learneth the hidden things of the Scriptures."[73] Wesley does not object to the term "stillness" in

---

69. Kempis, §§2.5.2–3; Wesley, *CP*, §§2.5.2–3, 38.
70. Kempis, §§1.14.1–2; Wesley, *CP*, §§1.11.1–2, 21.
71. Kempis, §3.1.1; Wesley, *CP*, §3.1.1, 51.
72. Kempis, §3.23.8; Wesley, *CP*, §3.18.3, 74.
73. Kempis, §1.20.6; Wesley, *CP*, §1.15.4, 26.

the sense of being patient for God to work in our lives, and he believes that we cannot earn our salvation or attain it on our own. However, he strongly rejects the notion that we are to do nothing toward our own salvation.[74] Wesley thus reacted against the Quietists, preferring the notion of cooperation to stillness.[75] For him, salvation is a divine-human synergism, and Richard Heitzenrater points out that this can be traced back to his days at Oxford. "The pervasive synergism of Wesley's mature theology, with its tension between 'faith alone' and good works, testifies to the solid grounding he had at Oxford in the synergistic perspective of the holy living tradition."[76] Consequently, when Kempis claims that God teaches human beings more in an instant that can be learned in ten years of education, Wesley reduces the claim to the assertion that God can give even the immature a clearer understanding than can be taught by human beings.[77] While Kempis believes that God can "perfectly fill [us] with knowledge," Wesley simply says that God instructs us.[78]

After reading Kempis, Wesley stated, "I began to see that true religion was seated in the heart and that God's law extended to all our thoughts as well as words and actions. I was, however, very angry at Kempis for being too strict."[79] Indeed, Kempis contends that we should seek nothing but to suffer tribulations. Divine comfort is given after tribulation is borne.[80] A "perfect contempt of the world" and "submission to any adversity for love of Christ" are among the things that give "great confidence of a happy death."[81] Furthermore, God is a willing accomplice in this process, even to the point of withdrawing his presence and favor. Kempis reflects, "I have never found any man so religious and godly but that he felt sometimes a withdrawal of the divine favor and lack of fervor."[82] Wesley flatly rejects this view of spirituality, for he believes that the life of the Christian is one of light, life, and love, none of which are ever withdrawn.

74. Wesley journal, 8 September 1746, §1, *WW*, 20:136 [J 2:27].
75. Outler, "Towards a Re-Appraisal of John Wesley," in *Theological Heritage*, 45.
76. Heitzenrater, *Mirror and Memory*, 103.
77. Kempis, §3.43.3; Wesley, *CP*, §3.31.2, 87.
78. Kempis, §3.2.1; Wesley, *CP*, §3.2.1, 52.
79. Wesley journal, 24 May 1738, §4, *WW*, 18:243 [J 1:99].
80. Kempis, §§2.12.7–8.
81. Ibid., §1.23.4.
82. Ibid., §2.9.7.

The goal in all of this asceticism is the purification of motives, for it is only when the affections are cleansed that the soul will experience peace.[83] Our passions are one of the chief obstacles we face in attaining this state of purity. As such, "true peace is to be found in resisting passion, not in yielding to it."[84] Pure intentions seldom last because we quickly focus on pleasant things and are rarely free from self-seeking.[85] As a result, we must "rise above every creature" and perfectly forsake ourselves.[86] We should abase ourselves and "shrink from all self-esteem" so that what little bit of it we do have will be "swallowed up in the depths of nothingness."[87]

It should now be clear that Kempis does not allow self-love to have a positive role in loving God. Not only are the passions a hindrance to pure love, self-love is as well. Kempis does not believe that reason can rescue us from this dilemma, for he sets his sights on the mystical infusion of spiritual knowledge, and this transcends the natural means of learning. This is essentially the view of the Quietists, which Wesley rejects and labels as "mysticism." In Wesley's relationship with Law, the breach between Wesley and the mystics becomes acute to the point of effecting a complete departure between them.

Wesley's Initial Attraction to William Law

Green believes that Law's early writings reinforced Wesley's religious heritage and appealed to his personal inclinations.

> John Wesley was first attracted to William Law by the latter's presentation of an ethical ideal, which was rendered singularly attractive by reason of his own Puritan and High Church ancestry, his reasoning, disciplined mental habits, his continuous religious aspirations, and his reading of Kempis, Taylor, and Law himself.[88]

Wesley relates that reading Law's *Christian Perfection* and *Serious Call* spurred him to wholeheartedly keep God's law, both inwardly and

---

83. Ibid., §1.11.4.
84. Ibid., §1.6.2.
85. Ibid., §3.33.2.
86. Ibid., §3.31.1.
87. Ibid., §3.8.1.
88. Green, *John Wesley and William Law*, 211.

outwardly. However, he "was much offended at many parts of both."[89] Albert Outler surmises that Taylor, Kempis, and Law all generally reinforced the same notion for Wesley, namely, "that the Christian life is *devotio*, the consecration of the whole man in love to God and neighbor in the full round of life and death."[90]

For Law, being godly is essentially having a disposition to please God. "He is the devout man, therefore, who considers and serves God in everything and who makes all of his life an act of devotion by doing everything in the name of God and under such rules as are conformable to His glory."[91] Pure intention is thus the desire to please God in all our actions "as the best and happiest thing in the world."[92] This intention is initiated by gratefulness to God for his providence in our lives, which is signified by complete resignation to God's will.[93] In other words, if we are appreciative of God's providential care, then we will want to submit to it in every facet of our lives. However, this is not a self-serving type of gratitude or commitment, for it engenders deeper devotion and the acceptance of responsibility for oneself. Law states that his desire is to instill within people a fear of living in sloth and idleness as well as an earnest longing for higher degrees of devotion.[94] In fact, people are often insufficiently motivated, and this prevents them from progressing spiritually. Law says that "we have not that perfection which our present state of grace makes us capable because we do not so much as intend to have it."[95]

Virtue is thus defined along these lines: "The whole nature of virtue consists in conforming to the will of God and the whole nature of vice is declining from the will of God. All God's creatures are created to fulfill his will."[96] We must try to reduce our desires "to such things as nature and reason require," and this will help us avoid unnecessary temptation. However, this does not require us to deprive ourselves of

---

89. Wesley journal, 24 May 1738, §5, *WW*, 18:244 [J 1:99].
90. Outler, *John Wesley*, 7.
91. Law, *Serious Call*, 17.
92. Ibid., 24; cf. 21.
93. Ibid., 142.
94. Ibid., 27.
95. Ibid., 24.
96. Ibid., 140–41.

life's comforts.⁹⁷ Obviously, the paragon of following God's will is Christ himself, but we cannot imitate the actions of his life. Rather, we are to have the same "spirit and temper" as he had.⁹⁸ This "spirit and temper" is love, for there is nothing more acceptable to God than "a universal fervent love to all mankind, wishing and praying for their happiness." God's nature is love and he has thus created us with this capacity for our happiness.⁹⁹ Harald Lindström posits that for Law our love for others must model God's love for us—pure and universal.¹⁰⁰

In these early works, Law sees self-love in a more positive light than Kempis. Indeed, self-love is central to loving God, which entails seeing God as our only source of happiness. This does, however, demand renunciation of the world.¹⁰¹ Even though temperaments vary from person to person, all must "equally look upon God as their sole happiness."¹⁰² In fact, the more we aspire to please God and conform to his will, the more we will enjoy God and increase our general happiness in life.¹⁰³ Hence, self-love is that which motivates us to seek God as the *Summum Bonum*, the source of true happiness. Proper self-love is also the standard of neighborly love. Consequently, the duty of loving others is based not only on the law of God, but likewise on human nature itself.¹⁰⁴

According to Law, there is nothing wrong with benefiting ourselves while we benefit others, but self-love cannot be the chief motivation of our actions.¹⁰⁵ Also, we are expected to make sacrifices for both God and others. Nevertheless, the sacrifices that religion commands us to make are ultimately for our own welfare and happiness.¹⁰⁶ It is God's desire that we should be happy, and we will find this happiness in loving God and others. This does not involve self-abasement, as Kempis suggests. Indeed, abusing ourselves is just as disobedient to God as injuring our

---

97. Ibid., 74.
98. Law, *Christian Perfection*, 216.
99. Law, *Serious Call*, 130.
100. Lindström, *Wesley and Sanctification*, 166.
101. Law, *Christian Perfection*, 68.
102. Ibid., 71.
103. Law, *Serious Call*, 71.
104. Lindström, *Wesley and Sanctification*, 167–68.
105. Law, *Serious Call*, 33.
106. Ibid., 76.

neighbor.[107] What we should strive for is humility, and this is involves a right judgment of ourselves such that we do not value ourselves too much or too little.[108]

Nonetheless, Law underscores the importance of self-denial in the Christian life. It is "the very form and substance of every virtue."[109] In fact, self-denial must take place in every part of our lives. "If self-denial be a condition of salvation, all who would be saved must make self-denial a part of their everyday life." This includes humility, caring for the needy, loving our enemies, giving thanks to God in everything, and renouncing foolish and vain things "in every part of our daily life."[110] It also includes living a life free from sin, so far as one is able. Law believes that our inner disposition is what makes this possible. To be born of God is to have "a temper and mind so entirely devoted to purity and holiness" that it is impossible to sin.[111] However, when we do our best, we are not to be blamed for our imperfections, and yet, if they stem from "negligence and lack of sincere intentions," then they are inexcusable.[112]

Thus far, we see a conception of perfection that closely parallels that of Wesley. The emphases on love for God and others, pure intentions, conformity to God's will, proper self-love, self-denial, the unity of virtue and happiness, and living a life of victory over willful sin are all central Wesleyan themes. Moreover, these earlier works of Law recognize the importance of reason in perfection. Law maintains that God has designed the world according to his divine reason. Consequently, the best choices in life are made in consideration of what God, reason, eternity, and our own happiness require of us.[113] This rationality is not limited to the material realm, but extends to spiritual matters. For instance, Law declares that the "reason and fitness" of both repentance and self-denial can be seen.[114]

---

107. Ibid., 65.
108. Law, *Christian Perfection*, 103–4.
109. Ibid., 110.
110. Law, *Serious Call*, 19.
111. Law, *Christian Perfection*, 27.
112. Law, *Serious Call*, 26.
113. Ibid., 128.
114. Law, *Christian Perfection*, 85.

Since God has created the world according to the divine reason, we must use our God-given reason in conducting our lives. "All men, therefore, as men, have one and the same business: to act up to the excellency of their rational nature, to make reason and order the law of all their designs and actions."[115] Law even attributes a lack of devotion to ignorance, because the more we know about God and ourselves, the more we will be inclined to confess our sin and submit ourselves to God.[116] This leads him to adopt a philosophy of education similar to that of Wesley and Locke. "The only end of education is to restore our rational nature to its proper state. Education, therefore, is to be considered as a reason [sic] borrowed at second hand which is to supply, as far as it can, the loss of original perfection."[117] Wesley expresses his approval of Law's approach to education, quoting this passage at length.[118] Wesley and Law both see the need for a good education, and they believe that the most crucial element (but not the only element) of an education is religious instruction. As Law expresses it, religion is the cure for "the infatuation and ignorance of our fallen state." It teaches us knowledge about ourselves as well as the "true value of things," i.e., good and evil.[119]

Basically, we are approved by God when we are conformable to the highest reason.[120] There is thus a degree of congruence between the divine reason and our human nature, such that following the dictates of reason will lead us toward the divine will. Newton Flew indicates that for Law, "our tempers always follow the judgments and opinions of our minds."[121] This not only implies that we are responsible to shape our own dispositions, but it also suggests that the way to achieve holy dispositions is by aligning our thoughts with divine reason. "God is reason and wisdom itself, and he can no more call us to any tempers or duties, but such as are strictly reasonable in themselves, than he can

---

115. Law, *Serious Call*, 68.
116. Ibid., 152–54.
117. Ibid., 116.
118. Wesley, Sermon 95, "On the Education of Children," §3, *WW*, 3:348–49 [J 7:87].
119. Law, *Christian Perfection*, 100.
120. Ibid., 103.
121. Flew, *Perfection in Christian Theology*, 300.

act against himself, or contradict his own nature." Furthermore, God cannot impose tempers or dispositions on us.

> God can only will that reasonable creatures should be more reasonable, more perfect, and more like himself, and consequently can enjoin us no duties, or tempers of mind, but such as have this tendency. All his commands are for our sakes, founded in the necessities of our natures, and are only so many instructions to become more happy than we could be without them.[122]

Wesley and Law Part Company

Wesley's departure from Law came in two respects, the first of which began with Wesley's dealings with the Moravians, particularly Peter Böhler. When Wesley was struggling with his own faith, longing for some type of assurance, it was Böhler who exhorted him, "Preach faith *till* you have it, and then, *because* you have it, you *will* preach it."[123] Böhler was trying to dissuade Wesley from Law's influence. He had a somewhat confrontational meeting with Law, then he reported this meeting to Wesley, giving an account of it that conflicted with Law's recollection of events.[124] Böhler claimed that Law had nothing to say about faith in Christ. Rather, he only spoke in mystical terms. Böhler took this to be a "very dangerous" position.[125] Wesley subsequently corresponded several times with Law, putting Law on the defensive.

Wesley told Law that his emphasis on living by the law of God was too high, for people could not live up to it. He said that he had been freed from this "heavy yoke" by Böhler's teaching on justification by faith.[126] According to English, Wesley thus moved away from the mystical view of regeneration toward the Reformation view through the influence of the Moravians.[127] Wesley also rejected Law's view of the atonement, asserting that it is too speculative and unsupported by Scripture.[128] His assertion that speculative philosophy (like that espoused by Law) spoils

---

122. Law, *Christian Perfection*, 99.
123. Wesley journal, 4 March 1738, *WW*, 18:228 [J 1:86].
124. Harper, "Law and Wesley," 63–64.
125. Wesley to Law, 14 May 1738, *WWJ*, 12:52.
126. Ibid., *WWJ*, 12:51; cf. Walters, "Concept of Attainment," 16.
127. English, "Francis Rous," 28.
128. Collins, "Christian Mysticism," 301–3.

religion is based on his distinction between essential doctrines and opinions, a distinction that was part of a broader intellectual movement in eighteenth-century religious thought.[129] Basically, Wesley felt that essential doctrines should be closely linked to Scripture and historical Christian orthodoxy.

Many scholars suggest that Wesley's tirade against Law was unkind and unfair.[130] Part of this may be attributed to the fact that Wesley was experiencing a major turning point in his life. For one thing, Wesley's experience at Aldersgate altered his views on holy living. He came to believe that humans cannot earn God's grace, so he could no longer regard holy living as a part of justification. Instead, he saw it as a response to the living faith realized in regeneration.[131] As a result, Aldersgate marked Wesley's intellectual break with mysticism.[132] However, this is due to the fact that Wesley came to view mysticism as the antithesis of Reformation theology. As such, Wesley did not agree with the mystics' view of justification, but he never lost the thirst for perfection that he acquired from them. Nevertheless, Wesley was opposed to the mystics' method of pursuing perfection. In that regard, he sought to integrate the West's emphasis on pardon with the East's emphasis on grace as the power to heal our infirm nature.[133] It is an integration of pardon and participation (in the divine nature).[134]

Nevertheless, the aspect of Wesley's split with Law that is most pertinent to this project has to do with Law's increased involvement with mysticism. Wesley resonated with Law's earlier works, which were more practical and moralistic, but he broke with Law when the latter began interpreting the writings of the mystic Jacob Behmen.[135] Consistent with his critique of Law, Wesley accused Behmen, Tauler, and other mystics of muddling the doctrine of justification by faith.[136] However,

---

129. Newton, "The Ecumenical Wesley," 163–66.

130. See Harper, "Law and Wesley," 64–67; also see Lindström, *Wesley and Sanctification*, 58.

131. Nausner, "Christian Perfection," 75.

132. Tuttle, *Mysticism in the Wesleyan Tradition*, 105.

133. Maddox, *Responsible Grace*, 84–85.

134. Outler, "The Place of Wesley in the Christian Tradition," in *Theological Heritage*, 93.

135. Clarkson, "Law's Mysticism," 538–39.

136. Collins, "Christian Mysticism," 307–8.

Wesley displayed a certain contempt for Behmen. He exclaimed that Behmen's writings are "unintelligible nonsense" and that reading them is a "waste of time."[137]

Law's beliefs became increasingly mystical, and this was reflected in his later writings, which stand in sharp contrast against *Serious Call* and *Christian Perfection*, the two works that influenced Wesley.[138] He began to expand on the very themes that Wesley had purposely omitted in his extract of Kempis. For example, Law says,

> For be assured of this, as a certain truth, that [as] corrupt, fallen, and earthly as human nature is, there is nevertheless in the soul of every man the fire, and light, and love of God, though lodged in a state of hiddenness, inactivity, and death, till something or other, human or divine, Moses and the prophets, Christ or his apostles, discover its life within us.[139]

This not only contradicts Wesley's doctrine of original sin, it is at odds with Wesley's view of revelation, especially the role that human reason plays throughout. The earlier Law had emphasized the importance of reason, knowledge, and education. In contrast, the later Law asserted that education, science, etc. are only beneficial to the "natural" self. They are of little use in spiritual matters.[140] He contended that it is futile to reason about the mysteries of God, because there are no "rational explications" of them. Since God communicates to us through his very presence in us, to rely on "learning and philosophy" is "to turn from God and wander out of the way of all divine communication."[141] This clearly contradicts his earlier assertion that we are unable to discern the "invisible operation and assistance of God's Holy Spirit."[142] Nevertheless, his earlier writings reflect some curiosity with this type of mysticism. For instance, he says that the Holy Spirit brings us "secret inspirations," and we prepare ourselves to receive them through self-denial.[143]

---

137. Wesley, "Thoughts upon Jacob Behmen," §3, *WWJ*, 12:512.
138. Cannon, *Theology of John Wesley*, 57.
139. Law, "Divine Knowledge," 118.
140. Ibid., 124–25.
141. Ibid., 130.
142. Law, *Christian Perfection*, 134.
143. Ibid., 142.

The overall shift in Law's thought was anti-intellectual and quietistic. According to Tyson, "Law's ideal of separation from the things of this world" eventually evolved into "a sort of anti-intellectualism and quietistic withdrawal from society—both of which were intolerable to John Wesley."[144] Clearly, Wesley was attracted to the mystics' emphasis on perfection whenever the importance of reason was stressed. On the other hand, he shied away from construals that de-emphasized reason.

Quietism: The Most Objectionable Form of Mysticism

The quietism that bothered Wesley is perhaps best illustrated by the French Catholic mystics like Madame Guyon and her disciple Fénelon. Although he admired their devotion to God, Wesley was troubled by their view of revelation, especially their reliance on personal, inward impulses. He said that Madame Guyon's primary mistake was that she subjugated Scripture to "inward impressions." He asserted that she read Scripture "not to learn, but to teach."[145] Her contribution to the development of quietism is undeniable.

For example, Guyon states that if you feel the presence of God while praying, you should remain quiet there and "cherish this sensation while it continues." When it starts to wane, it may bring a feeling of peace.[146] You must "sink into yourself" so that you can find God "in your innermost center." She continues,

> When you have fully entered into yourself, you will sense within you the warm presence of God when the senses are recollected and withdrawn from the circumference to the center and the soul is sweetly and silently employed on the truths we have read, not in reasoning, but in feeding thereon.[147]

Hence, being "calmly united to God" in love gives one the devotion to contemplate "every divine mystery."[148]

Wesley reacted against this type of quietism, wherever it appeared. In addition to his complaints against the Moravians' "antinomianism,"

---

144. Tyson, "John Wesley and William Law," 72.
145. Wesley, preface to *An Extract of the Life of Madame Guion*, §7, *WWJ*, 14:277.
146. Guyon, *Union with God*, 28.
147. Ibid., 16–17.
148. Ibid., 46.

Wesley recoiled from their quietistic tendencies, too.[149] According to W. P. Stephens, this split began when Philip Molther started exhorting people to abstain from the means of grace and from good works while waiting for God.[150] Wesley strongly opposed this, because he believed not only that the means of grace are necessary for Christian growth, but also that one's inward temper must be expressed in outward life and character.[151] The Moravians asserted that anything other than stillness causes human activity to be confused with the operations of divine grace. In contrast, Wesley believed that stillness does not isolate or stifle human nature. Rather, this type of "stillness" makes people more susceptible to the whims of their own feelings. Scripture and the other means of grace are necessary if this degree of subjectivity is to be avoided.[152] As Ted Runyon expresses it,

> Wesley was forced to recognize that the advocates of this "stillness" doctrine had, in effect, absolutized their own feelings and merged them with Christ. There was no critical principle, no rational accountability to Scripture or tradition in order to judge the adequacy of feelings.... This kind of "mysticism," according to Wesley, could only undermine the genuine function of experience within Christian faith, including the legitimate but relative role of feelings.[153]

Nevertheless, the quietists also propagated a notion of love that did not allow a legitimate place for self-love. Madame Guyon claimed that we should pray with a "pure and disinterested love that seeks nothing from God but to please him and to do his will."[154] We are to surrender to God's will, and this involves "renouncing every private inclination as soon as it arises, however good it may appear, that we may stand in indifference with respect to ourselves, and only will what God has willed from all eternity."[155] In this way, the soul's surrender to God is passive.[156]

---

149. Stephens, "Wesley and the Moravians," 32–34. Also, see Collins, "Christian Mysticism," 304.
150. Stephens, "Wesley and the Moravians," 32.
151. Newton, "Perfection and Spirituality," 99.
152. Knight, *Presence of God*, 43.
153. Runyon, *The New Creation*, 155.
154. Guyon, *Union with God*, 28.
155. Ibid., 39, n. 22.
156. Ibid., 158.

In order for love to become increasingly passive, first the external senses must be conquered, especially with regard to one's appetites. Next, the inward activities of the soul are also destroyed. This leaves only "naked faith," i.e., utter "internal and external desolation."[157]

Madame Guyon's protégé Fénelon took this antipathy toward self-love even further. He defines "pure love" as loving God only for himself without any regard to the beatitude we receive from God's beauty.[158] He declares, "We ought to desire the glory of God more than our own interest or happiness, and not even so much as desire that but for his glory."[159] We are to "do violence" to ourselves (i.e., deny ourselves) to the extent that we "reach that degree of absolute indifference necessary to a Christian, whose only will is that of God his creator . . . who takes pleasure in considering God, and who fears not at all to be considered by him."[160]

For Fénelon, "The sure and shortest way [to attain pure love] is to renounce self, to forget self, to abandon self, and not to think any longer of self except by faithfulness to God."[161] Indeed, "transport, forgetfulness of self, and disinterestedness" all describe that which is most divine in love.[162] We must transcend our passions if we are to experience this kind of love, because "transport" of the passions is what allows infinite beauty to be loved strictly for its own sake.[163] Nevertheless, this transcendence cannot be accomplished through human effort. It requires supernatural activity. Essentially, when God circumcises the heart, he removes self-love like a surgeon.[164] This is what gives true freedom.

> Happy then [are] those whom God takes away from their own will to attach to his own! Those whom God is pleased to chain with his own hands are free and happy, as those who chain themselves by their passions are miserable. In this apparent captivity, they can no longer do what they wish. So much the better. They do from morning to night, against their inclinations, what

---

157. Ibid., 176–79.
158. Fénelon, *Christian Perfection*, 140.
159. Fénelon, *Pure Love*, 3.
160. Fénelon, *Christian Perfection*, 46.
161. Ibid., 54.
162. Fénelon, *Pure Love*, 5.
163. Ibid., 9.
164. Fénelon, *Let Go*, 86–87.

God wants them to do. He holds them bound hand and foot by the lines of his will.[165]

Since disinterested love for Fénelon allows no place for incentives, the person who possesses it can even face the possibility of being annihilated by God at any moment.[166] Fénelon realizes that most people will never attain this type of pure love, yet he attributes this shortcoming to the will of God. He feels that God pursues very few people to the point of conquering self-interest. The vast majority must join their interest to the interest of God. However, since they are dependent on self-interest, it would be harmful to try to strip it away from them.[167]

Wesley agrees with Fénelon that we should progress toward pure love, but he does not understand "disinterestedness" to involve this kind of self-debasement. He also does not accept Fénelon's conception of "dark faith," which trivializes the role of reason.[168] In fact, Fénelon alleges that it is vain to trust in our own intellects and in philosophy itself.[169] Knowledge does not help us die to self. On the contrary, it only builds up pride.[170] For Wesley, proper humility comes from a proper knowledge of both God and oneself.

Influences That Offer a More Cognitive Approach

When we examine the other Christian writers who influenced Wesley, we will again find that what appealed to Wesley was not quietistic mysticism, or anti-intellectual fideism, but an emphasis on loving God and others that sufficiently stresses the role of cognition and the need for human responsibility without undervaluing divine initiative and assistance. Perhaps one of the best examples of this kind of influence is Clement of Alexandria. Although Wesley's admiration for Clement's "Christian Gnostic" was tempered over time, he regarded it as the model of the ideal Christian.[171]

---

165. Fénelon, *Christian Perfection*, 13–14.
166. Ibid., 142–43.
167. Ibid., 149–50.
168. English, "French Catholic Tradition," 443–44.
169. Fénelon, *Let Go*, 65–66.
170. Ibid., 61.
171. A. Wood, *Burning Heart*, 43.

Clement defines perfection as being made like the Lord up to the measure of our capacity.[172] In this regard, the perfect Christian can be said to lack nothing.[173] Although we cannot be perfect in all virtues simultaneously while we are yet human, we can still excel in every virtue.[174] Like Wesley, Clement believes that true perfection consists in the knowledge and love of God.[175] However, he and Wesley do not agree on the pursuit of perfection. For instance, Clement avers that perfection comes at regeneration.[176] Also, he relates perfection to election, for he claims that those chosen by God are those who are perfected in love.[177] Campbell adds that Wesley does not retain Clement's emphasis on "the Christian's passionlessness and contemplation of the divine."[178]

Nevertheless, the disagreement between Clement and Wesley is not as great as it first appears. Clement clearly asserts that in this life, we try "to be as perfect as we can," aspiring to achieve perfect compliance with the will of God in order to restore "truly perfect nobleness and relationship." This requires that we live a life of victory over sin. Hence, abstinence from evil is "a step to the highest perfection." Moreover, we each have unique strengths and weaknesses, and these provide us with varying capacities for acquiring the several virtues. We can thus become perfect with respect to our particular proficiencies, and this is a relative state of perfection. Consequently, people should not be called perfect while on earth, because that distinction is reserved for eternity.[179] This might help to explain why Wesley never claimed to have achieved perfection in his own life even though he asserted its possibility.

The role of cognition is stressed throughout Clement's writings. He recognizes knowledge itself as the most perfect good.[180] Knowledge is what provides us with practical wisdom, and this leads to self-control.[181]

---

172. Clement, *Writings of Clement*, 2:415.
173. Ibid., 1:132.
174. Ibid., 2:199.
175. Ibid., 2:212.
176. Ibid., 1:131–32.
177. Ibid., 2:190.
178. Campbell, *Christian Antiquity*, 42.
179. Clement, *Writings of Clement*, 2:199–202.
180. Ibid., 2:361.
181. Ibid., 2:378.

The Gnostic thus studies "to acquire mastery over the passions."[182] Even philosophy is given respect by Clement, since he sees it as a God-given "preparatory discipline for the perfection which is by Christ."[183] Basically, Clement understands perfection to occur through illumination, i.e., it involves seeing God clearly.[184] This is a cognitive process, one that dispels ignorance.[185] Nonetheless, Clement is not advocating a state of passivity like the mystics. "The soul must be prepared and variously exercised, if it would become the highest degree good."[186]

According to Clement, the proper employment of those who are perfect is to rejoice in the enduring of the good, "holding festival with God."[187] The Gnostic does good "for the sake of its own excellence" and for the purpose of conforming to the image and likeness of God.[188] Once we ascend to knowledge, we will pray for the perfection of love. We will also pray that we will never fall from virtue, but become infallible. After we choose to live infallibly, we subject ourselves to training so as to stabilize our knowledge. Once the knowledge of God is attained, virtue is preserved and becomes incapable of being lost. Then, habit becomes virtue.[189] Although Wesley initially believed that the perfect can never fall from grace, he later rejected that view, since he had seen too much evidence to the contrary.

Another description of perfection that Wesley found intriguing was that proposed by Macarius, who saw perfection as the goal of the Christian life.[190] Campbell surmises,

> It is likely that the reason why Wesley was attracted to the *Spiritual Homilies* of Macarius was because of the stress that the *Homilies* laid on holiness and perfection.... Wesley saw "Macarius," then, as a fourth-century advocate of the quest for

---

182. Ibid., 2:454.
183. Ibid., 2:395.
184. Ibid., 1:131–32.
185. Ibid., 1:135.
186. Ibid., 2:356.
187. Ibid., 1:129.
188. Ibid., 2:202–3.
189. Ibid., 2:439–40.
190. Outler, *John Wesley*, 9–10.

holiness Wesley believed to have characterized the church as a whole in its purer ages.[191]

Campbell adds that Wesley's doctrine of Christian perfection harkens back to the ascetic goal of "deification" (i.e., theiosis or apotheiosis). However, when Wesley edited the *Spiritual Homilies* of Macarius, he replaced this term with the word "sanctification."[192]

Macarius asserts that the purpose of the Incarnation was to allow us to become partakers of the divine nature. "We must love the Lord, and be diligent every way in all virtues, and ask persistently and continually," so that we might receive the Holy Spirit "completely and to perfection." This equips us to "fulfill every commandment unblamably and purely."[193] According to Macarius, perfection enables us to fulfill the commandments, because it brings liberation from our sinful affections and re-creates the image of God within us.[194] The virtues that are obtained in perfection become a sort of second nature to us, yet this does not happen quickly. The process of perfection occurs gradually through much toil and suffering.[195] All of this is consistent with Wesley's view of perfection, and Wesley appreciated Macarius's claim that we can always grow in grace, regardless of the state of perfection we might obtain.[196]

Hoo-Jung Lee concludes that Wesley "remained too bound by the dominant focus on logic and reason that pervades Western culture" to be fully consonant with this type of affective spirituality.[197] Nevertheless, Macarius is not as naïve as Lee supposes. For one thing, Macarius realizes that human nature is not simplistic. He asserts that we can be spiritually healthy in some respects while deficient in others.[198] Moreover, he recognizes the interaction of the various faculties of the soul, especially reason. The "ruling factors" of the soul are will, conscience, intelligence, and love.[199]

---

191. Campbell, *Christian Antiquity*, 66–67.
192. Campbell, "Church Fathers," 65–66.
193. Macarius, *Fifty Spiritual Homilies*, §44.9, 280.
194. Lee, "Experiencing the Spirit," 209–10.
195. Flew, *Idea of Perfection*, 183.
196. Tuttle, *Mysticism in the Wesleyan Tradition*, 146.
197. Lee, "Experiencing the Spirit," 200.
198. Macarius, *Fifty Spiritual Homilies*, §15.7, 109.
199. Ibid., §1.3, 3.

One final example is also worthy of notice. Wesley had a deep admiration for Gaston Jean Baptiste de Renty, to whom he referred as a "burning and shining light."[200] He produced an extract of the biography of de Renty's life. In Tuttle's opinion, Wesley "goes to great lengths to record his depth of piety and work of charity." The abridgement "upholds a strong Christian ethic while playing down so much mystical theology."[201] What Wesley admired most about de Renty was his rational control over his emotions. His love for God did not wane during painful illness, neither did it falter when his wife died. He accepted the death with resignation, regarding it as the will of God.[202] Wesley cited this example when he chided Adam Clarke for grieving too much over the death of his child.[203] Wesley also admired Gregory Lopez for the same reasons that he esteemed de Renty. Eamon Duffy says that Lopez can be regarded as "a mystic for the age of enlightenment: cool, rational, impatient of gush and idle chatter."[204] Therefore, it seems that the type of mystic that Wesley found most appealing was the more rational kind.

Summary

Although Wesley read a wide variety of authors who address the subject of perfection, he was selective in formulating his own views and in endorsing the views of others. Overall, Wesley distanced himself from the mystical, quietistic approach to perfection. Instead, he sympathized most with the authors who at least recognized (if not underscored) the importance of reason throughout the process, even with respect to the affections. I have not attempted to give a comprehensive account of the intellectual sources of Wesley's doctrine of perfection. My goal has been to examine the major sources of the doctrine with respect to their emphasis on reason and cognition. Although the matter could certainly be investigated more fully, I still suggest that a comprehensive analysis of Wesley's sources will reveal the same pattern I have outlined.

---

200. Wesley, "A Farther Appeal to Men of Reason and Religion, Part II," §3.12, *WW*, 11:261 [J 8:190–91]; cf. Wesley journal, 6 January 1738, *WW*, 18:208 [J 1:71].
201. Tuttle, *Mysticism in the Wesleyan Tradition*, 93.
202. Wesley, Sermon 82, "On Temptation," §§3.5–6, *WW*, 3:166–67 [J 6:483].
203. Duffy, "Counter-Reformation," 9–11.
204. Ibid., 14.

6

The Cognitive Content of Emotions

THE FOCAL POINT OF THIS CHAPTER WILL BE THE FURTHER CORROBO-ration of my claim that Wesley's understanding of perfection can be construed along more cognitivist lines. I will highlight the fact that Wesley recognized the cognitive content of emotions evidenced in his writings, especially his abridgement of Jonathan Edwards' *Treatise Concerning Religious Affections*. A careful analysis of the abridgement reveals the main similarities and differences between Edwards' and Wesley's views on moral transformation. This analysis is both clarified and confirmed by their other writings, and it commends the possibility of a more cognitive account of emotions that is consonant with the Wesleyan doctrine of perfection. Moreover, it suggests some epistemic boundaries for religious experience.

Background: Locke's Theory of Motivation

It has long been accepted that both Wesley and Edwards were influenced by Locke, though scholars have not always agreed on the extent of that influence. However, a brief description of Locke's understanding of motivation will provide a good starting point for comparing their views. Locke contends that the mind has two faculties—understanding and will. Understanding is our ability to perceive (1) our ideas, (2) the "signification of signs" (i.e., the meaning of impressions on our minds), and (3) the agreement or disagreement of our ideas. Will is essentially the power to prefer and choose.[1] Since he defines liberty and freedom as the power to act or not act, Locke concludes that they exist only in our actions, not in the will itself. Some things are matters of necessity,

---

1. Locke, *Essay*, §2.21.5, 1:313–14.

because we have no power over them, regardless of what we may desire. For example, a person is free to jump or not jump off of a bridge, but a person cannot jump fifty feet into the air even though it be greatly desired. However, actions that lie within our ability are free, because we can choose to do them or not do them.[2]

In contrast, Locke claims that the will is always determined by desire, "which is an uneasiness of the mind for want of some absent good." In the first edition of the *Essay*, Locke followed what he considered to be the widely accepted maxim, namely, that will is determined by the greatest good. He later recanted and concluded that the will is actually determined by the greatest desire, regardless of whether or not such may in reality be the greatest good. In this regard, it might be said that the will chooses the greatest *perceived* good. Locke feels that if the will were always moved by the greatest good, then people would constantly be striving to get to heaven, but such is not the case. Instead, the will is most often determined by the most immediate feelings of uneasiness, especially those that are corporeal.[3]

Here is a point where Wesley apparently misunderstood Locke. In response to Locke's assertion that the will is moved by uneasiness, Wesley answers,

> Not always. Pleasure determines it as often as pain. But [Locke says,] "desire is uneasiness." It is not. We desire to enjoy pleasure as much as to avoid pain. But desire differs *toto genere*, both from one and the other. Therefore, all that follows, about pain alone determining the will, is wrong from end to end.[4]

However, Locke never claims this, for he alleges that happiness alone is what motivates desire.[5] Wesley regards this as a contradiction, but he does not seem to grasp the way Locke nuances his definition of pain and relates it to happiness. For Locke, pain is not only a negative feeling imposed upon the mind, it is also the longing one feels emotionally in the absence of a desired good. Thus, when we desire something, we do not experience pleasure, but feelings of uneasiness regarding the

---

2. Ibid., §§2.21.7–28, 1:315–30.
3. Ibid., §§2.21.29–41, 1:330–40.
4. Wesley, "Remarks upon Mr. Locke's *Essay*," *WWJ*, 13:456–57.
5. Locke, *Essay*, §§2.21.42–43, 1:340–41.

concomitant pleasure's lack. This type of pain (i.e., uneasiness) is not aversive, but anticipatory.

In a nutshell, Locke sees happiness as the determining factor of desire. In turn, desire is what determines the will. Ultimately, the passions themselves are moved by pleasure and pain.[6] Nevertheless, the understanding exerts an influence over the affections and is able to shape them to a degree. As Vere Chappell points out, in Locke's system the object of desire must be cognized, most specifically with regard to the pleasure it will bring.[7] In the fifth edition of the *Essay*, Locke returns to a more intellectualist position like the first edition in which desire is depicted as the product of judgment concerning the goodness or badness of the object.[8] Although pain and pleasure motivate, they do not sufficiently motivate action, and yet reason alone is also an insufficient motivator. This is why reward and punishment are necessary to motivate moral action in those who are not otherwise inclined to pursue virtue.[9]

Tito Magri suggests that for Locke, desire and uneasiness do not determine the will merely as a reflex, but as "a cognitively structured and reasoned attitude." Reason prevents the will from being motivated by sheer short-term pleasure. Rather, the ultimate goal is happiness, and this requires practical reasoning to attempt to determine the greatest good.[10] Locke believes that we have both the ability and the obligation to suspend the execution of our desires so that they may be evaluated by reason. In effect, will is determined by desire, but only as one's desires and actions come under the scrutiny of reason. Moreover, the pursuit of happiness is reasonable, so the mind should be focused on that end. "The highest perfection of intellectual nature lies in a careful and constant pursuit of true and solid happiness."[11]

Locke also claims that we can change our palates, i.e., the pleasure or displeasure we take in things. This is done both by determining the best means to particular ends and by forming habits, which cause us

---

6. Ibid., §2.20.3, 1:303; §2.20.43, 1:340.
7. Chappell, "Basis of Sin," 204.
8. Ibid., 206.
9. Drury, "Natural Law and Innate Ideas," 541.
10. Magri, "Suspension of Desire," 66–69.
11. Locke, *Essay*, §§2.21.48–53, 1:344–49.

to become accustomed to certain things.[12] However, it is our ability to reason that provides us with a degree of freedom in the will, because reason enables us to determine the greatest good. "The stronger ties we have to an unalterable pursuit of happiness in general, which is our greatest good, and which, as such, our desires always follow, the more are we free from any necessary determination of our will to any particular action."[13]

For Locke, our ultimate happiness comes from doing God's will. "Every man has an immortal soul, capable of eternal happiness or misery, whose happiness depending upon his believing and doing those things in this life which are necessary to the obtaining of God's favor, and are prescribed by God to that end."[14] Since human reason is limited, collective reason is better than individual reason, and divine reason is superior due to its perfection. Consequently, our inability to adequately determine the greatest good on our own necessitates the existence and enforcement of law.

Edwards' General Schema

Edwards basically agrees with Locke's representation, but he diverges from it in certain ways. He begins with the same faculties of the soul—understanding and will. Understanding performs the three basic functions of perception, speculation, and judgment. Will, which is also commonly referred to as character and heart, provides the functions of approbation and inclination.[15] The faculty of will is essentially our capacity for love and hate.[16] In this regard, the function of the will is to approve and disapprove. The same can be said of the emotions. According to Edwards, God made affections the source of our actions.[17] He says that the will and the affections are not separate from one another. The will acts from inclination, and the affections differ from will and inclination only in degree.[18] In other words, will is an inclination that effects

---

12. Ibid., §2.21.71, 1:362–63
13. Ibid., §2.21.52, 1:348.
14. Locke, *Let*, 46.
15. Edwards, *RA*, §1.1, p. 96; cf. Wesley, *WHS*, 51.
16. Edwards, *TV*, §4, 43.
17. Ibid., §1.2, 100–1; cf. Wesley, *WHS*, 53.
18. Edwards, *RA*, §1.1, 97–98; cf. Wesley, *WHS*, 52.

a choice, and affection is a strong inclination. Affections often result in the exercise of will, but not always.

This psychological model is very consistent with Locke's account, but the two views are distinctly different at several points. Moreover, Edwards later moved away from the Lockean phenomenology of experience, at least in his explanation of spiritual perception. William Spohn indicates that this is most evident in *The Nature of True Virtue*, where Edwards adopts language that is more characteristic of Neo-Platonism.[19] This will become more evident as the contrast between Edwards and Wesley unfolds. For now, it would be beneficial to point out how Edwards departs from Locke's view of will in order to support his own compatibilist view of will.

Edwards maintains that when Locke says that the will is moved by uneasiness, he is indicating that the will is always moved toward that which is "agreeable" (i.e., pleasurable) and away from that which is "disagreeable" (i.e., displeasurable). The will makes the choice that will bring the greatest effect in this regard.[20] Although Locke distinguishes desire and will, Edwards argues that they are intertwined. "A man never, in any instance, wills anything contrary to his desires or desires anything contrary to his will."[21] In fact, "moral causes" like inclinations and motives are connected by necessity in a matrix of cause and effect. Every act of will is an effect of prior causes, and it becomes a contributing cause for future effects.[22]

Liberty and freedom are not powers of self-determination for Edwards. Rather, liberty is the property of being free of both constraint (in which one is compelled) and restraint (in which one is hindered).[23] To say that the will is free in this sense is not to assert that it is indifferent to motives. Edwards believes that the will can attain no such state of indifference, for it is necessarily motivated in some way.[24] This is what makes self-determination an impossibility. For the will to be self-determining, it would need to achieve "perfect and absolute"

---

19. Spohn, "Union and Consent," 20.
20. Edwards, *FW*, §1.2, 143.
21. Ibid., §1.1, 139.
22. Ibid., §1.4, 156.
23. Ibid., §1.5, 164.
24. Ibid., §2.6, 199.

indifference, because an inclination does not need to be a certain strength to determine the will. It only needs to be the strongest inclination at the moment.[25]

Some have argued that, since will is also dependent on reason, reason itself is what grants the will freedom, but Edwards rejects that argument. He feels that although the will is dependent on the understanding's determination of the greatest good, the understanding itself also operates of necessity, being the product of previous understanding and acts of will. The mind must be motivated to focus its attention on a particular matter, and Edwards believes that this is also determined by previous states of mind.[26] Edwards' schema will be unpalatable to those who believe that this type of determinism abolishes moral value, since it does not view will as self-determining. Edwards likewise regards this line of reasoning as erroneous, for he claims that we do not attribute praise or blame to the will's ability to be self-determining. Rather, we attribute praise and blame to particular acts and to the dispositions that tend toward them.[27]

In the final analysis, although Edwards' understanding of moral psychology is largely Lockean, his compatibilist view of will is much more consistent with the compatibilism of Thomas Hobbes, another notable British empiricist. Hobbes' compatibilist account of will can be seen most clearly in the debate that he had with the Anglican bishop John Bramhill.[28] Edwards' general schema helps to illustrate how British empiricism was utilized by a spectrum of groups from the Deists to the predestinationists. They all had similar psychological models, but they differed, sometimes widely, with regard to other key issues (e.g., freedom, divine providence, realism, etc.). In Edwards' case, he apparently combined Lockean epistemology and Hobbesean compatibilism with Platonic metaphysical intuitionism. Nevertheless, it will not be necessary to probe Edwards any further, for our chief concern here is his influence on Wesley.

---

25. Ibid., §2.7, 204.
26. Ibid., §2.9, 217–24.
27. Ibid., §4.4, 360–61.
28. See Hobbes and Bramhill, *Hobbes and Bramhill on Liberty and Necessity*.

Edwards' Impact on Wesley

Wesley became acquainted with Edwards' writings just a few months after his experience at Aldersgate, when he read Edwards' *Faithful Narrative*. Richard Steele speculates that this book equipped Wesley with the "conceptual tools for diagnosing that experience."[29] Within the next decade, Wesley produced extracts of that work as well as Edwards' *Distinguishing Marks* and *Thoughts on the Present Revival*.[30] However, he was most likely unacquainted with *Religious Affections* until the Gordon edition was published in London in 1762, an edition that reduced the original by almost a third and reworded many passages. John Smith concludes that this edition was the one Wesley used in producing his own abridgment in 1773.[31] However, Wesley was not interested in producing a document that was all that faithful to the original, as he explains in the prefatory note entitled "To the Reader."

> The design of Mr. Edwards, in the treatise from which the following extract is made, seems to have been chiefly, if not altogether, to serve his hypothesis. In three preceding tracts, he had given an account of a glorious work in New England, of abundance of sinners of every sort and degree who were in a short time converted to God. But in a few years, a considerable part of these "turned back as a dog to the vomit." What was the plain inference to be drawn from this? Why, that a true believer may "make shipwreck of the faith." How then could he evade the force of this? Truly, by eating his own words, and proving, as well as the nature of the thing would hear, that they were no believers at all!
>
> In order to [do] this, he heaps together so many curious, subtle, metaphysical distinctions, as are sufficient to puzzle the brain, and confound the intellects, of all the plain men and women in the universe, and to make them doubt of, if not wholly deny, all the work which God had wrought in their souls.
>
> Out of this dangerous heap, wherein much wholesome food is mixed with much deadly poison, I have selected many remarks and admonitions which may be of great use to the

---

29. R. Steele, "*Gracious Affection*," 133.
30. Wesley, *WWJ*, 14:214.
31. J. E. Smith editor's introduction to Edwards, *RA*, 75–80.

children of God. May God write them in the hearts of all that desire to walk as Christ also walked![32]

There is still a variety of opinions as to why Edwards wrote this treatise. Ava Chamberlain points out that although Edwards defended the "affectional piety" of the Puritan New Lights, he was constantly warding off its excesses. He had to distinguish true and false affections. Mark Noll believes that *Religious Affections* was Edwards' attempt to qualify the Reformed emphasis on the direct witness of the Holy Spirit.[33] In this regard, Chamberlain suggests that Edwards' Calvinism ultimately led him to advocate "a life of persevering Christian practice as the only sound foundation on which to build a hope of salvation."[34] Actually, the matter of assurance was a perpetual problem for Calvinists, fostered by their predestinationism. In other words, how can people be sure that they are among the elect before they have finally persevered (at death)? Rodney Reed traces the doctrine of assurance from the time of Calvin to the time of Edwards and Wesley, and he outlines the various attempts that Calvinists made to reconcile the doctrines of election and assurance. He concludes that Wesley's Arminianism allowed him to avoid this dilemma and base assurance strictly on one's present state.[35]

This helps to explain how Wesley could have such mixed feelings about the treatise and yet still be influenced by it. I would suggest that the treatise helped shape Wesley's view of moral psychology in his later years, solidifying the impact that Lockean empiricism had on him. For instance, in his early years Wesley believed that there are three basic faculties of the human psyche: understanding, will, and freedom. This view, similar to that of Locke, is reflected in his sermon, "The Image of God," preached on November 15, 1730, in St. Mary's Cathedral.[36] However, over twenty years later his view had changed, for he twice identified the faculties of the soul as "understanding, will, and affections."[37] This is essentially the model employed by the Aristotelian Scholasticism, which

32. Wesley, *WWJ*, 14:269–70.
33. Noll, "John Wesley," 164.
34. Chamberlain, "Self-Deception," 555.
35. Reed, "Doctrine of Assurance," 31–43.
36. Wesley, §§1.1–4, *WW*, 4:293–95.
37. Wesley, *NNT*, Mk. 12:30; "The Doctrine of Original Sin," §2, "Objection 5," *WWJ*, 9:295.

came into vogue in the seventeenth century. According to Steele, that model emphasized three distinct mental faculties of intellect, will, and passions.[38]

Nevertheless, Wesley's view would change again. A year after he produced his abridgment of Edwards' *Religious Affections*, Wesley wrote "Thoughts upon Necessity," returning to Locke's (and Edwards') understanding of the will and affections. Nevertheless, Wesley still wanted a model that views human beings as free moral agents.

> God created man an intelligent being, and endued him with will as well as understanding. Indeed, it seems, without this, his understanding would have been given to no purpose. Neither would either his will or understanding have answered any valuable purpose, if liberty had not been added to them, a power distinct from both, a power of choosing for himself, a self-determining principle. It may be doubted whether God ever made an intelligent creature without all these three faculties, whether any spirit ever existed without them, yea, whether they are not implied in the very nature of a spirit. Certain it is, that no being can be accountable for its actions, which has not liberty, as well as will and understanding.[39]

Steele believes that Wesley essentially took Edwards' model (of understanding and will) and added a third faculty of liberty to it.[40] This does not seem to be the case. For one thing, Wesley's reading of Edwards evidently did not lead to the formation of a new model for him, because he apparently returned to the model with which he started. Moreover, when Wesley's explanation is examined closely, it appears that he was essentially attempting to modify the Aristotelian model by redefining the terms.

> It seems, they who divide the faculties of the human soul into the understanding, will, and affections, unless they make the will and affections the same thing, (and then how inaccurate is the division!) must mean by affections, the will, properly speaking, and by the term *will*, neither more nor less than *liberty*, the power of choosing either to do or not to do, (commonly called liberty of contradiction,) or to do this or the contrary, good

---

38. R. Steele, *"Gracious Affection,"* 10.
39. Wesley, "Thoughts upon Necessity," §3.8, *WWJ*, 10:468.
40. R. Steele, *"Gracious Affection,"* 311.

or evil (commonly called liberty of contrariety). Without the former at least, there can be nothing good or evil, rewardable or punishable.[41]

In other words, Wesley attempted to synthesize the Lockean understanding of the will and affections with the Aristotelian notion of freedom. We must recall that Locke and Edwards believed that the will and the affections differ only in degree. Will is exercised whenever the affections are sufficiently elevated to effect a choice. As such, affections are part of the will. In the Aristotelian schema, will is the vehicle of freedom, but in the Lockean model, freedom is redefined. For Locke, freedom is simply the power to act or not act, but for Edwards, everything is determined. Edwards sees freedom as the absence of constraint and restraint, not as the power of self-determination.

Wesley thus found himself in a dilemma, for although he accepted the proposition that will is a product of the affections, he could not accept anything less than a libertarian notion of freedom.[42] Instead, he saw humans as self-determined. Wesley recognized the force that passions, affections, and tempers exert on human action, yet he felt that action is nothing more than mere instinct without free choice.

> If all the passions, the tempers, the actions of men, are wholly independent of their own choice, are governed by a principle exterior to themselves, then there can be no moral good or evil; there can be neither virtue nor vice, neither good nor bad actions, neither good nor bad passions or tempers. The sun does much good, but it has no virtue; it is not capable of moral goodness. Why is it not? For this plain reason, because it does not act from choice. The sea does much harm. It swallows up thousands of men, but it is not capable of moral badness, because it does not act by choice, but from a necessity of nature, if indeed one or the other can be said to act at all.[43]

Steele suggests that Wesley added a faculty of freedom to Edwards' model, and although Wesley's earlier model eliminates this possibility, it might appear that this is precisely what Wesley did to Locke's view. However, I do not believe that this is what Wesley perceived himself to be doing. In the Aristotelian model, will represents the power to choose

41. Wesley, "Thoughts upon Necessity," §3.9, *WWJ*, 10:468–69.
42. Ibid., §§3.6–7, *WWJ*, 10:467.
43. Ibid., §3.1, *WWJ*, 10:463–64.

(as it does for Locke), yet this power is both free and independent of the affections. Even though Wesley could not be persuaded to relinquish the Aristotelian definition of freedom, he evidently became convinced that choice is to a great extent determined by the affections. Otherwise, Wesley would not have associated the will with the affections. In the Aristotelian model, will is more free than determined, so it remains separate from the affections. In the Lockean model, will is determined by the affections, so they are united in one faculty. Wesley consistently believed that human beings possess a certain power of self-determination, so he retained this power (which is all that remains from the Aristotelian faculty of will) in a faculty that he simply refers to as liberty. He asserted that liberty is not a property of will (according to the new definition), but is distinct from it. "It is a power of self-determination."[44]

In 1781, the same year that he made his comments on Locke's *Essay*, Wesley reiterated his explanation of the model.

> Now, "man was made in the image of God." But "God is a Spirit:" So therefore was man. Only that spirit, being designed to dwell on earth, was lodged in an earthly tabernacle. As such, he had an innate principle of *self-motion*. And so, it seems, has every spirit in the universe, this being the proper distinguishing difference between spirit and matter, which is totally, essentially passive and inactive, as appears from a thousand experiments. He was, after the likeness of his Creator, endued with *understanding*, a capacity of apprehending whatever objects were brought before it, and of judging concerning them. He was endued with a *will*, exerting itself in various affections and passions, and, lastly, with *liberty*, or freedom of choice, without which all the rest would have been in vain, and he would have been no more capable of serving his Creator than a piece of earth or marble. He would have been as incapable of vice or virtue as any part of the inanimate creation. In these, in the power of self-motion, understanding, will, and liberty, the natural image of God consisted.[45]

After Wesley published his abridgement of *Religious Affections*, he consistently used this model from that point forward, at least five times

---

44. Wesley, Sermon 116, "What Is Man?" §11, *WW*, 4:23–24 [J 7:228].
45. Wesley, Sermon 60, "The General Deliverance," §1.1, *WW*, 2:438–39 [J 6:242–43].

total.⁴⁶ He never again returned to the standard Aristotelian model. Indeed, it is not evident as to why he departed from the Lockean model for a number of years. The answer to that question would most likely help to explain why Wesley waited so long to comment on Locke's *Essay*. It is interesting to note that Wesley's comments on Locke's *Essay* were not published until eight years after his abridgment of Edwards' *Religious Affections* and seven years after he wrote "Thoughts upon Necessity," the essay that reflects the change in his thinking. Furthermore, all of Wesley's personal recommendations of Locke's *Essay* were made after his published comments.

It thus appears that the young Wesley was influenced by Locke, but for some reason he turned away from Locke's views and advocated the Aristotelian position. I believe that Edwards' treatise had an impact on Wesley, reconnecting him with his Lockean roots. Several years later, Wesley returned to Locke's *Essay*, a work with which he had general familiarity, and reexamined it more closely to solidify his view. Afterward, he felt comfortable enough with Locke's *Essay* to recommend it to others. In this regard, the influence of Edwards on Wesley was certainly crucial to the development of Wesley's mature thought.

Sections of "Religious Affections" That Wesley Omits

Wesley's abridgment of *Religious Affections* provides some insight into his understanding of the affections and their importance in the Christian life. A good place to start is with the sections that Wesley omits altogether, because some of these omissions are driven by theological concerns, and they do not necessarily indicate other types of disagreement. It is interesting to note that Wesley includes all of Edwards' criteria for identifying false affections. In contrast, Wesley drops several of Edwards' criteria for recognizing true affections, and we will examine each of these.

First, Wesley removes Edwards' second sign, which alleges that true religious affections have no reference to self-interest. For Edwards, self-love signifies either the pursuit of one's own pleasure or private

---

46. Wesley, Sermon 71, "Of Good Angels," §1.1, *WW*, 3:6 [J 6:362]; Sermon 67, "On Divine Providence," §15, *WW*, 2:540–41 [J 6:318]; "Some Thoughts on an Expression of St. Paul, in the First Epistle to the Thessalonians, v.23," *WWJ*, 11:447; also "Thoughts upon God's Sovereignty," *WWJ*, 10:362.

interest itself.[47] This love is both natural and normal. "Every being that has understanding and will necessarily loves happiness."[48] He adds, "That a man should love his own happiness, is as necessary to his nature as the faculty of the will is, and it is impossible that such a love should be destroyed in any other way than by destroying his own being." Indeed, even the saints and angels in heaven love their own happiness.[49]

Edwards believes that self-love can generate gratitude, since we appreciate things that bring us pleasure. According to Norman Fiering, "Gratitude in Edwards's analysis, becomes simply the granting of love to the mirror image of our own self-love, as it is reflected in the love of others to us."[50] In other words, gratitude is loving others simply because they love the object of our affections—us. It is an indirect way of loving ourselves. Edwards also believes that self-love can generate love for others when we regard the pleasure that particular people give us. Additionally, self-love can even generate a love for virtue, since virtue tends toward our good.[51]

We love those who are related to us in some way, and this results in natural affection for others.[52] The connection between self-love and relating the self to others is the basis for Edwards' assertion that pity itself is a product of self-interest.[53] Fiering argues that Edwards' concept of sympathy is similar to that of Hume, for it is ultimately grounded in a sense of desert.[54] For Edwards, self-love can be extended to include others, even one's own nation or humanity in general.[55] Nevertheless, regardless how far self-love is extended, it can never equal true love in either quality or scope. Self-love will always fall short of the "universality of existence."[56] Furthermore, the loyalties it generates will only be partial.[57]

47. Edwards, *TV*, §4, 42–44.
48. Ibid., §8, 101.
49. Edwards, *CF*, §8.1.1, 159.
50. Fiering, *Moral Thought*, 189.
51. Edwards, "Miscellany 473," *Misc1*, 514–15.
52. Edwards, *CF*, §8.3.2, 172–73.
53. Edwards, "Miscellany 782" *Misc2*, 458–59.
54. Fiering, *Moral Thought*, 142–44.
55. Edwards, *RA*, §3.2, 246–47.
56. Edwards, *TV*, §2, 19.
57. Lewis, "Springs of Motion," 280.

In Christian love, God and others are loved for the same motive—for the sake of holiness.[58] This includes both benevolence, which focuses on the good to be enjoyed *by* the beloved, and complacence, which focuses on the good to be enjoyed *in* the beloved.[59] Love for God does not proceed from self-love as human love does. When we fall in love with God, our hearts are united to God such that we are drawn to God prior to self-interest. However, it is still possible for human love to be motivated by beauty rather than by self-interest. Conversely, self-love can generate love for God and for Christ specifically, but this love is not true love because it is not based on the perception of God's beauty, which must be seen even before we can perceive that God loves us.[60] Since true love is rooted in the perception of God's beauty, people who have true religious experiences end up testifying to the beauty and perfection of Christ. In contrast, those who have false experiences tend to talk about themselves and the experiences they have had.[61]

According to Edwards, "The tendency of true virtue is to treat everything as it is, and according to its nature." God should be regarded for his own sake, for who he is. Regrettably, "this disinterested love to God, this pure divine affection" is very rare.[62] Noll says that for Edwards, the world exists in order to manifest God's glory. All other purposes, including human happiness are subordinate to this.[63] This does not imply that God is to be the sole object of our love. As Spohn points out, "God is not the only object of virtuous affection, but only if other beings are integrated into the love of God can they be loved virtuously."[64] Fiering concurs, asserting that Edwards did not think it necessary for the love of others to originate with the love of God. Rather, the agent must have a disposition of loving God supremely.[65]

It would be unfair, though, to leave the impression that Edwards disdained self-love, for such was not the case. He recognized self-love as a part of all love, including benevolence and complacence. Hence,

58. Edwards, *CF*, §1.1.1, 5.
59. Ibid., §5.2.1, 104.
60. Edwards, *RA*, §3.2, 240–66; cf. Proudfoot, "Perception and Love," 130.
61. Ibid., §3.2, 252.
62. Edwards, *OS*, §1.1.5, 144.
63. Noll, "God at the Center," 854.
64. Spohn, "Sovereign Beauty," 403.
65. Fiering, "Moral Thought," 337, n. 38.

he felt it impossible to be willing to be miserable for God's sake. Even when we renounce our private good for the sake of God's good, we still take delight or pleasure in God's good, and this pursuit of pleasure is reducible to self-love.[66] Fiering explains, "For Edwards, self-love, properly defined, is an irremovable and acceptable substratum in human motivation." It is also a part of God's psychology, for God's self-love is the paragon of proper self-love.[67] Moreover, self-love is presupposed in the Golden Rule, indicating that God does not expect us to eliminate it. As Spohn asserts, "Self-love exercises an auxiliary role in love of God, but appreciation for God's beauty as good in itself is what grounds genuine love for God."[68] Nevertheless, at one point Edwards asserts that Christians are not only motivated by the excellency of God, but also by the promise that they will receive an eternal weight of glory that outweighs any sufferings they may endure.[69]

For Edwards, selfishness is inordinate self-love, but not in loving ourselves too much. It can be the result of loving others too little, and it can also arise when we limit our happiness to our own selves. However, inordinate self-love is primarily attributable to a lack of divine love, which is needed to govern self-love. Without divine love, self-love tends to dominate us.[70] Edwards naturally includes self-interest in his definition of liberty. "True liberty consists in these two things: a liberty to do whatever tends to our own advantage, a liberty to do whatever is for our true pleasure and satisfaction." This is due to the fact that God "obliges us to do that which will bring us to the highest pleasure and the greatest delights."[71]

Clearly, Edwards is not advocating a view of love that denies any place for self-love whatsoever. He is proposing that our best interests are served when we seek what is in the best interest of God. "In seeking the glory of God and the good of your fellow-creatures you take the

---

66. Edwards, "Miscellany 530," *Misc2*, 75.
67. Fiering, *Moral Thought*, 152–54.
68. Spohn, "Sovereign Beauty," 413.
69. Edwards, *CF*, §12.2.3, 258.
70. Ibid., §8.1.2, 160–66.
71. Edwards, "Christian Liberty," *Ser1*, 626–69.

surest way to have God seek your interests and promote your welfare."[72] Steele summarizes Edwards' view of self-love as follows:

> The heart of Edwards' moral theory is the attempt to reconcile these two paradoxical insights: 1) a self cannot be a self without self-love, that is, without having interests, desires, and engagements, but 2) a self cannot find true happiness unless it achieves true holiness, that is, unless it attains a self-disinterested love of God and subordinates its own private interests, desires, and engagements to the glorification of God and the welfare of the neighbor.[73]

Wesley does not exhibit this kind of struggle with self-love, for he assigns it a more positive role. Granted, Wesley consistently asserts that love must be free of self-will, but this simply indicates that self-interest cannot be the chief motivating factor in love. It does not mean that love must transcend self-love, as Edwards suggests. Furthermore, Wesley concurs with Edwards that we naturally relish virtue and the happiness of others, but unlike Edwards, he does not attribute this to self-love.

> But is there not likewise a kind of internal sense, whereby we relish the happiness of our fellow-creatures, even without any reflection on our own interest, without any reference to ourselves, whereby we bear a part in the prosperity of others and rejoice with them that rejoice? . . . May we not likewise observe that there is a beauty in virtue, in gratitude, and disinterested benevolence?[74]

Hulley infers that self-love and social love are not incompatible from Wesley's perspective. However, love for neighbor is not extended self-interest, it is universal love.[75] Likewise, love for God is not threatened by self-love. On the contrary, love for God legitimizes it.[76] Wesley repeatedly declares that holiness and happiness are inseparably joined. Just as Nicholas Wolterstorff suggests that Locke was more eudemonistic than hedonistic, I would suggest that Wesley was more eudemonistic than ascetic. Initially, Wesley believed that perfection frees us of self-

---

72. Edwards, *CF*, §8.3.3, 183.
73. R. Steele, *"Gracious Affection,"* 283.
74. Wesley, "Thoughts upon Taste", §§9–10, *WWJ*, 13:467.
75. Hulley, *To Be and To Do*, 30.
76. Lindström, *Wesley and Sanctification*, 197.

will so that even ease of pain is not desired. In 1744, Thomas Church charged Wesley with espousing "a stoical insensibility" carried to "the very height of extravagance and presumption." In a later revision of *Plain Account of Christian Perfection*, Wesley recanted this position and came to view self-love more positively, as described here.[77] Nevertheless, Wesley never gave the topic of self-love the attention it should have received, given the importance that love holds in his thought.[78]

Second, Wesley omits Edwards' third sign: true holy affections are based on the loveliness of the excellency of divine things. Terrance Erdt feels that Edwards basically adopted Calvin's notion that the regenerate feel *suavitas* ("sweetness") when they hear the gospel.[79] It is doubtful that this notion is the source of Wesley's objection, for it seems to coincide with his doctrine of assurance. Most likely, Wesley omitted this section for either of two reasons. On the one hand, this point represents the core of Edwards' defense of predestination. He asserts that the beauty of Christ is only revealed to the elect, so they are the only ones who can experience true religious affections. Moreover, the revelation of Christ's beauty is a passive experience. Regeneration is not the fruit of a divine-human synergism, as Wesley argues. On the other hand, Wesley prefers an account of virtue that is derived directly from scriptural principles. He believes that it is futile to found religion "on the eternal *fitness* of things, on the intrinsic *excellence* of virtue and the *beauty* of actions flowing from it, on the reasons, as they term them, of good and evil, the relations of beings to each other." He surmises that even if such accounts of virtue do indeed correspond with Scripture, they essentially detract our attention away from the weightier matters of Scripture. However, if these accounts do not correspond with Scripture, then they actually subvert it.[80] It is unclear whether Wesley was flatly opposed to philosophically nuanced accounts of virtue altogether or simply felt that the moral climate of his day necessitated the need to cultivate basic morality first.

Edwards regards love as an "idea of reflection," i.e., we cannot conceive it abstractly, only reflect on our past experiences of it. Hence, the

---

77. Walters, "John Wesley's Footnotes," 22.
78. Cobb, *Grace and Responsibility*, 67–68.
79. Erdt, *Sense of the Heart*, 11.
80. Wesley, Sermon 17, "The Circumcision of the Heart," §2.3, WW, 1:410 [J 5:209].

unregenerate have no concept of divine love, because they have not experienced it.[81] Wesley concurs that our love for God must be preceded by God's love for us, yet he contends that God's love must be perceived, not experienced. We cannot love God until we know that God loves us, because that is how we can know that God is gracious and willing to forgive us.[82] In contrast with Edwards, Wesley does not view divine love as something to be experienced passively. As Stanley Johnson indicates, "While Wesley grounds love for God in prior movement of divinity, he does not deny the properly active role of the self's love for God."[83]

According to Edwards, "The moral excellency of an intelligent voluntary being is more immediately seated in the heart or will of moral agents. That intelligent being whose will is truly right and lovely, he is morally good or excellent." Holiness thus includes all the true human virtues: love for God and others, justice, charity, mercy, humility, and gentleness.[84] Notwithstanding the beauty of these virtues, "that consent, agreement, or union of being to being, which has been spoken of, viz. the union or propensity of minds to mental or spiritual existence, may be called the highest and primary beauty."[85] True virtue thus consists of "benevolence to being in general."[86] Since God is the "Being of beings," true virtue is ultimately love for God.[87] Even love for others is not of true virtue unless it arises out of love for being in general.[88] Edwin Gaustad says that for Edwards, true virtue can only be found where creaturely affection is "subordinate to a propensity or union of the heart to God."[89]

Edwards declares that all of the Christian graces "have the same root and foundation, namely, the knowledge of God's excellence."[90] For

---

81. Edwards, "Miscellanies 238–39," *Misc1*, 353–55; cf. "Miscellany 782," *Misc2*, 452–66.

82. Wesley, "An Earnest Appeal to Men of Reason and Religion," §61, *WW*, 11:70 [J 8:24].

83. W. Johnson, "Christian Perfection," 52.

84. Edwards, *RA*, §3.3, 255.

85. Edwards, *TV*, §3, 27.

86. Ibid., §1, 3.

87. Ibid., §2, 14.

88. Ibid., §1, 5.

89. Gaustad, "Nature of True Virtue," 46.

90. Edwards, *CF*, §13.2.3, 276.

one thing, the proper appreciation of God's excellency and perfection is what fosters humility.[91] Religious affections are similar to natural affections, but they exceed them in quality and depth, because the regenerate can perceive "kinds of excellency" that the natural person cannot.[92] Consequently, believers are transformed when they appreciate the divine holiness and thus move beyond self-interest.[93]

The presumption that Edwards makes is that humans innately have a sense of appreciation for the beauty of natural agreement and proportion. This appreciation gives us a sense of desert, and this causes us to approve justice. In turn, this leads to the approval of benevolence (since it tends toward justice) and the disapproval of malice (since it tends away from justice). Self-love reinforces this, since benevolence is beneficial and malice is harmful.[94] The supernatural sense surpasses all of this, for it is a sort of spiritual taste that perceives the "beauty of holiness," ultimately grounded in being, excellence, and perfection.[95]

Wesley's definition of true virtue also assumes the perception of spiritual realities, but it is less Platonic than Edwards' explanation.

> From hence we may clearly perceive the wide difference there is between Christianity and morality. Indeed nothing can be more sure than that true Christianity cannot exist without both the inward experience and outward practice of justice, mercy, and truth, and this alone is genuine morality. But it is equally certain that all morality, all the justice, mercy, and truth which can possibly exist without Christianity, profiteth nothing at all, is of no value in the sight of God, to those that are under the Christian dispensation . . . those that name the name of Christ . . . unless they have new senses, ideas, passions, tempers, they are no Christians! However just, true, or merciful they may be, they are but atheists still.[96]

---

91. Gaustad, "Nature of True Virtue," 53.
92. Edwards, *RA*, §3.1, 208–9.
93. Spohn, "Sovereign Beauty," 396.
94. Edwards, *TV*, §4.5, 58–59.
95. Edwards, *RA*, §3.3, 259–60.
96. Wesley, Sermon 130, "On Living without God," §14, *WW*, 4:174–75 [J 7:353].

Like Edwards, Wesley indeed believes that true virtue must have reference to God.[97] Everything must ultimately be motivated by love for God. Natural morality resembles true morality, but falls short of it.

> Good sense (so called) is but a poor, dim shadow of what Christians call faith. Good nature is only a faint, distant resemblance of Christian charity. And good manners . . . is but a dead picture of that holiness of conversation which is the image of God expressed.[98]

In this regard, Wesley seems less optimistic than Edwards about the ability of natural virtue to resemble and approximate true virtue.

However, Wesley's understanding of true virtue does not require self-love to be transcended, as it does for Edwards. Rather, Wesley seems to follow the Aristotelian notion that virtue aims at the chief good, except in this case the chief good is not happiness, but God himself. Self-love can be either an asset or a detriment to virtue, depending upon whether it draws one closer to God or diverts one away from God. Essentially, reason plays a crucial role in guiding the self toward the highest good, and it regulates the other affections accordingly. It is not necessary to have a transcendent, disinterested experience for the affections to be proper, as Edwards asserts. In the final analysis, Edwards sees the acquisition of true virtue as a passive experience, but for Wesley it is more dependent on the natural function of reason, because it exceeds mere perception in that it also requires the other functions of reason—judgment and discourse.

Next, Wesley excises Edwards' fourth sign, which asserts that gracious affections arise from the mind being enlightened to understand divine things. Edwards reiterates the idea that a new comprehension of the "excellent nature of God" is what produces true religious affections. In this sense, true religious affections are derived from knowledge and understanding. He asserts, "Knowledge is the key that first opens the hard heart and enlarges the affections." Human nature is such that it cannot be moved emotionally by something that our mind has not conceived. However, apprehensions or conceptions that do not originate

---

97. Monk, *John Wesley: His Puritan Heritage*, 133.
98. Wesley, "An Earnest Appeal to Men of Reason and Religion," §26, *WW*, 11:54 [J 7:11].

in knowledge or instruction do not benefit us and do not lead to true religious affections.[99]

There is a distinction, though, between the understanding that produces true religious affections and what Edwards refers to as "common illuminations."

> So men may be much affected from common illuminations of the Spirit of God, in which God assists men's faculties to a greater degree of that kind of understanding of religious matters, which they have in some degree, by only the ordinary exercise and improvement of their own faculties. Such illuminations may much affect the mind, as in many whom we read of in Scripture, that were once enlightened, but these affections are not spiritual.[100]

Religious dispositions do not necessarily displace natural ones. A person with a naturally kind disposition will be even more loving under the influence of divine grace. Moreover, that person will be better able to achieve Christian virtues than someone who is naturally unkind. Edwards suggests that experiencing true beauty creates a "rectified palate," i.e., a "sanctified taste" that is inclined toward holiness and averse to unholy things.[101] Seeing the divine glory not only removes the prejudices of the heart, it also clarifies reason.[102] As James Hoopes indicates, Edwards believed that even "strong reason" may not be able to overcome biases and prejudices.[103] However, God's word sheds light on our understanding by "giving the soul a spiritual sense or relish" of God and of divine things.[104]

Wesley also claims that the Holy Spirit does internally "illuminate the understanding of such as believe, that they may receive the truth."[105] Furthermore, he agrees with Edwards that it is impossible to see (i.e., comprehend) God without loving God as a consequence.[106] However,

---

99. Edwards, *RA*, §3.4, 266–68.
100. Ibid., §3.4, 269–70.
101. Ibid., §3.4, 281–84.
102. Ibid., §3.5, 307.
103. Hoopes, "Religious Psychology," 856.
104. Edwards, *RA*, §3.1, 225.
105. Wesley, "A Farther Appeal to Men of Reason and Religion, Part I," §5.23, *WW*, 11:164 [J 8:99–100].
106. Wesley, "A Farther Appeal to Men of Reason and Religion, Part II," §3.22, *WW*, 11:269 [J 8:198].

it does not appear that Wesley's understanding of illumination is quite as Platonic as Edwards' view, since he does not regard the perception of God as a passive state of complacence. According to Edwards, in the perception of spiritual beauty, the understanding and will are joined as the soul is essentially "possessed of taste, inclination, and will." It surpasses "a mere notional understanding, wherein the mind only beholds things in the exercise of a speculative faculty."[107]

Steven O'Malley states that whereas Wesley emphasized two parallel systems of sense faculties, Edwards tried to demonstrate the ontological unity between the two realms.[108] In reality, Edwards also believed in both natural and spiritual senses. Nonetheless, he found it necessary to stress the ontological unity between the physical and spiritual realms in order to support his assertion that although the excellence and beauty of God are experienced passively, the perception of them still communicates cognitive content about God. If the two realms are not unified, then a passive experience might only result in sheer ecstasy or in self-knowledge. This is why Edwards characterizes the perception as "consent."

The spiritual knowledge of which Edwards speaks does not include the immediate knowledge of one's duty.[109] Essentially, he does not want to validate those who claim to be directly guided by the Holy Spirit in their daily lives. Even so, he avers that true love for God makes doing our duty easier, because it gives us (1) "peace of conscience," (2) the "pleasures of communion with God," and (3) a "joyful hope of eternal glory."[110]

Edwards suggests that people who are emotionally and intellectually unstable are more susceptible to the delusions of Satan.[111] He reports instances in which various individuals were truly converted yet still exhibited imagination beyond what "could naturally arise from their spiritual sense of things."[112] Even in a genuine work of the Holy Spirit, people may be apt to place too much weight on their imagination and

107. Edwards, *RA*, §3.4, 272.
108. O'Malley, "Recovering the Vision of Holiness," 11.
109. Edwards, *RA*, §3.4, 279.
110. Edwards, "True Love to God," *Ser1*, 636–41.
111. Edwards, *RA*, §3.4, 289–90.
112. Edwards, *NSC*, §2, 52.

be unable to distinguish it from that which is "intellectual and spiritual." This is most common among "persons of less understanding and of distinguishing capacity." God seems to condescend to them and "deal with them as babes."[113] Edwards realizes that we generally cannot have intense thoughts without stirring the imagination. It is acceptable for strong affections to stir the imagination. Conversely, whenever the imagination gives rise to affections, these affections cannot be trusted, since they are not founded on spiritual knowledge.[114]

This section is another example of how Wesley often disagrees with Edwards' characterization of genuine religious experience, but still agrees with him regarding the types of experiences that should not be regarded as legitimate. Wesley is well aware of the dangers of over-active imaginations. In fact, the term "enthusiasm" was used in the eighteenth century to describe those who mistook their own imaginations for the voice of God, and Wesley had to fend off charges of enthusiasm leveled at him and the Methodists. This will be examined in the next chapter.

These are the only sections that Wesley omits in their entirety. He does subsume sign number seven under the preceding sign. The seventh sign asserts that true religious affections cause a change in nature. Wesley does not contest the general principle. His disagreement concerns the manner in which change is effected. The reductions he makes are consistent with his omissions of the sections discussed above. Surprisingly, Wesley retains sign number ten, which declares that true religious affections have symmetry and proportion. Edwards argues this point to close the circle on his overall schema. Wesley concurs with this specific point without conceding Edwards' claim that religious affections have symmetry and proportion because they are the result of perceiving God's symmetry and proportion.

Helpful Areas of Agreement

Several of the points on which Edwards and Wesley agree are beneficial to the paradigm that I wish to construct for Wesleyan ethics. For example, both men believed that affections are the central core of religion. Edwards states, "True religion, in great part, consists in holy

---

113. Edwards, *DM*, §1.4, 95–96; Wesley, *WHS*, 15–16.
114. Edwards, *RA*, §3.4, 291.

affections."[115] The central affection to be attained is love, since it is connected to all of the graces.[116] Consequently, true religion can be summarized by the word "love," which is "the chief of the affections and fountain of all other affections."[117]

Wesley likewise maintains that Christians have dispositions that are comprised of holy affections. In fact, as Gregory Clapper points out, "the presence or absence of certain affections is a test-case of Christianity" for Wesley.[118] In his doctrine of Christian perfection, this is true to an even greater extent. Wesley declares that being born of God in the "full sense" entails being freed from pride, self-will, evil thoughts, darkness (i.e., doubt and fear), and the wounds inflicted by temptations.[119] In general, we must have a "single eye" toward God. If we have an "evil eye" toward the "love of the world," we are ignorant of ourselves, our true interest, and our relation to God. The "love of the world" includes "the pleasures of sense, the pleasures of imagination, the praise of men, [and] riches."[120] In effect, our tempers, thoughts, and actions are regulated through a focus on the eternal realm.[121]

For Wesley, all of the "other divine tempers" spring from "disinterested love" (i.e., love that is free of "self-will").[122] He suggests that benevolence for one's neighbor can also be disinterested, but only through gratitude toward God.[123] This claim stands in stark contrast to Edwards' assertion that gratitude is born of self-love and cannot lead to any type of disinterestedness. However, Wesley agrees with Edwards that the love of neighbor can be that of *storge* (i.e., a familial love or loyalty) or

---

115. Edwards, *RA*, §1, 95; Wesley, *WHS*, 51.

116. Gaustad, "Nature of True Virtue," 44.

117. Edwards, *RA*, §1.2, 106; Wesley, *WHS*, 55.

118. Clapper, *Wesley of Religious Affections*, 38.

119. Wesley, preface to *A Collection of Hymns and Sacred Poems* (1740), §§7–8, 14:324–25.

120. Wesley, Sermon 125, "On a Single Eye," §2.1, *WW*, 4:123–24 [J 7:299].

121. O'Malley, "Recovering the Vision of Holiness," 8.

122. Wesley, "A Farther Appeal to Men of Reason and Religion, Part II," §3.23, *WW*, 11:269 [J 8:198].

123. Wesley, Sermon 70, "The Case of Reason Impartially Considered," §2.9, *WW*, 2:598 [J 6:359].

complacence, yet Wesley believes that the latter is only experienced by the righteous.[124]

For Edwards and Wesley, just as true religion resides in the affections of the heart, so does sin proceed from "hardness of heart." For Edwards, this implies a lack of pious affections. For Wesley, it means more specifically that the individual is insensitive to pious affections.[125] In either case, the presence of pious affections, especially longing, hungering, and thirsting after God and holiness, is the most vital part of true spirituality and devotion to God.[126] Consequently, true religious affections provide us with a continual desire to progress spiritually.[127] These men feel that spiritual things are so great, that it is absurd to be moved only moderately by them.[128] This is the reason that Christian love seeks to please and glorify God, even at a cost to ourselves. It also wants others to glorify God and enjoy him.[129] We cannot be complacent about our relationship with God, but we must continually strive to attain higher degrees of devotion to God.[130] For Edwards, this is somewhat a paradox, for although divine love is perceived complacently, it results in the active pursuit of it.

Even though Wesley stresses the need for the means of grace, he does not want them to be overemphasized, because the real goal is the attainment of holy affections.

> But in process of time, when "the love of many waxed cold," some began to mistake the *means* for the *end*, and to place religion rather in doing those outward works than in a heart renewed after the image of God. They forgot that "the end of" every "commandment is love, out of a pure heart, with faith unfeigned," the loving the Lord their God with all their heart, and their neighbor as themselves, and the being purified from pride, anger, and evil desire, by a "faith of the operation of God."[131]

---

124. Cubie, "Theology of Love," 128.
125. Edwards, *RA*, §1.2, 116–18; Wesley, *WHS*, 56.
126. Edwards, *RA*, §1.2, 104; Wesley, *WHS*, 54.
127. Edwards, *RA*, §3.11, 376–77; Wesley, *WHS*, 96.
128. Edwards, *DM*, §132, 94–95; Wesley, *WHS*, 15.
129. Edwards, *CF*, §§8.2.1–2, 166–71.
130. J. Smith, "Treatise Concerning Religious Affections," 222.
131. Wesley, Sermon 16, "The Means of Grace," §1.2, *WW*, 1:378 [J 5:185–86].

In contrast, the affections are not merely a means to outward holiness, they are to be sought for their own sake.¹³²

However, Edwards and Wesley both understand that the goal of the Christian life is not simply to be emotional. Edwards believes that genuine piety is fervent, but he does not see it as mere emotionalism that excludes both understanding and perception. On one hand, he believes that lack of education and intellect leads to enthusiasm. On the other hand, he believes that rationalism alone presents an insufficient account of religion.¹³³ Wesley also sees the dangers that can follow when reason and emotion get out of balance. For instance, he asserts that people of a "passionate temper and disposition" generally have difficulty getting along with others.¹³⁴ In spite of the great emphasis that Edwards and Wesley place on the affections, they realize that the affections must be controlled and guided by reason.

Edwards and Wesley know that affections are often complex. Edwards suggests that although the things of religion should move our emotions, the mere stirring of emotion does not necessarily produce religious affections.¹³⁵ For one thing, since we are a unity of body and soul, our physical condition often affects our emotions.¹³⁶ The presence of intense religious emotions is not always an accurate indicator of true religion, because these emotions can be generated by other factors.¹³⁷ For instance, self-denial can be motivated by self-righteousness as much as by humility.¹³⁸ Moreover, love and other virtues can be counterfeited by Satan and by other human beings.¹³⁹

Clapper contends that for Wesley, "the religious affections are not merely inner, subjective feelings, but instead are complex entities patterned by the reasoning process."¹⁴⁰ Wesley realizes that we can by mistaken about our emotions. Although happiness is a necessary product of holiness, people can still be happy without being holy. The fact that

---

132. Clapper, *Experience and Emotion*, 28.
133. J. Smith, "Testing the Spirits," 35–36.
134. Wesley, Sermon 100, "On Pleasing All Men," §1.3, *WW*, 3:420 [J 7:142].
135. Edwards, *RA*, §1.2, 122; Wesley, *WHS*, 58.
136. Edwards, *RA*, §1.1, 98; Wesley, *WHS*, 52.
137. Edwards, *RA*, §2.1, 127; Wesley, *WHS*, 59.
138. Edwards, *RA*, §3.6, 319; Wesley, *WHS*, 86.
139. Edwards, *RA*, §2.1, 146; Wesley, *WHS*, 67.
140. Clapper, *Experience and Emotion*, 28.

we need objectivity in gauging our emotions is one of the reasons we cannot neglect the "outward means." Wesley argues this point at length with Law.

> And he who has attained the love of God, may still want to know how he shall keep it. And he may still inquire, "May I not take my own passions, or the suggestions of evil spirits, for the workings of the Spirit of God?" (Page 198.) To this you answer, "Every man knows when he is governed by the spirit of wrath, envy, or covetousness, as easily and as certainly as he knows when he is hungry." (*Ibid.*) Indeed he does not, neither as easily nor as certainly. Without great care, he may take wrath to be pious zeal, envy to be virtuous emulation, and covetousness to be Christian prudence or laudable frugality. "Now, the knowledge of the Spirit of God in yourself is as perceptible as covetousness." Perhaps so, for this is as difficultly perceptible as any temper of the human soul. "And liable to no more delusion." Indeed it need not, for this is liable to ten thousand delusions.
>
> You add: "His spirit is more distinguishable from all other spirits, than any of your natural affections are from one another." (Page 199.) Suppose joy and grief: Is it more distinguishable from all other spirits, than these are from one another? Did any man ever mistake grief for joy? No, not from the beginning of the world. But did none ever mistake nature for grace? Who will be so hardy as to affirm this?
>
> But you set your pupil as much above the being taught by books, as being taught by men. "Seek," say you, "for help no other way, neither from men, nor books, but wholly leave yourself to God." (Spirit of Love, Part II., p. 225.)
>
> But how can a man "leave himself wholly to God," in the total neglect of his ordinances? The old Bible way is, to "leave ourselves wholly to God," in the constant use of all the means he hath ordained. And I cannot yet think the new is better, though you are fully persuaded it is. "There are two ways," you say, "of attaining goodness and virtue, the one by books or the ministry of men, the other by an inward birth. The former is only in order to the latter." This is most true, that all the externals of religion are in order to the renewal of our soul in righteousness and true holiness. But it is not true, that the external way is one and the internal way another. There is but one scriptural way, wherein we receive inward grace, through the outward means which God hath appointed.[141]

141. Wesley to Law, 6 January 1756, §2.6, *WWJ*, 9:504.

Here we clearly see that Wesley is well aware of the risk of self-delusion, and he believes that the outward means of grace, especially education, are necessary if one wishes to avoid this problem.

Consequently, this calls for a more cognitivist account of emotions, and I believe that Edwards and Wesley were attempting such an enterprise. Edwards asserts that our "intellectual faculties" let us understand the reasons God has given us to love him. Hence, they determine our capacity for love.[142] Along these same lines, God must give us an understanding of what our deliverance means before we can have a deep appreciation of it.[143] In other words, love can only be as deep as the knowledge that supports it. This clarifies Edwards' proposition that holiness can only be known to the mind as an "idea of reflection."[144]

Edwards does not presume any opposition between reason and emotion.[145] According to Steele, Edwards maintains that intense emotions are still thoroughly rational, and he denies that rational religion is incompatible with "raised affections."[146] Knowledge is essentially a stabilizing factor in emotion. Those who are lacking in knowledge will tend to be emotionally unstable. For instance, "it is from littleness of soul" that people are easily disturbed by the mistreatment of others. Small streams are easily disrupted, but "great and mighty streams" continue to flow "calmly and quietly with smooth and unruffled [surface]."[147] Steele adds that for Edwards, even the manner in which we fulfill our passions "does fall within the purview of reason and volition and is therefore praise- or blameworthy."[148]

Of course, delusion is also one of Edwards' chief concerns, and he identifies two basic types (1) basing justification on outward morality, and (2) misinterpreting our own emotions and experiences.[149] Wayne Proudfoot suggests that the problem of delusion in religious affections is ultimately a matter of self-knowledge.[150] It is a matter of distinguishing

---

142. Edwards, *RA*, §3.6, 325; Wesley, *WHS*, 87.
143. Edwards, *RA*, §2.1, 152; Wesley, *WHS*, 68.
144. Hoopes, "Religious Psychology," 859.
145. Lewis, "Springs of Motion," 294; cf. Smith, "Testing the Spirits," 33.
146. R. Steele, "*Gracious Affection*," 199–204.
147. Edwards, *Im*, §71, 70.
148. R. Steele, "*Gracious Affection*," 208.
149. Edwards, *RA*, §2.1, 173; Wesley, *WHS*, 74.
150. Proudfoot, "From Theology to a Science," 154.

the imagination from reality. Edwards knows that the imagination is at times vital in religious experience, but he also realizes that it is the source of many delusions.[151] As I indicated earlier, his Calvinism makes this concern even more crucial, because he does not feel that it is adequate simply to observe a person's affections at a given point in time. Rather, Edwards wants to identify dispositions that will persevere, but this is not empirically observable. For example, the appearance of love (which can be observed) is insufficient, but a loving nature (which cannot be observed) is sufficient.[152] In contrast, Wesley's Arminianism allows him to focus on the present state of the individual, but he must struggle more with the problem of self-delusion that is inherent in subjective experience.

Although the possibility of delusion is a looming problem for Wesley and Edwards, they do believe that affections can be evaluated within certain epistemic boundaries. Wesley seems to regard the affections not as mere feelings, but as analyzable dispositions.[153] Since Edwards believes that truly gracious and holy affections have symmetry and proportion, he concludes that true affections eliminate the gross imbalances caused by false affections. These imbalances include (1) joy without sorrow for sin, (2) partiality, (3) only valuing persons extrinsically (rather than intrinsically), (4) being critical of others while being blind to one's own faults, (5) claiming to be spiritual without being moral, and (6) inconsistency. Wesley agrees with this assessment, except he drops the first and last of the list, since he believes that believers may backslide, yet they may also experience victory over willful sin so as to be set free from guilt.[154]

Gracious affections will produce the desire to live according to God's will, according to the principles of Christianity.[155] Frederick Dreyer argues that Wesley's insistence that the fruits of faith can be perceived is what separates him from the mystics. This perception presupposes "nothing more than the believer's ordinary faculties of reflection and self-consciousness."[156] On one hand, Wesley and Edwards regard

---

151. Erdt, *Sense of the Heart*, 52.
152. Proudfoot, "From Theology to a Science," 157.
153. Clapper, *Experience and Emotion*, 164.
154. Edwards, *RA*, §3.10, 365–76; Wesley, *WHS*, 94–96.
155. Edwards, *RA*, §3.12, 383; Wesley, *WHS*, 97.
156. Dreyer, "Faith and Experience," 17.

good works as signs of sincerity.[157] On the other hand, they are not infallible signs, for we cannot discern the spirits of others. As Edwards explains,

> Our wisdom and discerning, with regard to the hearts of men, is not much to be trusted. We can see but a little way into the nature of the soul and the depths of man's heart. The ways are so many whereby persons' affections may be moved without any supernatural influence, the natural springs of the affections are so various and so secret, so many things have oftentimes a joint influence on the affections, the imagination (and that in ways innumerable and unsearchable), natural temper, education, the common influences of the Spirit of God, a surprising concourse of affecting circumstances, an extraordinary coincidence of things in the course of men's thoughts, together with the subtle management of invisible malicious spirits, that no philosophy or experience will ever be sufficient to guide us safely through this labyrinth and maze, without our closely following the clue which God has given us in his Word.[158]

Moral self-scrutiny exposes hypocrisy, yet this scrutiny must be disinterested if it is to effectively overcome the biases of the hypocrisy it is intended to reveal. As such, scrutiny often requires a third party in order for objectivity to be obtained.[159] For Edwards, "hypocrisy" is not necessarily intentional deception, but the incongruity between appearance and reality.[160] Either way, self-deception must be detected, whether or not it is intentional. The key is mutual accountability, for we must be able to scrutinize one another if we are to validate our own self-analysis. The comparison of our own consciences to our actions gives us a template for evaluating the sincerity of others, yet we can assess our own sincerity much better than we can the sincerity of others.[161] Overall, it seems that the evaluation of affections must be comprehensive, judging both actions and motives, and including both first-person and third-person perspectives. This explains why Wesley believed early on that the attainment of Christian perfection should be judged by observing

---

157. Edwards, *RA*, §3.12, 407–11; Wesley, *WHS*, 98–99.
158. Edwards, *RA*, §3.12, 460; cf. Wesley, *WHS*, 107.
159. Proudfoot, "Perception and Love," 130–32.
160. Chamberlain, "Self-Deception," 543.
161. Bell, "Trusting One's Heart," 107–8.

the claimant's tempers, words, and actions for a period of at least two to three years.[162]

For both Wesley and Edwards, the most reliable way to evaluate affections is in trials, because they (1) distinguish true and false religion, (2) reveal the "genuine beauty and amiableness" of true virtue, and (3) purify and increase true religion.[163] In moments of trial, we must gauge not only our behavior, but our motives as well. However, patterns of successful trials of faith provide a stronger evidential base than isolated instances.[164] From observing a person's behavior in varied circumstances, we attribute to her a set of beliefs and desires. By observing patterns of continuity in these beliefs and desires, we ascribe character traits.[165]

Wesley concludes that we are responsible for the tempers and dispositions of our hearts, since he believes that God will judge us according to them.[166] Although the affections are less enduring and habituated than the tempers, we are responsible for them as well.[167] We are even responsible to shape our taste, which includes (1) "perception," "judgment," or "discernment;" and (2) pleasure. The first part is rational and can be molded through knowledge. Although the second part is somewhat innate, we can still improve it by exposing ourselves to great things, e.g., "to be conversant with the writings of the best authors" or to have "conversation with men of genius."[168]

According to Newton Flew, Wesley's concept of experiencing God includes cognitive content. "The consciousness of God is not an ecstasy and often does not even include a feeling of gladness or joy. The experience is not merely an emotional individual and evanescent something . . . In our modern phrase, the experience has an intellectual content."[169] Wesley holds the opinion that we cannot love God without knowledge

---

162. Maddox, *Responsible Grace*, 189.

163. Edwards, *RA*, §1, 93; Wesley, *WHS*, 50; cf. Proudfoot, "Perception and Love," 125.

164. Chamberlain, "Self-Deception," 554–55.

165. Proudfoot, "Perception and Love," 126–27.

166. Collins, "Topography," 168.

167. Ibid., 171.

168. Wesley, "Thoughts upon Taste" (1780), §§6, 11, 16–17, *WWJ*, 13:466–69.

169. Flew, *Perfection in Christian Theology*, 318.

of God, and this requires the renewal of the image of God in us.[170] The knowledge of God also removes the sting of death.

> Indeed there is an effectual cure, even the knowledge and love of God. There is a knowledge of God which unveils eternity and a love of God which endears it. That knowledge makes the great abyss visible and all uncertainty vanishes away. That love makes it amiable to the soul, so that fear has no more place![171]

Wesley asserts that the understanding effectively guides the will and the affections.[172] For example, Wesley believes that repentance comes from a feeling of remorse about our sins. It is more than a mere conviction (i.e., realization) that we have sinned, and yet the thing that distinguishes repentance from mere conviction is an increase in self-knowledge. In other words, increased self-knowledge elevates the emotions.[173] The understanding and the affections influence one another. If a wrong opinion is held, then a contrary change in the affections will only be temporary and the subject will eventually revert to emotions that are based on the wrong opinion. Conversely, if the affections are improper, they will bias the mind against the truth.[174]

Randy Maddox points out that the popular psychology of Wesley's day stressed reason as the means of self-determination and the need to bring the passions under rational control in order to have moral rectitude.[175] However, Wesley also agreed with the commonly held belief that humans have more control over their affections than they do over their passions, since the latter are more closely tied to bodily appetites.[176] For Edwards, whereas passions evoke reactions that are largely beyond our control, affections evoke responses that reveal inclinations.[177] Wesley and Edwards thus believe that affections can be shaped rationally.

---

170. Todd, *Wesley and the Catholic Church*, 143.

171. Wesley, "A Farther Appeal to Men of Reason and Religion, Part II," §3.19, *WW*, 11:267 [J 8:196].

172. Wesley, *NNT*, Luke 10:27.

173. Wesley, Sermon 85, "On Working Out Our Own Salvation," §2.1, *WW*, 3:2–304 [J 6:509].

174. Wesley, Sermon 142, "The Wisdom of Winning Souls," §2, *WW*, 4:312–13.

175. Maddox, "A Change of Affections," 5.

176. Clapper, *Experience and Emotion*, 69.

177. J. Smith, "Treatise Concerning Religious Affections," 220.

Incorporating Edwards' Notions into the New Paradigm

Some of Edwards' emphases, even beyond those endorsed by Wesley, will be beneficial to the type of paradigm I am trying to construct for Wesleyan ethics. For example, although Wesley does not accept the way that Edwards construes knowledge of God, Edwards' stress on knowledge in the affections is still helpful. He equates "sentiments" with "ideas," highlighting their cognitive content.[178] He contends,

> All affections are raised either by *light* in the understanding or by some *error and delusion* in the understanding, for all affections do certainly arise from some apprehension in the understanding, and that apprehension must either be agreeable to truth or else be some mistake or delusion; if it be an apprehension or notion that is agreeable to truth, then it is *light in the understanding*.[179]

For instance, Edwards asserts that "Godly sorrow" is the result of "spiritual sight or knowledge."[180] There is also a connection between love for God and knowledge of God.

> Divine knowledge and divine love go together. A spiritual view of divine things always excites love in the soul and draws forth the heart in love to every proper object. True discoveries of the divine character dispose us to love God as the supreme good, they unite the heart in love to Christ, they incline the soul to flow out in love to God's people and to all mankind. When persons have a true discovery of the excellency and sufficiency of Christ, this is the effect. When they experience a right belief of the truth of the gospel, such a belief is accompanied by love. They love him whom they believe to be the Christ, the Son of the living God.[181]

It is not necessary to accept Edwards' Platonic notion of love as a passive and irresistible experience to appreciate the general principle that our thinking greatly affects our emotions. Edwards contends that particular beliefs that people hold (e.g., God's wrath, God's mercy, etc.)

---

178. Edwards, *TV*, §8.2, 104.
179. Edwards, *ThR*, §3.1, 239.
180. Edwards, *Im*, §173, 121.
181. Edwards, *CF*, §1.2.3, 21.

affect their emotional state (i.e., anguish, calmness, etc.).[182] This is why private affections can only extend to the "contracted limits of mind and the narrowness of views."[183] For the Christian, love is dependent on faith, yet love "enlarges and promotes faith."[184] Optimally, a balance is struck between thinking and feeling.

> As on the one hand, there must be light in the understanding, as well as an affected fervent heart, [for] where there is heat without light, there can be nothing divine or heavenly in that heart; so on the other hand, where there is a kind of light without heat, a head stored with notions and speculations, with a cold and unaffected heart, there can be nothing divine in that light, that knowledge is no true spiritual knowledge of divine things. If the great things of religion are rightly understood, they will affect the heart.[185]

Again, Edwards' analysis presupposes irresistible grace, but Wesleyans can still agree with the general argument.

Edwards believes that truth must take precedence, because moral transformation cannot take place apart from it. People must hear the truth, regardless of how it may affect them emotionally. Otherwise, they cannot be converted.[186] Even though I do not accept the way Edwards sets up a dichotomy between false and true affections, I believe that his analysis of affections reveals some of their complexities. He asserts that our emotions will be delusional if the presuppositions behind them are errant.[187] In other words, affections which are based on false beliefs will produce other affections with the same cognitive flaws. As affections produce other affections, it becomes increasingly difficult to maintain the purity of the intentions, since the affections become more complex.

The critique that Edwards provides of the notion of a direct witness of the Holy Spirit is also instructive. It is not apparent whether Edwards had Wesley in mind when he made this critique. As I indicated earlier, although Wesley was a vocal advocate of this notion, he was not the only person to embrace it. Furthermore, there is good reason to believe that

---

182. Edwards, *NSC*, §2, 27–32.
183. Edwards, *TV*, §7, 88.
184. Edwards, *CF*, §13.1.2, 271.
185. Edwards, *RA*, §1.2, 120.
186. Edwards, *ThR*, §3.2, 244–52.
187. Edwards, *RA*, §2.1, 172.

Edwards was relatively unfamiliar with Wesley, since the only Wesleyan source he apparently read was a hymnal.[188]

Regarding the claims people make of receiving direct revelations from God, Edwards insists,

> This is a quite different thing from the Spirit's enlightening the mind to understand the precepts of propositions of the word of God and know what is contained and revealed in them, and what consequences may be justly drawn from them, and to see how they are applicable to our case and circumstances, which is done without any new revelation, only by enabling the mind to understand and apply a revelation already made.[189]

Claiming to receive direct revelations from God only makes a person more susceptible to self-delusion. "As long as a person has a notion that he is guided by immediate direction from heaven, it makes him incorrigible and impregnable in all his misconduct."[190] Edwards thus recoils from what Wesley calls the "direct witness." On the other hand, Edwards' account of assurance bears a strong resemblance to Wesley's "indirect witness." He asserts that there is no genuine assurance without knowing that one has met the qualifications required by Scripture.[191] The witness of the Holy Spirit is not an "immediate suggestion" or a "secret voice or impression." It is indeed a declaration, but one that provides evidence so that the matter may be argued and proven to be true.[192]

According to Edwards, we can discern if we in fact possess "divine dispositions," and we can subsequently conclude that we have the Holy Spirit. In its most basic sense, this is the witness of the Spirit.[193] The saint can see and feel the union that exists between God and the soul, the union that is effected through divine love.[194] It would seem that Edwards is getting dangerously close to the view he wants to discredit. Nevertheless, he believes that we can identify dispositions by observing what is constant or generally occurring in them, especially in

---

188. R. Steele, "*Gracious Affection*," 138–41.
189. Edwards, *ThR*, §4.4, 312.
190. Ibid., §4.4, 308.
191. Edwards, *RA*, §3.1, 226.
192. Ibid., §3.1, 231.
193. Edwards, "Miscellany 375," *Misc1*, 447.
194. Edwards, "Miscellany 686," *Misc2*, 249.

a variety of circumstances, and most of all in adverse circumstances.[195] Ultimately, the real witness that we are God's children is that we behave toward God like his children.[196]

Although Edwards suggests that our dispositions should be judged objectively as much as possible, he places limits on this as well. In fact, "no external manifestations . . . are infallible evidences of grace. These manifestations that have been maintained are the best that mankind can have."[197] For example, it is possible for people to be convinced of religious matters when they are really being guided by self-interest.[198] Also, some hypocrites press forward in the Christian life, but not to love God more. Instead, they seek a clearer assurance, a greater experience of God's love, or an exalted status, or perhaps they simply do not want others to impugn their status as true saints.[199] Motives can be mixed even to the extent that positive and negative emotions can be joined in one emotion.[200] Hence, good works must not only be accompanied by a proper confession of faith, the confession itself must be fully understood and embraced for the right reasons.[201]

I believe that Edwards' analysis of motivation is most helpful, and I feel that it can be applied to Wesleyan ethics without accepting Edwards' theological presuppositions. Evaluating one's own spiritual state must include both psychological self-analysis and the scrutiny of one's dispositions, evidenced in outward conduct. The affections must be judged according to their purity, their strength, and their cognitive content. This does not preclude a direct witness of the Spirit. Instead, it assumes that the direct witness is always validated by the indirect witness, and this is precisely what Wesley wants to assert.

Edwards' Incompatibility with a Wesleyan Paradigm

Obviously, the theological differences between Wesley and Edwards will limit the utility of Edwards' approach. First, as I have already mentioned,

195. Edwards, OS, §1.1.1, 108.
196. Edwards, RA, §3.1, 238.
197. Ibid., §3.12, 420.
198. Ibid., §3.5, 310.
199. Ibid., §3.11, 382.
200. Ibid., §1.1, 98–99.
201. Ibid., §3.12, 413–16.

his doctrine of irresistible grace undergirds his construal of the perception of divine beauty. He declares that the only "mental things" we can apprehend are (1) our own cognitive processes and (2) things pertaining to the will (i.e., things that bring pleasure or displeasure). The "sense of the heart" properly includes both of these types of apprehension so that spiritual knowledge is not merely speculative, but a true apprehension.[202] In essence, Edwards is arguing that a full perception (i.e., a "spiritual perception") of spiritual things necessarily effects a proper emotional response, else the perception is merely speculative. This is why he contends that Satan has no spiritual knowledge of God, only notional, speculative knowledge. Satan lost his spiritual knowledge when he fell.[203] I restate my observation that this entire explanation is incompatible with a Wesleyan (i.e., Arminian) view of free will.

Erdt indicates that many Puritans regarded the "sense of the heart" as an indication of election. They were all well aware of the "remarkable emotional response that marked its presence."[204] Consequently, the "sense of the heart" seems to be the Calvinistic counterpart to Wesley's witness of the Spirit. In any event, this analogy, along with Edwards' overall description of the perception of divine beauty, not only contradicts a Wesleyan understanding of free will, it requires either the type of mystical experience from which Wesley distanced himself or a supernatural (monergistic) change in human nature, both of which I am excluding in my new paradigm. In fact, I believe that in particular ways, Edwards' perception of divine excellence comes much closer to quietism (especially that of Fénelon) than Wesley's experiential religion.

Second, a Wesleyan paradigm must allow the possibility that a believer might backslide and fall from grace, and Edwards is unwilling to make this concession. He says that true saints may *temporarily* backslide and even yield to great sins, but not to the extent of reneging on "universal obedience."[205] Those who ultimately fall away never were true converts, because true religious affections always persevere. In

---

202. Edwards, "Miscellany 782," *Misc2*, 458–59.
203. Edwards, "False Light and True," *Ser4*, 140–41; cf. Erdt, *Sense of the Heart*, 31.
204. Erdt, *Sense of the Heard*, 19.
205. Edwards, *RA*, §3.12, 390.

contrast, false affections soften the heart initially, but harden it in the end.[206] Allowances for individual temperaments must be made,

> But not such allowances as to allow men that once were wolves and serpents to be now converted without any remarkable change in the spirit of their mind. The change made by true conversion is wont to be most remarkable and sensible with respect to that which before was the wickedness the person was most notoriously guilty of.[207]

Edwards dismisses out of hand conversions that are not "remarkable," since they are not as likely to endure. This seems to betray a certain bias, given the fact that he is well aware that conversion experiences may vary greatly. He observes that awakening (i.e., conviction) occurs at different rates for different people.[208] The converting light is suddenly bright to some, gradually to others.[209] Moreover, the change of conversion is not necessarily a complete moral transformation. "In the new birth there is certainly a very great change in the soul . . . yet the sensible change is very gradual."[210] In other words, virtue must be increased gradually. Regeneration supplies the necessary tools for this increase. Consequently, many believers have rather imperfect behavior, yet they still have a "real zeal for God."[211] A genuine conversion always (1) increases esteem for Christ; (2) counters sin, evil, and worldliness; (3) causes greater regard for Scripture; (4) inclines the convert toward truth; and (5) results in love for God and others.[212] These tenets can be accepted without viewing conversion as an irreversible process or event.

Third, although Edwards' emphasis on the cognitive content in affection is most helpful, he comes dangerously close to viewing religious affections as rationally necessary. Richard Brantley and Clapper both speculate that Wesley probably omitted Edwards' fourth sign because

---

206. Ibid., §3.9, 357–58.
207. Ibid., §3.8, 357.
208. Edwards, NSC, §2, 23.
209. Ibid., §2, 41.
210. Edwards, "Miscellany 241," *Misc1*, 358.
211. Edwards, *DM*, §1.6, 101.
212. Edwards, *DM*, §§2.1–5, 109–15; Wesley, *WHS*, 23–30.

it comes too close to rationalism.[213] Consider the following passage in *Religious Affections*:

> And the degree of religion is rather to be judged of by the fixedness and strength of the habit that is exercised in affection, whereby holy affection is habitual, than by the degree of the present exercise; and the strength of that habit is not always in proportion to outward effects and manifestations, or inwards effects, in the hurry and vehemence, and sudden changes of the course of the thoughts of the mind. But yet it is evident, that religion consists so much in affection, as that without holy affection there is no true religion, and no light in the understanding is good, which doesn't produce holy affection in the heart, no habit or principle in the heart is good, which has no such exercise, and no external fruit is good, which doesn't proceed from such exercises.[214]

In effect, all "good light" in the understanding necessarily produces holy affections, which are revealed in their "fixedness." Once again, Edwards is bolstering his doctrine of irresistible grace. Since he wants religious affections to originate in a complacent love of divine beauty, one that transcends self-interest, it is necessary that one should be overwhelmed by the beauty of Christ. This also harkens back to Edwards' emphasis on a "full perception" of spiritual knowledge, which surpasses speculative, notional understanding and causes the proper affections.

I repeat my claim that this model is inconsistent with a Wesleyan view of free will. Wesley declares,

> We know indeed that wrong opinions in religion naturally lead to wrong tempers or wrong practices, and that, consequently, it is our bounden duty to pray that we may have a right judgment in all things. But still a man may judge as accurately as the devil and yet be as wicked as he.[215]

Whereas Edwards attributes the evil of Satan to a lack of knowledge, Wesley does not view any knowledge as irresistibly determinative, since he understands liberty to entail self-determination.

---

213. Brantley, "Common Ground," 143.
214. Edwards, *RA*, §1.2, 118–19.
215. Wesley, Sermon 127, "On the Wedding Garment," §15, *WW*, 4:146 [J 7:315–16].

Fourth, Edwards' uncertainty about the value of self-love is reflected in his understanding of love for others. He has difficulty explaining how godly people naturally love others given (1) self-love is a necessary part of all love, and (2) pure love transcends self-interest. As I have already indicated, Edwards at first believed that we can only love others out of self-interest, except for the complacent love of their beauty. By the time he wrote *True Virtue* at the end of his life, he had changed his mind. Here he takes his new definition of love as the consent of being to being and applies it to the love of others.

> I have observed from time to time, that in pure love to others, i.e. love not arising from self-love, there is a union of the heart with others, a kind of enlargement of the mind, whereby it extends itself so as to take others into a man's self: and therefore it implies a disposition to feel, to desire, and to act as though others were one with ourselves.[216]

He now makes a clear distinction between pure love to others and sympathy. Whereas pure love to others involves an "enlargement" of the self, sympathy is still a "substitution" of the self in the other's place.[217] He also differentiates pure love for others from natural affection, which is produced by self-love and a sense of desert.[218] Although this depiction of neighbor love is certainly an improvement on his earlier thought, it still does not fully address the paradox that Edwards clearly recognized. In *Religious Affections* Edwards contended that loving others is only a sign of godliness in the sense of keeping our duties toward them, not in the sense of having affections toward them. In other words, love for others is only virtuous to the extent that it obeys scriptural commands to love others.[219] It does not appear that Edwards ever revised this assertion, and this complicates the whole matter. Edwards essentially assigns self-love a positive role in natural affections, but he views it as a hindrance to true virtue.

Unfortunately, Edwards met an untimely death within a few years of *True Virtue*, and the book was published posthumously. In my opinion, Edwards was trying to resolve the paradox of pure love, but he ran

---

216. Edwards, *TV*, §5, 61.
217. Ibid., §5, 64.
218. Ibid., §4.3, 51.
219. Edwards, *RA*, §3.12, 437.

out of time. Nevertheless, I suspect that if Edwards had continued to remain a predestinationist, then a fuller development of his understanding of love would still be only partially compatible with a Wesleyan view of love. It is my belief that the most fruitful development of Edwards' analysis of love would be to more fully apply his theory that the purity of love is revealed in trials. He recognizes the complexity of motives and the difficulty we have in trying to separate and analyze them. He also believes that right affections produce particular results, yet these results can also be produced by impure motives. Edwards thus concludes that the purity of love is best revealed when love requires sacrifice or suffering. To me, this seems to be a most useful concept in evaluating love, both love for God and love for others.

Toward a More Intellectually Sophisticated Account

Edwards and Wesley utilized the intellectual resources that were available to them, but I believe that their account of religious affections can be developed intellectually in two particular ways. First of all, they set up a simplistic dichotomy between true and false affections. To a great extent, this can be attributed to their heavy emphasis on supernatural change in the human spirit. Even their definition of the term "spiritual" reveals this slant. They say that things are referred to as "spiritual" when they have some relationship to the Holy Spirit.[220] In a general sense, this seems like a solid definition, for Christianity has consistently asserted the active role of the Holy Spirit in salvation. However, Edwards wants to assign the Spirit a monergistic role in his predestinationist schema. Although Wesley does not desire this, he still sides with Edwards in trying to make true virtue the product of some supernatural change.

They claim that the affections brought by the Holy Spirit are entirely different from the natural affections.[221] The unregenerate person lacks the necessary faculties. Spiritual things (especially notions like benevolence) cannot be perceived by the unregenerate because they do not have a disposition toward them. Edwards suggests that we cannot have ideas of spiritual things without the prerequisite "adopted disposition

---

220. Edwards, *RA*, §3.1, 198; Wesley, *WHS*, 80.
221. Edwards, *RA*, §3.1, 205; Wesley, *WHS*, 81.

of mind," which can be "increased only by the practice of virtue and holiness."[222] This even applies to the understanding of Scripture.[223]

In conversion, God alters the mind's conception of good.[224] In this regard, the spiritual light of regeneration "not only directly evidences the truth of religion to the mind . . . it sanctifies the reasoning faculty and assists it to see the clear evidence there is of the truth of religion in rational arguments." It "removes prejudices" and "positively enlightens and assists" the mind.[225] Moreover, the Holy Spirit infuses new, supernatural faculties at regeneration.[226] This enables the believer to perceive "spiritual harmony."[227] According to William Wainwright, Edwards believes this spiritual perception to be objective in nature, since it agrees with the nature of things and it perceives spiritual realities.[228] The conclusion that Edwards and Wesley reach is that true divine love produces all Christian affections. In contrast, counterfeit love produces false affections.[229] For Edwards, true affections are those that endure. Even though people may have religious affections, believe the gospel, and change their behavior, it is not genuine if it does not last. Wesley agrees with this, but not to the degree that Edwards does.[230]

Edwards and Wesley focus on the purity of affections and on their cognitive content, but they do not focus enough on their strength. This overlooks the fact that an affection can be dominant not only because it is strong, but also due to the lack of competing affections. Hence, a weak affection can dominate temporarily but lose out to stronger competing affections in the long run. Even competing affections can be weakened by other opposing affections, yet regain their strength later on. For example, a person may be diagnosed as terminally ill and be converted, yet if the patient recovers, the conversion may be recanted if the other reasons supporting the conversion are weak and the reasons opposing conversion still have force. Neither Wesley nor

---

222. Edwards, "Miscellany 123," *Misc1*, 286–87.
223. Edwards, "Miscellany 126," *Misc1*, 289–91.
224. Edwards, "Miscellany 284," *Misc1*, 380–81.
225. Edwards, "Miscellany 628," *Misc2*, 156–57.
226. Edwards, *RA*, §3.1, 205–6; Wesley, *WHS*, 81–82.
227. Edwards, "Miscellany 141," *Misc1*, 297–98.
228. Wainwright, "Sense of the Heart," 55–56.
229. Edwards, *RA*, §2.1, 150.
230. Edwards, *RA*, §3.5, 293–94; Wesley, *WHS*, 83.

Edwards would disagree with this, but the real issue concerns deciding what constitutes a genuine conversion. Edwards argues that a genuine conversion is one that is never recanted. Wesley does not accept this, for he believes that a genuine convert may backslide. However, Wesley does not want to affirm "conversions" that are short-lived, yet his acceptance of Edwards' dichotomy gives him no conceptual framework for making finer distinctions.

Furthermore, pious affections can occur in varying degrees of strength and purity of intention. However, the requirements of regeneration (i.e., repentance, faith, etc.) imply that these affections must meet certain thresholds for these requirements to be met with sincerity. Interestingly enough, both Edwards and Wesley recognize a scale of assent. In their construal, this should imply a scale of strength in emotions. They admit that different believers have varying "degrees of strength of faith," yet they contend that true believers have certainty that exceeds mere probability.[231] I would suggest that they are on the right track, but need a more nuanced definition of certainty. Although they recognize both the cognitive content of emotions and the variability of assent, they do not make the connection to sufficiently recognize the variable strength of affections. The question is not whether we *truly* love God, it is whether we love God *sufficiently* and with *proper motive*.

The other shortcoming that Edwards and Wesley have is that they make appeals to grace in matters that today can be explained more fully in natural terms. For Edwards, this can be illustrated most aptly in the way that he develops his account of conscience. Initially, he claimed that the Spirit assists natural conscience through "common grace."

> Natural men may have convictions from the Spirit of God, but 'tis from the Spirit of God only as assisting natural principles, and not infusing any new and supernatural principle. That conviction of guilt which a natural man may have from the Spirit of God is only by the Spirit's assisting natural conscience the better and more fully to do its office. Therein common grace differs from special, that common grace is only the assistance of natural principles, special is the infusing and exciting supernatural principles. Or (if any of these words are too abstruse) common grace only assists the faculties of the soul to do that more fully, which they do by nature ... But special grace causes

---

231. Edwards, *RA*, §3.5, 304–7; Wesley, *WHS*, 83–84.

the faculties to do that that they do not do by nature, causes those things to be in the soul that are above nature, and causes them to be in the soul habitually.[232]

Although Edwards early believed that common grace permits natural conscience, he later attributed natural conscience to reason and self-interest, and he claimed that the regenerate possess an inner affective sense of the intrinsic nature of good and evil.[233] In natural conscience, we naturally desire to be consistent with ourselves, so our perceptions of our own consistency yield corresponding positive and negative feelings.[234] Moreover, we naturally take pleasure in the approval of others to the extent that their approval and disapproval determine our behavior as immediately as sensory experience.[235]

Edwards asserts that the moral sense theorists are wrong in claiming that humans universally have a benevolent disposition toward true virtue, which they believe is a disinterested moral sense. He argues that if natural conscience and the disposition to approve true virtue were one and the same, they would always occur in the same degree, but this is not the case. Edwards does believe, though, that natural conscience can operate from a sense of desert, and this operation is usually not a product of self-love.[236] Nevertheless, natural conscience falls short of a proper sensitivity to true morality. Even though Christianity is thoroughly rational and congruous to human reason, natural reason has been corrupted by sin. Hence, God has revealed truths in Scripture that are above natural reason.[237]

The real struggle that Edwards faced was in trying to determine the importance of natural faculties in true morality. On the one hand, he wants to assert God's absolute sovereignty in salvation, and this does not allow any room for human initiative, in his mind. It necessitates supernatural change in human faculties beyond that which can be effected through natural means. Moreover, it leads to false dichotomies between true virtue and natural morality, true and false affections,

---

232. Edwards, "Miscellany 626," *Misc2*, 155.
233. Fiering, *Edwards' Moral Thought*, 65.
234. Edwards, *TV*, §5.1, 65.
235. Ibid., §4, 45–46.
236. Ibid., §5.2, 70–71.
237. Edwards, "True Nobleness of Mind," *Ser2*, 231–34.

and between a moral sense and natural conscience. Whenever these dichotomies cannot be justified rationally, an appeal is made to grace. Some have it and some do not.

On the other hand, Edwards acutely observes human behavior and motivation, and his account of natural morality is arguably more nuanced than the other theories of his day. For this reason, these dichotomies and appeals to grace seem unnecessary, if not forced. Edwards notes that God typically accomplishes his work through means that are observable to us.[238] In fact, he says that it is "enthusiastical" to think that the Holy Spirit will operate on our minds without using some subservient means.[239] Although he believes that there is a lasting change in one's nature at regeneration, he still recognizes the change to be a relative one in which the person's natural temper is not eliminated or replaced, but significantly improved and corrected.[240] Harold Simonson points out that although conversion for Edwards constitutes an inward change, the individual is still vulnerable to the same sinful inclinations.[241]

Edwards is well aware that the development of conscience involves increasing both the breadth and the depth of one's moral perception. Enlightenment is what brings conscience from the private sphere to consider things in general. If conscience is thus well-informed, it will approve true virtue.[242] Moral perception must be broadened beyond the sphere of self-interest, even to the point of considering the universality of morality. Nevertheless, moral perception must also be able to focus inwardly on intentions and motives. Edwards observes that conversion generally requires a shift in focus from outward conduct to the condition of the heart.[243] He knows that moral reasoning is at times concrete and at other times abstract. In light of the many nuanced views that Edwards holds concerning morality and moral reasoning, I suggest that the dichotomies that he tries to justify are ultimately limitations to the development of this astute man's thought.

---

238. Edwards, *DM*, §1.5, 98; Wesley, *WHS*, 17.
239. Edwards, *RA*, §2.1, 138; Wesley, *WHS*, 64.
240. Edwards, *RA*, §3.7, 340–41.
241. Simonson, *Theologian of the Heart*, 61.
242. Edwards, *TV*, §5.2, 69.
243. Edwards, *NSC*, §2, 27.

Wesleyan ethics would be benefited by engaging in this type of critical analysis without using forced dichotomies or appealing to grace whenever the conceptual categories prove inadequate. In the next chapter, I will consider the implications of Wesley's belief that the grace of God typically operates through natural means. I believe that as our understanding of human nature becomes more sophisticated, our understanding of grace will become more naturalized. However, this does not make human beings less dependent on grace, it simply means that as our abilities increase, so do our responsibilities.

Summary

Wesley's abridgements of Edwards not only shed light on Wesley's understanding of moral psychology, they also suggest ways in which it can be developed. In the words of Clapper:

> We can see in the *Treatise*, then, all of the major points of Wesley's heart-centered theology: the close relations between reason and emotion, the constant checks against self-deception, the transitive or objective [sic] nature of the affections, the central importance of the love of, and joy in, God, and, finally, the dispositional nature of the emotions—the fact that the truly Christian affections compel the believer to live constructively in the social world.[244]

Edwards' thought is a good resource for the development of Wesleyan ethics, especially its understanding of moral psychology. Noll asserts that evangelicals at large can benefit from Edwards' approach to theology. "The anti-intellectualism nourished by evangelicals could not be further from Edwards' patient attention to what we would today call psychology, metaphysics, and natural science."[245] I believe that if Wesleyan ethics is able to appropriate Edwards in its own development, it could thus make a greater impact on evangelicalism and Christianity in general.

---

244. Clapper, *Experience and Emotion*, 148.
245. Noll, "God at the Center," 857.

Conclusion

Wesley was driven by the pursuit of perfection, but he never envisioned perfection as the result of a mystical experience. He understands perfection to be a state of perfect love, yet he does not regard love merely as something to be passively experienced. Early on, Wesley was inclined to pursue perfection through ascetic moral rigorism, but this only added to the inner turmoil and confusion that he felt within. He discovered a certain freedom in experiential religion. However, his followers carried things to extremes that he did not want to permit, and still he displayed a great deal of tolerance in that regard. In the end, he still saw perfection as loving God with our whole hearts and loving our neighbors as ourselves, and this is a state that results in a consistent pattern of victory over willful sin. The pure love of Christian perfection is not disinterested to the extent that self-love must be transcended. Rather, it is a love in which self-will is continually surrendered to the divine will out of complete trust. Wesley realizes that love is more than a mere experience. Consequently, the continued development of his doctrine of perfection requires a more cognitive view of emotion and a more comprehensive definition of sin.

PART THREE

Constructing *a* New Paradigm

7

The Basic Conceptual Elements

THIS CHAPTER WILL OUTLINE THE WAY THAT PARTICULAR CONCEPTS need to be developed in order to construct the intellectual paradigm that I am proposing for Wesleyan ethics. The nature of each of these developments is suggested by Wesley's own concerns. As such, most of this development will build upon the analysis of Wesley's thought performed in the previous chapters. However, some additional developments will also be suggested by the broader intellectual context in which Wesley is located. To be specific, I will engage British empiricism and its interlocutors, including strands of rationalism (especially in Kant's philosophy) that respond to British empiricism in particular ways. Since I am suggesting that the new paradigm be acceptable by intellectual standards that are higher than those which have formerly been associated with Wesleyan ethics, some of the developments proposed in this chapter will be reinforced through appeals to sources that are more recent. Many of the sections in this chapter will summarize and develop arguments that were presented in previous chapters. As the book progresses, the developments will increasingly utilize other sources.

To start, epistemic certainty will need to be objectified to some extent. Since empiricism relies upon personal perception, it naturally contains a subjective element. Moral certainty should require some type of objective validation, and this also implies that it should not be based solely (if primarily) upon subjective mystical experiences. Of course, Scripture will need to be retained as an authoritative source of moral knowledge in a Wesleyan paradigm, and moral certainty must be founded upon and be congruent with scriptural truth. Next, I am suggesting that a Wesleyan view of grace can be construed so as to yield a more naturalized interpretation of grace. In the Wesleyan paradigm I am developing, although God is not limited to acting in particular ways, God generally acts through natural means so that divine influence is usually subtle. Supernatural acts can by and large be confirmed according to the natural means they utilize, but our ability to understand the means to particular ends does not preclude belief in any underlying divine providence. Finally, love must be seen as more than a passive feeling, because the emotions are rooted in cognitive content. I will explain this in some detail and briefly allude to some contemporary accounts of emotion that are constructed along these lines.

Making Certainty Less Subjective

Wesley asserts that believers can be sure of their salvation, especially through the witness of the Holy Spirit. This claim, along with his general willingness to grant experience an epistemic role, led his critics to accuse him of "enthusiasm" (i.e., mistaking one's own imagination for the voice of God). Wesley understands that his belief in supernatural involvement in human affairs makes him an "enthusiast" in the eyes of naturalists like the Deists. However, he says that he is not a "rank enthusiast," because he limits the epistemic role of experience and he insists on subjecting experience to objective criteria by which its validity may be tested.

Part of the difficulty that Wesley faces is that empiricism relies upon personal perception and thus contains a subjective element. Locke stresses the subjective element rather heavily, claiming that we only perceive particulars, not universals. He also claims that when we classify objects, we do not speak of the objects themselves, but of our ideas of them. Wesley distances himself from this type of nominalism, because he believes in the integrity of language. He feels that we can intelligently communicate ideas about the real essences of objects. Like Reid, Wesley tries to counter the subjective element of empiricism by recognizing self-evident maxims by which perceptions can be judged. Even though Wesley does not allow as broad a range of self-evident maxims as Reid, his strong faith in the authority of Scripture compensates for this difference with regard to moral matters. It will lie beyond the scope of this project to fully explore the compatibility of empiricism with this type of realism. In this chapter, it will simply be noted that although empirical perception is subjective, it can be objectified to a significant extent by reason, which provides the necessary means for translating experience into knowledge.

With regard to spiritual knowledge, both Wesley and Edwards appeal to a "spiritual sense" analogy in order to maintain the certainty of assurance in conversion, and this has already been explained in detail. In this chapter, I will build upon my previous arguments and restate my assertion that Wesley's spiritual sense analogy needs to be abandoned. Instead, Locke and Browne provide a more beneficial way of construing epistemic certainty, and this is applicable to the knowledge of spiritual matters as well as to other types of knowledge.

Was Wesley an Enthusiast?

Many of Wesley's critics complained that he gave too much credence to personal experience, that his epistemology was too subjective. This negative appraisal is reflected in the charges of "enthusiasm" leveled against him. I contend that although Wesley may have been guilty of "enthusiasm," especially as defined by the Deists, he was not guilty of what he called "rank enthusiasm." Obviously, enthusiasm could be avoided altogether if religious experience were simply discarded, but this would not be consistent with the core commitments of Wesleyanism. Hence, Wesleyan spirituality must allow a certain degree of subjectivity, and yet I feel that the epistemic role of religious experience can be sufficiently limited so as to discourage (if not practically eliminate) notions and practices that engender "enthusiasm." Again, Wesley himself is a good example of this type of balanced approach, for he made no personal claims of perfection, and he never advocated an inner experience of assurance apart from the scrutiny of objective criteria. Thus, he should be judged more on this basis than on the basis of what he permitted in pastoral practice.

Although the term "enthusiasm" was widely used in the seventeenth and eighteenth centuries, it was Locke's definition that was generally used by the Deists and others in leveling accusations against Wesley and the Methodists. Locke described the term as such:

> This I take to be properly enthusiasm, which, though founded neither on reason nor divine revelation, but rising from the conceits of a warmed or overweening brain, . . . [causes people to be] most forwardly obedient to the impulses they receive from

> themselves ... For strong conceit, ... when got above common sense, and freed from all restraint of reason and check of reflection, it is heightened into a divine authority, in concurrence with our own temper and inclination.[1]

Locke asserts that those who believe in such immediate revelations take them to be self-evident, infallible, and above reason.[2] These perceptions would not be so problematic were they verifiable by strict reasoning or by empirical observation. In effect, people accept whatever "groundless opinion" is impressed strongly upon their minds as the illumination of the Holy Spirit, and they regard some strong inclination or impulse as "a call or direction from heaven."[3] Immediate revelation thus exhibits a sort of intellectual laziness, since it is "a much easier way for men to establish their opinions and regulate their conduct than the tedious and not always successful labor of strict reasoning."[4] To counter such enthusiasm, Locke issued what has been called the "evidentialist challenge."[5] Claims and propositions are only as strong as the evidence that supports them.

Stephen Gunter outlines the four general types of enthusiasm of which Wesley and the Methodists were accused: (1) they made claims to special inspirations and revelations, (2) they fostered an anti-clerical attitude, (3) they allowed lay people to preach and to pray in public, and (4) they asserted that it is possible to live without sin.[6] However, Gunter points out that the definition of enthusiasm that circulated at the time of the Methodist revival predominantly defined the term as a pretense to divine revelation.[7] Indeed, Wesley felt that this was the precise thing of which he was being accused.

> I believe, thinking men mean by *enthusiasm* a sort of religious madness, a *false imagination* of being inspired by God, and by an enthusiast one that *fancies* himself under the influence of the

---

1. Locke, *Essay*, §4.19.7, 2:432–33.
2. Ibid., §4.19.8, 2:443.
3. Ibid., §4.19.6, 2:432.
4. Ibid., §4.19.5, 2:431.
5. Wolterstorff, *Ethics of Belief*, 118–19.
6. Gunter, *The Limits of "Love Divine,"* 13–14.
7. Ibid., 119.

Holy Ghost when, in fact, he is not. Let him prove me guilty of this who can.⁸

Although some have contended that Wesley's doctrine of perfection is a source of his enthusiasm, he limits his definition of sin sufficiently so as to deny the charge that his doctrine is one of "sinless perfection," so he is not guilty of enthusiasm in that sense of the word. Rather, the point at which Wesley is most vulnerable to charges of enthusiasm is his doctrine of the direct witness of the Spirit. Wesley maintains that the truest and worst type of enthusiasm is mistaking your own imagination for the witness of the Spirit so as to assume that you are acceptable to God while you are "doing the works of the devil."⁹ He believes that the witness of the Spirit must be antecedent to assurance, because we can only know that we are holy after we know that we love God. However, we can only know this after we become aware that God loves us, and this in turn requires knowledge that our sins have been forgiven.¹⁰

The ultimate problem, as Wesley sees it, is that assurance can often be vague. However, "the direct witness may shine clear, even while the indirect one is under a cloud."¹¹ The two witnesses (i.e., direct and indirect) thus jointly prevent delusion.¹² Randy Maddox claims that Wesley's reasons for maintaining his doctrine of the witness of the Holy Spirit were to avoid works righteousness and to maintain that true virtue comes from within as a response to God's love.¹³ This assessment is accurate, but it is so for a specific reason. As I indicated earlier, Wesley was driven by an ascetic moral rigorism. On one hand, this made him reluctant to claim that he had attained perfection. On the other hand, it gave him great anguish and doubt regarding his own justification, and his experience at Aldersgate (later interpreted as the direct witness of the Spirit) set him free from his inner struggle to be acceptable to God.

---

8. Wesley, "A Farther Appeal to Men of Reason and Religion, Part I," §5.27, *WW*, 11:170–71 [J 8:106].

9. Wesley, Sermon 10, "The Witness of the Spirit, Discourse I," §1, *WW*, 1:269 [J 5:111].

10. Ibid., §1.8, *WW*, 1:274 [J 5:115]; cf. Wesley, Sermon 11, "The Witness of the Spirit, Discourse II," §3.5, *WW*, 1:290 [J 5:127].

11. Wesley, Sermon 11, "The Witness of the Spirit, Discourse II," §4.3, *WW*, 1:294 [J 5:130].

12. Ibid., §4.8, *WW*, 1:295 [J 5:131].

13. Maddox, *Responsible Grace*, 130.

Wesley insisted that Christian tradition is on his side in the matter of assurance.

> I know likewise that Luther, Melancthon, and many other (if not all) of the Reformers, frequently and strongly assert that every believer is conscious of his own acceptance with God, and that by a supernatural evidence, which if any choose to term immediate revelation he may.[14]

This does not imply that he accepted the Reformers' doctrine of assurance itself, because he could not concur with their doctrine of election.[15] Although Wesley did not see his doctrine as problematic for Anglicanism, he believed that he was ultimately expelled from the Anglican churches for propagating it, for preaching "inward salvation, now attainable by faith."[16] He regarded this as unjust, since the Methodists were being faithful to the Church of England in promoting "living faith," the preaching of Scripture, and the administration of the sacraments.[17] Wesley argued that the Methodist revival was "so pure from superstition, so thoroughly scriptural."[18]

Mary Ryder points out that Samuel Johnson, one of the acknowledged intellectual leaders of the age, never referred to the Methodists as "enthusiasts." She asserts that zeal, which is generally a good thing, lies at the heart of enthusiasm. When zeal is not dictated by reason, it often leads to violence and pride. This is why Johnson and Wesley both insisted that zeal must be "continually controlled by reason, ingrained with humility, and directed toward doing good" through charity. In particular, enthusiasm often entailed claims of supernaturally granted gifts of insight and power. Ryder indicates that Wesley and Johnson were skeptical of such claims to supernatural revelations.[19]

Wesley is not overly concerned about delusion, because he believes that self-deceivers can be exposed by their lack of several scriptural

---

14. Wesley to Richard Thompson, 5 February 1756, *WWJ*, 12:469.
15. Cobb, *Grace and Responsibility*, 90.
16. Wesley, "An Earnest Appeal to Men of Reason and Religion," §70, *WW*, 11:74 [J 8:28].
17. Ibid., §78, *WW*, 11:77–78 [J 8:31].
18. Wesley, "A Farther Appeal to Men of Reason and Religion, Part III," §1.9, *WW*, 11:277 [J 8:206].
19. Ryder, "Wesley and Johnson on Enthusiasm," 214–20.

marks, e.g., repentance, humility, and obedience.[20] Furthermore, if we know that we are being "led by the Spirit of God into all holy tempers and actions," then we know we are the children of God.[21] The result of the witness of the Spirit is the fruit of the Spirit, and the witness cannot continue without the fruit.[22] Ultimately, we all must be judged by the quality of our character. "Yet all this is no other than rational evidence, the witness of our spirit, our reason or understanding."[23] In contrast, the true witness is "immediately and directly perceived, if our spiritual senses are rightly disposed."[24] This is what Wesley refuses to relinquish.

Nevertheless, Wesley knows that this type of divine testimony cannot be empirically verified. As such, the objective testimony of our spirit is the most intimate and certain.[25] Gradual growth in the knowledge and love of God brings gradual improvement in "grace and goodness," and this provides a basis for assurance.[26] Wesley feels that this emphasis on the objective criteria of assurance is what separates him from the real enthusiasts.[27] He does believe in "immediate inspiration" to the extent that God's spirit acts directly upon our spirits. He says, "God pours his love into your heart . . . God, a Spirit, acts upon your spirit. Make it out any otherwise if you can."[28] He proceeds to cite the Anglicans Cranmer, Ridley, Latimer, and Hooper, the Anglican *Homilies*, and the church fathers Origin, Chrysostom, and Athanasius as supporting the belief that the Holy Spirit operates on all believers. Rex Matthews suggests that inasmuch Wesley claims that we can have personal knowledge of

---

20. Wesley, Sermon 10, "The Witness of the Spirit, Discourse I," §§2.3–7, *WW*, 1:277–81 [J 5:118–20].

21. Ibid., §1.2, *WW*, 1:271–72 [J 5:113].

22. Wesley, Sermon 11, "The Witness of the Spirit, Discourse II," §2.1, *WW*, 1:286 [J 5:124].

23. Wesley, Sermon 10, "The Witness of the Spirit, Discourse I," §1.4, *WW*, 1:272 [J 5:114].

24. Ibid., §§2.9–10, *WW*, 1:282 [J 5:121].

25. Ibid., §§1.11–12, *WW*, 1:275–76 [J 5:117].

26. Wesley, "A Farther Appeal to Men of Reason and Religion, Part I," §3.6, *WW*, 11:126 [J 8:66].

27. Noll, "John Wesley," 174.

28. Wesley, "A Farther Appeal to Men of Reason and Religion, Part I," §5.28, *WW*, 11:171–72 [J 8:107].

God, he cannot be regarded as an enthusiast (in that sense of the word) any more than Edwards.[29]

Wesley acknowledges that he could be validly called an enthusiast by the Deists, but he is not bothered by that, since he considers their view of Scripture (and Christianity in general) to be too low.[30] Gunter notes that:

> Wesley was willing to be labeled an "improper enthusiast," which to him meant that he was not an enthusiast at all. Against his accusers Wesley asserted that he had joined experiential religion and sound reasoning. Even the enthusiastic excesses of some of his preachers failed to convince Wesley that there was any validity to the accusations of the Anglicans.[31]

Wesley argued that if he and his followers were truly enthusiasts, then their doctrine would eventually prove fallacious. In his mind, his doctrine was sound, because he had never been refuted. This reinforced his belief that he was not a bona fide enthusiast.[32] This is not to say that Wesley agreed with the way many of his critics defined enthusiasm. For example, he declared that it is not enthusiasm to love God with our whole hearts.[33] Moreover, experiencing happiness as a part of fulfilling the love commandments cannot reasonably be regarded as enthusiasm, for it is a central part of vital Christianity.[34] Rather than dispute trivial matters, as these critics often did, Christians should focus on what is really important.

> I will not quarrel with you about any *opinion*. Only see that your heart be right toward God, that you know and love the Lord Jesus Christ, that you love your neighbor and walk as your Master walked, and I desire no more. I am sick of opinions; I am weary to hear them. My soul loathes this frothy food. Give

---

29. Matthews, "Religion and Reason Joined," 369–70.

30. Wesley, "A Farther Appeal to Men of Reason and Religion, Part I," §5.31, WW, 11:175 [J 8:110].

31. Gunter, *The Limits of "Love Divine*," 271.

32. Wesley, "A Farther Appeal to Men of Reason and Religion, Part I," §5.32, WW, 11:176 [J 8:111].

33. Wesley, "A Farther Appeal to Men of Reason and Religion, Part III," §1.10, WW, 11:277–78 [J 8:206].

34. Wesley, "A Farther Appeal to Men of Reason and Religion, Part II," §3.23, WW, 11:270 [J 8:199].

me solid and substantial religion. Give me an humble, gentle lover of God and man, a man full of mercy and good fruits, without partiality, and without hypocrisy, a man laying himself out in the work of faith, the patience of hope, the labor of love. Let my soul be with these Christians, wheresoever they are, and whatsoever opinion they are of. "Whosoever *thus* doeth the will of my Father which is in heaven, the same is my brother, and sister, and mother."[35]

In other words, Wesley decided that he would not be hindered in pursuing holy affections short of being disproven by Scripture. He did not try to make others conform to his preferences, and he expected to be given the same latitude. "But as to all opinions which do not strike at the root of Christianity, we think and let think."[36]

It is important to note that Wesley tempered his views on assurance over time. Early on, he believed that unless one had divine assurance, one was not a genuine Christian.[37] He later started speaking of degrees of faith and assurance, and he came to believe that while assurance is possible, it is not necessary for justifying faith. As Maddox observes,

> In short, the mature Wesley rejected his immediate post-Aldersgate assumption of an absolute connection between being the recipient of God's pardoning grace and having a clear assurance of that pardon. He allowed for broader variability in the manner that the Holy Spirit effects justification in individuals.[38]

Gunter adds that Wesley's brother Charles had an influence on him in this regard. Charles was less tolerant of emotional outbursts from people, because he was rather skeptical as to their authenticity. He had a gradual influence on John, and the amount of hysterical demonstration began to diminish. Rather than emphasize a conversion experience as a sign of divine grace, Charles believed that the desire to seek God itself is an indication of grace at work.

Matthews suggests that for Wesley, knowledge of God is just as "reasonable" as knowledge of the natural world.

---

35. Wesley, "A Farther Appeal to Men of Reason and Religion, Part III," §4.10, *WW*, 11:321 [J 8:244].
36. Wesley, "The Character of a Methodist," §1, *WW*, 9:34 [J 8:340].
37. Wesley, Sermon 2, "The Almost Christian," §2.5, *WW*, 1:139 [J 5:23].
38. Maddox, *Responsible Grace*, 126–27.

> In either case knowledge results from the application of the faculty of reason, in its three-fold functioning, to the data of sensory experience. Consequently Wesley could claim that his doctrine of assurance does not, in fact, amount to "enthusiasm," because it agrees with both parts of Locke's definition: the truth so embraced is, in Wesley's view, both "consonant to the *revelation* in the written word of God," and "conformable to the dictates of right *reason*."[39]

According to Wallace Gray, emotion is not the most significant element of assurance for Wesley. Rather, emotion accompanies it.[40] In the final analysis, religious experience for Wesley is rooted in the knowledge of God given in Scripture and in self-knowledge. Its primary function is not instructional, but motivational. As such, its epistemic function is to reaffirm what is known and confirmed by natural means.

It is my contention that Wesley should be judged more by his own life and less by what he permitted in pastoral practice. Some may be uncomfortable with Wesley's emphasis on experiential religion, but he should not be faulted for this, since this is what ultimately brought him inner peace.[41] Even Ronald Knox admits that although Wesley may have been sympathetic with "enthusiasm," he never got carried away with it himself.[42] He was overly harsh and scrupulous with himself, but very tolerant of others. Indeed, he initially gave too much weight to individual professions, and this is evidenced in the way that he eventually modified his views.[43] Furthermore, he did not want to see the Methodist revival stray toward enthusiasm either. As Todd indicates, Wesley "did not want the mystical utterances of his followers disseminated."[44]

Henry Knight concludes that Wesley ultimately sought a mediating position between formalism, which tends toward forgetting God, and enthusiasm, which leads to self-deception.[45] According to Franz Hildebrandt, there is an early picture of Wesley in Nicolson Square

---

39. Matthews, "Reason and Religion Joined," 370.
40. Gray, "Place of Reason," 191.
41. Gunter, *The Limits of "Love Divine*," 276.
42. Knox, *Enthusiasm*, 451–52.
43. Miley, *Systematic Theology*, 2:361.
44. Todd, *Wesley and the Catholic Church*, 129–31.
45. Knight, *Presence of God*, 47.

Church, Edinburgh, under which is a quote attributed to Wesley that captures this sentiment:

> Preach our doctrine, inculcate experience, urge practice, enforce discipline. If you preach doctrine only, the people will be antinomians; if you preach experience only, they will become enthusiasts; if you preach practice only, they will become Pharisees; and if you preach all of these and do not enforce discipline, Methodism will be like a highly cultivated garden without a fence, exposed to the ravages of the wild boar of the forest.[46]

Empiricism and Subjectivity

At this point, it will be useful to review the basic principles of Wesley's epistemology in order to reiterate the point that for him, reason is able to give knowledge an objective basis, even though it is ultimately rooted in subjective experience. In empiricism, knowledge is based on experience, and although this involves a subjective element of perception, this aspect of empirical observation can be objectified to a great extent.

We should recall that reason for Wesley has three functions: (1) apprehension, (2) judgment, and (3) discourse. As such, reason must ultimately be rooted in some type of experience, i.e., "apprehension." For both Wesley and Locke, knowledge is ultimately the product of rational discourse about experience. In other words, experience only provides sensations. Knowledge is produced after experience is interpreted by reason.

Of course, reason can also produce speculative knowledge, either by formulating analytic truths or by engaging in theoretical reflection regarding experience. This suggests that experience could be said to also include impressions made upon the mind. In general, this can be attributed to the workings of reason itself. However, Wesley also believes that God can and often does communicate with us by placing impressions on our minds, yet this is perhaps the most subjective type of experience and thus needs to be objectified. This illustrates the fact that speculative knowledge, when it is not based on logical necessity, is generally not as reliable as practical knowledge, since it is further removed from empirical data. Consequently, subjective experiences like the direct witness of the Spirit must be reinforced by the empirical witness of conscience.

46. Quoted in Williams, *Wesley's Theology Today*, 36.

Consequently, as long as the senses can be trusted, experience itself cannot be regarded as "false." Rather, the interpretation of experience can be true or false, and this determines the truth value of the knowledge it produces. For example, the "enthusiasts" were not criticized for having particular impressions or feelings. Rather, they were criticized for the interpretations they gave these experiences, i.e., they were criticized for mistaking their own imaginations for the voice of God. In the final analysis, the integrity of knowledge is directly dependent on reason. False beliefs cannot be attributed merely to the subjectivity of experience, but rather to wrong reasoning. This is why Wesley was quick to attribute Locke's "nominalism" to a neglect of logic.

As we have already seen, Wesley strongly objects to mystical claims of divinely imparted knowledge. Such claims can only be scrutinized by their logical consistency with present knowledge. Otherwise, they are invulnerable to criticism. Indeed, Wesley is very reluctant to lend credence to claims that are both unfalsifiable and uncorroborated by acceptable evidence, and yet he is willing to consider propositions that meet at least one of these criteria. For instance, although the resurrection of Christ is apparently unfalsifiable, it is corroborated by Scripture and tradition, so Wesley accepts it as true. Locke is not nearly as willing to accept such testimony.[47] Conversely, if a person claims to experience the new birth and receive the witness of the Spirit, others may not be able to corroborate the person's sincerity. However, Wesley and Edwards both believe that this claim is falsifiable, because a genuine conversion will bring about particular effects in the person's life that can be scrutinized. As such, Wesley says that if the person is trustworthy, then the testimony can be accepted so long as the claim is not falsified.

Wesley thus asserts the criteria of "the law and the testimony" (i.e., Scripture and Christian tradition) to prevent the subjectivity engendered by Locke's type of nominalism. Again, this supports my proposition that experience for Wesley is subject to the scrutiny of Scripture, tradition, and reason. In the end, making experience accountable to

---

47. Of course, producing the remains of Jesus of Nazareth would indeed falsify claims of his resurrection. However, even if the supposed remains of Jesus were discovered, there would most likely be some room for doubt concerning their authenticity. Consequently, the claim that Jesus rose from the dead can apparently only be validated or falsified through testimony. This testimony is foundational to both Scripture and tradition, and although Wesley regards it as reliable, Locke does not.

these criteria allows it to be evaluated and greatly reduces its degree of subjectivity.

To summarize, reason can objectify experiential knowledge to a significant degree. Experiences should be interpreted within the context of other experiences. In turn, the interpretation of experience is subject to logic. Furthermore, the interpretation of experience must either be corroborated by reliable evidence or be falsifiable. Optimally, it should meet both criteria.

Abandoning the Spiritual Sense Analogy

In the second chapter, I argued that the spiritual sense analogy should be discarded for several reasons. First, it does not coincide with Wesley's fundamental definition of faith. He maintains that faith is both assent and trust, and not only are both of these founded on cognitive content, neither of them suggests the need for a spiritual sense. Second, analogies such as the spiritual sense rely on intuition, and I will argue a little later that intuitionism is incompatible with the Wesleyan ethical paradigm I am constructing. Wesley and Edwards invoked this analogy in their attempt to explain how cognition is affected in conversion. Today, what is needed is a more sophisticated understanding of religious conversion, not an analogy that creates false dichotomies.

Furthermore, Wesley's own intellectual milieu is incongruent with the spiritual sense analogy. Locke and Browne both argue that knowledge of God is indirect and mediated. In fact, Browne contends that we receive no new faculties for the discernment of divine knowledge. He says that we only learn through our five senses and our reason, and this is true of our knowledge of God as well. To a certain extent, it is somewhat surprising that Wesley would invoke an analogy like the spiritual sense, for he regards moral knowledge as more cognitive than intuitive. It is only consistent to claim that the same should hold true for spiritual knowledge.

The Certainty of Assurance

Wesley recognizes the need for the direct witness of the Spirit to be validated by the indirect witness of conscience, and this can be accounted for in empirical terms. In other words, even though Wesley employs the analogy of the spiritual sense, he ultimately appeals to his empiricism in order to maintain epistemic certainty. Believing in a spiritual sense may grant momentary satisfaction, but it cannot provide assurance that has a significant amount of longevity. Rather than base the certainty of assurance on an analogy like the spiritual sense, the Wesleyan notion of certainty should remain true to Wesleyan epistemology, especially its commitment to empiricism. It is in this regard that Locke's and Browne's views on epistemic certainty are most informative.

John Culp feels that contemporary Wesleyan epistemology must have three themes. First, it must assert that knowledge of God is possible, including knowledge derived from experiencing God. Second, it must claim that knowledge is active, not passive, and this implies that we must direct and modify our perceptions of our experiences. Third, it must regard knowledge as more probable than certain.[48] This is a good synopsis, because it integrates Wesley's core epistemic concerns. Additionally, I believe that Wesleyan epistemology can affirm the possibility of attaining a significant degree of certainty in knowledge, just not absolute certainty. It should be remembered that Wesley adheres to a scale of assent, and this suggests that certainty can be attained in various degrees. Indeed, Wesley believes that all knowledge requires some degree of faith, for even scientific laws are mere descriptions of reality.[49]

According to Locke, all belief is supported by evidence. He proposes that there are three degrees of assent: (1) *assurance* is achieved when the experience of all other people constantly concurs with our experience; this approaches knowledge and is practically certain; (2) *confidence* results when our experience generally coincides with the experiences of many reliable witnesses; and (3) *unavoidable assent* is produced when we receive unsuspected testimony on an indifferent matter.[50] Locke asserts that "any testimony, the further off it is from the original truth, the less force and proof it has."[51]

Since Browne has a higher view of Scripture than Locke, his insights are all the more useful. He builds upon Locke, but since he is not as skeptical as Locke, he has a broader epistemic base, especially with regard to Scripture. Browne's basic scheme regarding knowledge

---

48. Culp, "A Wesleyan Contribution," 260–61.
49. L. Wood, "Wesley's Epistemology," 53.
50. Locke, *Essay*, §§4.16.6–8, 2:375–76.
51. Ibid., §4.16.10, 2:377.

can be divided into two basic categories. Immediate knowledge consists of knowledge acquired from the senses and from self-consciousness. Mediate knowledge, i.e., that which is produced by reason, includes logical demonstration, moral certainty, opinion, and testimony.[52] The category most relevant to this discussion is moral certainty. Taking a brief look at Browne's comparison between logical demonstration and moral certainty is perhaps the easiest way to determine the boundaries and thresholds of moral certainty.

In logical demonstration, the intellect is compelled to assent, because the evidence that supports it is "infallible." In contrast, assent is not compelled in moral certainty, but its evidence is still "indubitable." In this case, the will can promote or obstruct assent, and this leaves room for "passion and prejudice" to influence moral reasoning. Moreover, moral certainty "admits of several degrees of certainty." Whereas logical demonstration excludes faith, moral certainty requires it.[53] Consequently, those who reject the Christian faith because they demand the strictest proof are driven by their passions and prejudices to ignore the evidence that exists. This is especially true of those who otherwise accept natural morality or natural religion.[54]

Nevertheless, Browne avers that faith must be more than mere opinion, which he characterizes as "a medium between knowledge and ignorance," being comprised of both. Hence, "mere opinion cannot arise from sensation, self-consciousness, logical demonstration, moral certainty, or sufficient testimony" (human or divine), because it is not based solely on knowledge, but also on imagination. As such, opinion can vary in probability, so it leaves room for varying degrees of doubt. In contrast, moral certainty leaves no reasonable doubt.[55] Mere opinion cannot be a foundation for faith, because it is not "clear and certain" knowledge.[56]

To recapitulate, moral certainty is supported by "indubitable" evidence. This does not compel assent, but allows for several degrees of certainty. For this reason, it requires faith, but this must be more than

52. Winnett, *Peter Browne*, 114.
53. Browne, *Limits of Human Understanding*, 232–40.
54. Ibid., 248–51.
55. Ibid., 264–65.
56. Ibid., 270–71.

mere opinion. In the end, moral certainty leaves no room for reasonable doubt, and this seems to be a rather balanced approach to empiricism, one that can be applied to assurance and one that has been endorsed by a number of thinkers. For instance, William James states that the empirical method does not necessarily lead to skepticism. It simply requires that we be liable to correction and only claim reasonable probability for our conclusions, rather than absolute certainty.[57] John Miley, Methodist theologian of the late nineteenth century, likewise asserts that assurance itself is not absolute, but occurs in degrees.[58] Edwards also admits that there is a great difference in the degree of hope and satisfaction that new converts have.[59]

There must be some type of certainty in Wesleyan assurance. Since Wesleyan ethics believes in the possibility of apostasy, it cannot claim that we can be certain of our perseverance in salvation. However, we can be rather certain of our present state, and this provides a basis for assurance. This will be sketched out in the final chapter.

Scripture Retained as an Authoritative Source of Moral Knowledge

Taking a more cognitivist approach to Wesleyan ethics will give greater authority to reason. During the Enlightenment, this type of emphasis generally eroded the authority of Scripture, and this is why many people are averse to systems of religion that incorporate elements of Enlightenment thought. However, I believe that the Wesleyan paradigm I am proposing can maintain the authority of Scripture without resorting to skepticism or fideism.

At the time of Wesley, the freethinkers believed that true, primitive Christianity had been turned into superstition, but they also felt that the philosophers had preserved the true religion of nature.[60] Similarly, Hume did not see his attack on religion as a threat to morality. Rather, he saw religious superstition and enthusiasm as the real threat.[61] The vast majority of the opponents of enthusiasm wanted to exclude

57. James, *Varieties of Religious Experience*, 364.
58. Miley, *Systematic Theology*, 2:351–52.
59. Edwards, NSC, §2, 48.
60. Rivers, *Reason, Grace, and Sentiment*, 2:51.
61. Ibid., 328.

modern claims to new inspiration and yet retain the claims of the ancient prophets and apostles.[62] Locke was sympathetic with this project. He trusted divine revelation, but he felt that we must be sure that we are properly identifying and understanding divine revelation.

> Only we must be sure that it be a divine revelation, and that we understand it right, else we shall expose ourselves to all the extravagancy of enthusiasm and all the error of wrong principles if we have faith and assurance in what is not divine revelation. And therefore, in those cases, our assent can be rationally no higher than the evidence of its being a revelation and that this is the meaning of the expressions it is delivered in.[63]

A number of scholars have noted the way that the Enlightenment tended to erode Scriptural authority. For example, Adam Seligman asserts,

> Pascal's wager of the seventeenth century, of reason for faith, was replaced in the eighteenth century by a wager over the terms of sacrality . . . we have eschewed any idea of the revealed truth of a transcendent Being in favor of "self-evident" truths, thought to be as amenable to reason as the principles of Euclidian geometry.[64]

He refers to this as "modernity's wager." He continues,

> As society secularized, religion retreated from the public domain, reduced its claims on the public sphere, and became more and more a matter of the congregant's internal value disposition—with the result of a concomitant growth in tolerance of other faiths. But pluralism and tolerance seem to hold only as long as religion is privatized.[65]

Seligman argues that the Kantian emphasis on intentionality located morality itself within the individual, and this led to shifting the source of moral authority to the individual as well.[66]

---

62. Beiser, *Sovereignty of Reason*, 186.
63. Locke, *Essay*, §4.16.14, 2:383.
64. Seligman, *Modernity's Wager*, 12.
65. Ibid., 13.
66. Ibid., 42–43.

> Morality and moral authority came to be founded on the dialectic of reason, inherent in but (as yet) transcending individual conscience. The governing principle of sociability became the autonomous moral subject constituted by transcendental reason and united by compacts or contracts.[67]

Protestantism initially emphasized the justification of the individual solely by transcendent grace, but "with secularization, the transcendent referent was replaced by a transcendental one, rooted in the workings of human reason and no longer dependent on divine grace."[68] Seligman concludes that we need to counter these corrosive influences by retaining an authoritative source of the sacred as well as the idea of the self as relational, situated within a particular community.[69]

Frederick Beiser offers a similar analysis. He suggests that the seventeenth-century philosophers merely established that we have "a right to ask the reasons for the truth of Scripture, tradition, or inspiration," but this was enough to make reason the ultimate authority. There was an attempt to find universal standards of morality, but this ultimately failed. The failure of universal morality thus anticipated postmodern skepticism. The main defense against such skepticism was to assert that epistemic certainty varies, depending upon the nature of the belief in question. An appeal was made to pragmatism, but this led to relativism, since this approach regards beliefs as only means, not as ends. Another appeal was made to universal principles in human nature, but since human sentiments seem to vary with culture, this attempt was also unsatisfactory.[70]

There is no easy solution to this dilemma, and although I do not pretend to offer a superior alternative, I do believe that there is a Wesleyan response to this particular problem. According to William Abraham, Wesley himself struggled with this dilemma.

> In the manner of Aquinas and in contrast to the approaches adopted more recently by Kierkegaard and Barth, Wesley engaged in a whirlwind of apologetic arguments appealing to reason and experience. He insisted that there be arguments for the proper identification of divine revelation, so he offered various

---

67. Ibid., 115.
68. Ibid.
69. Ibid., 119.
70. Beiser, *Sovereignty of Reason*, 323–62.

proofs for the divine inspiration of Scripture. What this means is that beneath his theological foundationalism he was forced to appeal to inference and experience to get the whole operation off the ground. Hence there was the constant danger that revelation would be displaced by reason and experience. After all, revelation now rested on inference and experience, hence it was essentially secondary. Moreover, once revelation was allowed to be confirmed by reason and experience, there was the constant danger that revelation would be displaced all over again from a different direction. It was as if revelation was being eaten away both from below and from above at the same time; divine revelation was like a mountain being undermined from the bottom and eroded from the top.[71]

Abraham believes that the Wesleyan tradition thus needs a more contemporary account of knowledge of God, but one different from the Reformed view.

> However that account is played out, it must, if it is to be recognizably Wesleyan, exploit the epistemic significance of conversion, taking that in a rounded sense as the work of God in the human heart and soul. It must also find room for a robust account of special divine revelation that is intimately related to Scripture.[72]

Wesley upholds the authority of Scripture as an act of faith. However, this is neither skepticism nor fideism. On one hand, it does not require logical certainty. On the other hand, it requires a view of divine revelation with a certain level of sophistication. I believe that it requires a certainty akin to Browne's moral certainty. We cannot prove the truth of Scripture from logical necessity, neither can we verify with the certainty of empirical science the belief that Scripture is divinely inspired. Nevertheless, reason, tradition, and experience together offer numerous reasons for regarding these claims as reliable. As we have already observed, Wesley recognizes a certain logic in Scripture, and this gives him confidence that Scripture can withstand scrutiny.

The authority of Scripture is foundational in a Wesleyan paradigm. For Wesley, true virtue must have reference to God and must ultimately be motivated by love for God. However, we cannot love God without

---

71. Abraham, "The Epistemology of Conversion," 180.
72. Ibid., 190.

knowledge of God, and this requires special revelation. Nonetheless, Wesley insists that it is "rank enthusiasm" to insist that Scripture should be our only source of knowledge.[73] As Abraham indicates, these other sources of authority should be regarded as norms "not for the truth of Scripture, but for the right interpretation of the truth given by God in Scripture. This is a much cleaner and simpler analysis of Wesley" than has frequently been offered.[74]

Robert Chiles feels that the attempt to relieve the tension between revelation and reason is what caused Scripture to be subjected to external validation.[75] I contend that this tension should not be relieved, because it is a vital part of Wesleyan epistemology. Scripture can be upheld as the authoritative source for moral knowledge, but this does not mean that it cannot be scrutinized at all. Rather, Locke's claim that we must determine what is to be regarded as divine revelation is valid, for that is precisely what takes place in canonization. However, Wesleyan epistemology cannot be as skeptical as Locke in accepting the canon of Scripture. Wesley asserts the "law and the testimony" as our rule of faith and conduct, and this requires a certain amount of trust in the authority of Scripture. At the same time, this trust is supported by the witness of Christian tradition. The tension between reason and revelation exists because Scripture must be properly identified and interpreted, as Locke suggests, but then reason must in turn be subjected to the authority of Scripture, and Locke is less willing to do this than is Wesley.

A More Naturalized Interpretation of Grace

Wesley rejects mystical approaches to religion that neglect or disdain the use of natural means. This emphasis on the natural means of grace is indicative of his belief that God generally works through ordinary channels. Although Wesley believes that salvation begins with divine initiative, he still places great emphasis on human responsibility. As such, salvation itself should be viewed as a synergism initiated by God. Human beings must cooperate with God's grace in order to be saved from sin and damnation.

---

73. Wesley, "Minutes of Several Conversations between the Rev. Mr. Wesley and Others, 1744–1789," Q32, *WWJ*, 8:315.

74. Abraham, "John Wesley's Conception," 10–11.

75. Chiles, *Theological Transition*, 191–93.

For Wesley, the atonement of Christ avails the grace of God to all humanity in some degree, if only through prevenient grace. This fundamental type of grace fosters the preservation of society and draws us toward justifying grace. Prevenient grace is thus Wesley's way of explaining things like natural morality and natural conscience. If a more naturalized view of grace is adopted, Wesley's doctrine of prevenient grace will still serve an important role, but it will be less mystical, understood more in natural terms. For instance, conscience can be understood as being grounded in empirical self-knowledge, but this does not imply that God is not involved with conscience, nor does it suggest that conscience cannot be regarded as the indirect voice of God in the soul. In the final analysis, a Wesleyan view of grace teaches that the natural and the supernatural are not separate spheres. Rather, divine grace operates through natural channels.

Wesley's Rejection of Mysticism Recalled

In the previous chapter, Wesley's rejection of mysticism was described in detail. Although he sympathizes with the spiritual ideals and concerns of the mystics, he strongly opposes their neglect of the means of grace. Consequently, spirituality for Wesley involves the use of reason and natural means. In fact, Wesley believes that humanity's general neglect of reason can be attributed in large part to humanity's sinfulness.[76]

James enumerates four characteristics of mysticism: (1) ineffability, (2) supernaturally imparted knowledge, (3) transience, and (4) passivity.[77] From what we have seen, Wesley is opposed to each one of these traits, for he believes that true knowledge of God is understood in terms of Scripture, requires the active engagement of the mind, is mediated and confirmed through natural means (excepting the divine inspiration of Scripture), and produces a real change of character. However, Wesley would not concur with James' general critique of religious experience. James believes that religion is merely subjective and that theology is formulated for the purpose of validating religious experience. He simply regards mysticism as the worst case since it cannot be scrutinized.[78] This reflects a certain bias in James' thought. Essentially,

---

76. Gray, "Place of Reason," 109.
77. James, *Varieties of Religious Experience*, 414–15.
78. Ibid., 470.

he ignores the fact that our religious beliefs shape our perceptions of our religious experiences.[79]

James takes an easy way out, resorting to skepticism and regarding religious experience as wholly subjective. In contrast, Wesley and Edwards affirm the centrality of religious experience, but they are aware of its epistemic limitations. Unlike James, they see the role that cognition plays in religious experience, and this provides them with a basis for objectifying its subjective element. On the other hand, Wesley and Edwards are unwilling to embrace mystical notions of spiritual knowledge, for they know that such subjectivity has no epistemic value.

Stressing Human Responsibility

Maddox prefers to characterize Wesley's understanding of grace as "responsible grace" because he sees grace as enabling us to respond to more grace, making us ultimately responsible for ourselves.[80] He says that this emphasis is "an abiding orienting concern" that guides Wesley's theology.[81] According to Wesley himself, to say that God's grace is at work in us implies not only that we are able to work out our own salvation, it also implies that we are obligated to do so in response to God's action.[82] As we saw earlier, even solitude (i.e., time spent alone with God) should not be pursued at the expense of good works, for God expects us to be actively expressing our love for him and for others. For Wesley, the stress on human responsibility and duty does not impugn God's governance of the world, for in "true predestination . . . promise and duty go hand in hand."[83]

Mildred Bangs Wynkoop opposes the model of instantaneous supernatural change that has often been embraced by the Wesleyan traditions. She contends that it cannot be the case that the Holy Spirit changes our sinful impulses at a sub-conscious level because that suggests (1) the possibility that all impulse toward sin can be removed, but this would essentially end free will as Wesley understood it; and (2) the

---

79. Proudfoot, "From Theology to a Science," 165.
80. Maddox, *Responsible Grace*, 92.
81. Ibid., 254.
82. Wesley, Sermon 85, "On Working Out Our Own Salvation," §3.2, WW, 3:206 [J 6:511].
83. Wesley, *NNT*, I Pet 1:2.

impossibility of changing our impulses at the level of consciousness.[84] Rather, she suggests,

> When God's grace begins to operate upon the person, it is at this point of moral responsibility. Grace awakens into sharp awareness everything that *moral* means. Both persons, God and Man, confronting each other, maintain personal integrity. Neither is merged into the other, nor is identity submerged in an irrational shadowland. The coming of the Spirit does not occasion an eclipse of human rationality and consciousness.[85]

Stressing human responsibility within the operation of divine grace also underscores the fact that God deals with each of us according to our abilities and capacities. For instance, Culp points out that overlooking the human involvement in sanctification and focusing only on divine activity leads to excessive claims and ignores the fact that individuals will possess and express perfect love in different ways.[86] The goal of divine grace is to transform us so that we might conform to the image of God. We must be involved in our own transformation and pursue the means that are best suited to that end.

Salvation as Synergism

Consequently, a Wesleyan view of salvation must be synergistic, because it teaches that divine grace anticipates a human response. In general, theology always seeks to define the dividing line between divine and human activity. Every theology (or system of religion) runs the risk of setting the dividing line improperly. For example, both Locke and Kant emphasize human responsibility, but they limit God to the role of providing divine aid to supplement our human efforts. As such, their notion of divine grace is more limited than Wesley's, and they approach religion from an anthropological perspective, rather than from a theological one. In contrast, Edwards' predestinationism leads him to maintain God's sovereignty in salvation to such an extent that human beings have no control in the matter. The elect will inevitably respond to God's irresistible grace, but the reprobate will be damned beyond all hope.

---

84. Wynkoop, *Theology of Love*, 216.
85. Ibid., 220.
86. Culp, "Supernatural and Sanctification," 161.

Wesleyan theology attempts to strike more of a balance between divine and human activity. Salvation begins with God's initiative, and this is what enables human response. Divine action does not obviate human responsibility; neither does it override human freedom. As Thomas Oden affirms, the will is not remade through coercion, but through gradual persuasion.[87] For Wesley, divine grace enables human freedom, and this is the source of human responsibility. Hence, Wesley's doctrine of grace is more theological than that of Locke and Kant. On the other hand, it is more naturalistic than Edwards' view of grace.

Is Prevenient Grace Superfluous?

Since a more naturalized view of grace is being proposed for Wesleyan ethics, it is valid to ask whether or not such a shift will obviate Wesley's doctrine of prevenient grace, since that is the way that he explains how human beings have some basic goodness in spite of their depravity. I believe that this doctrine is necessary in any type of Wesleyan theological framework, but it will not have the same function in a more naturalized construal of grace.

The doctrine of prevenient grace offered Wesley a way to retain the reformed doctrine of total depravity while maintaining free will, natural conscience, and natural morality. In David Bennett's opinion, although Wesley is indeed an Arminian, his emphasis on the corruption of human nature places him close enough to Calvin to almost be regarded as a Calvinist by contemporary Arminians.[88] Leo Cox feels that the Wesleyan doctrine of prevenient grace is much like the Calvinistic doctrine of common grace, except prevenient grace prepares people for salvation and enables them to enter into it freely.[89] Although this may seem to overstate the case, this assessment is not much different from the way that Wesley viewed himself in this regard.

> Q. 22. Does not the truth of the gospel lie very near both to Calvinism and Antinomianism?
>
> A. Indeed it does, as it were, within a hair's breadth, so that it is altogether foolish and sinful, because we do not quite agree either with one or the other, to run from them as far as ever we can.

---

87. Oden, *Transforming Power*, 96.
88. Bennett, "How Arminian was John Wesley?" 248.
89. Cox, "Prevenient Grace," 144.

Q. 23 Wherein may we come to the very edge of Calvinism?
A.   (1.) In ascribing all good to the free grace of God, (2.) In denying all natural free-will and all power antecedent to grace, and (3.) In excluding all merit from man, even for what he has or does by the grace of God.

Q. 24. Wherein may we come to the edge of Antinomianism?
A.   (1) In exalting the merits and love of Christ; (2.) In rejoicing evermore.[90]

Albert Knudson notes that the popularization of Arminian libertarianism can largely be attributed to Methodism.[91] As we have already seen, Wesley agreed with Edwards that the affections determine the will, but he upheld a libertarian account of will, retaining the separate faculty of will from the Aristotelian model and simply calling it "freedom." In the final analysis, the importance of the doctrine of prevenient grace in Wesley's general system of thought is unmistakable. As Elton Hendricks states,

> No other Protestant theologian has given to Prevenient Grace the important role assigned by Wesley. It was the means by which he maintained a Reformation-like depravity without losing the concept of free will; it is also the means by which he avoided advocating a "works righteousness" without falling prey to an irresistible grace and election. Man as the object of prevenient grace has had restored to him many of the capacities lost in the Fall.[92]

Nevertheless, it seems that there is some disparity between Wesley's claim that God uses natural means to accomplish his purposes and the highly supernatural account of free will, natural conscience, and natural morality that is characteristic of his doctrine of prevenient grace. I believe that the problem does not lie in Wesley's doctrine of grace, but in the Reformed doctrine of total depravity. That is to say, the doctrine of total depravity is not compatible with Wesley's general doctrine of grace. As a result, Wesley's doctrine of prevenient grace is cast in terms emphasizing the supernatural in order to reconcile Wesley's libertarianism with total depravity. It seems that if the doctrine of total depravity

---

90. Wesley, "Minutes of Some Late Conversations between the Rev. Mr. Wesley and Others," Conversation II, 2 August 1745, QQ. 22–24, *WWJ*, 8:284–85.

91. Knudson, *Doctrine of Redemption*, 142.

92. Hendricks, "Wesley and Natural Theology," 11.

were relinquished, free will, natural conscience, and natural morality could be explained in more naturalistic terms, and this would yield a doctrine of prevenient grace that is likewise more naturalized and more consistent with Wesley's general doctrine of grace.

Explaining free will is perhaps the most difficult of the three. For example, Kant believes that transcendental freedom can be described, but it cannot be explained beyond its existence.[93] For Kant, moral autonomy is thus an "ideal conception," one that must be assumed for practical purposes.[94] Likewise, freedom must be presupposed if we are to regard ourselves as rational beings.[95] Without true freedom, obligation would have no meaning for Kant.[96] In this regard, moral obligation is a concomitant of our rationality, since rationality is the basis of freedom.[97] This is why Kant grounds morality in reason itself. Morality requires freedom, and our freedom comes from our rationality. The freedom which morality requires is freedom in the greatest sense of the word, for it is a transcendental, libertarian type of freedom.[98] This is what brings Patrick Riley to the conclusion that,

> Ultimately there is only *one* will in Kant: the consciousness of a capacity to be an uncaused cause; but this will will [sic.] be free in a "positive" sense (of conformity to reason) only when it goes beyond mere freedom from causality to self-determination through reason.[99]

Locke and Wesley agree that the nature of morality presupposes that the will is free.[100] Moreover, we must recall that for Locke too, free will comes from our ability to reason. This is especially true with respect to our ability to ascertain the greatest good, because such is what ultimately determines the will. However, this concept of freedom is different from Kant's concept of transcendental freedom. J. B. Schneewind thus criticizes Kant for providing a new view of morality.

---

93. Guevara, *Kant's Theory of Moral Motivation*, 81.
94. Willey, *English Moralists*, 299.
95. Kant, *GMM*, 50 [4:447–48].
96. Cragg, *The Church and the Age of Reason*, 252.
97. Kemp, *Reason, Action, and Morality*, 66.
98. Guevara, *Kant's Theory of Moral Motivation*, 41 n. 21.
99. Riley, "Kant on Will," 121.
100. Dreyer, "Faith and Experience," 22.

> The new outlook that emerged by the end of the eighteenth century centered on the belief that all normal individuals are equally able to live together in a morality of self-governance. All of us, on this view, have an equal ability to see for ourselves what morality calls for and are in principle equally able to move ourselves to act accordingly, regardless of threats or rewards from others.[101]

Indeed, Locke's understanding of freedom is preferable, because it allows for degrees of freedom. For Locke, freedom is the result of rationality, but since people have varying degrees of reasoning power, it follows that people will consequently have varying degrees of freedom. Moreover, the Lockean account of freedom is not transcendental, but empirical. As such, it affirms that threats and rewards are necessary for morality, because our empirical nature cannot be ignored.

Natural conscience can also be explained in more natural terms. In fact, although Wesley defines conscience in terms of grace, he explains the inner workings of conscience in natural terms. Conscience can still be regarded as the vehicle through which the Holy Spirit speaks to us, but this does not imply that the Holy Spirit provides superadded knowledge. Oden suggests that conscience is not an act of will, an emotion, or the direct voice of God.

> Rather, God speaks indirectly through conscience, which is the moral self-awareness that accompanies consciousness even amid myriad variables of cultural conditioning. Whatever one's acculturation, God the Spirit meets each one in the depths of moral self-awareness and there alone challenges each individually to truthful disclosures.[102]

In the next chapter, I will explore more fully the possibility of situating a more naturalistic account of conscience in Wesleyan ethics.

Finally, natural morality can likewise be explained without making such a strong appeal to supernaturalism. Oden believes that it is an overstatement to say that unbelievers can only sin or are completely lacking in virtue or "grace-enabled goodness."[103] Sociobiology teaches that humans are predisposed toward selfishness, yet we still have

---

101. Schneewind, *Invention of Autonomy*, 4.
102. Oden, *Transforming Power*, 72.
103. Ibid., 101–2.

tendencies toward altruism. Stephen Pope has constructed an account of love (and human nature) that he feels is needed in contemporary Catholic theology. His account seeks to reconcile sociobiology with the thought of Thomas Aquinas.[104] I believe that a similar reconciliation can be made with Wesley's thought, and this is certainly a worthwhile project for the future.

In effect, Wesley emphasized the doctrine of depravity to such an extent that he had to counter it with a strongly supernatural doctrine of prevenient grace. If we were to relinquish the notion that human beings are *utterly* depraved with no vestige of natural goodness left after the fall, much of what Wesley accounted for through prevenient grace could be explained in natural terms. Nevertheless, even though relinquishing the doctrine of total depravity will yield a more naturalized version of prevenient grace, the doctrine of prevenient grace will still be needed in several respects.

First, prevenient grace is Wesley's way of emphasizing the loving extension of God's grace to all people. In other words, it asserts that grace is freely offered to both the sinner and the saint. Second, the doctrine of prevenient grace is necessary for stressing God's initiative in salvation. We do not take the first step, but we are enabled to respond and come to experience deeper levels of God's grace. Third, God's mercy is extended to children and to those who otherwise cannot be held morally accountable, and we refer to this as prevenient grace. Fourth, prevenient grace also signifies the various ways that God subtly influences the unregenerate. Without violating free will, God draws sinners away from evil and toward goodness, and this helps to preserve society and minimize its corruption. Whenever the gospel is presented to unregenerate persons, the Holy Spirit gently invites them to repent and be converted. In summary, the doctrine of prevenient grace should not be used as a metaphysical reinterpretation of things that can be explained in natural terms, but it still remains a vital part of Wesley's general doctrine of grace and theological framework because it describes God's interaction with the unregenerate.

---

104. Pope, *Evolution of Altruism and the Ordering of Love*.

Supernatural Activity in the Natural Realm

As I have repeatedly stated, a key claim in Wesley's doctrine of grace is that even though God is not limited in the way that he relates to humanity, he still generally operates through natural means. Dean Blevins states that for Wesley, grace is manifested through holiness of heart and life. Since this can occur in a variety of ways, a number of practices could be regarded as means of grace.[105] Wesley refers to these as "prudential means" of grace, and they "reflect God's ability to use any means, in addition to those instituted [by Scripture], in accordance with different times and circumstances."[106] Wesley considers specific practices as prudential means of grace if they tend toward holiness of heart and life, mediating prevenient, justifying, or sanctifying grace. Redemptive grace can be either individual or social, so the means of grace can be focused on either or both of these ends.[107] Ole Borgen concurs with this assessment: "Whatever is conducive to holiness and love becomes, to that extent, a means of grace."[108] In the means of grace, the participant gains new self-knowledge and knowledge of God. It is logical to assume that God is active in this process of learning in some fashion.[109]

Consistent with his opposition to mystical, superadded knowledge, Wesley is a staunch advocate of education and intellectual inquiry. Indeed, Wesley was interested in philosophy and science so long as they did not contradict Scripture.[110] Moreover, he had no real concern about potential conflicts between science and the Bible.[111] For instance, many people of Wesley's day believed lightning to be an expression of God's anger, so they were disturbed by Franklin's discovery of electricity. In contrast, Wesley did not view the discovery as a threat to his belief in the supernatural. In fact, he conducted his own experiments using electricity.[112]

---

105. Blevins, "John Wesley and the Means of Grace," 287.
106. Blevins, "Toward a Wesleyan Praxis," 79.
107. Blevins, "John Wesley and the Means of Grace," 345.
108. Borgen, *John Wesley on the Sacraments*, 105.
109. Blevins, "John Wesley and the Means of Grace," 278–79.
110. Gray, "Place of Reason," 95.
111. Ibid., 141.
112. Sweet, "John Wesley," 591–92.

To restate the matter, the real issue is the division of responsibility between God and human beings. Belief in the supernatural (and in supernatural activity) is a matter of faith (i.e., trust), so it can be neither proven nor disproven. Consequently, asserting that we can understand the natural means by which God operates does not deny God's involvement altogether. Wesley faulted Voltaire, Rousseau, and Hume for attempting to establish morality independent of special revelation and the concept of God.[113] In contrast, the earlier writings of William Law assert the invisible operation and assistance of the Holy Spirit but claim that we are unable to discern it. It is of little wonder that Wesley was attracted to these first works by Law but repelled by his later works, which represent a clear departure from this position.

Love as More than Passive Feelings

It is my contention that taking a more cognitivist approach will not necessarily commit Wesleyan ethics to some type of rationalism that devalues the role of emotion in moral reasoning. On the contrary, a cognitive approach will recognize the emotions as cognitively rooted. Furthermore, since emotions have a cognitive core, they can be controlled and shaped within certain limits. Viewing the emotions as cognitively based also suggests that they can be rationally scrutinized. Such an account of emotion is actually quite compatible with some current theories, and this will be briefly elaborated.

The Cognitive Core of Emotion

There are several contemporary theories of emotion that recognize its cognitive basis. Interestingly enough, Wesley's own view of emotion is much closer to these theories than it is to mystical accounts. I will note the way that contemporary theorists emphasize the role of cognition in emotion, then I will briefly comment on the import that this has for Wesleyan ethics.

Antonio Damasio suggests that neither reason nor emotion can be disassociated from biological regulation. In fact, feelings can only be fully understood in reference to biology and culture.[114] Richard and

---

113. Wesley, Sermon 120, "The Unity of the Divine Being," §§19–20, *WW*, 4:69 [J 7:271].

114. Damasio, *Descartes' Error*, 245–46.

Bernice Lazarus concur with this assessment. They indicate that emotions help us survive and flourish in three ways: (1) they give us strength in emergencies, (2) they help us cope with emergencies, and (3) they signal our state of mind to others.[115] However, the most significant thing to note is that both the arousal and control of our emotions are controlled by our reasoning.[116] The better we understand the rationality of our emotions, the more we can trust them and the more we will learn about ourselves, even the way our reasoning functions.[117] Along these same lines, Martha Nussbaum has recently argued that emotions should be regarded as "intelligent responses to the perception of value." As such, they must be considered a vital part of ethical reasoning.[118]

According to Ted Runyon, a Wesleyan emphasis on experience must be rooted in rationality.[119] This encompasses the whole of experience, even its emotional elements. This is what leads Gregory Clapper to assert that religious affections need not be understood as "supernatural and mystical infusions of the Spirit of God."[120] For Wesley, understanding gives us reasons for loving, i.e., it gives us an appreciation of the beloved. There is thus a reasonableness in loving others and living by the Golden Rule.[121] Wesley clearly asserts that God's love must be perceived as well. We must know that God loves us before we will be able to properly love him. In general, emotions are based upon presuppositions and apprehensions, whether they be true or false. Since these are all dependent on knowledge, it is beneficial to view the emotions cognitively.

Les Steele echoes these sentiments in his proposal for a Wesleyan approach to education. He claims that education has tended to bifurcate reason and emotion. As a result, there has been a repeated fluctuation between a transmission model and an experiential model of education. He asserts that affective development needs to be framed more cognitively. Moreover, Christian formation must be affective such that emotions are organized into an "orderly and motivating pattern," and the

---

115. Lazarus and Lazarus, *Passion and Reason*, 179.
116. Ibid., 199.
117. Ibid., 203–4.
118. Nussbaum, *Upheavals of Thought*, 1.
119. Runyon, "Orthopathy," 300.
120. Clapper, *Experience and Emotion*, 73.
121. Wesley, "An Earnest Appeal to Men of Reason and Religion," §21, WW, 11:52 [J 8:9].

affections must be "educated" so that this pattern can form character. Finally, discernment must be cultivated so that self-deception can be avoided. Steele concludes, "We must seek to treat the affections as true sources of knowing and to overcome the dichotomy of knowing as either objective or subjective." We must also understand the development of the affections.[122]

Controlling the Emotions

If the emotions can be regarded as cognitively based, then the aspiration to control one's emotions is not as lofty as it may seem. Earlier it was noted that Wesley admired de Renty and Gregory Lopez for their rational control over their own emotions. In contrast, Wesley faulted Hume and Lord Kames for espousing a fatalistic view of "tempers" (i.e., reasoned dispositions), a denunciation that is reminiscent of his criticism of Edwards.[123] For Locke, reason can shape the affections to a degree. Objects must be cognized regarding the pleasure or pain they will bring. In other words, they must be judged as good or bad, at least in a general sense. Hence, pleasure, pain, and reason are all necessary elements of motivation.

Clapper indicates that for Wesley, our freedom enables us to determine and makes us responsible for "the frame, the contents, the intentions of our heart. The shape of our heart rests on our own evaluations, judgments, and decisions." Moreover, since our impulses can be misguided, we must never suspend our judgment and rely solely on them.[124] The Wesleyan view of self recognizes the fact that we are shaped empirically, yet it contends that we are able to achieve some transcendence over our empirical selves through the self-determining power of reason. Wynkoop suggests that there is a part of our self-consciousness that "is not bound into the cause/effect matrix of the natural," enabling us to transcend mere naturalism. It is thus the freedom of self-determination that essentially makes us "spiritual" beings.[125]

---

122. L. Steele, "Educating the Heart," 230–34.

123. Wesley, Sermon 128, "On the Deceitfulness of the Human Heart," §3, *WW*, 4:151 [J 7:336].

124. Clapper, *John Wesley on Religious Affections*, 31.

125. Wynkoop, *Theology of Love*, 173.

In the previous chapter, we saw that Wesley believes that knowledge stabilizes the emotions. In fact, he claims that we can shape even our taste through reason and experience. Les Steele maintains that although we have involuntary feelings, our emotions can be shaped through knowledge. Our positive emotional states can be habituated into virtues (i.e., long-standing dispositions), and this shapes our emotions and gives them stability.[126] Viewing the emotions as controllable is pragmatic as well, since regarding the emotions as uncontrollable often leads to self-indulgence and impulsiveness. As Richard Steele expresses it,

> For by leading us to believe that our passions are irrational, involuntary, and episodic, it suggests that they are incorrigible, unmanageable, and outside the domain of either human control or divine command. If we believe this, we will see no point in learning how to tame or harness them, and we will have a ready-made excuse for self-indulgence and impulsiveness.[127]

Over a century ago, Miley insisted that moral agency must include power over one's motives and volitions.[128] In his mind, "The reflection and judgment upon end and impulse ... should precede any volition toward the end, and must precede it if life is to be conducted rationally."[129] In essence,

> We have no immediate power of volition to prevent or repress a motive state, but we have immediate power to defer any volition or deed toward its end. Then through reflection and judgment we may realize the motives of reason and conscience, and direct our life from them.[130]

Today, we can assert our ability to at least take steps toward the prevention of certain emotions and the cultivation of others, even though this control is limited. As Les Steele notes, self-control does not equal suppressing emotion. Rather, our emotions must be controlled by

---

126. L. Steele, "Educating the Heart," 228–29.
127. R. Steele, "The Passion," 248.
128. Miley, *Systematic Theology*, 2:290.
129. Ibid., 2:296.
130. Ibid., 2:301–2.

"the master passion of faith."[131] In a Wesleyan perspective, faith itself is cultivated through participation in the means of grace.[132]

Evaluating the Emotions

Along these same lines, we should be able to scrutinize the cognitive content of emotions and judge them accordingly. In the most basic sense, when we make progress toward our goals we experience positive emotions, but when we fail to progress toward our goals, negative emotions are the result.[133] Consequently, evaluating our goals and motivations is the first step in evaluating our emotions.

Runyon argues that a Wesleyan account of the emotions must transcend mere subjectivism.[134] It can only do this if the emotions are scrutinized by some type of objective criteria. We should recall that Wesley argued at length with Law concerning the necessity of using outward means in order to gauge the validity of our emotions.[135] Emotions must also be evaluated by a third party, and there must be accountability for them. It only stands to reason that we are accountable for our emotions to the extent that we can exert control over them.

It is crucial to evaluate our emotions, due to the fact that they play a vital role in morality itself. As Knudson surmises, "Feeling, and at times even ecstatic feeling, has its place in Christian experience. Instead of weakening a person's moral purpose, it may greatly reinforce it."[136] To be sure, Wesley and Edwards both believe that it is reasonable to experience strong feelings of love for God. It should be understood that emotions are not being discounted here, for they are at the heart of moral motivation. Indeed, their importance in morality is what makes the critical evaluation of them a moral imperative.

---

131. L. Steele, "Educating the Heart," 256–57.
132. Ibid., 264–65.
133. Lazarus and Lazarus, *Passion and Reason*, 214.
134. Runyon, "Orthopathy," 296–97.
135. Wesley to Law, 6 January 1756, §2.6, *WWJ*, 9:504.
136. Knudson, *Doctrine of Redemption*, 426.

Conclusion

Since the emotions can be evaluated and controlled to a significant degree, they need to be regarded as more than passive states of feeling. Hence, a mystical view of religious affection is unsuitable. Instead, Wesleyan ethics should adopt a more cognitivist approach to religious experience. This will actually heighten the amount of moral progress that can be achieved by individuals.

8

Incorporating Kantian Concepts

MY BASIC PROJECT HAS BEEN TO CONSTRUCT A MORE COGNITIVIST paradigm for Wesleyan virtue ethics. As I have indicated, I believe that the most basic way to locate Wesley intellectually is as a Lockean empiricist with strong Aristotelian commitments. As such, the type of development I am proposing will be facilitated by allowing Wesley's concepts to interact with later strands of thought that react in some way to the Lockean empiricism and Aristotelian scholasticism of Wesley's day. In my opinion, the best source for this type of critique is the thought of Kant, because it serves as a corrective to these traditions without abandoning their concerns altogether. In fact, I will argue that Kant and Wesley actually shared some of the same concerns, and yet they addressed these concerns in much different ways. This will offer some options for the development of Wesley's concepts.

Kant will thus prove to be a helpful resource in the construction of the new paradigm. This chapter will discuss the particular developments to Wesley's thought that can benefit from an engagement with Kant's concepts. First, I contend that it is no longer suitable to regard conscience as some type of intuition. Rather, conscience should be regarded as a product of practical reasoning. Second, as I suggested earlier, sin should be more broadly defined as the neglect of duty. One of the key advantages to this approach is that this broader definition will incorporate the notion of sins of omission, which Wesley had difficulty emphasizing within his own definition of sin. Third, expanding the Wesleyan definition of sin in this way will also place greater emphasis on the morality of actions in general and not merely focus on the purity of one's intentions. This has strong implications for the development of Wesley's doctrine of perfection, and Kant's own version of perfection will provide some interesting and helpful insights in that regard. Fourth, the new paradigm will also require a more cognitivist portrayal of moral action. I will propose that Kant's model of maxim-making can be helpful in this regard, and this coincides with my suggestion that conscience should be regarded as a type of practical reasoning.

Wesleyan Ethics Informed by Kantian Concepts

Thus far I have argued that Wesley's doctrines of assurance and Christian perfection have not, to an adequate extent, been developed intellectually. Rather, they have either been distorted or ignored altogether. I believe that an important factor in this scenario is the fact that some of Wesley's own terms and categories are not broad enough, or it is simply the case that Wesley himself does not nuance them enough. As such, the cognitivist paradigm that I am attempting to develop will need to be broader than Wesley's own conceptual framework.

What I am suggesting at this point is that a more cognitivist Wesleyan paradigm can take some of its cues from Kant. The ethical thought of Kant provides some concepts that can be adapted and incorporated into a Wesleyan paradigm. Kant and Wesley share some common concerns, and since Kant construes them in a different way than Wesley does, Kant's way of framing these issues suggests ways in which Wesley's concepts can be expanded. However, this expansion must be limited in particular ways if Wesley's theological and epistemic commitments are to be honored. Consequently, it will be necessary to examine these concepts in sufficient detail so that they can be properly nuanced without compromising Wesley's commitments or misrepresenting Kant's thought.

The Appropriateness of Kant in a Wesleyan Paradigm

At first glance, Wesley and Kant seem to be rather unlikely conversation partners. For one thing, although Kant published his critical works in the decade preceding Wesley's death, there is no evidence that they were familiar with one another whatsoever. In fact, it does not appear that even Locke's thought had a direct influence on Kant. However, Locke's religious views were received favorably in Germany at that time.[1] In

---

1. Fischer, "John Locke," 446.

addition, Kant and other popular German philosophers of his day were indeed interested in British empiricism and grappled with some of the issues they raised.[2] According to Lewis White Beck, Kant's historical position must be understood in relation to four strands of thought: (1) the rationalism of Leibniz and Wolff, (2) German "popular philosophy," (3) British psychological ethics, and (4) the philosophy of Rousseau.[3] Kant initially gravitated toward the moral sense theorists, but he later rejected the notion of a moral sense since it views moral knowledge as *a posteriori*.[4] He also distanced himself from this moral philosophy because he believed that much of it ultimately exalts self-love.[5]

Wesley and Kant were both raised in pietistic homes, but they later separated themselves from pietism. In Wesley's case, he not only gradually distanced himself from Pietists like the Moravians, he aligned himself with the Anglican moderates on a number of issues.[6] As far as Kant is concerned, although he was a rationalist, it can be argued that he never completely severed himself from his pietistic roots, intellectually speaking. However, he asserted that true pietism involves more than feelings. He defined piety as "moral conduct in accordance with the divine beneficent will."[7] Nevertheless, his ties to pietism were loose at best, for he also separated himself from traditional orthodox Christianity in key ways, reflected most sharply in the way that he sterilized many religious terms and themes. It should therefore be noted that when Kant uses language that is characteristic of Wesley's thought, he is not indicating quite the same thing as Wesley. Then again, I believe that there is enough overlap in meaning such that Kant's general concepts can be adapted to fit within a Wesleyan paradigm.

The Limits of Kant's Usefulness

Kantian concepts cannot be used unqualifiedly in Wesleyan ethics, because Kant's view of religion is vastly different from that of Wesley. In the first place, Kant makes religion subservient to morality. Indeed, he

2. Ibid., 442.
3. Beck, *Philosophy of Kant*, 6.
4. Ibid., 29.
5. Teale, *Kantian Ethics*, 14.
6. English, "Anglican Moderates," 205–16.
7. Kant, *LE*, 42.

claims that morality essentially has no need of religion, for it only requires pure practical reason.[8] Felicitas Munzel points out that although Kant does not need religion to define morality, it can still contribute to the moral progress of individuals. Religion not only provides the encouragement given by its moral exemplars, it also gives needed discipline to the individual through the constraint of conscience.[9] As such, religion plays an important role in the formation of a moral society.

Kant asserts that children should be instilled with a hate and a disgust for evil actions, starting at the earliest stages of infancy. Evil actions are to be abhorred not merely because they are punishable or harmful, but due to the fact that they are detestable in and of themselves.[10] Here is a good example of the way that Kant seems to presume that people will have a common conception of moral good. He does not want morality to be empirically determined, since that would be subjective, so he upholds the notion that moral concepts must be *a priori*. Obviously, he believes that people will generally agree on the universalizability of various laws and principles, but it is not clear why this should be the case. For a Christian empiricist like Wesley, this dilemma is one of the reasons that special revelation is needed. In particular, Scripture is most instrumental in providing us with an account of moral good, since it can be accessed directly by each person. Wesley agrees that morality must have an objective basis, but he does not think that this can be derived strictly from the nature of reason itself, as Kant supposes. This is another example of how the rationalistic tendencies of Wesley pale in comparison to the rationalism of Kant.

In Kant's thought, religious concepts are essentially reduced until they are merely moral ones. For example, he claims that the concept of God is a byproduct of morality.

> In theological morality the concept of God must determine our duties. But this is just the opposite of morality. For men picture all sorts of terrible and frightening attributes as part of their concept of God. Now of course such pictures can beget fear in us and move us to follow moral laws from compulsion or through fear of punishment. But they do not make the object interesting.

---

8. Kant, *Rel*, 33 [6:4].
9. Munzel, *Kant's Conception of Moral Character*, 295.
10. Kant, *LE*, 46.

> For we no longer see how abominable our actions are; we abstain from them only from fear of punishment. Natural morality must be so constituted that it can be thought independently of any concept of God, and elicit our most zealous devotion solely on account of its own inner worth and excellence. But it serves to increase our devotion if after we have taken an interest in morals itself, to take interest also in the existence of God, a being who can reward our good conduct. And then we will obtain strong incentives which will determine us to the observance of moral laws. This is a highly necessary hypothesis.[11]

In other words, Kant claims that morality is independent of the concept of God, as well as many other religious concepts. As a result, religion is relegated to a position inferior to morality. Whereas morality is necessary in and of itself, religious concepts like the concept of God are construed as practically necessary moral concepts.[12] For Kant, the nature of morality dictates that virtue and morality ultimately be rewarded, and this requires the existence of God as the grand rewarder. This is the crux of what Kant calls the moral argument for God's existence, but even this is not an objective proof, for it is an assumption dictated by morality itself. It is not the case that morality must presuppose the existence of God. Instead, morality necessitates this assumption.[13] As R. Z. Friedman states the matter, Kant asserts that we cannot have logical certainty *about* God's existence, yet we must have logical certainty *of* it.[14]

Kant says that from morality we also deduce that God must be "a holy lawgiver, a benevolent sustainer of the world, and a just judge."[15] In this regard, we cannot be moral without believing in God.[16] The teleology of morality essentially leads us to the concept of God. Hence, Kant understands religion itself to be little more than recognizing all our duties as God's commands.[17] Religion is not only dependent on morality, religion is essentially derived from it. For Kant, the foundation of religious faith is morality, and he does not regard this as a detriment. On

---

11. Kant, *LPT*, 31.
12. Ibid., 110.
13. Kant, *CJ*, §87, 381, n. 1.
14. Friedman, "Kant and Kierkegaard," 9.
15. Kant, *LPT*, 112.
16. Kant, *LE*, 81.
17. Kant, *CJ*, §91, 423.

the contrary, he believes that reducing the basis of religion to morality solidifies religious faith, since "nothing firmer or more certain can be thought in any science than our obligation to moral actions."[18]

For the moment, let us return to Kant's claim that objective matters cannot be empirically determined. Even his concept of God is one that is free from empirical conditioning, but is dictated by the nature of morality itself. He suggests that even if we could perceive God empirically, we would still need a prior pure concept of God in order to be certain that we were perceiving God.[19] For Wesley, our concept of God comes from Scripture, and this concept becomes both the basis of our faith in God and the criterion for assessing what we believe to be our encounters with God. Wesley agrees with Kant that faith must have a rational basis, but he disagrees as to what that rational basis should be. Moreover, Wesley feels that faith must also have a subjective element, for it must be personal.

Given the fact that Wesley regards right affections to be the core of morality, his declaration that "true religion, in the very essence of it, is nothing short of holy tempers"[20] might be interpreted as conveying the same message as Kant, that religion must be founded on morality. This is incorrect on two counts. First, Wesley is not alleging that morality is the basis of religion, but that religion cannot fall short of morality, for morality is indeed at the heart of religion. It is religion that points us to morality, not vice versa.

Second, Wesley believes that love for God is the primary affection in morality, an affection for which Kant has little, if any, use at all. Kant does speak of the duty of gratitude, and it could be argued that this implies the necessity of having gratitude toward God.[21] However, given the hypothetical nature of Kant's concept of God, it is difficult to conceive how love for God can be nearly as personal for Kant as it is for Wesley. The kind of personal love for God that Wesley advocates requires, at the very least, that we see the God of Scripture as relevant to our daily personal lives. Indeed, Wesley's own experience of assurance led him to believe that it requires more than this, for he came to believe that we

---

18. Kant, *LPT*, 40.
19. Ibid., 161.
20. Wesley, Sermon 91, "On Charity," §3.12, *WW*, 3:306 [J 7:56].
21. Kant, *MM*, 203–4 [6:454–56].

can only properly love God if we have a personal conviction that our sins are forgiven.[22]

If Kant has any place for love to God, it falls far short of this standard. Besides God's role as the rewarder of virtue in the afterlife, Kant only recognizes one type of divine activity in this life—the divine aid required in moral regeneration, but even this is another hypothetical proposition that must be logically presupposed. Kant does recognize Christ as our moral exemplar, but it is not apparent that this requires anything more than an idealization of Christ.[23] In other words, it is not important whether or not Christ actually lived a perfect life, died for the sins of the world, and rose again from the dead. What apparently matters for Kant is that we hold this ideal of Christ in our minds. A Wesleyan understanding of religious faith cannot succumb to such a hollow definition of Christianity, for even though Kant feels that his type of faith is more objective, the object of his faith ends up being more subjective.

Kant as a Useful Resource

Within the scope of these limitations, I believe that Kant is a worthwhile resource for Wesleyan ethics. As we have already seen, Wesley is far more committed to a rational assessment of religion and morality than is commonly assumed. He wants a robust account of religion and morality that fully utilizes the resources of Scripture, reason, tradition, and experience. This separates him from many of his predecessors and contemporaries who tend to neglect one or more of these epistemic sources. I believe that Wesley's broad epistemic base thus helps to explain his eclecticism. Wesley simply turned to sources that informed the different facets of his thought.

Of the many authors that Wesley admired, there were a number whose epistemology relied significantly on speculative reason. For example, Wesley's reliance on Locke and Aristotle is undeniable. Furthermore, Wesley advised his ministers to understand "the depths of the Schoolmen, the subtleties of Scotus [and] Aquinas." He also suggested that they be able to "read with ease and pleasure" the metaphysical

---

22. Wesley, "An Earnest Appeal to Men of Reason and Religion," §61, *WW*, 11:70 [J 8:24].

23. Kant, *Rel*, 79–84 [6:60–66].

works of authors such as Henry More, Samuel Clarke, Malebranche, and Isaac Newton, among others.[24] These authors represent an approach to religion and morality that places great emphasis on rationality and speculative knowledge, an approach akin to that of Kant. In that regard, although Wesley did not have access to Kant's writings, I cannot help but feel that he would have found Kant to be a useful resource.

In this project, Kantian themes will be appropriated for a Wesleyan paradigm in several ways. Since these concepts will be nuanced so as not to presuppose Kant's more rationalistic context, I believe that they can be adapted for a different type of project, like the one I am constructing. First, the Wesleyan concept of love, which is personal in nature, will be expanded to include the respect for morality, including a devotion to the duties and principles that characterize morality. As has already been noted, Wesley believes that the love of God and the love of morality are already joined together, since God's nature cannot be separated from God's will. Second, there will be a broadened definition of sin that is comprised of omissions as well as commissions. Attitudes, states of mind, etc. will also fall under the realm of moral accountability inasmuch as they can be controlled. Third, maxims will be regarded as the rational principles that guide human behavior. In a Wesleyan paradigm, they will be informed by Scripture, reason, tradition, and experience, and they will be applied to concrete situations in producing moral action. As such, some maxims will be broad and general while others will be specific and contextualized.

Conscience as a Product of Practical Reasoning

Conscience for Wesley is the faculty whereby we judge ourselves according to Scripture. I believe that it is improper to construe this either as divine command ethics or as some form of intuitionism. Instead, Wesley's view of conscience is more aptly characterized as a product of practical reasoning. On one hand, since I am proposing that the Wesleyan definition of sin be expanded to include duties not specifically commanded by Scripture, the function of conscience will need to be more expansive than a divine command theory might allow. On the other hand, an intuitionist theory of conscience is not consistent with Wesley's general theory of knowledge, as I shall explain shortly.

---

24. Wesley, "Address to the Clergy," §2.1.(5), *WWJ*, 10:492.

Of course, an empirical view of conscience is needed. Specifically, it should be based on Lockean empiricism, denying the existence of innate moral ideas. A number of Wesley's contemporaries developed views of natural conscience that were adaptations of Lockean empiricism, yet most of these theories base conscience on intuition. Some even regard conscience as a "moral sense." These theories are unsuitable for a Wesleyan paradigm, because none of them allows for the types of moral considerations Wesley thinks we need, especially the reflective incorporation of Scripture. Nevertheless, these theories still offer emphases that should be included in a Wesleyan view of conscience.

Theories of Conscience in Wesley's Day

During the eighteenth century a number of thinkers adapted the thought of Locke in a number of ways. With respect to their various views of conscience, since they all denied the existence of innate moral ideas, another basis was sought for natural conscience. First, there were those who based conscience on self-interest or self-love. Joseph Butler is the foremost example of this approach. He says that "reasonable self-love and conscience are the chief or superior principles" in human nature. Our true happiness is found where they agree.[25] Moreover, benevolence and self-love naturally coincide. "We can scarcely promote one without the other."[26] Consequently, humans are closely united in nature, and this gives us a natural desire for relationship.[27] However, virtue requires that lower principles (i.e., passion) be subordinated to higher ones.[28] The Earl of Shaftesbury, Anthony Ashley Cooper, also bases conscience on self-interest, because he feels that it is in the private interest of everyone to work toward the general (i.e., public) good. To neglect to do this not only hinders our own happiness and welfare, it makes us our own direct enemies.[29]

The second view of conscience is best represented by Francis Hutcheson, who bases conscience on universal benevolence. He views human nature very favorably, for he declares, "We neither have malicious

---

25. Butler, Sermon 3, "Upon Human Nature," 39.
26. Ibid., Sermon 1, "Upon Human Nature," 20.
27. Ibid., 23.
28. Frey, "Self-Love and Benevolence," 252–53.
29. Shaftesbury, *Inquiry Concerning Virtue*, 110.

affections naturally nor is there any probability, in our present constitution, of promoting a private interest separately from, or in opposition to, the public."[30] Rather, he believes that we naturally have benevolence, and this is the sole ground of moral approbation.[31] The benevolence that we have toward others produces a "moral sense" within us, and this causes us to esteem laws and moral principles.[32] However, the moral sense is not conformity to law, truth, or some other type of fitness.[33] Instead, we judge the morality of actions according to the dispositions that produce them.[34] When we perceive benevolence in others, it generates benevolence within us.[35] This is not to say that the moral sense always functions properly, because the moral sense is often overcome with self-love.[36] However, if the obstacles to self-love are removed, it can guide us to benevolence.[37] When benevolence and self-love work together, they make us desire the happiness of others without any self-interest on our part.[38]

Third, there were theorists who believed that conscience is rooted in sympathy. For example, David Hume suggests that in moral judgment, reason must assess the "tendency of qualities and actions, and point out their beneficial consequences to society and to their possessor." There must also be an underlying sentiment that desires the happiness of mankind and resents its misery.[39] As such, "sympathy is the chief source of moral distinctions." We are affected by the happiness of others through sympathy alone. It is the source of moral approbation.[40] Nevertheless, affections play a much greater role in sympathy than does reason. Consequently, "morality . . . is more properly felt than judged of."[41] For Hume, moral sentiment reflects human psychology in

30. Hutcheson, *Illustrations*, 154.
31. Hutcheson, *Inquiry*, 197–98.
32. Ibid., 274–75.
33. Hutcheson, *System*, 56–57.
34. Hutcheson, *Inquiry*, 169.
35. Bishop, "Moral Motivation," 281.
36. Hutcheson, *Inquiry*, 242.
37. Ibid., 269.
38. Hutcheson, *Illustrations*, 118–19.
39. Hume, *Enquiry*, Appendix 1, 157–58.
40. Hume, *Treatise of Human Nature*, §3.3.6, 618–19.
41. Ibid., §3.1.2, 470.

general. The ultimate ends of human action are guided by sentiment without any dependence on the intellectual faculties.[42]

Adam Smith also bases conscience on sympathy, but he gives reason a more active role. He too claims that moral approbation and disapprobation are derived from sympathy. We approve or disapprove the conduct of others to the extent that we can or cannot entirely sympathize with the "sentiments and motives which directed it." In the same way, we approve or disapprove our own conduct to the extent that we can or cannot view ourselves from the perspective of others and still sympathize with our own sentiments and motives.[43] Smith believes that we naturally desire the praise of individuals, and we want to be praiseworthy from an impartial perspective.[44] Essentially, conscience is only as strong as the feeling of sympathy that supports it. As a result, properly judging between our interests and the interests of those with whom we have no particular connection requires the perspective of an impartial third party.[45] Moreover, our passions cause self-deceit, but this bias can be corrected by observing the behavior of others and forming general rules of conduct.[46] In the final analysis,

> The man of the most perfect virtue, the man whom we naturally love and revere the most, is he who joins, to the most perfect command of his own original and selfish feelings, the most exquisite sensibility both to the original and sympathetic feelings of others.[47]

The fourth way that Lockean empiricism was adapted to explain natural conscience was to base it on rational, self-evident principles. Richard Price is a thinker who holds this view of conscience. He declares that our perceptions of right and wrong come from understanding and perception.[48] These perceptions are simple (i.e., "uncompounded") ideas.[49] Sense perceives the outward while reason perceives the inward

---

42. Hume, *Enquiry*, Appendix 1, 162.
43. A. Smith, *Theory of Moral Sentiments*, §3.1, 161.
44. Ibid., §3.2, 166–67.
45. Ibid., §3.2, 192.
46. Ibid., §3.4, 221–24.
47. Ibid., §3.3, 214.
48. Price, *Principle Questions in Morals*, 14.
49. Ibid., 16.

nature of things.⁵⁰ Price believes that our actions are right or wrong independent of the sensations they cause.⁵¹ Clearly distinguishing himself from Locke, he asserts that pleasure and pain are the concomitants of the perception of right and wrong, they are not the perceptions themselves.⁵² Ultimately, when we become consciously aware that an action brings a sense of satisfaction, we approve the action and perceive it to be right.⁵³ Since moral truths are necessary truths, we instinctively intuit our duty and are motivated toward it.⁵⁴

Thomas Reid likewise asserts that conscience testifies to self-evident, first principles of moral reasoning from which all knowledge of duty is deduced.⁵⁵ Moral motivation naturally follows, since knowledge of the good contains the desire for it.⁵⁶ Hence, moral judgments are accompanied by feelings and affections.⁵⁷ Reid feels that conscience is not strong enough to prevent "errors in speculation." It "needs the aid of instruction, education, and habit, as well as our other natural powers." This is why some people have better moral judgment than others.⁵⁸ However, there is less variety in moral opinions than is commonly believed. The differences are attributable to errors associated with speculation, not in distinguishing right and wrong.⁵⁹ In the end, the judgments of conscience are not infallible, but must be assessed rationally.⁶⁰

Wesley's Objection to Wholly Natural Accounts of Conscience

Considering the eclecticism of Wesley's thought, and given the fact that all of these options were available to him, it is interesting that he did not substantively incorporate any of these theories into his thought. Again, much of this can probably be attributed to his loyalty to the

50. Dreyer, "Edmund Burke," 115.
51. Price, 70–71.
52. Ibid., 63.
53. Ibid., 91.
54. Schneewind, *Invention of Autonomy*, 382–85.
55. Reid, *Active Powers*, §3.3.6, 233.
56. Ibid., §3.3.2, 206.
57. Ibid., §3.3.7, 238.
58. Ibid., §3.3.8, 247–49.
59. Ibid., §3.3.5, 226.
60. Stecker, "Thomas Reid," 463.

doctrine of total depravity, since he rejected the moral sense as a purely natural sense.[61] For instance, Wesley specifically faulted Hutcheson for espousing natural conscience without prevenient grace.[62] Richard Steele notes three major criticisms that Wesley leveled against Hutcheson: (1) he postulated an autonomous moral sense in place of the theonomous conscience of traditional Christian ethics, (2) he rendered an overly optimistic appraisal of human nature, and (3) he equated virtue with disinterested benevolence, and this effectively downplayed religious piety.[63]

Nevertheless, I surmise that Wesley's objections are more theological in nature than they are epistemological. For example, Hutcheson claims that the moral sense judges the morality of laws, even divine ones.[64] Although Wesley would react negatively to this claim inasmuch as it seems to undermine the authority of divine law, Wesley would most likely agree that conscience can evaluate the fitness of laws, i.e., their congruence with the nature of things and with reason. It is a well-known fact that Wesley did much of his reading while traveling on horseback, and we have already noted some places where Wesley apparently missed the subtle nuances of Locke's writing. It is not unreasonable to suppose that Wesley may have missed some of the subtleties of other authors like Hutcheson. Furthermore, we also know that Wesley reacted strongly against those who challenged orthodoxy in a significant way, like Hume. It is also very likely that Wesley found the lack of evangelical focus in Hutcheson's writings to be distasteful, given the fact that Hutcheson was generally regarded as a Christian thinker.

In short, Wesley's rejection of these natural accounts of conscience was most likely due to his commitment to the doctrine of total depravity. Nevertheless, even if that doctrine is relinquished, as I have suggested, none of these theories can be incorporated into a Wesleyan paradigm in its entirety, as we shall now see.

---

61. R. Steele, "*Gracious Affection*," 335.
62. Wesley, Sermon 105, "On Conscience," §1.9, WW, 3:484 [J 7:189].
63. R. Steele, "*Gracious Affection*," 333.
64. Hutcheson, *Inquiry*, 273.

Reconciling Natural Conscience with Wesleyan Ethics

Even if it can be argued that Wesley dismissed these views of conscience too quickly, the question still remains as to whether any of these approaches can be applied to Wesley's ethics. Some type of development is needed in Wesley's understanding of conscience if it is to (1) satisfactorily handle the expanded definition of sin that is being proposed and (2) remain consistent with Wesley's general theory of knowledge. In that respect, it will be helpful to examine the extent to which the theories discussed above can inform a Wesleyan view of conscience.

First, it does not seem that a Wesleyan view of conscience will regard it as being based on self-love or self-interest. To be sure, Wesley does allow a legitimate role for self-love. However, he feels that self-interest tends to be degenerative, so it cannot be trusted to the extent of allowing it to form our moral judgments. Moreover, proper self-love for Wesley is more than enlightened self-interest. It is valuing the self neither too much nor too little, and it is also valuing the self for the right reasons (e.g., fulfilling the Love Commandments, etc.). For both Wesley and Edwards, proper self-love can serve as a template for loving others properly. Nevertheless, self-interest still cannot be a major factor in conscience, since (1) we naturally pursue it, whether our purposes are good or evil; and (2) God's commandments are for our benefit, indicating that our best interests are served by submitting ourselves to the will of God in our lives.

Second, a Wesleyan conception of conscience will not be based on benevolence either. For Wesley, benevolence is one of the aims of perfection. As such, it is attainable, but the natural state of affairs for (unregenerate) human beings is to be guided by self-interest, which tends to be narrow. Even the regenerate struggle with self-will in the process of pursuing perfection. Although conscience can be informed by universal benevolence once it is achieved, conscience cannot generally be based on it.

Third, Wesleyan ethics could perhaps relate conscience to sympathy, but in a different way. To start, this would not be applicable to love for God, because our feelings of moral obligation toward God do not originate in feelings of sympathy. On the other hand, regarding conscience as being rooted in sympathy is helpful in loving others, as Hume and Smith both explain. I believe that viewing conscience this way is consistent with both empiricism and the moral principles of Scripture. However, Wesley does not view reason as the slave of the passions or emotions, as does Hume. The Wesleyan understanding of sympathy is more cognitive, based on value judgments. Rather than control reason, sympathy is both shaped and scrutinized by it.

Fourth, basing the Wesleyan understanding of conscience on self-evident principles is also questionable. Wesley recognizes self-evident principles, but these are propositions of logical necessity about the nature of God, mathematics, metaphysics, or logic itself.[65] For Wesley, moral principles are not self-evident. Some basic moral principles can be derived from human nature and from the natural order of the world, but Scripture is still the authoritative source of moral knowledge. Although this explanation of conscience is more cognitive than the other explanations, it is still intuitionist at its core, and this is unsuitable for a Wesleyan paradigm. I will elaborate on this point shortly.

To summarize, Wesleyan conscience can use proper self-love as a template for loving others, but not as a guide for moral discernment. Conscience can be aided by universal benevolence once it is achieved, but since this is a part of perfection, most will not attain it until near death. Sympathy, when exercised within the confines of scriptural principles, can be helpful in understanding how to love others, but it is not very useful (perhaps not useful at all) in understanding how to love God. A Wesleyan view of conscience is cognitive, but not based on self-evident moral principles. Not only would this neglect relying on Scripture for the basic principles of morality, it would rely on intuition, which is not a desirable account of conscience in a Wesleyan paradigm.

Intuitionism as Insufficient for Wesleyan Ethics

According to Locke and Wesley, moral ideas are complex ideas that require "intermediate ideas." As such, they are not understood through mere intuition.[66] Moreover, Wesley asserts the need for special revelation, because the sinful state of the world precludes immediate moral perception. William Hudson points out that in times when social mores are unquestioned, it is not surprising to find agreement among people

---

65. Wesley, "A Compendium of Logic, Book II," §1.4, *WWJ*, 14:179.
66. Drury, "Natural Law and Innate Ideas," 532.

concerning their duty.⁶⁷ In the eighteenth century, the general consensus that existed regarding the fundamental principles of morality perhaps led these various theorists to overestimate the homogeneity that exists in human nature. If they had lived in a more diverse society, they may not have been so optimistic about moral intuition. In this regard, ethical intuitionists have difficulty explaining why some have more or less scruples than others.⁶⁸

According to Stephen Darwall, we must be able to distinguish naturalness from intrinsic worth. Otherwise, we are in danger of committing the naturalistic fallacy (i.e., implying "ought" with "is").⁶⁹ It seems that intuitionism runs this risk. In a Wesleyan schema, the world is naturally in a sinful state, so we cannot judge morality merely by the state of affairs. Even though Wesley recognizes that morality is, to a significant degree, based on the "fitness of things," he feels that people are unable to attain a sufficient degree of moral knowledge without special revelation. This is why Wesley has two goals in education: evangelism and morality.⁷⁰ Achieving one's full moral potential thus includes both religious commitment and moral development, especially in knowledge.

Regarding Moral Knowledge as Cognitive

Overall, Wesley sees moral knowledge as more cognitive than intuitive. He believes that conscience, since it is a product of reason, can only operate properly if it has freedom. Conversely, it is the truth which sets us free. This is why unholy people try to restrict the conscience of others.⁷¹ For Wesley and Locke, conscience is shaped by education and is limited to the knowledge it derives from empirical experience and intellectual speculation. This is the kind of view that William Law held early on, when Wesley resonated with his thought.

Conscience can be regarded as the vehicle through which God speaks to us. However, this does not imply that conscience always echoes the voice of God. Conscience remains empirical, so it does not receive

---

67. Hudson, *Ethical Intuitionism*, 61.
68. Ibid., 58–60.
69. Darwall, *The British Moralists*, 270.
70. Blevins, "John Wesley and the Means of Grace," 124.
71. Wesley, "A Farther Appeal to Men of Reason and Religion, Part I," §7.8, *WW*, 11:194 [J 8:128].

superadded knowledge from God. Wesley thus asserts that even feelings of grief for our sins are not only scriptural, they are also reasonable.[72] Kant insists that conscience does not judge the objective truthfulness of our beliefs, but whether we really regard our beliefs as objectively true.[73] He likewise makes a distinction between conscience and moral feeling. "Conscience" is the judgment of practical reason as to our conformity to duty, and "moral feeling" is the accompanying feeling of pleasure or displeasure that is produced by this judgment.[74]

In formulating his own views on conscience, Wesley cites the sermon of his own grandfather, Dr. Annesley, on the same subject. As he is discussing the manner in which a good conscience is to be maintained, Annesley makes several assertions that suggest a cognitive view of conscience. These are (1) "consult duty, not events;" (2) "what advice you would give another, take yourself;" (3) "do nothing on which you cannot pray for a blessing;" (4) "think and speak and do what you are persuaded Christ himself would do in your case, were he on earth;" and (5) "let every action have reference to your whole life and not to a part only."[75] Every one of these assertions requires moral reflection, and this emphasizes the importance that Wesley places on cognition and reason in the function of conscience. It also suggests that, with respect to his account of conscience, Wesley is in fact closer to Kant than he is to most of his contemporaries.

Sin As the Neglect of Duty

Wesley's definition of sin is as follows: "Nothing is sin, strictly speaking, but a voluntary transgression of a known law of God. Therefore, every voluntary breach of the law of love is sin; and nothing else, if we speak properly."[76] This definition needs to be expanded, because it lends itself to interpreting Wesleyan ethics as a type of divine command ethics, and it does not provide sufficient impetus toward moral progress and development, which Wesley certainly wants to maintain. I suggest that

72. Ibid., §7.13, *WW*, 11:197-98 [J 8:130-31].
73. Kant, "On the Miscarriage of All Philosophical Trials in Theodicy," in *Rel*, 27 [8:268].
74. Kant, *MM*, 160 [6:399-400].
75. Wesley, Sermon 105, "On Conscience," §§1.19.7-10, *WW*, 3:489-90 [J 7:193-94].
76. Wesley to Elizabeth Bennis, 16 June 1772, *WWJ*, 12:394.

sin be defined more broadly as the neglect of duty, for it seems that this definition is superior in several ways: (1) it better captures Wesley's own concerns, (2) it retains the commitments of Wesley's original definition, and (3) it underscores the need for continual moral progress.

The Need for an Expanded Definition

According to John Tyson, Wesley's recognition that willful and cognitive factors are at the heart of human sin is what separated him from the Westminster definition of sin as "any want of conformity unto, or transgression of, the law of God."[77] Indeed, Wesley incorporated the notions of both law and love in his understanding of sin, and this is evidence of his desire to include both actions and intentions in his understanding of morality. Nevertheless, the emphasis is clearly on the intentions, for only intentional transgressions can "properly" be called sins. Even though involuntary transgressions still require the atonement of Christ, they can only "improperly" be referred to as sins.[78]

William Sangster thinks that Wesley defined sin as he did in order to delimit the extent to which we can be freed from it.[79] The Wesleyan doctrine of perfection is shaped to a great extent by the Wesleyan doctrine of sin, because perfection entails purity of heart, i.e., moral purity. Truly, there was a point of tension in Wesley's thought with respect to his claim that perfection is possible in this life, especially in the sense of living victoriously over sin. In order to claim this, he effectively had to limit his definition of sin to willful acts within the scope of one's knowledge. In other words, it is only a sin to do something that you already believe is wrong. However, he felt that sin could not be strictly limited this way. As such, he claimed that although we can objectively judge particular actions and motives to be right or wrong, God will not hold us accountable for that which is beyond our control and beyond our knowledge at the time. When his critics accused him of proclaiming "sinless perfection," he acknowledged sin in the broader sense but said that this cannot "properly" be called sin.[80]

---

77. Tyson, "Sin, Self and Society," 78.
78. Wesley, "A Plain Account of Christian Perfection," §19, *WWJ*, 11:396.
79. Sangster, *Path to Perfection*, 30.
80. Wesley, "A Plain Account of Christian Perfection," §19, *WWJ*, 11:394–97.

Historically, Wesleyans have espoused the narrow definition of sin, because it helps to support the claim that people can be freed from the power of sin in this life. This is particularly the case with those who advance the notion that perfection can be and should be attained in a single, momentary experience. However, construing perfection in this manner led to seeing it as a plateau, not as a continuing process with thresholds and/or a culmination point. Consequently, it contributed to the anti-intellectual attitude that was generally characteristic of American evangelicalism from the mid-1800's through the mid-1900's. In effect, the only type of knowledge that was regarded as spiritually relevant was a commonsense understanding of Scripture. Even the recognition of one's own rebellious nature did not require deep analysis and self-scrutiny. Once people were "entirely sanctified," they tried to grow in grace, but they did so under the assumption that they no longer had any sinful inclinations whatsoever.[81]

Sangster feels that the greatest failure of Wesley's doctrine of sin is in its inability to address sins of omission.[82] Indeed, Wesley wanted to exclude transgressions that are beyond our control, but in so doing he also excluded areas of neglect that should be included. Albert Knudson asserts that Wesley's definition of sin needs to be expanded to include "moral imperfection for which an agent is, in God's sight, accountable."[83] Wesley does acknowledge "involuntary transgressions," but these are not covered by his definition of sin.[84] For both Wesley and Kant, sin is essentially an act of the will. Kant regards an unintentional transgression as a fault, but he calls an intentional transgression a crime.[85] Wesley also makes a distinction between voluntary and involuntary transgressions, and this stresses moral and ethical responsibility.[86]

If a broader conception of sin can be developed for Wesleyan ethics, then it would be easier to produce a more robust account of Wesleyan perfection as well. I believe that Kant's concept of duty can add this needed breadth. To be specific, I am suggesting that sin be

---

81. For a fuller explanation of the reformulation of Wesley's doctrine of perfection, see Lowery, "Wesleyan Road," 187–222.

82. Sangster, *Path to Perfection*, 155.

83. Knudson, *Basic Issues*, 119.

84. Hynson, *To Reform the Nation*, 103.

85. Kant, *MM*, 16 [6:224].

86. Bence, *Teleological Hermeneutic*, 68.

understood as the neglect of duty. This would retain Wesley's emphasis on intentionality, but it would also require more than merely intending to do one's duty to the extent that it can be perceived. Instead, we would be expected to try to gain a deeper knowledge of our duty. Furthermore, we would be obligated to actually perform our duty, not just weakly intend to do it at some future time. However, Kant's concept of duty does not entail limitless obligation, for Kant maintains that only those things which are possible to do in experience can qualify as duties, i.e., "ought implies can."[87]

The concept of duty is thus limited to the conscious, yet it points toward the unconscious. Sangster asserts that human motives are often so entangled that it is almost impossible to clearly distinguish the conscious from the unconscious and the selfish from the unselfish.[88] Wesley's definition of sin is focused on the conscious, but it lacks emphasis on our obligation to explore the unconscious and gradually bring it under the control of the conscious. The concept of duty places this obligation on our shoulders, for duty is something that exists beyond us. In contrast, intentions are limited to the control of the moral agent. The more mystical developments of Wesleyanism assumed that God supernaturally changes us beyond the realm of our consciousness, but Sangster points out that this view essentially robs us of our moral worth, because nothing outside of our control can be regarded as a duty.[89]

Wesley's Stress on Moral Duty

Wesley frequently refers to positive duties that he feels Christians must fulfill. He refers to the neglect of these as "sins of omission." These need to be more adequately incorporated into his definition of sin. Recall that for both Wesley and Locke, moral good is determined by conformity with law. This can lead to interpreting Wesley as a divine command ethicist. However, Wesley repeatedly asserts positive duties, and he considers the neglect of them to be "sins of omission."[90] To be

---

87. Kant, "On the Proverb: That May Be True in Theory, But Is of No Practical Use," in *PP*, 62 [8:277].

88. Sangster, *Path to Perfection*, 75.

89. Ibid., 121–23.

90. Wesley, Sermon 14, "The Repentance of Believers," §1.14, *WW*, 1:343 [J 5:163]; Sermon 35, "The Law Established through Faith, Discourse I," §3.8, *WW*, 2:31–32 [J 5:457]; and Sermon 98, "On Visiting the Sick," §3.9, *WW*, 3:397 [J 7:127].

specific, Wesley refers to "transgression" as the "commission of sin" and to "disobedience" as the "omission of duty."[91] Consequently, God's grace and mercy not only deliver us from his wrath, they motivate us to perform our duty.[92] Fulfilling our moral obligation is thus a part of our salvation. Moreover, sins of omission cannot be ignored, because they tend to quench the Spirit gradually and slowly.[93]

For Wesley, all duties are founded on Scripture, but they are not specifically commanded by Scripture. He looked to Christian antiquity to validate practices not specifically commanded by Scripture. Therefore, when Wesley refers to himself as *"homo unius libri"* (i.e., a man of one book), we should understand that Scripture for him is the ultimate authority, but not the sole source of moral knowledge. In fact, Wesley avers, "A Christian acts in all things by the highest reason, from the mercy of God inferring his own duty."[94] Of course, duties are somewhat subjective, because they do not apply equally to everyone. What is a duty for some may not be a duty for others.[95]

The Derivation of Specific Duties

This broader definition of sin will retain Scripture as the authoritative source of moral knowledge. However, it will require the derivation of duties founded upon scriptural principles but not specifically commanded by Scripture. As Wesleyan ethics becomes less associated with divine command theory, it will need to be interpreted from another context. Although I am not prepared at this point to suggest precisely what this context should be, I feel strongly that Wesleyan ethics would be better served by a teleological approach to ethics, rather than a deontological one. I thus ally myself with a number of Wesleyan voices who make this very claim, albeit in a different way. For instance, Ray Dunning claims,

> Since guidelines for Christian behavior are grounded in the will of God, and people of his kingdom are called on to obey these guidelines, we clearly have a deontological dimension. But

---

91. Wesley, *NNT*, Heb 2:2.
92. Ibid., Rom 12:1.
93. Wesley, Sermon 46, "The Wilderness State," §2.3, *WW*, 2:209 [J 6:81].
94. Wesley, *NNT*, Rom 12:1.
95. Ibid., Matt 19:21.

> on the other hand, it seems clear that divinely revealed ethical guidelines are informed by a purpose or goal that God desires to accomplish in the lives of his people, so there is also a teleological element.
>
> . . . I have come to the conclusion that Christian ethics, especially when viewed from a Wesleyan perspective, is thoroughgoingly teleological. A careful study of John Wesley's own ethical instruction reveals that he self-consciously understood ethics in this fashion. In fact his whole understanding of the Christian life is cast in these terms, and he repeatedly points out that the end (*telos*) that God is seeking to produce in our lives is a renewal of the divine image. Thus Wesley defines the essence of the Christian life as the divine activity of renewing human persons in the image of God. Here, I believe, is the clue to a proper understanding of Christian ethics.[96]

Being renewed in the image of God is indeed the telos of Wesleyan ethics. This is encapsulated in the Wesleyan emphasis on perfection, and as Mildred Bangs Wynkoop points out, it specifically requires a teleological context.

> Never is perfection absolute in an abstract sense but is always relative to an end appropriate to any particular case, that is, in respect of a particular standard. But it is equally true to say that the end as a goal is in harmony with the nature and possibility of that which is to be brought to perfection. Perfection is something that *ought to be the case*, in a particular situation, *and can become so* under grace. That which, in man, is to be considered under the term perfection was endowed with the capacity for perfection and must proceed to that goal if one is not to repudiate the grace given to this end. This simply means that evangelical perfection is not only consistent with the human probationary status, but is essential to it in that it marks out the goal of probation.[97]

At first glance it might appear that the derivation of specific duties is inconsistent with Wesley's position on Scripture. Let us take a second look at a pertinent passage from Wesley.

> The faith of the Protestants, in general, embraces only those truths as necessary to salvation which are clearly revealed in

---

96. Dunning, *Reflecting the Divine Image*, 34–35.
97. Wynkoop, *Theology of Love*, 294.

> the oracles of God. Whatever is plainly declared in the Old and New Testament is the object of their faith. They believe neither more nor less than what is manifestly contained in, and provable by, the Holy Scriptures. The word of God is "a lantern to their feet, and a light in all their paths." They dare not on any pretense go from it to the right hand or to the left. The written Word is the whole and sole rule of their faith, as well as practice. They believe whatsoever God has declared, and profess to do whatsoever he hath commanded. This is the proper faith of the Protestants; by this they will abide, and no other.[98]

It is also helpful to remember that Wesley contends that whatever Scripture does not forbid or require is morally neutral and should not be a concern of conscience.[99] Furthermore, Wesley defines a "scrupulous" (i.e., overly sensitive) conscience as one that assumes duties that are not enjoined by Scripture.[100]

I do not find these assertions to be too restrictive so as to thwart my overall agenda. The moral principles contained in Scripture are sufficiently broad so as to encompass morality. For example, Christ says that the Love Commandments summarize all the law and the prophets. It seems that these general principles are relevant to every aspect of human experience. Even though Scripture cannot yield context specific rules for every possible circumstance, it still gives us laws, principles, illustrations, etc. that provide a lot of moral insight. As such, there must be some compulsion to derive particular duties that are not specifically addressed in Scripture, yet are still based on scriptural principles.

Wesleyan ethics already focuses on the morality of intentions (i.e., the morality of the agent). What Wesleyan ethics needs to do, in particular, is to determine the morality of actions. Wesley believes that the natural world yields specific duties that all people are obligated to keep. Christianity does not destroy these natural duties. Rather, it perfects them.[101] The question is: What type of methodology should Wesleyan ethics use, or what moral theory should it employ, in the derivation of specific duties? Given Wesley's cognitivist account of conscience and

---

98. Wesley, Sermon 106, "On Faith," §1.8, *WW*, 3:496 [J 7:198].

99. Wesley, Sermon 12, "The Witness of Our Own Spirit," §§5–8, *WW*, 1:302–4 [J 5:136–37].

100. Wesley, Sermon 105, "On Conscience," §§1.16–17, *WW*, 3:487 [J 7:191].

101. Wesley, *NNT*, I Tim 5:8.

teleological construal of perfection, it seems that the best overall approach to Wesleyan ethics would be a teleological one.

This would entail several things. First, it should be based upon a hierarchical system of values and ends. This would be derived primarily from Scripture and secondarily from practical reason informed by tradition and experience. In general, Wesleyan ethics must include the goals of moral perfection and natural perfection. These will be discussed shortly. Second, it would involve a framework of general principles, structured according to the system of values and ends. These would be formulated in the same manner. Third, a teleological approach to Wesleyan ethics must also have the flexibility to adapt to extraordinary situations. Wesley believed that many of the means of grace apply to all persons, but he recognized that there are also particular prudential means of grace, the relevance of which is derived from a particular context for a particular person. Similarly, a teleological approach to ethics demands a certain flexibility in the obligations it places upon people. This is only a brief sketch of what a viable Wesleyan ethic might look like, but attempting to provide a fuller account extends beyond the scope of this project.

Emphasizing the Morality of Actions

Wesley was attracted to a duty-oriented type of piety. Consequently, his emphasis on experience always extended beyond piety to include practical matters.[102] This likewise suggests that Wesleyan ethics must broaden its scope beyond the morality of intentions and also focus on the morality of actions. In this section, I will attempt to show that the way Kant relates moral and natural perfection is relevant to Wesley's concerns.

Kant's Broader Definition of Perfection

Kant asserts that we, as moral agents, have a duty to pursue our own perfection in two respects. First, we must cultivate our faculties (i.e., natural predispositions), especially our understanding, since it is the highest faculty we possess. Second, we must cultivate the will for two reasons: (1) so that we might minimize the influence of self-love in our

---

102. Maddox, "Enriching Role," 109–11.

dispositions by setting ends for ourselves, diminishing our ignorance, and correcting our errors, and (2) so that the moral law itself might become our incentive for conforming with duty.[103] There is thus a distinction between quantitative and qualitative perfection, and both must be pursued.[104]

Kant claims that the perfection of our faculties is necessary so that the dictates of the will can be made operative.[105] However, since morality excludes everything that does not contribute to the perfection of our inner moral worth, it cannot dictate the manner in which all our powers and capacities should be perfected, for that is a pragmatic affair. One thing is certain, our mental powers must be perfected most of all, because they have the greatest influence on our moral conduct.[106] Moral perfection requires not only strength of will, but also proper judgment.[107] More generally, the duty to develop one's natural perfection is derived from Kant's demand that we treat humanity as an end in itself. Again, this does not necessitate endorsing particular maxims of perfection, it only requires the acceptance of the goal of natural self-improvement.[108]

Nonetheless, the aspect of personal perfection that morality does dictate is the perfection of the will itself. As Allen Wood explains,

> Hence the moral good cannot be a mere formal condition of ends, but must consist in an end which is unconditionally and unqualifiedly good, an end whose promotion follows directly from the formal condition of all good ends. This end is virtue, man's moral strength of will, which consists in the perfection of the disposition to make duty (or the legislative form of his maxim) a sufficient motive of action. Each morally good act *is* good only if it does promote this end by exemplifying this striving in its formally legislative maxim, by contributing to the "labor of moral reconstruction" and fulfilling every man's duty to increase his own moral perfection.[109]

---

103. Kant, *MM*, 150–51, 154–55 [6:386–87, 391–93].
104. Kant, *CJ*, §15, 78.
105. Kant, *LE*, 26.
106. Ibid., 141–42.
107. Denis, "Kant on the Perfection of Others," 23.
108. Denis, *Moral Self-Regard*, 113.
109. A. Wood, *Kant's Moral Religion*, 73–74.

For Kant, perfection concerns the will itself and the motives that guide it, not merely the knowledge that informs it.[110] Humanity is thus completed and perfected in the realization of "personality," i.e., a good will.[111] As Lara Denis indicates, the attainment of a good will is regarded as a type of perfection because it is "our fullest realization as autonomous, but human, rational beings." We are perfect inasmuch as we can will both from duty and in accordance with it, and as we are fit to fulfill all of our morally permissible ends. She defines Kantian perfection as such: "One is morally perfect to the extent that one is able to discern what is morally required, needs no non-moral inducements to act rightly, and fully discharges one's duties."[112] Philip Quinn adds that "complete moral perfection is constituted of both a morally good disposition to act purely on the incentives provided by the moral law and a morally good course of life full of deeds in harmony with that disposition."[113]

Kant does make a distinction between being holy, i.e., having a pure disposition to duty, and being perfect, i.e., "fulfilling all one's duties and ... attaining completely one's moral end with regard to oneself."[114] Moral perfection is thus subjective with respect to one's inner disposition to duty, but objective with respect to the fulfillment of duty and the achievement of one's own moral end.[115] Also, Kant makes a distinction between virtue and holiness: "Virtue implies ability and readiness to overcome our inclination to evil on moral principles ... Thus holy beings are not virtuous, for the reason that they have no evil inclinations to overcome; their will is of itself sufficient for compliance with the law."[116] In this way, a holy will, i.e., one that is absolutely good, can only belong to God, since God is the only being that has no evil inclinations. Humans can only aspire to holiness by acting from duty in spite of subjective inclinations and desires.[117]

According to Kant, "The moral condition which [we] can always be in is virtue, i.e. moral disposition in conflict, and not holiness in

---

110. Rossvaer, *Kant's Moral Philosophy*, 23.
111. Korsgaard, *Kingdom of Ends*, 123–24.
112. Denis, "Kant on the Perfection of Others," 22–23.
113. Quinn, "Christian Atonement," 447.
114. Kant, *MM*, 196 [6:446].
115. Denis, *Moral Self-Regard*, 113.
116. Kant, *LE*, 244.
117. T. Williams, *Categorical Imperative*, 2–3.

the supposed possession of perfect purity of the dispositions of will."[118] In other words, given the fact that virtue involves overcoming evil inclinations while holiness is the absence of evil inclinations altogether, human beings can be virtuous, but not holy. On the other hand, God can be holy, but not virtuous. As Wood puts it,

> We can now see why Kant's doctrine of radical evil is the true exposition and ground for the dialectic of practical reason which leads to the first antimony. The attainment of holiness of will is impossible for finite rational beings as we know them in the world of sense because this attainment by man would require not simply an overcoming of particular moral obstacles, but the overcoming of the source of these obstacles in his own moral nature itself. It would thus require not a progress in *degree* of virtue, but the attainment of a different *kind* of moral volition. But because the radical evil of man's own nature is both imputable to him (as a propensity of his free *Willkür*) and inextirpable by him in time, the transition from virtue to holiness is unattainable by him.[119]

Finite practical reason can thus attain virtue but not holiness. However, it can achieve certainty that constant moral progress can be made, extending into eternity.[120]

Kant says that the first command of the duties we have to ourselves is to know ourselves not with respect to our natural perfection, but with respect to our moral perfection.[121] Even though we cannot be conscious of performing our duty from completely unselfish motives, it is still what morality requires of us.[122] It can thus be said that Kant views moral motivation as opaque, since he thinks that we cannot be absolutely certain of the purity of our motives.[123] Nevertheless, self-knowledge is crucial to being moral, according to Kant. As Wood indicates, self-knowledge is our "primary instrument of enlightenment and self-improvement," both in morality and in religion.[124] In fact, self-scrutiny is what enables

---

118. Kant, *CPr*, 88 [5:84].
119. A. Wood, *Kant's Moral Religion*, 115–16.
120. Munzel, *Moral Character*, 169.
121. Kant, *MM*, 191 [6:441].
122. Kant, "On the Proverb," in *PP*, 68 [8:284].
123. Guevara, 23.
124. A. Wood, *Kant's Moral Religion*, 201.

us to think for ourselves and be the kind of autonomous agents that Kant believes us to be.[125] As Denis explains,

> [The duty to know oneself] requires not merely that the agent not deceive herself about her motive in particular cases, but rather that she adopt self-knowledge as an end . . . This duty is both similar to and intertwined with the duty of moral perfection. Moral self-improvement depends on striving to be honest with oneself about one's deepest motives; self-knowledge with regard to one's relation to one's duty depends on striving to do one's duty from duty, thus giving oneself whatever "practical proof" one can of one's purity and strength of will. The foundational nature of the duties of moral self-improvement and self-knowledge—i.e., the way in which they underlie other duties and structure the agent's life—reflects the central role of character and self-government in Kant's moral theory.[126]

Obviously, Kant's concept of perfection is notably different from Wesley's doctrine of Christian perfection. Even the motivation is fundamentally different. Kant says that in its complete perfection, we do not possess virtue; rather, virtue possesses us.[127] Perfection is thus motivated by a love and respect for virtue and for the moral law itself. I believe that Wesleyan perfection should be more comprehensive than this, for it should emphasize a love and respect for morality as well as a personal love for God and others.

Granted, it can be argued that the motivation behind Kantian perfection is ultimately grounded in respect for our own rational nature.[128] For instance, J. B. Schneewind indicates that "Rousseau convinced Kant that everyone must have the capacity to be a self-governing moral agent, and that it is this characteristic that gives each person a special kind of value or dignity."[129] Patrick Riley proposes that Kant did not regard the respect for the dignity of persons as ends-in-themselves as a sensible impulse, i.e., a motive stemming from happiness or pleasure, and this leads him to conclude that Kant's ethics is not formal to the point of

---

125. Munzel, *Kant's Theory of Moral Motivation*, 229.
126. Denis, *Moral Self-Regard*, 115.
127. Kant, MM, 165 [6:406].
128. Denis, "Kant on the Perfection of Others," 21.
129. Schneewind, "Autonomy, Obligation, and Virtue," 314.

only emphasizing universality.[130] In spite of these arguments, there is little evidence to suggest that the Kantian stress on treating people as ends in themselves is anything more than a respect for rationality itself, so it does not seem that this aspect of Kant's thought can be cleared of the charge of formalism.

All of that aside, I mentioned earlier Wesley's belief that holiness and happiness are joined in love, and I believe that this encompasses personal love as well as a love of righteousness, i.e., morality. And yet, the Wesleyan emphasis on respecting the moral law will view the moral agent as the agent of God's will, fulfilling the law of love first and foremost. Consequently, the Wesleyan respect for the moral law is tied to personal love for God and for others. It is my belief that this comprehensive emphasis is present in Wesley, but has been neglected by the Wesleyan traditions. Kant's account of perfection elucidates the neglected emphasis of respect for morality much better than Wesley does. In this way, a Wesleyan account of perfection can be informed by many of Kant's points.

Wesley's Dual Emphasis

According to Wesley, virtue includes both pure intentions and moral action. The two cannot be separated without compromising virtue in some fashion.

> This then is real, genuine, solid virtue. Not truth alone, nor conformity to truth. This is a property of real virtue, not the essence of it. Not love alone, though this comes nearer the mark, for *love*, in one sense, "is the fulfilling of the law." No, truth and love united together are the essence of virtue or holiness. God indispensably requires "truth in the inward parts," influencing all our words and actions. Yet truth itself, separate from love, is nothing in his sight.[131]

Wesley uses two particular phrases that best capture for him this dual emphasis on the morality of both intentions and actions. First, he declares that we must aspire to "holiness of heart and life." This includes the inner disposition of the heart as well as outward conduct.[132] Second,

---

130. Riley, "Kant on Persons," 48.
131. Wesley, Sermon 90, "An Israelite Indeed," §2.11, *WW*, 3:289 [J 7:45].
132. Blevins, "John Wesley and the Means of Grace," 127.

he maintains that we must have both "simplicity and Godly sincerity." In other words, our intentions must be pure and our actions must be conducive to the glory of God. This means that true religion will be pragmatic to some extent. Weakly intending to live a holy life is insufficient. Our intention to be pure must be sufficiently strong such that we actively pursue our own perfection, both morally and naturally, and we seek to act in ways that will bring glory to God and benefit others. This is why Wesley admits, "I find more profit in sermons on either good tempers, or good works, than in what are vulgarly called Gospel sermons."[133]

Conclusion

These two expressions ("holiness of heart and life" and "simplicity and Godly sincerity") essentially describe the telos of Wesleyan ethics. Wesleyan ethics aims at inward and outward holiness, both subjectively (according to personal conscience) and objectively (according to Scripture and the dictates of morality). Kant's way of relating moral perfection to natural perfection sheds useful light on the way that these concerns can be integrated. In a Wesleyan schema, moral perfection is the primary goal of perfection. However, pursuing moral perfection requires that we also seek our natural perfection. Furthermore, moral perfection requires that both types of perfection be scrutinized by objective standards.

A More Cognitivist Portrayal of Moral Action

Since I am attempting to construct a more cognitivist account of Wesleyan ethics, it will be necessary to understand moral action along more cognitivist lines. Wesley himself displays particular tendencies that suggest that moral action should be portrayed more cognitively. These tendencies are sufficient to show the feasibility of such a development, but they are merely tendencies and will not allow this development to be made primarily from Wesley's own thought. Rather, this development will need to draw on other sources. I propose that Kant's model of maxim-making can be usefully adapted for the new Wesleyan paradigm in a way that is consistent with Wesley's own cognitivist tendencies.

133. Wesley to Miss Bishop, 18 October 1778, *WWJ*, 13:35–36.

Wesley's Cognitivist Tendencies

Most of Wesley's cognitivist tendencies have already been laid out in previous chapters. For instance, Wesley highly esteems logic and gives it a central role in his epistemology. He does not understand ideas to be mere mental pictures or images. Instead, ideas are conceptual in their content, and this allows them to be shaped, scrutinized, and related to one another, even propositionally. Moreover, Wesley asserts that true virtue requires an active role for reason. He agrees with Edwards' claim that human learning gives believers even "greater ability and advantage to do service."[134] In short, Wesley believes that knowledge lies at the root of moral action.

Kant's Paradigm of Maxim-Making

In chapter 6, we saw that Wesley and Edwards believe that the will is moved by the affections. I am contending for a more cognitivist account of the emotions as part of the paradigm I am trying to construct. Kant gives an account of moral action that places greater stress on the role of reason, and this type of approach will be helpful in that regard.

Wood asserts that for Kant, the will always chooses according to rules; it never chooses only particular acts.[135] According to Barbara Herman, Kant regards motives as neither desires nor causes. Rather, they are the agent's reasons for acting.[136] Moral motivation for Kant is ultimately grounded in belief. However, it also seems to stem from his "mysterious doctrine of respect."[137]

Kant believes that each of us acts according to subjective principles, which he calls maxims. He claims that human beings are not evil because of the acts they perform, but because their constitution allows the inference of evil maxims. Consequently, the ground of evil is not in a determining power of inclination, but in the exercise of freedom in forming maxims.[138] In essence, good and evil are not found in the nature of things, but in the exercise of reason. The same principle holds true for actions as well, for the moral worth of duties performed does

---

134. Edwards, *DM*, §3.2, 142; cf. Wesley, *WHS*, 45.
135. A. Wood, *Kant's Moral Religion*, 45.
136. Herman, *Moral Judgment*, 11–12.
137. Timmons, "Possibility of Moral Motivation," 394.
138. Kant, *Rel*, 46–47 [6:20–21].

not come from the purposes they achieve, but from the maxims that determine them.[139] The mere conformity of an action with law is its legality, but the conformity of an action's motive with the incentive of duty is its morality.[140]

Maxims are subjective principles that are valid only for the will of the subject. In contrast, practical laws are objective principles that are valid for the will of every rational being.[141] Maxims are not rules or prescriptions for all possible contexts.[142] Instead, they include particulars about the agent and the circumstances the agent is facing.[143] For Kant, moral action involves not only general maxims that must be objectively valid, but also specific maxims of choosing the most efficient means to a given end in particular circumstances, and these specific maxims aim at fulfilling the general maxims.[144] Some maxims can be regarded as material, since they are formed from both reason and inclination, which is empirically grounded. These maxims have subjective ends. Other maxims are formal, because they are formed by reason alone and hence have universal ends. Only formal maxims have moral value in themselves.[145]

Wood notes that maxims reflect both the empirical and the rational nature of human beings.

> Maxims manifest both man's reason and his finitude, both his freedom and his subjection to the conditions of sensibility. They are "determined by reason," but "in accordance with the conditions of the subject." The former feature of maxims distinguishes the human will from subrational animal will, and the latter feature distinguishes it from the divine holy will.[146]

The desired goal is for reason to control and shape the empirical self without being conditioned by it. In that regard, Munzel outlines three of Kant's distinct maxims of human understanding: (1) the maxim of the

139. Kant, *GMM*, 12–13 [4:399].
140. Kant, *MM*, 20 [6:219].
141. Kant, *CPr*, 17 [5:19].
142. O'Neill, *Constructions of Reason*, 117.
143. Herman, *Moral Judgment*, 75.
144. Beck, *Philosophy of Kant*, 168.
145. T. Williams, *Categorical Imperative*, 20.
146. A. Wood, *Kant's Moral Religion*, 43.

understanding, i.e., thinking for oneself; (2) the maxim of judgment, i.e., thinking from a universal perspective; and (3) the maxim of reason, i.e., thinking resolutely. The last maxim is achieved through a union of the first two.[147] Kant insists that our maxims must be universalizable if they are to carry any moral obligation.[148] Our maxims ultimately reflect our conception of the laws on which they are founded.[149] If they are to be universalizable, then we must learn to think universally, and this first requires taking the conceptions of others into account when forming our maxims.[150]

Walter Schaller suggests that our maxims of action must be tested by the categorical imperative, and our maxims of incentive are judged according to their respect for the moral law.[151] However, there is a limit to the universalizability of our maxims. According to Kant, our maxims can only be regarded as universal laws due to their form, not their content.[152] The form of a maxim is its generality as a rule or principle. The content of a maxim is the particular end adopted by the will through the faculty of desire when it acts according to that maxim.[153] Essentially, the more specific and contextualized our maxims become, the less universalizable they will be. Nevertheless, morality requires us to form specific maxims so that we may keep our duty. Even our specific maxims should still have a general form that can be universalized.

Application

In the paradigm I am constructing, it will be beneficial to regard maxims as the foundation of moral action, because they represent the reasons that we have for acting. Maxims are essentially the subjective application of objective principles. This coincides with Wesley's assertion that there are prudential means of grace, i.e., subjective means that lead individuals toward holiness from within a given context. In a Wesleyan paradigm, however, maxims will not be motivated solely by a respect

---

147. Munzel, *Moral Character*, 223.
148. Kant, *GMM*, 14 [4:402].
149. Korsgaard, *Kingdom of Ends*, 57.
150. Munzel, *Moral Character*, 231.
151. Schaller, "Should Kantians Care," 34.
152. Kant, *CPr*, 26 [5:27].
153. A. Wood, *Kant's Moral Religion*, 43–44.

for duty, as they are for Kant. Rather, they will also be motivated by personal love for God and for others.

Still, this does not imply that they are based on passive feelings. Instead, maxims themselves are founded upon value judgments. As such, our maxims and the value judgments on which they are founded can be scrutinized and shaped. This is consistent with the belief that experience can be scrutinized and shaped. In Wesleyan ethics, maxims are not judged by their universalizability, as they are in Kantian ethics. Rather, maxims are founded upon and subject to the four pillars of Wesleyan epistemology: Scripture, reason, tradition, and experience.

9
Reformulating Wesley's Two Distinctive Doctrines

THE UNDERLYING PREMISE OF THIS BOOK HAS BEEN THAT TWO OF Wesley's most distinctive doctrines, i.e., his doctrines of assurance and Christian perfection, have not been intellectually developed to a sufficient degree. Rather, these doctrines, to a great extent, have either been distorted or neglected. I have suggested that Wesleyan ethics needs to be recast in a paradigm that more adequately emphasizes the cognitive aspects of religious knowledge and moral development.

A new paradigm was thus constructed in two stages. First, the cognitivist roots of Wesley's thought were explored, beginning with his reliance upon Lockean empiricism. I thus contended that Wesleyan epistemology should remain more closely tied to empirical knowledge and distance itself from mystical and intuitionist models like Wesley's own "spiritual sense" analogy. Additionally, by carefully examining Wesley's view of emotions, I showed that Wesleyan ethics should not regard emotions as something to be passively experienced. Rather, emotions have cognitive content that allows them to be shaped. This perspective becomes evident in light of Wesley's rejection of mystical approaches to spirituality in favor of a more cognitive approach to spiritual and moral development. It is also reflected in the way that Wesley appropriates Edwards' view of the religious affections. Second, the new paradigm was completed as I suggested ways that some of Wesley's own concepts should be revised and expanded. The goal is to allow more of Wesley's concerns to be incorporated into the paradigm without sacrificing his core commitments.

The final task will be to provide a sketch of what the doctrines of assurance and perfection will look like in the new paradigm. Essentially, assurance will be based on religious faith and on self-knowledge, both empirical and psychological, and perfection will be understood in a more teleological context. Hopefully, the end result will be a version of Wesleyan ethics that is a more faithful development of Wesley's own thought and can withstand the scrutiny of higher intellectual standards.

Assurance

A central part of the Wesleyan doctrine of assurance is the belief in the witness of the Spirit. As such, it cannot and should not be excised from a Wesleyan account of assurance. There are two aspects of this teaching, the direct witness made by the Spirit and the indirect witness made by conscience, and Wesley asserts that both aspects are necessary. The direct witness is needed for obtaining a clear conscience, but it must be confirmed by the indirect witness if assurance is to have any epistemic weight. In the new Wesleyan paradigm I am constructing, the indirect witness will need to be understood along more cognitivist lines without destroying the need for the direct witness.

Surprisingly, Kant offers a helpful way of addressing this concern as well, for he defines assurance as faith in the satisfaction of one's sins and faith that one is becoming well-pleasing to God. I believe that this basic model can be adapted to provide a more empirical account of assurance that attempts to maintain tension between justification by faith and the need for both moral action (i.e., good works) and moral progress. Wesley's teaching on the direct witness of the Spirit will still have great significance, but its epistemic value will be limited. Instead, the certainty of assurance will largely be derived from empirical self-knowledge.

The Witness of the Holy Spirit

Believing in the witness of the Holy Spirit is beneficial to the regenerate. William James maintains that Methodism's emphasis on sudden conversion is not only "healthier-minded" than other models of conversion, it is psychologically more complete. However, there is also ample evidence "that saints of the once-born type exist, that there may be a gradual growth in holiness without a cataclysm."[1] In that regard, it is important to note that the significance of Aldersgate for Wesley changed

---

1. James, *Varieties of Religious Experience*, 251.

over time. As Richard Heitzenrater states, "The irony of Aldersgate, however, is that its theological significance rests in Wesley's eventual modification of nearly every aspect of his perception and explanation of the event at the time."[2] In essence, the most important part of Wesley's concept of conversion is not the manner in which conversion takes place, be it sudden or gradual. Rather, the cornerstone of a Wesleyan view of conversion is that the regenerate receive assurance that they have been "born in the Spirit."

The real issue that must be addressed, one of which Wesley himself was well aware, is how to discern self-delusion and determine precisely what constitutes a true conversion. Even though Wesley does not see conversion from within a predestinationist context like Edwards, both men want an account of conversion that is empirically verifiable nonetheless. Consequently, they both assert the direct and indirect (i.e., the supernatural and the natural) aspects of assurance. We have already noted that Edwards interprets the witness of the Spirit as a declaration, one that provides evidence that may be scrutinized. He insists that we must evaluate our own motives. Similarly for Wesley, the direct witness of the Spirit must be accompanied by the indirect witness of conscience. As John Miley explains, although there are two witnesses (i.e., the witness of the Holy Spirit and the witness of our spirit), there is only one unified state of assurance.[3]

Kant's Model of Assurance

It is my contention that Kant's model of assurance can be adapted for a Wesleyan doctrine of assurance. According to Kant, saving faith entails faith in the satisfaction of one's sins and faith that one can become well-pleasing to God.[4] It is Gordon Michalson's opinion that Kant's "belief in atonement really only amounts to a belief in our own rational capacity to become well-pleasing to God—a potential savior figure, in whom we would believe, merely embodies a moral capacity available to all."[5] In light of Kant's assertion that God regards our moral progress as a completed whole, it could be argued that Kant means more than this, that he

---

2. Heitzenrater, "Great Expectations," 91.
3. Miley, *Systematic Theology*, 2:351.
4. Kant, *Rel*, 123 [6:116].
5. Michalson, *Fallen Freedom*, 102.

at least understands satisfaction to involve an act of divine forgiveness. However, this would still fall far short of a traditional Christian view of atonement. Philip Quinn surmises that Kant's real objection is to the belief that human sinfulness is somehow transferred from generation to generation: "Any doctrine of vicarious atonement will be difficult, if not impossible, to square with a conviction that is central to the conceptual scheme of common sense morality," namely, that "moral credits and debits are neither transferable nor transmissible."[6]

Wesley does not recoil from the traditional doctrine of original sin as such. Nonetheless, the basic elements of Wesley's account of assurance bear some resemblance to Kant's description. Frederick Dreyer asserts that Wesley understands faith to be manifested through confidence in one's pardon (i.e., the witness of the Spirit) and through the manifestation of holy affections (i.e., the fruit of the Spirit).[7] In that regard, Miley suggests that as a mental state, assurance is "the resulting persuasion of truth in what we have believed."[8] In other words, we must be convinced that our sins have been forgiven and that we have been transformed sufficiently such that Christian virtues are evident in our lives.

The doctrine of assurance must thus maintain tension between the excesses of antinomianism and legalism. Without the doctrine of justification by faith, the result is works righteousness. However, emphasizing justification by faith can lead to trivializing the need for good works. Henry Knight believes that a mediating position can be supported if the Christian life is understood as a dynamic process.[9] Wesley tried to resolve this tension by asserting that although salvation is by faith, it must be preceded by repentance that surpasses mere sorrow for one's sins and includes an entire change of heart and life.[10]

A similar tension exists in Kant's thought, for he recognizes that the belief in justification by faith counters the belief that we shall be held responsible for the conduct of our lives. On one hand, justification by faith tends to undermine the incentive we have to progress morally. On the other hand, it is necessary for having a clear conscience

6. Quinn, "Christian Atonement," 458–59.
7. Dreyer, "Evangelical Thought," 183.
8. Miley, *Systematic Theology*, 2:339–40.
9. Knight, 90–91.
10. Maddox, *Responsible Grace*, 162–63.

(i.e., being able to regard oneself as pleasing to God).[11] In fact, the need for a clear conscience is ongoing. Accordingly, Kant asserts that our moral shortcomings do not need to torment us, because as long as we are progressing morally, God regards our infinite moral progress as a completed whole.[12] John Hare speculates that this assertion could be regarded as Kant's version of the doctrine of imputed righteousness. Like his insistence on faith in satisfaction, it is one of his attempts to preserve Reformation doctrines.[13]

Both Wesley and Kant consider moral progress to be an integral part of salvation, and this primarily involves the purification and the perfection of the will. Even though they hold different standards of moral purity, they both assert that the will must be properly motivated. For Kant, moral motivation comes from a respect for duty itself. For Wesley, it comes from love for God and for others. In both cases, pure motives are not self-centered. Consequently, it appears that moral purity can only be achieved if one's conscience is clear, and this is only possible if moral agents can believe that God has forgiven them of their sins. Otherwise, good works cannot be morally pure since they will in part be an attempt to earn justification.

Wesley subscribes to the traditional view that divine forgiveness is bestowed by the grace of God when one trusts in the merits of Christ's atonement. When believers truly believe that their sins have been forgiven, their guilt and shame are dispelled, and they are given a fresh start in life with a clear conscience. Of course, attaining a clear conscience regarding the harm we have caused others requires more than this, because we must also ask for their forgiveness and try to make restitution for our sins toward them. In regard to one's attitude toward God, although a convert's motives may be self-interested in seeking justification, the justified believer does not need to be concerned with meriting the favor of God, and good works can now be done through unselfish love. Agents are thus enabled to move beyond self-interest and progress toward moral purity.[14]

11. Kant, *Rel*, 86–87n [6:69–70n].
12. Ibid., 85 [6:67].
13. Hare, *Moral Gap*, 54–55.
14. Wesley, Sermon 12, "The Witness of Our Own Spirit," §§15–16, *WW*, 1:309–10 [J 5:140–41].

I suggest that this particular point is one that Kant cannot ultimately make, since he refuses to embrace the notion of unmerited grace. Instead, he claims that we must make ourselves worthy of divine assistance, the respect of others, and happiness. Kant places such heavy emphasis on human responsibility that it becomes inappropriate to see salvation as a free gift from God. Granted, he would most likely argue that salvation is free in the sense that God is not obligated to forgive us. However, he still suggests that we must strive to earn God's forgiveness. As a result, it does not appear that he can ever assert anything more than works righteousness, and this certainly counteracts his standard of moral purity, i.e., performing duty for its own sake and not for one's own sake. In general, Kant gives no explanation as to how moral purity can be achieved, given the other assumptions he makes.

Wesley wants his standard of moral purity to be attainable, so he carefully defines the limits of human moral responsibility. Specifically, he contends that believers are not condemned for (1) past sins (since they have already been forgiven), (2) present sins (since believers do not commit them), (3) inward sinful inclinations (since we are not responsible for their existence, only for our cultivation of them), (4) impure (i.e., mixed) motives, (5) "sins of infirmity" (i.e., transgressions committed out of ignorance), and (6) that which is beyond our control.[15] However, Wesley is not attempting to reduce our moral responsibility, for he insists that we must strive for the highest attainments of holiness. In William Cannon's mind, Wesley's assertion "that man can be righteous and indeed must be righteous if he is to be Christian means that his final salvation includes moral attainment and personal purity as essential elements. Without inherent personal holiness, Wesley says, no man can see God."[16] Of course, Wesley believes that true morality is not found in keeping the letter of the law, but in keeping the spirit of the law. In this way, our righteousness exceeds that of the Pharisees.[17]

For Wesley, moral transformation should be judged by the results it produces. As Cannon points out, "And always in defending the validity of his preaching and the work of his movement, John Wesley pointed to the moral successes, to the fact that men's lives were changed and

---

15. Wesley, Sermon 8, "The First Fruits of the Spirit," §§2.1–13, *WW*, 1:237–43 [J 5:89–94].

16. Cannon, *Theology of John Wesley*, 225.

17. Dillman, "Law in Discourse," 62.

that they produced in deeds and character the fruit of their faith."[18] A Wesleyan understanding of assurance must therefore include both the belief that one's sins have been forgiven as well as a firm conviction that one's life has been changed to the extent that significant moral progress is being made and will continue to be made.

Assurance, even its emotional aspect, is cognitive at its roots. Wesley's protégé Adam Clarke concurs, for he declares that with respect to assurance, the intellect is "the place or faculty to which such information can properly be brought."[19] Of course, Wesley feels that basing assurance merely on having a clear conscience or on the presence of particular virtues is a fallible approach, because the possibility of self-delusion always exists.[20] However, what is needed to bridge this gap is not a mystical experience, but a deeper understanding of our own motivations.

In summary, Kant bases assurance on faith in satisfaction and faith that one is becoming well-pleasing to God (i.e., is progressing morally). A more empirical account of Wesleyan assurance can be portrayed in a similar fashion. It is still founded on the tenet that we are saved by grace through faith. This is not antinomianism, but it recognizes the need for believers to do good works and to pursue perfection, and this involves moral progress. Such an account corresponds with Wesley's insistence that the direct witness must be accompanied by the indirect witness of conscience.

The Importance of the Direct Witness

The notion of the direct witness of the Spirit will need to be retained in the Wesleyan doctrine of assurance. Its importance is linked to the stress placed on justification by faith. Wesley says that if we believe Scripture, we must believe that the Holy Spirit testifies to us that we are God's children such that we are able to perceive this testimony.[21] Moreover, moral purity requires a clear conscience, and this requires some type of immediate assurance. Wesley's full explanation of this principle is as follows:

18. Cannon, *Theology of John Wesley*, 25.
19. Clarke, *Christian Theology*, 150.
20. Maddox, *Responsible Grace*, 129–30.
21. Wesley to John Smith, 25 March 1747, §8, *WW*, 26:233 [J 12:86].

That the "testimony of the Spirit of God" must, in the very nature of things, be antecedent to the "testimony of our own spirit," may appear from this single consideration: we must be holy in heart and life before we can be conscious that we are so. But we must love God before we can be holy at all, this being the root of all holiness. Now we cannot love God, till we know he loves us: "We love him, because he first loved us." And we cannot know his love to us, till his Spirit witnesses it to our spirit. Till then we cannot believe it; we cannot say, "The life which I now live, I live by faith in the Son of God, who loved me, and gave himself for me."

> Then, only then we feel
> Our interest in his blood,
> And cry, with joy unspeakable,
> Thou art my Lord, my God!

Since, therefore, the testimony of his Spirit must precede the love of God, and all holiness, of consequence it must precede our consciousness thereof.[22]

The direct witness of the Spirit is both scriptural and reasonable, i.e., it proceeds from the nature of faith itself. Even from a natural standpoint, it stands to reason that when we truly repent and believe that we are forgiven, we will have a sense of forgiveness. However, the subjectivity of this event requires it to be scrutinized objectively. Wesley recognized this and thus stressed the need for the indirect witness. The indirect witness actually gives believers assurance that they have truly experienced the direct witness.[23]

Miley regards the direct witness of the Spirit as being comparable to the conviction of sin.[24] Although we can perceive the conviction that we are God's children, we cannot perceive the means by which we receive it.

> Therein [the Spirit's] testimony is given simply in the mode of an impression in our consciousness, an impression in the form of an assurance that we are the children of God, and we are

---

22. Wesley, Sermon 11, "The Witness of the Spirit, Discourse II," §3.5, *WW*, 1:289–90 [J 5:127].
23. Monk, *John Wesley: His Puritan Heritage*, 61.
24. Miley, *Systemic Theology*, 2:347.

directly cognizant only of that impression, not of the agency of the Spirit whereby it is produced.[25]

Wesley's problem was in reconciling the witness of the Spirit with his belief that believers may backslide and eventually lose their salvation. In defending the direct witness of the Spirit, Wesley was forced to conclude that backsliders would have it erased from memory.[26] It is not necessary to assert this. If one truly believes that salvation can ultimately be forfeited, then backsliding will essentially erode the indirect witness of conscience and assurance will gradually be lost. In Wesley's mind (and Kant's), we must believe that we are accountable for the moral conduct of our lives, even after justification, else we will be in danger of espousing antinomianism.

Nevertheless, it may be argued that Wesley's belief that salvation may ultimately be forfeited essentially reduces his view of salvation to works righteousness, because believers must continue to merit God's forgiveness. Here, the key is the distinction Wesley makes regarding the nature of good works, which I prefer to refer to as *works righteousness* and *works of righteousness*. The former is done in order to obtain saving faith, but the latter is done as an expression of the saving faith that one already has. Even though we are saved by faith alone, proper faith will produce repentance, love, and good works. This, in turn, informs the indirect witness of conscience and thus helps to establish assurance. Hence, proper faith surpasses mere assent, which even the demons give, and includes trust in the merits of Christ's atonement for salvation. In Wesley's mind, this kind of trust can only be exercised if one is truly sincere, and this is what qualifies proper faith, that which produces love and righteousness.[27] Overall, it is Wesley's belief in justification by faith that separates him from Kant, and it is his definition of sincere faith that distances him from antinomianism.

Assurance as Empirical Self-Knowledge

A Wesleyan view of assurance requires moral certainty regarding one's present spiritual state. However, this need for certainty is not absolute, for Wesley admits that it is possible to be justified without clear

---

25. Ibid., 2:381.
26. Wesley to John Smith, 25 March 1747, §5, *WW*, 26:231 [J 12:84].
27. Wesley, Sermon 2, "The Almost Christian," §§2.4–5, *WW*, 1:138–39 [J 5:22–23].

assurance.[28] In any event, the moral certainty of assurance does need to be objectified to a significant degree. For Wesley, this takes place in the indirect witness of conscience, which confirms the direct witness of the Spirit. Therefore, the certainty of assurance is directly dependent upon the reliability of conscience. According to Wesley, conscience ascertains three things: (1) knowledge of the moral law, (2) knowledge of self, and (3) congruence of the two.

Earlier, I suggested that conscience should be regarded as the product of practical reasoning. Since Scripture must be retained as an authoritative source of moral knowledge in a Wesleyan schema, it will be the primary source of knowledge of the moral law. Reason is the secondary source of moral knowledge, and it is also the vehicle through which moral knowledge is attained. It must be allowed to formulate duties that are not specifically enjoined by Scripture. Nevertheless, tradition and experience are also sources of moral knowledge that inform our understanding of Scripture. In addition to the moral knowledge it gains from Scripture, reason, tradition, and experience, conscience must also have an empirical knowledge of self and be able to objectively evaluate the self in the light of its moral knowledge.

Assurance thus begins with the assessment of one's psychological state. First, we must have faith that our sins have been forgiven. We must believe that God accepts us and no longer holds us accountable for the sins of the past. Second, we must be able to gauge our own sincerity. Only we know within ourselves if we are truly sorry for our sins and are fully repentant, having every intention of living a holy life.

Our psychological state can be assessed since the emotions are more than passive feelings. They are cognitive in content and can thus be shaped and evaluated. However, our bodily conditions can affect us emotionally and so skew our assurance. Wesley observes, "Possibly some may be in the favor of God, and yet go mourning all the day long, but I believe this is usually owing either to disorder of body or ignorance of the Gospel promises."[29] Consequently, assurance must be based on something else besides psychological self-assessment.

In a cognitivist paradigm, a proper psychological state will cause one's actions to be congruent in several ways. First and foremost, actions

---

28. Wesley to Richard Thompson, 18 February 1756, *WWJ*, 12:472–73.
29. Wesley to Dr. Thomas Rutherford, 28 March 1768, §1.4, *WW*, 9:376 [J 14:348].

will be congruent with Scripture, for since this is the authoritative source of moral knowledge, a clear conscience cannot be obtained if Scripture is disregarded or disobeyed. Next, a proper mental state will yield actions that are consistent with one's truest intentions. In reality, our actions reveal what our true intentions really are, as well as their strength and purity. Also, the actions of the regenerate should have congruence amongst themselves. In other words, our actions should be consistent and coherent, reflecting the purity of our psychological state. Finally, a proper psychological state will produce actions that conform to duty. There will be an earnest desire to live a moral life and to fulfill one's obligations to God and to others. In a previous chapter, we saw that for Wesley, the fact that ideas can be associated with one another yields a holistic view of human nature. Although regeneration begins as a psychological state, it will affect every aspect of life and existence, because our thoughts determine who we are and what we can become.

In the long run, the certainty of assurance is strengthened through evidence of moral progress. Since the fruit of the Spirit represents a set of virtues whose presence can be judged outwardly by others, this provides objective evidence of moral progress and hence confirms the subjective experience of conversion. In contrast, inward motives must be judged by personal conscience.[30] However, this inner self-scrutiny is also confirmed by evidence of moral progress. As Ted Runyon maintains, a Wesleyan approach to salvation will thus regard religious experience as transforming.[31] It entails more than warm feelings and a sense of assurance, since "we should not be satisfied until we see actual change."[32]

As Wesley indicates, the ordinary influences of the Spirit are felt in particular virtues, especially love, joy, peace, patience, gentleness, and meekness.[33] Nonetheless,

> A clear conviction of the love of God cannot remain in any who do not walk closely with God. And I know no one person who has lost this without some voluntary defect in his conduct,

---

30. Wesley, Sermon 10, "The Witness of the Spirit, Discourse I," §§2.1–14, *WW*, 1:277–84 [J 5:117–23].

31. Runyon, "Orthopathy," 297–98.

32. Runyon, "Importance of Experience," 106.

33. Wesley to Dr. Thomas Rutherford, 28 March 1768, §3.1, *WW*, 9:381 [J 14:353–54].

though perhaps at the time he was not conscious of it, but upon prayer it was revealed to him.[34]

In essence, assurance is a state, so it must be ongoing. However, it can be disrupted by sin and restored once again through repentance.[35]

Summary

The Wesleyan doctrine of assurance acknowledges the importance of both the direct witness and the indirect witness. A sense of assurance is prerequisite to a clear conscience, and this must be obtained in order for good works to have moral purity. As such, the direct witness provides the immediate sense of assurance that is needed at conversion. However, due to its highly subjective nature, it must be validated by the indirect witness. This second witness is that of conscience, and in the new Wesleyan paradigm, it entails empirical self-knowledge. Conscience testifies to one's psychological state, the congruence of one's actions, and the extent of one's moral progress.

Perfection

In the new paradigm I have constructed, perfection should be understood as a teleological pursuit, not as an event constituted of ontological change. This will better maintain and develop Wesley's understanding of perfection as a process that reaches a point of culmination. It will also allow the ends and goals of human perfection to be related to the telos of creation itself, although this will not be explored here.[36] The claim that I am making is that a Wesleyan account of perfection must assert the attainability of particular thresholds while emphasizing the need for continual moral progress. I will discuss a key threshold of perfection that has been historically asserted by Wesleyans, a threshold that maintains the tension between attainment and progress.

Wesley insists that perfection includes victory over willful sin. If the definition of sin is expanded to include the notion of duty, perfection will also now include the fulfillment of duty. Nevertheless, a Wesleyan account of perfection will still focus mainly on the affections,

---

34. Wesley to Richard Thompson, 16 March 1756, *WWJ*, 12:473.
35. Starkey, "Wesleyan Witness," 75–76.
36. See Bence, "Teleological Hermeneutic".

so perfection will entail wholehearted love for God, love for others, and purity of motives. This cognitivist approach to Wesleyan ethics recognizes the cognitive content of the emotions, and this gives us the ability to evaluate and to shape them. This principle is useful in the doctrine of perfection in particular.

Teleological, not Ontological

Earlier I pointed out the disparity between Wesley and the Wesleyan traditions regarding the nature of the moral transformation that takes place in perfection. Wesley believes that perfection involves gradual moral transformation that reaches a point of culmination. In contrast, the Wesleyan traditions have tended to portray perfection as an instantaneous moral transformation. In order to justify this, the change has often been regarded as an ontological one, supernaturally effected beyond natural means. This emphasis sometimes led to defining sin as a type of spiritual "substance." I have already referred to a number of recent Wesleyan voices who, for this reason and others, reject an ontological account of perfection in favor of a teleological approach. As Robin Lovin states, "The fundamental Wesleyan message of the possibility of real change and the link between these changes and the will and the affections is worth rethinking and incorporating into whatever ethical system we find more adequate on the whole."[37]

Once again, I find Kant to be a helpful resource. Although the bulk of Kant's ethics is deontological in that it relies on the formation of rules and principles, it is still a good example of how the broader issues of ethics can be construed in the context of a teleological framework. In a teleological system, all things should tend toward their proper end. According to Christine Korsgaard, Kant believes that we always have an end in view.

> It is Kant's view throughout his moral philosophy that every action "contains" an end; there is no action done without some end in view. The difference between morally worthy action and morally indifferent action is that in the first case the end is adopted because it is dictated by reason and in the second case the end is adopted in response to an inclination for it.[38]

37. Lovin, "Physics of True Virtue," 271.
38. Korsgaard, *Kingdom of Ends*, 107.

Although the ends we embrace may be personal, there are also universal ends, which morality dictates. Indeed, Kant claims that "the universal end of mankind is the highest moral perfection."[39] As William Hund points out, even Kant's general imperative to always do the most perfect act possible seems to presuppose a teleological view of human nature.[40] We thus have a duty to pursue perfection, not merely for its own sake, but we must cultivate our natural powers as "means to all sorts of possible ends."[41]

For Kant, the path to perfection is what leads people toward true freedom. Obedience is not something that God coerces. Rather, God desires that we should always act freely.

> Christianity's objective is to promote love of the concern for observing one's duty, and in addition it elicits this love, for its founder speaks not as a commander who requires obedience to *his will*, but as a friend of mankind who places in the hearts of his fellow men their own well-understood wills, i.e. the will in accord with which they would themselves freely act.[42]

According to Kant, God commands something because it is a moral law and because his will coincides with the moral law.[43] The congruence between God's will and the moral law does not hamper God's perfect freedom in any way. Similarly, our freedom is not threatened by our conformity with the moral law. Freedom is part of our autonomy, and this is preserved in our ability to be self-motivated. Kant declares, "The more a man can compel himself, the freer he is. The less he need be compelled by others, the greater is his inner freedom."[44] Consequently, the ultimate end of perfection does not hinder freedom. Rather, it promotes freedom, since it leads us to become even more autonomous.

Morality itself dictates that we progress toward a kingdom of ends. For this reason, Kant maintains that all maxims must (1) be universalizable, (2) have an end in which relative ends are limited by the intrinsic end of rational nature itself, and (3) conform their ends to a unified

---

39. Kant, *LE*, 252.
40. Hund, "Human Perfection as a Moral Determinant," 344.
41. Kant, *MM*, 194 [6:444].
42. Kant, "The End of All Things," in *PP*, 102 [8:338].
43. Kant, *LE*, 40.
44. Ibid., 30.

kingdom of ends.[45] He thus believes that since the dictates of morality are objectively determined by the nature of reason itself, people can follow these dictates autonomously and yet achieve moral unity. R. W. Hall feels that this joint pursuit—of our own perfection and the happiness of others—specifically brings about the realization of this kingdom of ends, because the pursuit "brings about the harmonization of purposes among rational beings."[46] Ultimately, the harmonization of human will is legislated by practical reason.[47]

Even Kant's concept of the highest good, i.e., the "furtherance of happiness in harmony with morality," can be regarded as the actualization of the final purpose of creation.[48] Hence, the highest good represents the perfection and the unification of nature and morality. As Jacqueline Mariña states, "Morality thus commits us to the hope that the natural world is ordered in accordance with an ethico-teleological purpose."[49] When stated this way, Kant's general belief in the eventual attainment of a kingdom of ends can be applied not only to Wesleyan ethics, but to any theological or moral system that strives for the perfection of all creation.

A Wesleyan emphasis on perfection implies that religious experience itself should be teleological.[50] To be specific, it must promote the various facets of Christian perfection, which are (1) wholehearted love for God, (2) love for others, (3) purity of intention, (4) the imitation of Christ, and (5) victory over willful sin. It should be noted, however, that fully intending to live a Godly life is expected at regeneration. In perfection, this is realized more fully in the purification of motives and in the fulfillment of duty.

As we have already observed, the general ends of perfection are "holiness of heart and life" and "simplicity and Godly sincerity." These ends imply that we must not only be morally pure, we must also be effective in a practical sense. In short, Wesleyan perfection focuses on both motive and action. Wesley himself states this most plainly.

45. Kant, *GMM*, 41–42 [4:436].
46. Hall, "Ethical Formalism," 438.
47. O'Leary-Hawthorn and Howard-Snyder, "Reflections on Aquinas and Kant," 241.
48. Lindstedt, "Postulate of Practical Reason," 139–40.
49. Mariña, "Making Sense," 351.
50. Runyon, "Orthopathy," 302–3.

> Good works are so far from being hindrances of our salvation; they are so far from being insignificant, from being of no account in Christianity that, supposing them to spring from a right principle, they are the perfection of religion. They are the highest part of that spiritual building whereof Jesus Christ is the foundation. To those who attentively consider the thirteenth chapter of the First Epistle to the Corinthians, it will be undeniably plain that what Saint Paul there describes as the highest of all Christian graces, is properly and directly the love of our neighbor. And to him who attentively considers the whole tenor both of the Old and New Testament, it will be equally plain, that works springing from this love are the highest part of the religion therein revealed. Of these our Lord himself says, "Hereby is my Father glorified, that ye bring forth much fruit." Much *fruit*! Does not the very expression imply the excellency of what is so termed? Is not the tree itself for the sake of the fruit? By bearing fruit, and by this alone, it attains the highest perfection it is capable of, and answers the end for which it was planted. Who, what is he then, that is called a Christian, and can speak lightly of good works?[51]

Finally, Wesleyan ethics must also promote the perfection of all creation, in both the spiritual and natural realms. Just as we must pursue our own natural perfection as a necessary means to our moral perfection, we must also seek to promote the natural perfection of the world, so that God might be glorified and the ends of his kingdom might be realized on earth as they are in heaven.

Wholehearted Love for God and Love for Others

Wesley insists that true religion must include both love for God and love for others. He believes that too many Christian thinkers emphasize one to the neglect of the other. For example, whereas he criticizes Hutcheson for ignoring love for God, he disparages Wollaston for overlooking the importance of love for others.[52] Darlene Fozard Weaver suggests that the same type of imbalance still exists in Christianity. "The relative silence in contemporary Christian ethics about love for God yields an anemic theological anthropology. Too often, the person's

---

51. Wesley, Sermon 99, "The Reward of the Righteous," §1.6, *WW*, 3:405 [J 7:130-31].

52. Wesley, Sermon 90, "An Israelite Indeed," §§1-4, *WW*, 3:279-81 [J 7:37-39].

self-transcendence is truncated and the religious dimension of human life is neglected."[53]

What is needed is a robust integration of spirituality and ethics. For Wesley, this integration is rooted in the connection between faith and love. He does not regard faith as an end in itself, but as the means to the end of love. "Let this love be attained, by whatever means, and I am content; I desire no more. All is well if we love the Lord our God with all our heart and our neighbors as ourselves."[54] Wesley feels that we often try to compensate for the lack of love in our hearts. In I Cor 13, St. Paul indicates that the absence of love for God is often replaced with a hierarchy of lesser substitutes: (1) eloquence, (2) knowledge, (3) faith, and (4) good works. However, "nothing is higher than this, but Christian love, the love of our neighbor flowing from the love of God."[55]

There must also be a legitimate place for self-love in Wesleyan perfection. According to Weaver, love for God serves as a norm for self-love, ruling out works righteousness as well as a quietism that reduces love to a faith that presupposes that God's grace essentially nullifies human freedom and responsibility.[56] Mildred Bangs Wynkoop argues that self-interest has a legitimate place in Wesleyan ethics, for both self-interest and other-interest are "absolutely essential to mental health." As such, self-love is only sinful when it crowds out "other selves."[57] Albert Outler agrees, asserting that both self-loathing and narcissism should be avoided, since they corrupt the relationships that we have with others.[58]

Indeed, Wesley recognizes the need to limit self-love and place it in proper perspective, for he believes that arrogance is pervasive and morally destructive. As a matter of fact, he condemned both the skeptics and the enthusiasts for their pride.[59] However, rather than view self-love as something that should be eliminated, Wesley believes that love for God and love for others is ultimately what prevents "pride, vanity,

---

53. Weaver, *Self Love and Christian Ethics*, 45.
54. Wesley to John Smith, 25 June 1746, §9, WW, 26:203 [J 12:78–79].
55. Wesley, Sermon 91, "On Charity," §2.6, WW, 3:300 [J 7:51].
56. Weaver, *Self Love and Christian Ethics*, 136.
57. Wynkoop, *Theology of Love*, 203.
58. Outler, *Wesleyan Spirit*, 83.
59. Gray, "Place of Reason," 216.

and self-will" from tainting our words and actions.[60] True moral motivation includes humility, and the primary way humility is displayed is through obedience and submission to God.

Essentially, a Wesleyan theology of love teaches that God must be loved supremely and for the right reasons. In other words, God must be loved wholeheartedly, above all else, unconditionally, and primarily for his own sake; love of God for our own sake is secondary to loving God for God's sake. Then, we must love others (1) as Christ loves us, aspiring to his ideal of unconditional love; (2) as Christ loves them, seeing them as Christ sees them; (3) as ourselves, regarding them as equals; (4) for God's sake, because everything we do should be for the glory of God; (5) for their sake, since people must be valued as ends in themselves; and (6) for our own sake, realizing that we were created to be in relationship and will only feel fulfilled if we cultivate this dimension of our personalities. Proper love for others is undergirded by the demands of justice, but it exceeds these demands, requiring sacrifice.

Pure Motives

Wesley sees the person as a psychosomatic unity. He thus does not bifurcate the material and the spiritual elements of our existence as the idealists and the materialists do.[61] He also does not bifurcate the rational and the empirical as is the tendency of Kant and other rationalists. Rather, Wesley understands moral purity to involve the proper ordering and regulation of our affections, and this is not easily accomplished. It is this emphasis that leads Isabel Rivers to regard Wesley's concept of perfection as "more demanding and ambitious" than the concept of benevolence proposed by Shaftesbury, Hutcheson, or Hume.[62] As Ray Dunning suggests, if Wesleyan perfection is to entail a change of character, then it must include the transformation of dispositions, perceptions, and intentions.[63]

There is no doubt that the emphasis of Wesleyanism is personal. As Wynkoop states, "It has always been the most profound conviction

60. Wesley, "An Earnest Appeal to Men of Reason and Religion," §51, *WW*, 11:64 [J 8:20].
61. Runyon, *The New Creation*, 156.
62. Rivers, *Reason, Grace, and Sentiment*, 1:234.
63. Dunning, "Christian Perfection," 159.

of Wesleyanism that the Bible speaks to the moral relationships of men and not about sub-rational, non-personal areas of the self."[64] For Wesley, the power of sin is expelled by the power of affection—specifically, love for God and for others.[65] This can be seen in the way that Wesley describes the perfect person:

> This man can now testify to all mankind, "I am crucified with Christ; nevertheless I live, yet not I, but Christ liveth in me." He is holy, as God who called him is holy, both in life and in all manner of conversation. He loveth the Lord his God with all his heart, and serveth Him with all his strength. He loveth his neighbor (every man) as himself, yea, as Christ loved us, them in particular that despitefully use him and persecute him, because they know not the Son, neither the Father. Indeed, his soul is all love, filled with bowels of mercies, kindness, meekness, gentleness, long suffering. And his life agreeth thereto, full of "the work of faith, the patience of hope, the labor of love." And whatsoever he doeth, either in word or deed, he doeth it all in the name, in the love and power, of the Lord Jesus. In a word, he doeth the will of God on earth as it is done in heaven.
>
> This it is to be a perfect man, to be sanctified throughout, created anew in Jesus Christ, even "to have a heart all flaming with the love of God," (to use Archbishop Usher's words,) "so as continually to offer up every thought, word, and work as a spiritual sacrifice, acceptable unto God through Christ;" In every thought of our hearts, in every word of our tongues, in every work of our hands, to show forth His praise who hath called us out of darkness into his marvelous light. O that both we, and all who seek the Lord Jesus in sincerity, may thus be made perfect in one![66]

Although Kant's view of love is not compatible with Wesley's, Kant's analysis cannot be ignored completely. He is correct to point out the subjective nature of personal love. If love becomes too personal, then it becomes too subjective and often leads to self-deception about one's motives. For this reason, personal commitment must be judged objectively. Lara Denis believes that even though the assistance of other people may not be necessary in the pursuit of our own perfection, they

---

64. Wynkoop, *Theology of Love*, 167.

65. Vick, "Teaching Concerning Perfection," 207–8 n. 16.

66. Wesley, preface to "A Collection of Hymns and Sacred Poems" (1745), §§5–6, *WWJ*, 14:329–30.

can still contribute to it in key ways.⁶⁷ I suggest that one of the most beneficial ways others can contribute to our moral progress is by providing us with a third person perspective so that we might be judged as objectively as possible. To be sure, Wesley recognizes the dangers of self-deception and narrowness of perspective. As such, he consistently stresses the need for Christians to be accountable to one another.

In contrast, Kant espouses a more rationalistic view of love that is indeed objective, but he takes matters too far and ends up with an impersonal, abstract love. For Kant, everything revolves around the respect for duty, so we respect others to the extent that they respect duty. He is right when he claims that we naturally respect the goodness of the will in people who love us, but this respect cannot be attributed entirely to an admiration of their moral character. Rather, we also appreciate sincere love because it indicates that others value us. This is why we can find it flattering to be loved even by those whose moral character is not admirable. It is true that personal love can be selfish, but in its highest form personal love demands that we value people for their own sake, that they be treated as ends and not merely as means to other ends. However, personal love values others for many reasons besides their respect for duty or their status as rational beings.

Wesley provides a rather extensive description of universal love, which integrates many of these points.

> Above all, remembering that God is love, [the perfect Christian] is conformed to the same likeness. He is full of love to his neighbor, of universal love . . . Neither does he love those only that love him, or that are endeared to him by intimacy of acquaintance . . . For he loves every soul that God has made, every child of man, of whatever place or nation. And yet this universal benevolence does in nowise interfere with a peculiar regard for his relations, friends, and benefactors, a fervent love for his country, and the most endeared affection to all men of integrity, of clear and generous virtue.
>
> His love, as to these, so to all mankind, is in itself generous and disinterested, springing from no view of advantage to himself, from no regard to profit or praise, no, nor even the pleasure of loving. This is the daughter, not the parent, of his affection. By experience he knows that social love, if it mean the love of our neighbor, is absolutely different from self-love, even of the

---

67. Denis, "Kant on the Perfection of Others," 35.

most allowable kind, just as different as the objects at which they point. And yet it is sure that if they are under due regulations, each will give additional force to the other, till they mix together never to be divided.

And this universal, disinterested love is productive of all right affections . . . It makes a Christian rejoice in the virtues of all and bear a part in their happiness at the same time that he sympathizes with their pains and compassionates their infirmities . . .

The same love is productive of all right actions . . . It guides him into a uniform practice of justice and mercy, equally extensive with the principle whence it flows. It constrains him to do all possible good, of every possible kind, to all men, and makes him invariably resolved, in every circumstance of life, to do that, and that only, to others, which, supposing he were himself in the same situation, he would desire they should do to him.

And as he is easy to others, so he is easy in himself. He is free from the painful swellings of pride, from the flames of anger, from the impetuous gusts of irregular self-will. He is no longer tortured with envy or malice, or with unreasonable and hurtful desire. He is no more enslaved to the pleasures of sense, but has the full power both over his mind and body, in a continued cheerful course of sobriety, of temperance and chastity. He knows how to use all things in their place, and yet is superior to them all. He stands above those low pleasures of imagination which captivate vulgar minds . . .

And he who seeks no praise, cannot fear dispraise. Censure gives him no uneasiness, being conscious to himself that he would not willingly offend, and that he has the approbation of the Lord of all . . . So that, in honor or shame, in abundance or want, in ease or pain, in life or in death, always, and in all things, he has learned to be content, to be easy, thankful, happy.[68]

Notice that when Wesley speaks of "disinterested love," he is not indicating the absence of self-love altogether. What he asserts is that genuine love for others is not ultimately motivated by self-love. Rather, people are loved for their own sakes. In fact, Wesley claims that self-love and universal love, when properly regulated, can actually strengthen one another. As such, Wesley emphasizes universality in love without sacrificing personal love or self-love in the process. Moreover, love

---

68. Wesley to the Rev. Dr. Conyers Middleton, 4 January 1749, §§6.1.5–11, *WWJ*, 10:68–70.

is not confined to personal affection, but encompasses a respect for morality and duty.

Nonetheless, the dichotomy of true and false affections espoused by Edwards and Wesley must be rejected. In our attempts to analyze an individual's ability to persevere, we must consider both the strength of the motives and the strength of competing motives. It is too simplistic to say that a person's failure to persevere is an indication of false affections, attributed to either delusion or insincerity. This false dichotomy is especially unsuitable from a Wesleyan perspective, given the fact that Wesley believes that even the highest spiritual state attainable in this life may still be lost. In other words, even the holiest saints on earth can have incentives that tend to impede their moral and spiritual progress. Regression (i.e., backsliding) will result to the extent that these incentives are followed.

Therefore, it is not always the case that some have true affections while others do not. Affections can arise from a variety of motives, many of them ulterior. In his sermon on doing our alms in secret (Matt 6:1–15), Wesley gives a description of moral purity that is worthy of consideration:

> But it is not only the having an eye to the praise of men which cuts us off from any reward in heaven, which leaves us no room to expect the blessing of God upon our works, whether of piety or mercy. Purity of intention is equally destroyed by a view to any temporal reward whatever. If we repeat our prayers, if we attend the public worship of God, if we relieve the poor, with a view to gain or interest, it is not a whit more acceptable to God than if it were done with a view to praise. Any temporal view, any motive whatever on this side eternity, any design but that of promoting the glory of God, and the happiness of men for God's sake, makes every action, however fair it may appear to men, an abomination unto the Lord.[69]

Wesley seems to take a rather rigorous stance. Reflecting a position reminiscent of Augustine, he indicates that we are to have but one moral motive—to promote the glory of God. Even the happiness of others is to be sought for God's sake. As is the case with Kant, there is apparently no room for the assistance of non-moral motives. Wesley clearly states

---

69. Wesley, Sermon 26, "Upon Our Lord's Sermon on the Mount, Discourse VI," §2.2, *WW*, 1:576 [J 5:331].

that purity of intention is *destroyed* by the presence of additional motives. This ostensibly makes moral purity a virtual impossibility since (1) it is difficult to conceive a moral act that is not accompanied by additional incentives and (2) we would regard someone as psychologically unhealthy who would not be motivated by those incentives to some extent. For example, when we perform acts of kindness for others, we often receive their gratitude and respect, and yet it would be unnatural not to value the gratitude and respect of others at all.

I propose that an alternative reading (or at least a development) of Wesley is also needed, similar to the one Kant has been given.[70] Specifically, the moral purity of motives should not necessitate the absence of all other incentives. To be sure, moral purity should exclude immoral motives, but it does not have to exclude non-moral motives. Instead, the moral motive should be the sufficient one that consistently produces moral action regardless of the presence or absence of other incentives. For Kant, this moral motive is respecting duty for its own sake, but for Wesley, it is loving God and others for their own sake.

Wesley persistently emphasizes loving God supremely and loving others as oneself, but the above passage from Wesley leaves us with the impression that the only true incentive is loving God, that others are only loved for God's sake. I question whether such feelings could really be regarded as love for others, for it seems that the truest form of love requires that something be loved for its own sake. It seems that the best way to interpret (or develop) Wesley on this point is to say that we are to love others for their own sake, but this cannot be for their sake alone, for God cares about each of us. In other words, when I love my neighbor, I am doing something that is pleasing to God. As such, my love for others is also an expression of my love for God. If Wesley is understood in this way, then proper moral motivation will entail (1) direct love for God to the exclusion of all other incentives and (2) loving others directly for their own sake, which still expresses love for God indirectly.

In a cognitivist paradigm, the purity of our affections is revealed by their cognitive content. Identifying the cognitive content of our affections allows us to evaluate their coherence and consistency, and this directly bears upon the purity of our motives. However, the purity of

---

70. See Guevara; Herman; A. Wood, "The Emptiness of the Moral Will"; Dean; Johnson, "Kant's Conception of Merit," 310–34; R. Johnson, "Expressing a Good Will," 147–68.

the affections is primarily revealed in trial and testing, especially when sacrifice is required, because this forces us to choose between two competing incentives, revealing the purity and strength of our motives. In essence, sacrifice exposes the value system that lies beneath the affections, i.e., it exposes the relative strength of each affection. It also reveals the overall strength of each motive.

In general, the affections must not only be properly ordered, they must have sufficient strength. This is particularly true with respect to the thresholds (e.g., repentance and consecration) that must be attained in the Christian life. Crossing these thresholds does in fact indicate that the motive has attained a particular strength overall. However, this does not reveal the purity of the motive, for an action or a commitment can be based on a number of motives. For Edwards, this is a problem, because a true conversion must always result in perseverance. Since Wesley believes in the possibility of backsliding to the point of forfeiting one's salvation, perseverance itself becomes more important than having a certain degree of moral purity in crossing the various thresholds. In a Wesleyan schema, it is important that (1) our intentions be sincere, that we not be guided by ulterior motives; and (2) that we constantly seek to further purify our motives as part of the pursuit of perfection. We must love God and others as they deserve to be loved, but we can only be expected to do this according to our affective capacities.

Integrity of Maxims

The early Holiness Movement taught that entire sanctification (i.e., Christian perfection) results in the instantaneous eradication of one's "carnal nature" (i.e., inclinations toward sin). This was later rejected by the proponents of the Keswick Movement and by some Methodists. They understood perfection to be repression, not eradication. For example, Miley asserts that in Christian perfection, sinful proclivities are repressed by love. However, new affection comes from developing a capacity that is latent in the mind, not a newly created power.[71]

I believe that both of these approaches are inappropriate to a certain extent. On one hand, we cannot simply rely on supernatural change that exceeds natural means. On the other hand, mere repression falls short of Wesley's insistence on moral purification. The proper way

---

71. Miley, *Systematic Theology*, 2:365.

to frame the issue is according to the more naturalized interpretation of grace that I have suggested. In the more cognitivist paradigm that I am proposing, perfection involves reordering and reformulating one's value system and maxims. This entails real moral change while emphasizing both human responsibility and divine assistance.

As has already been demonstrated in previous chapters, this type of cognitivist approach is compatible with the kind of writings on perfection that Wesley found most attractive. For example, William Law held such a view early in life. He writes, "All men, therefore, as men, have one and the same business: to act up to the excellency of their rational nature, to make reason and order the law of all their designs and actions."[72] He proposes that holy dispositions come from aligning our thoughts with the divine reason. Likewise, Clement contends that we must ascend to knowledge and pray for the perfection of love. According to Clement, the first step we need to take is to choose to live infallibly. In other words, we must resolve to fully aspire to perfection before we can approximate it. Once we have done this, we must stabilize knowledge so that love will continue to be perfected and virtue will be preserved.

Wesleyan perfection involves the purity of one's disposition, and although this is primarily understood as having right affections for God and for others, in a more cognitivist paradigm it will also entail integrity in one's maxims. Since I am suggesting that sin be more broadly understood as the neglect of duty, it necessarily follows that sinfulness (i.e., the disposition toward sin) should be regarded as the disposition to neglect or breach one's duty. This includes both the duty to have moral motives as well as the duty to perform moral acts. Thus, sinfulness is twofold, corresponding to the two aspects of duty. On one hand, we are sinful to the extent that our motives are not moral. On the other hand, we can also be deemed to be sinful inasmuch we are inclined to produce actions that fall short of the highest moral standards.

The concept of maxims is what relates the morality of motive to the morality of actions. As Michalson indicates, Kant stresses that "a morally good will is reflected through maxims that contain the moral law as their end."[73] In this regard, Wesleyan perfection should include

---

72. Law, *Serious Call*, 68.
73. Michalson, *Fallen Freedom*, 33.

integrity in one's maxims to the extent that they reflect not only personal affection for God and others, but also a respect for morality itself. Furthermore, the integrity of maxims should demand that pure motives lead to moral actions.

Wesley acknowledges the existence of sin in the believer, for he asserts that sin can reside even in places where it does not reign. For instance, a person may generally have character that is humble and meek and still have particular tempers (e.g., pride and anger) that are excessive in certain respects.[74] Wesley asserts, "Christ indeed cannot *reign* where sin *reigns*, neither will he *dwell* where any sin is *allowed*. But he *is* and *dwells* in the heart of every believer who is *fighting against* all sin, although it be not yet purified."[75] Therefore, when one becomes a Christian (i.e., experiences the "new birth"), one must be committed to living a holy life, at least to the extent that good impulses predominantly win out over evil impulses. In perfection, the commitment to holiness becomes unconditional and comprehensive such that good impulses consistently rule one's inner disposition. Whereas regenerate believers strive to be holy in their outward conduct, perfected believers become holy in their inner dispositions.

Terrance Williams explains that being moral requires us to examine the integrity of our maxims.

> On Kant's view moral living is a reflective process and it is only in so far as an agent overcomes these difficulties and becomes aware of the real maxims of his actions—through a process of critical self-analysis as he lives his life—that his actions can have moral worth. It is only in so far as a man is aware of what he is doing and of the quality of his actions that he can be regarded as acting morally.[76]

Randy Maddox observes that later in life Wesley likewise began to recognize "the need for continual awakenings to remaining sin within the Christian life, not simply an initial awakening to begin this life."[77] In other words, Wesley placed much emphasis on continuous self-scrutiny, and this certainly includes the evaluation of one's maxims.

---

74. Wesley, Sermon 13, "On Sin in Believers," §4.10, *WW*, 1:330–31 [J 5:153–54].
75. Ibid., §3.8, *WW*, 1:323 [J 5:149].
76. T. Williams, *Categorical Imperative*, 18.
77. Maddox, *Responsible Grace*, 161.

For both Wesleyans and Kantians, morality requires that we not only act in accordance with our maxims, our motivations must also arise from them.[78] Walter Schaller argues that the traditional view of Kantian good will fails to differentiate between higher- and lower-order maxims. He believes that adopting a morally good supreme maxim in one's disposition does not guarantee the moral rightness of lower maxims that govern our actions and incentives.[79] Wesleyan perfection can benefit from this analysis, for loving God wholeheartedly, loving our neighbors as ourselves, and being unconditionally and fully committed to being holy does not ensure that our actions and lower incentives will be fully commensurate with our general dispositions. We must continually scrutinize all of our maxims to see if they conform to our supreme maxims, and this requires careful rational analysis. It is no coincidence that Wesley later modified his earlier statements that downplayed the role of reason in Christian perfection.[80] Thomas Oden thus concludes that real "enthusiasts" are those "who tend to substitute their own dreams and emotive life for rational analysis."[81]

Fulfillment of Duty

For Wesley, perfection involves victory over sin, but his emphasis is clearly on willful sin. Therefore, if the concept of sin is expanded so as to entail a breach or neglect of duty, then perfection must necessarily be broadened to include the fulfillment of duty. This corresponds with Jeremy Taylor's assertion that even the best intentions do not purify or justify unholy actions. It also is supported by the claim I made in the previous chapter—that perfection must include the morality of actions—and this was illustrated by Kant's dual emphasis on moral and natural perfection. In essence, both motives and actions can be judged according to their morality, but the morality of one does not necessarily lead to the morality of the other.

However, since motive is the cause of action, Wesleyan ethics places the greatest stress on motive. After all, if our motives are pure, then we will strive to always act morally, even if our actions fall short

---

78. O'Neill, *Constructions of Reason*, 153.
79. Schaller, "Relation of Moral Worth," 353.
80. Walters, "John Wesley's Footnotes," 27.
81. Oden, *Scriptural Christianity*, 73.

of the moral law. There is thus the possibility for what could be termed "moral mistakes." In contrast, actions that otherwise conform to moral law can originate with impure motives, and we do not regard such actions as moral. Rather, we refer to them as hypocritical, Pharisaical, etc. These illustrate the fact that "proper" actions do not necessarily lead to the purification of motives. In fact, they can be used in the attempt to justify or rationalize impure motives.

For Kant, duty can only be imposed within the confines of what lies within our control. However, the perfection of our natural capacities and abilities lies within our control, so this itself is a duty. When considered together, these two claims imply that we have a duty to expand our various spheres of duty. We cannot become morally complacent, but must strive for perfection in both the quality and the quantity of our fulfillment of duty. In a Wesleyan paradigm, this again reinforces the notion that God's grace is focused on our becoming more responsible.

The Wesleyan notion of perfection must consequently aim at the fulfillment of our moral duties, and this includes both inner duties of disposition and outer duties of action. For Kant, pragmatic rules are needed to make our actions consistent with our will. However, these rules cannot bring our actions into harmony with the wills of others. He concludes that we must therefore have universal, *a priori* rules that "are derived from the universal ends of mankind."[82] He feels that if morality were based on inclination, there would essentially be no moral law, since morality would then be entirely subjective.[83] In his mind, the only truly objective basis for morality is the nature of rationality itself.

The focus of Wesleyan ethics should be similarly broader than the integrity of one's personal maxims, for it must also emphasize general principles that can unite individuals in a shared conception of morality. However, in a Wesleyan paradigm, the quest for moral objectivity will not be limited to the nature of rationality, because Wesley acknowledges two other objective bases of morality. First, Scripture is the Christian's standard of faith and conduct. Second, Wesley assumes a certain commonality in human nature. He believes that the moral law does indeed agree with the "fitness of things," because God has willed to create the

---

82. Kant, *LE*, 17.
83. Ibid., 37.

world in a certain way.[84] Not only can we benefit from the scientific study of the world, the perspectives of other people are valuable as well. This is why tradition and experience are granted a role in Wesley's epistemology.

In Wesleyan ethics, the core duties will be defined by and derived from Scripture, since it is an authoritative source of moral knowledge. However, duties not specifically commanded by Scripture will still need to be formulated. Although any full account of ethics will entail a number of duties, Wesleyan ethics will require several in particular. First, we have a duty to love. According to Wesley, Christ's sacrifice lays "obligations to love and duty" upon us.[85] Our foremost duty is to love God wholeheartedly. This is a delightful duty, because we find our happiness to the extent that we love God. Wesley asserts, "We give God our heart when we not only seek but find happiness in him . . . And according to the degree of our love is the degree of our happiness."[86] Of course, the duty to love extends to others.[87] Moreover, it also includes loving oneself, which "is not a sin, but an indisputable duty."[88]

Second, Wesleyan ethics will include a duty to believe, i.e., place one's trust in God, in the atonement of Christ, in the authority of Scripture, etc. As has already been discussed, Wesley adheres to the doctrine of salvation by faith, that which is evidenced in repentance and good works. Essentially, the duty to believe is more than mere assent, for it must also be an affective response to the Gospel, resulting in moral transformation.

Third, Wesleyan ethics will stress our duty to keep the moral law. In contrast to Kant, Wesley does not regard love as a hindrance to keeping one's duty. Rather, love is the specific motivation for keeping the law.[89] In Wesley's mind, God's will cannot be separated from God's nature.[90]

---

84. Wesley, Sermon 34, "The Origin, Nature, Properties, and Use of the Law," §§3.6-9, *WW*, 2:12-13 [J 5:440-41].

85. Wesley, *NNT*, I Cor. 11:24.

86. Wesley, Sermon 90, "An Israelite Indeed," §1.2, *WW*, 3:283 [J 7:40].

87. Wesley, *NNT*, Rom 13:8.

88. Ibid., Eph 5:28.

89. Dillman, "Law in Discourse XXV," 64.

90. Wesley, Sermon 34, "The Origin, Nature, Properties, and Use of the Law," §3.7, *WW*, 2:13 [J 5:441].

Consequently, love for God naturally includes a love for God's will, i.e., the moral law.

Fourth, a Wesleyan account of ethics will also incorporate duties to ourselves. Since I am suggesting adapting Kant's basic portrayal of perfection, Kantian duties to oneself will be relevant to Wesleyan ethics as well. Kant claims that if we fail in our duty to ourselves, then we have no moral worth at all. Consequently, our duty to ourselves must be fulfilled before we can fulfill our duty to others.[91] Denis argues that duties to oneself are more fundamental to Kantianism than duties to others for at least three reasons: (1) they are directly related to maintaining inner freedom, (2) they thus help to maintain a sense of one's moral capacity, and (3) they provide a heuristic for understanding and recognizing duties to others.[92] If we are to be of moral worth to others, then we must achieve a certain measure of self-mastery. Denis continues,

> The principle of self-mastery is universal respect for one's own person in relation to the essential ends of humanity or human nature. This is the principle of duties to oneself and the objective condition of morality. The self-regarding duties are conditions under which alone the other duties can be performed.[93]

Felicitas Munzel indicates that in Kant's mature thought "virtue is in effect self-control characterizing the human processes of thinking, specifically of choice making or the subjectively practical use of reason in human moral life."[94]

To recapitulate, perfection involves the fulfillment of duty. It requires that the realm of our moral responsibility be ever-increasing according to our abilities and capacities. The authoritative source for defining moral duty is Scripture (understood through reason, tradition, and experience). However, we must be able to extrapolate beyond the specific commands of Scripture and formulate other duties that are more contextualized. In the end, certain duties should be regarded as essential to Wesleyan ethics, namely, duties to love God and others, to believe (i.e., trust), to keep the moral law, and to tend to our own well-being and moral progress.

---

91. Kant, *LE*, 118.
92. Denis, *Moral Self-Regard*, 158–59.
93. Ibid., 138.
94. Munzel, *"Critical" Link of Morality*, 165.

Thresholds and Degrees of Perfection

Cannon points out that for Wesley, true Christianity cannot be separated from moral obligation, especially our duty to pursue perfection. If being a Christian does not include "the highest ethical attainments, then it means nothing at all."[95] William Sangster indicates that the very nature of Wesleyan perfection thus invites moral scrutiny.

> To say, "I know I am forgiven" gives all the glory to God. To say, "I know I am holy" may carry with it a similar desire for God's glory, but it intrudes the self and invites psychological and ethical proof of the uttermost kind. Entire sanctification is an ethical claim which cannot be surpassed on this earth, and it must submit to ethical tests.[96]

For Wesley, perfection entails having our affections governed by love for God and others such that we live victoriously over sin and strive to bring glory to God. Consequently, a Wesleyan view of perfection teaches that it must be possible to attain some noticeable degree of perfection in this life. However, if perfection is given the broader definition that I am proposing, then it is mistaken to believe that perfection can be achieved in its entirety. Consistent with the distinctions he makes in his basic definition of Christian perfection, Wesley more generally recognizes that perfection is actually attained in degrees. "Now this perfection does certainly admit of degrees. Therefore, I readily allow the propriety of that distinction—perfection of kinds, and perfection of degrees. Nor do I remember one writer, ancient or modern, who excepts against it."[97] Wesley knows that the standard must be set properly, neither too high nor too low. The lower the standard of attainment is, the more people will be able to achieve it, but the less content it will have.

The Wesleyan traditions have historically debated as to whether perfection should be characterized primarily as a process or as an event. It now seems more appropriate to say that perfection is a process that has specific thresholds, i.e., degrees of attainment. These can be called culmination points, but by no means should they be regarded as termini of any kind, for even that which is attained at the threshold can still be improved. Wesley himself asserts this.

95. Cannon, *Theology of John Wesley*, 221.
96. Sangster, *Path to Perfection*, 103.
97. Wesley, "An Answer to the Rev. Mr. Dodd," §§3, *WWJ*, 11:451.

> Yea, and when ye have attained a measure of perfect love, when God has circumcised your hearts, and enabled you to love him with all your heart and with all your soul, think not of resting there. That is impossible. You cannot stand still; you must either rise or fall. Rise higher or fall lower. Therefore the voice of God to the children of Israel, to the children of God, is, "Go forward!"[98]

There could be any number of thresholds in perfection, each one representing either the realization of virtue or the conquering of vice. For example, becoming a compassionate person might be regarded as a threshold of perfection. The same might be said of gaining control over one's anger. Both of these represent the culmination of various processes, yet they can still be perfected further, so they lead to subsequent progress and growth.

This is actually a very Aristotelian approach to virtue ethics, and Wesley even adheres to Aristotle's notion that virtue is a mediation between opposite extremes, and this is what allows many of the thresholds of perfection to be attainable. For instance, Wesley asserts,

> Christian meekness . . . keeps clear of every extreme, whether in excess or defect. It does not destroy but balance the affections, which the God of nature never designed should be rooted out by grace, but only brought and kept under due regulations. It poises the mind aright. It holds an even scale with regard to anger and sorrow and fear, preserving the mean in every circumstance of life and not declining either to the right hand or the left.[99]

This implies that the thresholds of perfection are not attained in the same manner for every person. While the lack of virtue in some may be due to a deficiency, in others it may be due to excess. In the example given above, it is presumably more virtuous to possess a moderate amount of anger, rather than be apathetic or furious. Then again, it also seems that the reasons that motivate anger determine its morality in part. Likewise, anger should occur in proportion to the importance of the matter that incites it. Hence, it becomes evident that defining the

---

98. Wesley, Sermon 106, "On Faith," §2.5, *WW*, 3:501 [J 7:202].

99. Wesley, Sermon 22, "Upon Our Lord's Sermon on the Mount, Discourse II," §1.3, *WW*, 1:489 [J 5:263].

thresholds of perfection is not always easy, because virtue and vice are often multifaceted and are not as simple as we might suppose.

For Wesley, even love must be moderated, since "it is always exercised εν καλω, in that which is good, so it is always *proportioned* to that good, to the degree of goodness that is in its object."[100] Since there is a basic dignity in human nature, derived from being created in the image of God, we should love and respect others equally with ourselves on that basis. Of course, since God is infinitely good, God is always deserving of our wholehearted love. God is to be loved supremely for his own sake.

In that regard, the Wesleyan traditions have long taught that perfection entails entire consecration, i.e., complete, unconditional surrender to God and to God's will. In fact, Wesley himself regards consecration as an evidence of perfection, namely, "total resignation to the will of God, without any mixture of self-will."[101] Although there may be a number of thresholds in perfection, entire consecration seems to be one of key importance. It can be regarded as a threshold, because it is both the culmination of certain aspects of perfection as well as a point of initiation for other aspects of perfection that transform the deepest part of our moral character.

There is an interesting parallel in Kant's thought. In effect, he believes that we act according to maxims, and this implies that our moral rectitude can be judged by (1) the universalizability of our maxims and (2) the extent to which our maxims are founded on the respect for duty itself. With regard to the latter requirement, Kant understands each of us to be ultimately guided by a supreme maxim that reflects the degree of our commitment to morality. We are either unconditionally committed to it or our motives are impure to some extent. Kant thus claims that if we desire to be fully moral, we must adopt a morally good supreme maxim through what he refers to as a "moral revolution." I feel that this can be tailored to serve as a model of the consecration that is needed as part of perfection. The nature of the commitment will obviously be different in a Wesleyan framework, but it is complete and unconditional in both cases.

---

100. Sermon 92, "On Zeal," §2.6, *WW*, 3:314 [J 7:61].
101. Wesley, "A Plain Account of Christian Perfection," §25.Q23, *WWJ*, 11:422.

According to Kant, in order to be morally pure, we must have a morally good supreme maxim, i.e., a maxim to be unconditionally committed to being moral. We are always influenced by both moral and sensuous motives.[102] Happiness is necessarily the desire of every rational being. Consequently, good and evil in the human will is not in the presence or absence of incentives, but in the subordination of one incentive to another.[103] However, humans cannot be part good and part evil, for each person has a single basic disposition to morality that either is or is not fully committed to being moral.[104] This basic disposition to morality is for all intents and purposes a "supreme maxim," which serves as the ground of all other maxims.[105] After all, our general attitude toward morality largely determines the particular morals we embrace and practice.

Kant espouses the view that human beings are naturally "radically evil." The radical evil of human nature cannot be extirpated by human forces, but it can be overcome.[106] Quinn thinks that this particular doctrine is Kant's rationalistic version of the traditional doctrine of original sin.[107] Kant regards the fall symbolically, as the triumph of self-love over duty within each individual.[108] The radically evil disposition is personally adopted through a free, non-temporal choice.[109] Denis Savage interprets this point as meaning that the disposition to evil is chosen after the disposition to morality is developed. However, since the human tendency to hedonism precedes reason, it has the upper hand and ultimately wins out.[110] Richard Dean explains how a single decision can result in a change of disposition. "When one chooses to act immorally, one must take oneself to be choosing not only a particular prohibited action, but also choosing to abandon the unconditional commitment to morality. One must take oneself to be sacrificing one's good will."[111]

102. Michalson, "Moral Regeneration," 261.
103. A. Wood, *Kant's Moral Religion*, 42.
104. Kant, *Rel*, 49–50 [6:24–25].
105. Michalson, *Fallen Freedom*, 54.
106. Kant, *Rel*, 59 [6:37].
107. Quinn, "Original Sin," 197.
108. Reardon, "Kant as Theologian," 254.
109. Kant, *Rel*, 62 [6:40].
110. Savage, "Kant's Rejection of Divine Revelation," 68–73.
111. Dean, "End in Itself," 276.

For Kant, although one's moral disposition cannot be both good and evil, there are still three degrees of the propensity to evil: (1) frailty—the good maxim is weaker than competing maxims; (2) impurity—the good maxim requires additional incentives in order to be adopted; and (3) corruption/perversity—the order of moral incentives is inverted.[112] In each case, the agent is not unconditionally committed to being fully moral. And yet, Kant asserts that the perversity of the human heart is not diabolical, i.e., evil is not chosen for its own sake.[113] Munzel believes that in his effort to explain why human beings must be radically evil but not diabolical, Kant is trying to avoid two undesirable alternatives. On one hand, if he construes choice as being determined by the object of one's inclination, then human autonomy is relinquished. In other words, he cannot claim that humans necessarily choose evil, because this would contradict his understanding of human freedom. On the other hand, if he suggests that humans are naturally evil because it is impossible for us to choose the good, then the maxim to choose evil itself would become the ground of all our other maxims, but this would be diabolical.

The only way that one can be freed from radical evil and adopt a morally good supreme maxim is through a moral revolution. Kant contends that we can become legally good through a change in mores, but becoming morally good requires a revolution (i.e., a rebirth) in the disposition through a "single and unalterable decision." The revolution occurs in the mode of thought, but gradual reformation takes place in the mode of sense.[114] In Munzel's mind, there must be a "singular commitment," i.e., a "fundamental act of resolve," before the rational human being can take a straight course in life and stop vacillating between command and incitement.[115] According to Kant, divine assistance is needed for moral progress, especially a moral revolution, but we must be worthy of receiving it.[116]

Michalson feels that Kant's comments on divine aid or grace are his attempt to counterbalance the motivational problems encountered

112. Kant, *Rel*, 53–54 [6:29–31].
113. Ibid., 60 [6:37].
114. Ibid., 67–68 [6:47–48].
115. Munzel, *"Critical" Link of Morality*, 172.
116. Kant, *Rel*, 65 [6:44].

by a lack of assurance of moral regeneration.[117] Moreover, Kant's insistence that we merit God's grace is essentially a safeguard against irresponsibility.

> The concept of divine aid, in particular, is misused if we invoke it while passively awaiting its benefits; yet it is properly and morally used if we invoke it when we find ourselves at the limits of our moral efforts and have done all we can to improve ourselves, though our efforts may be imperfect.[118]

Kant finds it necessary to appeal to divine aid in order to preserve both radical evil and human autonomy.[119] Michalson believes that, in the end, Kant espouses a type of human-divine synergism.

> Kant apparently has in mind some sort of cooperative endeavor that involves both an element of autonomous human effort toward moral recovery and an element of divine grace that makes up the inevitable shortfall in the fallen moral agent's effort . . . Kant depicts something like a divine/human alliance in the recovery from radical evil, a partnership in the drive toward moral improvement.[120]

In one respect, Kant's account suggests that the experience of religious conversion should involve a moral revolution of some sort, and this is certainly relevant for Wesleyan ethics. To simply say that a conversion experience is needed is too vague, because these experiences can be very diverse and often do not have the same moral content.[121] Wesley certainly emphasizes the need for repentance and faith in conversion, yet Kant's account of moral action reframes the matter along more cognitivist lines. The emphasis must be shifted away from experience toward the need for a revolution in the mind that is both religious and moral.

Evangelicals in general have traditionally emphasized the experience of conversion, but this has sometimes led to a mere stirring of emotion, particularly in the practice of "hell and brimstone" preaching. Wesley himself did not feel that a fear of hell is effective in driving people

---

117. Michalson, *Fallen Freedom*, 95–96.
118. Michalson, "Moral Regeneration," 265.
119. Michalson, *Fallen Freedom*, 126.
120. Michalson, "Problem of Salvation," 323.
121. Tyson, "John Wesley's Conversion at Aldersgate," 41.

to salvation. Rather, it tends to harden the unbelievers and discourage the believers. In his sermons there are only four references to hell, in his letters there are eleven, and in his journal there are none.[122]

Wesleyan ethics must find a way to recognize the importance of experience without stressing it inordinately or improperly. In the words of Runyon,

> The mistake of nineteenth-century popular Methodism was not that it took experience seriously, but that it lost sight of both the *source* and the *aim* of religious experience, focusing on subjective consciousness and tending to equate human decision and human feelings with salvation.[123]

Wesley stresses a real change in nature at conversion because he believes that good works are only righteous if they are done for God's glory.[124] In other words, moral transformation must take place so that the convert will be properly motivated. Wesleyan ethics must recapture this emphasis, but in a deeper, more meaningful way.

Nevertheless, perhaps the most appropriate way that Wesleyan ethics can adapt Kant's model of moral revolution is as a template for complete consecration, which is a key threshold in perfection. This is commensurate with Clement's assertion that we must fully commit ourselves to living infallibly before love and virtue can be perfected in us. It is also reminiscent of the Wesleyan traditions' stress on entire consecration. The Wesleyan traditions have often interpreted this as the attainment of perfection itself, but it should be seen as a threshold, representing a type of perfection, not perfection in its entirety. Moral progress does not occur automatically or through a single step. For one thing, it is too simplistic to assert that every inclination toward evil can be eradicated in its entirety. As Mariña indicates, "Once an evil disposition has been operative in our lives, it adversely affects the structure of our desiring *even after we have resolved to become better persons.*"[125]

Free Methodist Bishop Leslie Marston suggests that perfection is much broader than what can be experienced, emotionally or otherwise. This is due to the fact that our intellectual powers are always capable of

---

122. Wilson, "Importance of Hell," 12–14.
123. Runyon, *The New Creation*, 149.
124. Hulley, *To Be and To Do*, 21.
125. Mariña, "Transformation and Personal Identity," 490.

further perfection.[126] Moreover, as John Cobb indicates, the presence of love does not guarantee knowledge or understanding. Granted, a certain knowledge of the beloved is requisite to love. However, people who love God and others may not understand the benefit or harm of their actions, nor may they always agree as to "what actions properly express love."[127]

The Holiness traditions have specifically stressed the experience of perfection (i.e., "entire sanctification") as a crisis, but Wesley believes that self-knowledge of one's own sinfulness, achieved after justification, does not necessarily lead to a state of darkness.

> It is allowed, there will be a far deeper, a far clearer and fuller knowledge of our injured sin, of our total corruption by nature, after justification, than ever there was before it. But this need not occasion darkness of soul. I will not say that it *must* bring us into heaviness.
>
> Were it so, the Apostle would not have used that expression, *if need be*, for there would be an absolute, indispensable need of it, for all that would know themselves, that is, in effect, for all that would know the perfect love of God and be thereby "made meet to be partakers of the inheritance of the saints in light." But this is by no means the case. On the contrary, God may increase the knowledge of ourselves to any degree and increase, in the same proportion, the knowledge of Himself and the experience of his love. And in this case there would be no "desert, no misery, no forlorn condition" but love, and peace, and joy, gradually springing up into everlasting life.[128]

Again, this corresponds with Wesley's rejection of the mystics' emphasis on states of spiritual darkness (e.g., John of the Cross).

In a Wesleyan view of perfection, there needs to be a threshold of full, unconditional surrender to God, both in personal devotion and in one's commitment to being moral. This means that one is willing to be transformed and to keep pursuing perfection without hesitation or reservation. Consecration of this kind does not need to be a crisis in which one struggles against the subtle influences of the Holy Spirit. Of course, our sinful inclinations can make consecration difficult, but

---

126. Marston, "The Crisis-Process Issue," 9–10.

127. Cobb, *Grace and Responsibility*, 114.

128. Wesley, Sermon 47, "Heaviness through Manifold Temptations," §3.9, *WW*, 2:230–31 [J 6:99].

so long as we willingly and freely respond to God's grace, a crisis need not ensue. Rather, it can be attained in due course as part of the path to perfection. This type of commitment, as constituting a supremely good moral maxim, will serve as the basis for all other maxims and motivate even further moral progress and devotion to God and others.

Continual Moral Progress

As has been consistently argued throughout this book, continual moral progress is necessary in the Christian life. Wesley views salvation as being renewed in God's image. It is "begun on earth, but perfected in heaven."[129] Although Wesley was optimistic regarding the possibility of attaining the perfection of motives in this life, he was still wary of emphasizing its instantaneous attainment, for it tends to encourage a static idea of perfection overall.[130] For example, Wesley came to admit that even the perfect might have wandering thoughts for various reasons.[131] Roberta Biondi suggests that a truly Wesleyan concept of perfection thus contrasts with the Aldersgate model of sudden change in two ways: (1) deep attitudes of the heart do not come suddenly, but must be developed over time; and (2) human nature is complex, so we must engage in self-reflection and not be discouraged by occasional setbacks and difficulties.[132] Consequently, Wesleyan ethics should not only regard perfection as an end that may be attained in particular respects, but it should also consider perfection as a broader end to which we continually aspire.

Although Wesley does not represent perfection in a strictly moralistic fashion like Kant, his teaching on the subject does contain a strong moral emphasis. As Outler points out, "Wesley's real concern with 'perfection' was that it held soteriology and ethics together in vital balance and so signified the fullness and integrity of the Christian life."[133] Cannon adds, "There is no other theologian in the entire range of Christian history who was any more concerned with the direct relationship between Christianity and morality than was John

---

129. Wesley, preface to *A Collection of Hymns and Sacred Poems* (1740), §4, *WWJ*, 14:323.
130. Walters, "Concept of Attainment," 28.
131. Walters, "John Wesley's Footnotes," 23.
132. Biondi, "Aldersgate and Patterns," 24–26.
133. Outler, "John Wesley: Folk Theologian," 53.

Wesley."[134] There is little doubt that one of John Wesley's primary objectives was to integrate spirituality and ethics.[135] This integration is most evident in his doctrine of perfection.

Wesley repeatedly asserts that perfection is not a static state, but that it entails continual moral progress. He claims that in regeneration the hearts of believers are genuinely renewed, yet this is generally not a complete renewal.[136] Although those who attain perfection achieve a type of dispositional purity, there is still a need for constant growth and development. We must seek to overcome our weakness and ignorance, yet we must not allow our awareness of them to shake our faith.[137] Wesley did believe that moral progress is only likely to occur when some type of attainment is expected. However, even though he started with the "twice-born" model of the Moravians, his interpretation of his own spiritual progress became more gradualist over time.[138] Maddox suggests that while the emphasis on expecting Christian perfection presently is *distinctive* of Wesley, the emphasis on progression is more *characteristic* of him.[139] Moreover, even though Wesleyans have always prided themselves in upholding Scripture as the foremost authority, there is no clear Scriptural sanction for claiming that one can have assurance of achieving perfection.[140] Perhaps this at least partially explains why Wesley never claimed to have achieved perfection even though he believed that Scripture teaches its possibility in this life, at least in certain respects.

As we have seen, certainty occurs in degrees for Locke, Browne, and Wesley. If moral certainty is to be attained, then there must be reliable evidence to support it. In the case of perfection, it seems that we can be rather certain of attaining particular thresholds, especially the key threshold of entire consecration. However, since perfection is ongoing, it is never completed. Hence, there cannot be assurance that it has been completed. What Wesley desires is the degree of perfection at

---

134. Cannon, "Doctrine of Sanctification," 94.
135. Outler, "Focus on the Holy Spirit: Spirit and Spirituality in John Wesley," 165.
136. Wesley, Sermon 13, "On Sin in Believers," §§4.1–2, *WW*, 1:325–27 [J 5:150–51].
137. Wesley, Sermon 8, "The First Fruits of the Spirit," §3.5, *WW*, 1:246–47 [J 5:97].
138. Maddox, *Responsible Grace*, 154–55.
139. Ibid., 190.
140. Staples, "Doctrine of the Holy Spirit," 103.

which believers live victoriously over sin and have all of their affections governed by love. It is feasible to believe that we could be certain of this at a given point in time, but not certain that it would necessarily be sustained. Moreover, this type of assurance, since it involves a higher attainment of perfection, cannot be as certain as lower thresholds.

Overall, the standard of perfection must be sufficiently high so that it will be more than mere feelings of delight. The notion of perfection must have moral content and demand continual moral progress. Likewise, keeping expectations at a reasonable level will also be easier if the claims of moral attainment remain modest. Sangster feels that it is dangerous to claim that one has attained perfection for the following reasons: (1) the claim is only as valid as the conscience of the person making it; (2) while one might be able to claim perfection at a given moment, claiming it as a state is impractical; (3) we cannot fully understand the complexity of our motives anyway; and (4) making such claims can foster pride.[141] The Wesleyan doctrine of perfection is far more defensible as Wesley expressed it himself, and it should be remembered that the claims that he made concerning his own spiritual and moral attainments remained modest throughout his life.

Conclusion

In the final analysis, assurance must be understood as something that is divinely granted, yet empirically verified. As such, we must accept some responsibility in the strengthening of our own assurance. Wesley's translation of 2 Pet 1:10 accurately reflects his feelings on the matter: "Wherefore, brethren, be the more diligent to make your calling and election firm; for if ye do these things, ye shall never fall."[142]

Likewise, perfection should be promoted as an achievable end, not as an experience. The question is, "How much should we promote perfection and urge others to pursue it?" The Wesleyan traditions have long been divided over this very issue. In that regard, Kant concludes, "Since God's providence is universal, I may not be indifferent to the happiness of others." We have "an obligation to be mindful of the welfare of others," because "we all have an equal right to the good things which

---

141. Sangster, *Path to Perfection*, 164–65.
142. Wesley, *NNT*.

nature has provided."[143] However, we must go beyond mere sensitivity and actively promote the happiness of others since this helps to remove obstacles from their moral progress. As such, the moral integrity of others is the ultimate end, not happiness in and of itself. Others can choose for themselves what they think will make them happy, but we can refuse to help them with ends that we feel are harmful to them.[144] Since perfection involves adopting ends in accordance with one's own conception of duty, we are not obligated to make the perfection of others our end, nor are we obligated to promote it.[145]

Perhaps Kant is overstating the case. On one hand, it is obvious that I cannot take someone else's adoption of a particular end and make that adoption my own end, since I can only adopt ends that are within my control. Such is the case with perfection, because we must all adopt that end for ourselves. On the other hand, it seems that I still can make the promotion of perfection my end, at least the promotion of it in general. In other words, although I cannot control the decisions of others, I can still try to influence them. I cannot be responsible for the perfection of others, but I can help to put others in a position to make this choice. This is especially true in the case of those for whom we have responsibility, e.g., our children.[146] The importance that Kant places on education and organized religion indicates that we should, at the very least, promote the moral good of others.[147]

The doctrines of assurance and perfection must be kept in tension. We must know that we are forgiven by God and are acceptable in God's sight. However, we cannot be complacent, but must have a continual desire to progress spiritually and morally. This should not result in perfectionism or self-doubt, yet our progress should reinforce the assurance we have.

This approach to ethics that I have represented is founded on the premise that moral transformation begins in the mind. In essence, our beliefs and feelings are all shaped by the way we think. In order to change who we are, we have to change our thinking. However, morality

143. Kant, *LE*, 192.
144. Kant, *MM*, 151–52, 155–56 [6:387–88, 393–94].
145. Ibid., 150 [6:386].
146. Korsgaard, *Kingdom of Ends*, 220 n. 36.
147. A. Wood, *Kant's Moral Religion*, 78.

is more than propositional knowledge, for our morals are based on our core values. As such, moral transformation requires shaping and properly ordering our values. In this type of a cognitivist, empirical paradigm, reason must work with the data supplied to it by perception, inner consciousness, and memory. In general, God subtly interacts with us through these natural means, but God is not limited in the manner or extent of his involvement in our lives.

Albert Knudson proposes that Methodism has historically been too preoccupied with practical piety to develop Christian doctrine.

> But on the whole the pietistic movement did not contribute much to the development of theology . . . The Methodists and Pietists in general accepted the more fundamental Christian doctrines that had come down from the past without making any serious attempt to refashion them. In their own vivid religious experience they found a verification of the truth of Christianity, but they themselves were too much absorbed in the promotion of practical piety to realize the importance of reconstructing the traditional theology and making it conform more closely with the demands of their own experimental religion.[148]

Interestingly enough, this was not Wesley's intent, for he expressed his willingness to develop and revise his doctrine, particularly his doctrine of perfection.

> I will thank you for showing me any mistake I am in, being not so tenacious of my opinions now as I was twenty or thirty years ago. Indeed, I am not fond of any opinion as such. I read the Bible with what attention I can, and regulate all my opinions thereby, to the best of my understanding. But I am always willing to receive more light, particularly with regard to any less common opinions, because the explaining and defending of them takes up much time, which I can ill spare from other employments. Whoever, therefore, will give me more light with regard to Christian perfection will do me a singular favor. The opinion I have concerning it at present, I espouse merely because I think it is scriptural. If therefore I am convinced it is not scriptural, I shall willingly relinquish it.
>
> I have no particular fondness for the term. It seldom occurs either in my preaching or writings. It is my opponents who thrust it upon me continually, and ask me what I mean by it.[149]

---

148. Knudson, *Present Tendencies*, 153–54.
149. Wesley, "An Answer to the Rev. Mr. Dodd," §§1–2, *WWJ*, 11:450.

Indeed, even though Wesley defended his doctrines of assurance and perfection, he was neither dogmatic nor inflexible. His goal was to discover the truth as it is revealed in Scripture, aided by the guides of reason, tradition, and experience. It was his desire to develop these doctrines so that they would continue to be relevant in days to come. Perhaps our great reverence for Wesley himself has caused many to shy away from the attempt to improve upon his thought. Whatever the motivation, it does not seem that the development of these doctrines has been sufficient. Colin Williams lifts out a quote from R. W. Dale (given in 1903, at the bicentennial of Wesley's birth), which is right on the mark.

> There was one doctrine of John Wesley's—the doctrine of perfect sanctification—which ought to have led to a great and original ethical development; but the doctrine has not grown; it seems to remain where John Wesley left it. There has been a want of genius or the courage to attempt the solution of the immense practical questions which the doctrine suggests. The questions have not been raised, much less solved. To have raised them effectively, indeed, would have been to originate an ethical revolution which would have had a far deeper effect on the thought and life—first in England and then of the rest of Christendom—than was produced by the Reformation of the sixteenth century.[150]

This quote is just as pertinent to the state of Wesleyan theology today as it was a century ago. I believe that Wesley's doctrines of assurance and perfection can significantly contribute to discussions on the dynamics of Christian living, especially in the integration of spirituality and morality. I have endeavored to lay the foundation for what I regard as the most fruitful approach to developing these doctrines. Extra care has been taken to explore the most germane facets of Wesley's intellectual context, so that the new development will be consistent with his own aims and motivations. Hopefully, this study will contribute to the continued intellectual development of both Wesley's thought and the theological tradition that he founded.

---

150. R. W. Dale, quoted in *Wesley Bicentennial, 1703-1903*; quote given by C. W. Williams, *John Wesley's Theology Today*, 181.

Bibliography

Primary Sources

Basil, Saint. *Gateway to Paradise: Basil the Great*. Vol. 1, translated by Tim Witherow and edited by Oliver Davies. Brooklyn: New City, 1991.
Browne, Peter. *The Procedure, Extent, and Limits of Human Understanding*. 1728. Reprint, New York: Garland, 1976.
Butler, Joseph. *Butler's Fifteen Sermons Preached at the Rolls Chapel; and, A Dissertation of the Nature of Virtue*. London: SPCK, 1970.
Clement, of Alexandria. *The Writings of Clement of Alexandria*. 2 vols. Translated by William Wilson. Edinburgh: T. & T. Clark, 1871–1872.
Edwards, Jonathan. *Charity and Its Fruits*. Edited by Tyron Edwards. Reprint, Carlisle, PA: Banner of Truth, 1969.
———. *The Distinguishing Marks of a Work of the Spirit of God*. 1741. Reprint, in *Jonathan Edwards on Revival*. Edinburgh: Banner of Truth, 1999.
———. *Freedom of the Will*. Edited by Paul Ramsey. Vol. 1, *The Works of Jonathan Edwards*. New Haven, CT: Yale University Press, 1957.
———. *Images or Shadows of Divine Things*. Edited by Perry Miller. Westport, CT: Greenwood, 1977.
———. *The "Miscellanies" (Entry Nos. a–z, aa–zz, 1–500)*. Edited by Thomas A. Schafer. Vol. 13, *The Works of Jonathan Edwards*. New Haven, CT: Yale University Press, 1994.
———. *The "Miscellanies" (Entry Nos. 501–832)*. Edited by Ava Chamberlain. Vol. 18, *The Works of Jonathan Edwards*. New Haven, CT: Yale University Press, 2000.
———. *A Narrative of Surprising Conversions*. 1736. Reprint, in *Jonathan Edwards on Revival*. Edinburgh: Banner of Truth, 1999.
———. *The Nature of True Virtue*. Ann Arbor: University of Michigan, 1960.
———. *Original Sin*. Edited by Clyde A. Holbrook. Vol. 3, *The Works of Jonathan Edwards*. New Haven, CT: Yale University Press, 1970.
———. *Religious Affections*. Edited by John E. Smith. Vol. 2, *The Works of Jonathan Edwards*. New Haven, CT: Yale University Press, 1959.
———. *Sermons and Discourses, 1720–1723*. Edited by Wilson H. Kimnach. Vol. 10, *The Works of Jonathan Edwards*. New Haven, CT: Yale University Press, 1992.
———. *Sermons and Discourses, 1723–1729*. Edited by Kenneth P. Minkema. Vol. 14, *The Works of Jonathan Edwards*. New Haven, CT: Yale University Press, 1997.
———. *Sermons and Discourses, 1734–1738*. Edited by M. X. Lesser. Vol. 19, *The Works of Jonathan Edwards*. New Haven, CT: Yale University Press, 2001.

———. *Thoughts on the Revival of Religion in New England*. 1740. Reprint, New York: American Tract Society, [18—].

Fénelon, François de Salignac de la Mothe. *The Archbishop of Cambray's Dissertation on Pure Love*. London: Hinde, 1735.

———. *Christian Perfection*. Reprint, New York: Harper, 1947.

———. *Let Go*. Originally published under the title *Spiritual Letters*. Translated by Mildred Whitney Stillman. Reprint, New Kensington, PA: Whitaker, 1973.

François de Sales, Saint. *An Introduction to a Devout Life*. Translated by John K. Ryan. New York: Harper, 1966.

Guyon, Madame Jeanne. *Experiencing Union with God through Inner Prayer*. Edited by Harold J. Chadwick. Gainesville, FL: Bridge Logos, 2001.

———. *The Way and Results of Union with God*. Edited by Harold J. Chadwick. Gainesville, FL: Bridge Logos, 2001.

Hobbes, Thomas and John Bramhill. *Hobbes and Bramhill on Liberty and Necessity*. Edited by Vere Chappell. Cambridge: Cambridge University Press, 1999.

Hume, David. *An Enquiry Concerning the Principles of Morals*. Edited by Tom L. Beauchamp. Oxford: Oxford University Press, 1998.

———. *Treatise of Human Nature*. Amherst, NY: Prometheus, 1992.

Hutcheson, Francis. *Illustrations on the Moral Sense*. Edited by Bernard Peach. Cambridge, MA: Belknap, 1971.

———. *An Inquiry into the Origin of Our Ideas of Beauty and Virtue*. New York: Garland, 1971.

———. *A System of Moral Philosophy*. New York: Kelley, 1968.

Ignatius of Loyola, Saint. *Ignatius of Loyola: Spiritual Exercises and Selected Works*. Edited by George E. Ganss and Edward J. Malestesta. New York: Paulist, 1991.

Kant, Immanuel. *Critique of Judgment*. Translated by J. H. Bernard. Amherst, NY: Prometheus, 2000.

———. *Critique of Practical Reason*. Translated and edited by Lewis White Beck. New York: Macmillan, 1993.

———. *Critique of Pure Reason*. Translated by Norman Kemp Smith. Reprint, Boston: Bedford, 1965.

———. *Grounding for the Metaphysics of Morals*. Translated by James W. Ellington. Indianapolis: Hackett, 1981.

———. *Lectures on Ethics*. Translated by Louis Infield. Indianapolis: Hackett, 1963.

———. *Lectures on Philosophical Theology*. Translated by Allen W. Wood and Gertrude M. Clark. Ithaca, NY: Cornell University Press, 1978.

———. *Metaphysics of Morals*. Translated and edited by Mary Gregor. Cambridge: Cambridge University Press, 1996.

———. *Observations on the Feeling of the Beautiful and Sublime*. Translated by John T. Goldthwait. Berkeley: University of California Press, 1960.

———. *Perpetual Peace and Other Essays*. Translated by Ted Humphrey. Indianapolis: Hackett, 1983.

———. *Religion within the Boundaries of Mere Reason and Other Writings*. Translated and edited by Allen Wood and George di Giovanni. Cambridge: Cambridge University Press, 1998.

Kempis, Thomas à. *The Imitation of Christ*. Uhrichsville, OH: Barbour, 1984.

Law, William. *A Practical Treatise upon Christian Perfection.* Reprint. Vol. 3, *The Works of William Law.* Eugene, OR: Wipf & Stock, 2001.
———. *A Serious Call to a Devout and Holy Life.* Edited by John W. Meister et al. Louisville: Westminster John Knox, 1955.
———. *Selected Mystical Writings.* Translated and edited by Stephen Hobhouse. New York: Harper, 1948.
Locke, John. "A Discourse of Miracles." In *The Reasonableness of Christianity*, edited by Ian T. Ramsey. Stanford: Stanford University Press, 1991.
———. *Essay Concerning Human Understanding.* 2vols., collated and annotated by Alexander Campbell Fraser. NY: Dover, 1959.
———. *A Letter Concerning Toleration.* New York: Macmillan, 1988.
———. *The Reasonableness of Christianity.* Edited by Ian T. Ramsey. Stanford: Stanford University Press, 1991.
Macarius the Egyptian, Saint. *Fifty Spiritual Homilies.* Translated by A. J. Mason. London: SPCK, 1921.
Price, Richard. *A Review of the Principal Questions in Morals.* New York: Benjamin Franklin Reprints, 1974.
Reid, Thomas. *Essays on the Active Powers of the Human Mind.* Cambridge, MA: M.I.T. Press, 1969.
———. *Essays on the Intellectual Powers of Man.* Edited by A. D. Woozley. London: Macmillan, 1941.
Shaftesbury, Anthony Ashley Cooper, Earl of. *An Inquiry Concerning Virtue, or Merit.* Manchester: Manchester University Press, 1977.
Smith, Adam. *The Theory of Moral Sentiments.* Amherst, NY: Prometheus, 2000.
Taylor, Jeremy. *Holy Living.* Edited by Hal M. Helms. Brewster, MA: Paraclete, 1988.
Wesley, John. *The Christian's Pattern, or An Extract of "The Imitation of Christ" by Thomas à Kempis.* Reprint, Salem, OH: Schmul, n.d.
———. *Explanatory Notes upon the New Testament.* London: Epworth, 1976.
———. *The Work of the Holy Spirit in the Human Heart.* Abridgement of *The Distinguishing Marks of a Work of the Spirit of God* and *A Treatise on the Religious Affections*, by Jonathan Edwards. 1857. Reprint, Salem, OH: Schmul, 1998.
———. *The Works of John Wesley.* Begun as "The Oxford Edition of the Works of John Wesley," Oxford: Clarendon, 1975–83. Continued as "The Bicentennial Edition of the Works of John Wesley." Nashville: Abingdon, 1984–. 35 total vols. to be printed.
———. *The Works of John Wesley.* 14 vols. Edited by Thomas Jackson. London: Wesleyan Methodist, 1872. Reprinted often.

Primary Sources—Wesleyan Traditions

Barker, John H. J. *This Is the Will of God: A Study in the Doctrine of Entire Sanctification as a Definite Experience.* Reprint, Salem, OH: Schmul, 1984.
Brengle, Samuel. *Helps to Holiness.* 1896. Reprint, Avonmore, PA: West, 2000.
Clarke, Adam. *Christian Theology*, compiled by Samuel Dunn. 1835. Reprint, Salem, OH: Schmul, 1967.
Cook, Thomas. *New Testament Holiness.* 1950. Reprint, Salem, OH: Schmul, 1986.
Dunning, H. Ray. *Grace, Faith, and Holiness.* Kansas City: Beacon, 1988.

Foster, R. S. "Christian Purity, or The Heritage of Faith." 1871. Reprint, in *Christian Perfection: A Compilation of Six Holiness Classics.* Vol. 1. Salem, OH: Schmul, 1974.
Grider, J. Kenneth. *A Wesleyan-Holiness Theology.* Kansas City: Beacon, 1994.
Hills, A. M. *Scriptural Holiness and Keswick Teaching Compared.* Reprint, Salem, OH: Schmul.
Keen, S. A. "Faith Papers: A Treatise on Experimental Aspects of Faith." 1888. Reprint, in *Six Holiness Classics.*
Knudson, Albert C. *Basic Issues in Christian Thought.* New York: Abingdon-Cokesbury, 1950.
———. *The Doctrine of Redemption.* New York: Abingdon-Cokesbury, 1933.
———. *Present Tendencies in Religious Thought.* New York: Abingdon-Cokesbury, 1924.
Miley, John. *Systematic Theology.* 2 vols. New York: Hunt and Eaton, 1893. Reprint, Peabody, MA: Hendrickson, 1989.
Pope, William Burt. *A Higher Catechism of Theology.* New York: Hunt and Eaton, 1889.
Steele, Daniel. *Defense of Christian Perfection.* 1896. Reprint, Salem, OH: Schmul, 1984.
———. *Milestone Papers.* 1878. Reprint, Salem, OH: Schmul, 1976.
Taylor, Richard S. "The Relation of the Holy Spirit to the Self." *Wesleyan Theological Journal* 22, no. 2 (1987) 84–91.
———. *A Right Conception of Sin.* Kansas City: Beacon, 1945.
———. *The Theological Formulation.* Vol. 3, *Exploring Christian Holiness.* Kansas City: Beacon, 1985.
Wiley, H. Orton. *Christian Theology.* 3 vols. Kansas City: Beacon, 1952.
Wogaman, J. Philip. *Christian Moral Judgment.* Louisville: Westminster John Knox, 1989.
Wynkoop, Mildred Bangs. *A Theology of Love: The Dynamic of Wesleyanism.* Kansas City: Beacon, 1972.

Secondary Sources

Abraham, William J. "The Epistemology of Conversion: Is There Something New?" In *Conversion in the Wesleyan Tradition,* edited by Kenneth J. Collins and John H. Tyson, 175–91. Nashville: Abingdon, 2001.
———. "John Wesley's Conception and Use of Scripture (Bibliographic Essay and the 1995 Book of Scott Jones)." *Wesleyan Theological Journal* 33 (1998) 5–13.
Andrews, Stuart. "John Wesley and the Age of Reason." *History Today* 19 (1969) 25–32.
Ayling, Stanley. *John Wesley.* Nashville: Abingdon, 1980.
Bassett, Paul Merritt. "The Theological Identity of the North American Holiness Movement." In *The Variety of American Evangelicalism,* edited by Donald W. Dayton and Robert K. Johnston, 72–108. Knoxville: University of Tennessee, 1991.
Beck, Lewis White. *Studies in the Philosophy of Kant.* Indianapolis: Bobbs-Merrill, 1965.

Beiser, Frederick C. *The Sovereignty of Reason: The Defense of Rationality in the Early English Enlightenment*. Princeton: Princeton University, 1996.

Bell, Richard H. "On Trusting One's Heart: Scepticism in Jonathan Edwards and Soren Kierkegaard." *History of European Ideas* 12 (1990) 105–16.

Bence, Clarence L. "John Wesley's Teleological Hermeneutic." PhD diss., Emory University, 1981.

Bennett, David. "How Arminian Was John Wesley?" *Evangelical Quarterly* 72 (2000) 237–48.

Biondi, Roberta C. "Aldersgate and Patterns of Methodist Spirituality." In *Aldersgate Reconsidered*, edited by Randy L. Maddox, 21–32. Nashville: Kingswood, 1990.

Bishop, John D. "Moral Motivation and the Development of Francis Hutcheson's Philosophy." *Journal of the History of Ideas* 57 (1996) 277–95.

Blevins, Dean G. "John Wesley and the Means of Grace: An Approach to Christian Religious Education." PhD diss., Claremont School of Theology, 1999.

———. "Means of Grace: Toward a Wesleyan Praxis of Spiritual Formation." *Wesleyan Theological Journal* 32 (1997) 69–83.

Borgen, Ole E. *John Wesley on the Sacraments: A Definitive Study of John Wesley's Theology of Worship*. Grand Rapids: Asbury, 1972.

Boshears, Onva K. "The Books in John Wesley's Life." *Wesleyan Theological Journal* 3 (1967) 48–56.

Brantley, Richard Estes. "The Common Ground of Wesley and Edwards." *Harvard Theological Review* 83 (1990) 271–303.

———. *Locke, Wesley, and the Method of English Romanticism*. Gainesville: University of Florida Press, 1984.

Campbell, Ted A. "The Interpretive Role of Tradition." In *Wesley and the Quadrilateral: Renewing the Conversation*, edited by W. Stephen Gunter, et al., 63–75. Nashville: Abingdon, 1997.

———. *John Wesley and Christian Antiquity: Religious Vision and Cultural Change*. Nashville: Kingswood, 1991.

———. "Wesley's Use of the Church Fathers." *Asbury Theological Journal* 50–52, no. 2–1 (1995–1996) 57–70.

Cannon, William Ragsdale. "John Wesley's Doctrine of Sanctification and Perfection." *Mennonite Quarterly Review* 35 (1961) 91–95.

———. *The Theology of John Wesley: With Special Reference to the Doctrine of Justification*. New York: Abingdon-Cokesbury, 1946.

Cell, George Croft. *The Rediscovery of John Wesley*. Lanham, MD: University Press of America, 1935.

Chamberlain, Ava. "Self-Deception as a Theological Problem in Jonathan Edwards' *Treatise Concerning Religious Affections*." *Church History* 63 (1994) 541–56.

Chappell, Vere. "Locke on the Intellectual Basis of Sin." *Journal of the History of Philosophy* 32 (1994) 197–207.

Chiles, Robert E. *Theological Transition in American Methodism: 1790–1935*. New York: Abingdon, 1965.

Cho, John Chongnahm. "Adam's Fall and God's Grace: John Wesley's Theological Anthropology." *Evangelical Review of Theology* 10 (1986) 202–13.

Christensen, Michael J. "Theosis and Sanctification: John Wesley's Reformation of a Patristic Doctrine." *Wesleyan Theological Journal* 31, no. 2 (1996) 71–94.

Clapper, Gregory S. *John Wesley on Religious Affections: His Views on Experience and Emotion and their Role in the Christian Life and Theology.* Metuchen, NJ: Scarecrow, 1989.

Clarkson, G. E. "John Wesley and William Law's Mysticism." *Religion in Life* 42 (1973) 537–44.

Cobb, John B. *Grace and Responsibility: A Wesleyan Theology for Today.* Nashville: Abingdon, 1995.

Collins, Kenneth J. "John Wesley and the Means of Grace." *Asbury Seminarian* 40, no. 2 (1985) 23–31.

———. "John Wesley's Assessment of Christian Mysticism." *Lexington Theological Quarterly* 28 (1993) 299–318.

———. "John Wesley's Platonic Conception of the Moral Law." *Wesleyan Theological Journal* 21 (1986) 116–28.

———. "John Wesley's Topography of the Heart: Dispositions, Tempers and Affections." *Methodist History* 36 (1998) 162–75.

Cox, Leo George. "Prevenient Grace: A Wesleyan View." *Journal of the Evangelical Theological Society* 12 (1969) 143–49.

Cragg, Gerald R. *The Church and the Age of Reason, 1648–1789.* London: Penguin, 1990.

Crocker, Robert. "Mysticism and Enthusiasm in Henry More." In *Henry More (1614–1687) Tercentenary Studies*, edited by Sarah Hutton. Dordrecht: Kluwer Academic, 1990.

Cubie, David L. "Wesley's Theology of Love." *Wesleyan Theological Journal* 20, no. 1 (1985) 122–54.

Culp, John. "Supernatural and Sanctification: Comparison of Roman Catholic and Wesleyan Views." *Wesleyan Theological Journal* 31, no. 2 (1996) 147–66.

———. "A Wesleyan Contribution to Contemporary Epistemological Discussions." In *Thy Nature and Thy Name Is Love*, edited by Bryan P. Stone and Thomas Jay Oord, 239–62. Nashville: Abingdon, 2001.

Damasio, Antonio R. *Descartes' Error: Emotion, Reason, and the Human Brain.* New York: Bard, 1994.

Darwall, Stephen. *The British Moralists and the Internal Ought: 1640–1740.* New York: Cambridge, 1995.

Dayton, Donald W. *Theological Roots of Pentecostalism.* Metuchen, NJ: Scarecrow, 1987.

Dean, Richard. "What Should We Treat as an End in Itself?" *Pacific Philosophical Quarterly* 77 (1996) 268–88.

Denis, Lara. "Kant on the Perfection of Others." *Southern Journal of Philosophy* 37 (1999) 21–41.

———. *Moral Self-Regard: Duties to Oneself in Kant's Moral Theory.* New York: Garland, 2001.

Dillman, Charles N. "Wesley's Approach to the Law in Discourse XXV on the Sermon on the Mount." *Wesleyan Theological Journal* 12 (1977) 60–65.

Dorr, Donald J. "Total Corruption and the Wesleyan Tradition." *Irish Theological Quarterly*, 31 (1964) 303–21.

Dreyer, Frederick. "Edmund Burke and John Wesley: the Legacy of Locke." In *Religion, Secularization, and Political Thought: Thomas Hobbes to J. S. Mill*, edited by James E. Crimmins, 111–29. London: Routledge, 1989.

———. "Evangelical Thought: John Wesley and Jonathan Edwards." *Albion* 19 (1987) 177–92.

———. "Faith and Experience in the Thought of John Wesley." *American Historical Review* 88 (1983) 12–30.

Drury, S. B. "John Locke: Natural Law and Innate Ideas." *Dialogue* 19 (1980) 531–45.

Duffy, Eamon. "Wesley and the Counter-Reformation." In *Revival and Religion Since 1700: Essays for John Walsh*, edited by Jane Garnett and Colin Matthews, 1–19. London: Hambledon, 1993.

Dunning, H. Ray. "Christian Perfection: Toward a New Paradigm." *Wesleyan Theological Journal* 33, no. 1 (1998) 151–63.

———. *Reflecting the Divine Image: Christian Ethics in a Wesleyan Perspective*. Downer's Grove, IL: InterVarsity, 1998.

Edwards, Maldwyn. *John Wesley and the Eighteenth Century*. London: G. Allen and Unwin Ltd., 1953.

English, John C. "John Wesley and Francis Rous." *Methodist History* 6, no. 4 (1968) 28–35.

———. "John Wesley and the Anglican Moderates of the Seventeenth Century." *Anglican Theological Review* 51 (1969) 203–20.

———. "John Wesley and the English Enlightenment: An 'Appeal to Men of Reason and Religion.'" *Studies on Voltaire and the Eighteenth Century* 263 (1989) 400–403.

———. "John Wesley and the French Catholic Tradition." *Studies on Voltaire and the Eighteenth Century* 303 (1992) 441–44.

———. "John Wesley and the Rights of Conscience." *Journal of Church and State* 37 (1995) 349–63.

———. "John Wesley's Indebtedness to John Norris." *Church History* 60 (1991) 55–69.

———. "John Wesley's Scientific Education." *Methodist History* 30 (1991) 42–51.

———. "John Wesley's Studies as an Undergraduate." *Proceedings of the Wesley Historical Society* 47 (1989) 29–37.

Erdt, Terrence. *Jonathan Edwards: Art and the Sense of the Heart*. Amherst, MA: University of Massachusetts, 1980.

Fiering, Norman. *Jonathan Edwards' Moral Thought and Its British Context*. Chapel Hill: University of North Carolina, 1981.

Fischer, Klaus P. "John Locke in the German Enlightenment: An Interpretation." *Journal of the History of Ideas* 36 (1975) 431–46.

Flage, Daniel E. "Locke and Natural Law." *Dialogue* 39 (2000) 435–60.

Flew, R. Newton. *The Idea of Perfection in Christian Theology: An Historical Study of the Christian Ideal for the Present Life*. New York: Humanities, 1968.

Frey, R. G. "Butler on Self-Love and Benevolence." In *Joseph Butler's Moral and Religious Thought: Tercentenary Essays*, edited by Christopher Cunliffe, 243–67. Oxford: Clarendon, 1992.

Friedman, R. Z. "Kant and Kierkegaard: The Limits of Reason and the Cunning of Faith." *International Journal for Philosophy of Religion* 19 (1986) 3–22.

Gaustad, Edwin S. "The Nature of True — and Useful — Virtue: From Edwards to Franklin." In *Benjamin Franklin, Jonathan Edwards, and the Representation of American Culture*, edited by Barbara B. Oberg and Harry S. Stout, 42–57. New York: Oxford, 1993.

Gray, Wallace G. "The Place of Reason in the Theology of John Wesley." PhD diss., Vanderbilt University, 1953.

Green, J. Brazier. *John Wesley and William Law*. London: Epworth, 1945.

Guevara, Daniel. *Kant's Theory of Moral Motivation*. Boulder, CO: Westview, 2000.

Gunter, W. Stephen. "Aldersgate, the Holiness Movement, and Experiential Religion." In *Aldersgate Reconsidered*, edited by Randy L. Maddox, 121–31. Nashville: Kingswood, 1990.

———. *The Limits of "Love Divine": John Wesley's Response to Antinomianism and Enthusiasm*. Nashville: Kingswood, 1989.

———. "The Quadrilateral and the 'Middle Way.'" In *Wesley and the Quadrilateral*, 17–38.

Hall, R. W. "Kant and Ethical Formalism." *Kant Studien* 52 (1960) 433–39.

Hare, John E. *The Moral Gap: Kantian Ethics, Human Limits, and God's Assistance*. Oxford: Clarendon, 1996.

Harper, K. "[William] Law and [John] Wesley." *Church Quarterly Review* 163 (1982) 61–71.

Hauerwas, Stanley. "Characterizing Perfection: Second Thoughts on Character and Sanctification." In *Wesleyan Theology Today*, edited by Theodore Runyon, 251–63. Nashville: United Methodist, 1985.

Heitzenrater, Richard P. "God with Us: Grace and the Spiritual Senses in John Wesley's Theology." In *Grace upon Grace*, edited by Robert K. Johnston, L. Gregory Jones, and Jonathan R. Wilson, 87–109. Nashville: Abingdon, 1999.

———. "Great Expectations: Aldersgate and the Evidences of Genuine Christianity." In *Aldersgate Reconsidered*, edited by Randy L. Maddox, 49–91. Nashville: Kingswood, 1990.

———. *Mirror and Memory: Reflections on Early Methodism*. Nashville: Kingswood, 1989.

Hendricks, M. Elton. "John Wesley and Natural Theology." *Wesleyan Theological Journal* 18, no. 2 (1983) 7–17.

Herman, Barbara. *The Practice of Moral Judgment*. Cambridge, MA: Harvard University, 1993.

Hoopes, James. "Jonathan Edwards' Religious Psychology." *Journal of American History* 69 (1983) 849–65.

Hudson, William Donald. *Ethical Intuitionism*. London: Macmillan, 1967.

Hulley, Leonard D. *To Be and To Do: Exploring Wesley's Thought on Ethical Behavior*. Pretoria: University of South Africa, 1988.

Hund, William B. "Kant's Attitude toward Human Perfection as a Moral Determinant." In *Proceedings of the Third International Kant Congress*, edited by Lewis White Beck. Dordrecht: Reidel, 1972.

Hynson, Leon O. "John Wesley's Concept of Liberty of Conscience." *Wesleyan Theological Journal* 7, no. 1 (1972) 36–46.

———. *To Reform the Nation: Theological Foundations of Wesley's Ethics*. Grand Rapids: Francis Asbury, 1984.
———. "The Wesleyan Quadrilateral in the American Holiness Tradition." *Wesleyan Theological Journal* 20, no. 1 (1985) 19–33.
James, William. *The Varieties of Religious Experience*. New York: Modern Library, 1999.
Johnson, Robert N. "Expressing a Good Will: Kant on the Motive of Duty." *Southern Journal of Philosophy* 34 (1996) 147–68.
———. "Kant's Conception of Merit." *Pacific Philosophical Quarterly* 77 (1996) 310–34.
Johnson, W. Stanley. "Christian Perfection as Love for God." *Wesleyan Theological Journal* 18, no. 1 (1983) 50–60.
Jones, Charles Edwin. *Perfectionist Persuasion: The Holiness Movement and American Methodism, 1867–1936*. Metuchen, NJ: Scarecrow, 1974.
———. "Tongues-Speaking and the Wesleyan-Holiness Quest for Assurance of Sanctification." *Wesleyan Theological Journal* 22, no. 2 (1987) 117–24.
Jones, Scott J. *John Wesley's Conception and Use of Scripture*. Nashville: Abingdon, 1995.
———. "The Rule of Scripture." In *Wesley and the Quadrilateral*, 39–61.
Kemp, J. *Reason, Action, and Morality*. New York: Humanities, 1964.
Kingdon, Harold. "John Wesley: Bible Scholar Extraordinaire." *Asbury Seminary Journal* 40, no. 1 (1985) 39–54.
Knight, Henry H., III. *The Presence of God in the Christian Life: John Wesley and the Means of Grace*. Metuchen, NJ: Scarecrow, 1992.
Knox, Ronald A. *Enthusiasm: A Chapter in the History of Religion*. Notre Dame, IN: University of Notre Dame Press, 1994.
Korsgaard, Christine M. *Creating the Kingdom of Ends*. Cambridge: Cambridge University, 1996.
Lazarus, Richard S., and Bernice N. Lazarus. *Passion and Reason: Making Sense of Our Emotions*. New York: Oxford University Press, 1994.
Lee, Hoo-Jung. "Experiencing the Spirit in Wesley and Macarius." In *Rethinking Wesley's Theology for Contemporary Methodism*, edited by Randy L. Maddox, 197–212. Nashville: Kingswood, 1998.
Lemos, Noah M. "Commonsensism and Critical Cognitivism." In *A Companion to Epistemology*, edited by Jonathan Dancy and Ernest Sosa, 71–74. Oxford: Blackwell, 1992.
Lewis, Paul. "The Springs of Motion: Jonathan Edwards on Emotions, Character, and Agency." *Journal of Religious Ethics* 22 (1994) 275–97.
Lindstedt, David. "Kant: Progress in Universal History as a Postulate of Practical Reason." *Kant Studien* 90 (1990) 129–47.
Lindström, Harald. *Wesley and Sanctification: A Study in the Doctrine of Salvation*. 1946. Reprint, with a foreword by Timothy L. Smith, Wilmore, KY: Francis Asbury, 1980.
Long, D. Stephen. *John Wesley's Moral Theology: The Quest for God and Goodness*. Nashville: Kingswood, 2005.
Lovin, Robin W. "The Physics of True Virtue." In *Wesleyan Theology Today*, 264–72.

Lowery, Kevin T. "A Fork in the Wesleyan Road: Phoebe Palmer and the Appropriation of Christian Perfection." *Wesleyan Theological Journal* 36, no. 2 (2001) 187–222.

———. "Wesley's Limited Alliance with Lockean Empiricism." Paper presented at the Graduate Student Theological Seminar of the Wesleyan and Free Methodist Churches, Indianapolis, IN, October 2000.

Maddox, Randy L. "A Change of Affections: The Development, Dynamics, and Dethronement of John Wesley's Heart Religion." In *"Heart Religion" in the Methodist Tradition and Related Movements*, edited by Richard B. Steele, 3–31. Lanham, MD: Scarecrow, 2001.

———. "The Enriching Role of Experience." In *Wesley and the Quadrilateral*, 107–27.

———. "Reclaiming an Inheritance: Wesley as Theologian in the History of Methodist Theology." In *Rethinking Wesley's Theology for Contemporary Methodism*, edited by Randy L. Maddox, 213–26. Nashville: Kingswood, 1998.

———. *Responsible Grace: John Wesley's Practical Theology*. Nashville: Kingswood, 1994.

Magri, Tito. "Locke, Suspension of Desire, and the Remote Good." *British Journal for the History of Philosophy* 8 (2000) 55–70.

Mariña, Jacqueline. "Making Sense of Kant's Highest Good." *Kant Studien* 91 (2000) 329–55.

———. "Transformation and Personal Identity in Kant." *Faith and Philosophy* 17 (2000) 479–97.

Marsden, George M. *Fundamentalism and American Culture: The Shaping of Twentieth-Century Evangelicalism, 1870–1925*. Oxford: Oxford University Press, 1980.

Marston, Leslie. "The Crisis-Process Issue in Wesleyan Thought." *Wesleyan Theological Journal* 4 (1969) 3–15.

Matthews, Rex D. "Religion and Reason Joined: A Study in the Theology of John Wesley." ThD diss., Harvard University, 1986.

Michalson, Gordon E. Jr. *Fallen Freedom: Kant on Radical Evil and Moral Regeneration*. Cambridge: Cambridge University Press, 1990.

———. "Moral Regeneration and Divine Aid in Kant." *Religious Studies* 25, no. 3 (1989) 259–70.

———. "The Problem of Salvation in Kant's *Religion within the Limits of Reason Alone*." *International Philosophical Quarterly* 37, no. 3 (1997) 319–28.

Miles, Rebekah L. "The Instrumental Role of Reason." In *Wesley and the Quadrilateral: Renewing the Conversation*, edited by W. Stephen Gunter, et al., 77–106. Nashville: Abingdon, 1997.

Monk, Robert C. *John Wesley: His Puritan Heritage*. Nashville: Abingdon, 1966.

Moore, Don Marselle. "Development in Wesley's Thought on Sanctification and Perfection." *Wesleyan Theological Journal* 20 (1985) 29–53.

Moore, J. T. "Locke on the Moral Need for Christianity." *Southwestern Journal of Philosophy* 11, no. 1 (1980) 61–68.

Munzel, G. Felicitas. *Kant's Conception of Moral Character: The "Critical" Link of Morality, Anthropology, and Reflective Judgment*. Chicago: University of Chicago, 1999.

Nausner, Helmut. "Some Notes on Christian Perfection." *Quarterly Review* 3 (1983) 71-82.
Newton, J. A. "The Ecumenical Wesley." *Ecumenical Review* 24 (1972) 160-75.
———. "Perfection and Spirituality in the Methodist Tradition." *Church Quarterly* 3 (1970) 95-103.
Noll, Mark A. "God at the Center: Jonathan Edwards on True Virtue." *Christian Century* 110 (1993) 854-58.
———. "John Wesley and the Doctrine of Assurance." *Bibliotheca Sacra* 132 (1975) 161-77.
———. *The Scandal of the Evangelical Mind*. Grand Rapids: Eerdmans, 1994.
Nussbaum, Martha C. *Upheavals of Thought: The Intelligence of Emotions*. Cambridge: Cambridge University, 2001.
Oakley, Francis. "Locke, Natural Law, and God — Again." *History of Political Thought* 18 (1997) 624-51.
Oden, Thomas C. *Doctrinal Standards in the Wesleyan Tradition*. Grand Rapids: Francis Asbury, 1988.
———. *John Wesley's Scriptural Christianity: A Plain Exposition of His Teaching on Christian Doctrine*. Grand Rapids: Zondervan, 1994.
———. *The Transforming Power of Grace*. Nashville: Abingdon, 1993.
O'Leary-Hawthorn, John and Daniel Howard-Snyder. "Are Beliefs about God Theoretical Beliefs? Reflections on Aquinas and Kant." *Religious Studies* 32 (1996) 233-58.
O'Malley, J. Steven. "Recovering the Vision of Holiness: Wesley's Epistemic Basis." *Asbury Theological Journal* 41, no. 1 (1986) 3-17.
O'Neill, Onora. *Constructions of Reason: Explorations of Kant's Practical Philosophy*. Cambridge: Cambridge University, 1989.
Outler, Albert C. *John Wesley*. New York: Oxford, 1964.
———. "Pietism and Enlightenment: Alternatives to Tradition." In *Christian Spirituality: Post-Reformation and Modern*, edited by Louis Dupré and Don E. Saliers, 240-56. New York: Crossroad, 1989.
———. *Theology in the Wesleyan Spirit*. Nashville: Tidings, 1975.
———. *The Wesleyan Theological Heritage: Essays of Albert C. Outler*. Edited by Thomas C. Oden and Leicester R. Longden. Grand Rapids: Zondervan, 1991.
———., et al. "Wesley Studies." In *The Future of the Methodist Theological Traditions*, edited by M. Douglas Meeks, 53-66. Nashville: Abingdon, 1985.
Peters, John Leland. *Christian Perfection and American Methodism*. New York: Abingdon, 1956.
Piette, Maximin. *John Wesley in the Evolution of Protestantism*. London: Sheed and Ward, 1938.
Proudfoot, Wayne. "From Theology to a Science of Religions: Jonathan Edwards and William James on Religious Affections." *Harvard Theological Review* 82 (1989) 149-68.
———. "Perception and Love in Religious Affections." In *Jonathan Edwards' Writings*, edited by Stephen J. Stein, 122-36. Bloomington: Indiana University, 1996.
Quanstrom, Mark R. "The Doctrine of Entire Sanctification in the Church of the Nazarene: From the Conquest of Sin to a New Theological Realism, 1905-1997." Ph.D. diss., Saint Louis University, 2000.

Quinn, Philip L. "Christian Atonement and Kantian Justification." *Faith and Philosophy* 3, no. 4 (1986) 440–62.

———. "Original Sin, Radical Evil and Moral Identity." *Faith and Philosophy* 1, no. 2 (1984) 188–202.

Reardon, Bernard M. G. "Kant as Theologian." *Downside Review* 93 (1975) 252–68.

Reed, Rodney L. "Calvin, Calvinism, and Wesley: The Doctrine of Assurance in Historical Perspective." *Methodist History* 32 (1993) 31–43.

Reist, Irwin W. "John Wesley and George Whitefield: A Study in the Integrity of Two Theologies of Grace." *Evangelical Quarterly* 47 (1975) 26–40.

Riley, Patrick. "Kant on Persons as 'Ends in Themselves.'" *Modern Schoolman* 57 (1979) 45–56.

———. "Kant on Will, 'Moral Causality,' and the Social Contract." *Modern Schoolman* 54 (1977) 107–22.

Rivers, Isabel. *Reason, Grace, and Sentiment*. 2 vols. Cambridge: Cambridge University, 1991–2000.

Rossvaer, Viggo. *Kant's Moral Philosophy: An Interpretation of the Categorical Imperative*. Oslo: Universitetsforlag, 1979.

Runyon, Theodore H. "The Importance of Experience for Faith." In *Aldersgate Reconsidered*, edited by Randy L. Maddox, 93–107. Nashville: Kingswood, 1990.

———. *The New Creation: John Wesley's Theology Today*. Nashville: Abingdon, 1998.

———. "Orthopathy: Wesleyan Criteria for Religious Experience." In *"Heart Religion" in the Methodist Tradition and Related Movements*, edited by Richard B. Steele, 291–305. Lanham, MD: Scarecrow, 2001.

———. "The Role of Experience in Religion." *International Journal for Philosophy of Religion* 31 (1992) 187–94.

Ryder, Mary R. "Avoiding the 'Many-Headed Monster': Wesley and Johnson on Enthusiasm." *Methodist History* 23 (1985) 214–22.

Sangster, William Edwin. *The Path to Perfection: An Examination and Restatement of John Wesley's Doctrine of Christian Perfection*. 1943. Reprint, London: Epworth, 1984.

Savage, Denis D. "Kant's Rejection of Divine Revelation and His Theory of Radical Evil." In *Kant's Philosophy of Religion Reconsidered*, edited by Philip J. Rossi and Michael Wreen, 54–76. Bloomington: University of Indiana, 1991.

Schaller, Walter E. "The Relation of Moral Worth to the Good Will in Kant's Ethics." *Journal of Philosophical Research* 17 (1992) 351–82.

———. "Should Kantians Care about Moral Worth?" *Dialogue* 32 (1993) 25–40.

Schneewind, J. B. "Autonomy, Obligation, and Virtue: An Overview of Kant's Moral Philosophy." In *The Cambridge Companion to Kant*, edited by Paul Guyer, 309–41. Cambridge: Cambridge University, 1992.

———. *The Invention of Autonomy*. Cambridge: Cambridge University, 1998.

Seligman, Adam B. *Modernity's Wager: Authority, the Self, and Transcendence*. Princeton: Princeton University, 2000.

Simonson, Harold P. *Jonathan Edwards: Theologian of the Heart*. Grand Rapids: Eerdmans, 1974. Reprint, Macon, GA: Mercer University, 1982.

Smith, John E. "Testing the Spirits: Jonathan Edwards and the Religious Affections." *Union Seminary Quarterly Review* 37 (1981) 27–37.

———. "A Treatise Concerning Religious Affections, by Jonathan Edwards, 1746." *American Presbyterians* 66 (1988) 219–22.

Snook, I. A. "John Locke's Theory of Moral Education." *Educational Theory* 20 (1970) 364–67.

Spellman, W. M. *John Locke and the Problem of Depravity*. Oxford: Clarendon, 1988.

Spohn, William C. "Sovereign Beauty: Jonathan Edwards and the Nature of True Virtue." *Theological Studies* 42 (1981) 394–421.

———. "Union and Consent with the Great Whole: Jonathan Edwards on True Virtue." *Annual of the Society of Christian Ethics* 5 (1985) 19–32.

Staples, Rob L. "John Wesley's Doctrine of the Holy Spirit." *Wesleyan Theological Journal* 21 (1986) 91–115.

Starkey, Lycurgus M. "The Holy Spirit and the Wesleyan Witness." *Religion in Life* 49 (1980) 72–80.

Stecker, Robert. "Thomas Reid on the Moral Sense." *Monist* 70 (1987) 453–64.

Steele, Les L. "Educating the Heart." In *"Heart Religion" in the Methodist Tradition and Related Movements*, 225–44. Lanham, MD: Scarecrow, 2001.

Steele, Richard B. *"Gracious Affection" and "True Virtue" According to Jonathan Edwards and John Wesley*. Metuchen, NJ: Scarecrow, 1994.

———. "The Passion and the Passions." In *"Heart Religion" in the Methodist Tradition and Related Movements*, 245–71. Lanham, MD: Scarecrow, 2001.

Stephens, W. P. "Wesley and the Moravians." In *John Wesley: Contemporary Perspectives*, edited by John Stacey, 23–36. London: Epworth, 1988.

Stoeffler, F. Ernest. "Pietism, the Wesleys and Methodist Beginnings in America." In *Continental Pietism and Early American Christianity*, edited by F. Ernest Stoeffler, 184–221. Grand Rapids: Eerdmans, 1976.

Sweet, W. W. "John Wesley and Scientific Discovery." *Christian Century* 40 (1923) 591–92.

Teale, A. E. *Kantian Ethics*. London: Oxford, 1951.

Telford, John, ed. *The Letters of the Rev. John Wesley*. 8 vols. London: Epworth, 1931.

Thorsen, Donald A. D. "Experimental Method in the Practical Theology of John Wesley." *Wesleyan Theological Journal* 24 (1989) 117–41.

———. *The Wesleyan Quadrilateral: Scripture, Tradition, Reason, and Experience as a Model of Evangelical Theology*. Grand Rapids: Zondervan, 1990.

Timmons, Mark. "Kant and the Possibility of Moral Motivation." *Southern Journal of Philosophy* 23 (1985) 377–98.

Todd, John Murray. *John Wesley and the Catholic Church*. London: Hodder and Stoughton, 1958.

Towns, Elmer L. "John Wesley and Religious Education." *Religious Education*, 65 (1970) 318–28.

Tracy, Wesley D. "Christian Education in the Wesleyan Mode." *Wesleyan Theological Journal*, 17, no. 1 (1982) 30–53.

Tuttle, Robert G. *Mysticism in the Wesleyan Tradition*. Grand Rapids: Francis Asbury, 1989.

Tyson, John R. "John Wesley and William Law: A Reappraisal." *Wesleyan Theological Journal* 17, no. 2 (1982) 58–78.

———. "John Wesley's Conversion at Aldersgate." In *Conversion in the Wesleyan Tradition*, edited by Kenneth J. Collins and John H. Tyson, 27–42. Nashville: Abingdon, 2001.

———. "Sin, Self and Society: John Wesley's Hamartiology Reconsidered." *Asbury Theological Journal* 44, no. 2 (1989) 77–89.

Vick, E. W. H. "John Wesley's Teaching Concerning Perfection." *Andrews University Seminary Studies* 4 (1966) 201–17.

Wainwright, William. "Jonathan Edwards and the Sense of the Heart." *Faith and Philosophy* 7 (1990) 43–62.

Wallace, Charles. "Susanna Wesley's Spirituality: The Freedom of a Christian Woman." *Methodist History* 22 (1984) 158–73.

Walters, O. S. "Concept of Attainment in John Wesley's Christian Perfection." *Methodist History* 10, no. 3 (1972) 12–29.

———. "John Wesley's Footnotes to Christian Perfection." *Methodist History* 12, no. 1 (1973) 19–36.

Weaver, Darlene Fozard. *Self Love and Christian Ethics*. Cambridge: Cambridge University, 2002.

Willey, Basil. *The English Moralists*. London: Chatto and Windus, 1964.

Williams, Colin W. *John Wesley's Theology Today*. Nashville: Abingdon, 1960.

Williams, Terrence Charles. *The Concept of the Categorical Imperative: A Study of the Place of the Categorical Imperative in Kant's Ethical Theory*. Oxford: Clarendon, 1968.

Wilson, David Dunn. "The Importance of Hell for John Wesley." *Proceedings of the Wesley Historical Society* 34 (1963) 12–6.

———. "John Wesley and Mystical Prayer." *London Quarterly and Holborn Review* 193 (1968) 61–9.

Winnett, Arthur Robert. *Peter Browne: Provost, Bishop, Metaphysician*. London: SPCK, 1974.

Wolterstorff, Nicholas. *John Locke and the Ethics of Belief*. Cambridge: Cambridge University, 1996.

Wood, A. Skevington. "The Contribution of John Wesley to the Theology of Grace." In *Grace Unlimited*, edited by Clark H. Pinnock, 209–22. Minneapolis: Bethany, 1975.

———. *John Wesley: The Burning Heart*. Grand Rapids: Eerdmans, 1967.

Wood, Allen W. *Kant's Moral Religion*. Ithaca, NY: Cornell University, 1970.

———. "The Emptiness of the Moral Will." *Monist* 72 (1989) 454–83.

Wood, Laurence W. "Wesley's Epistemology." *Wesleyan Theological Journal* 10 (1975) 48–59.